Facing Zero Population Growth

STUDIES IN SOCIAL AND ECONOMIC DEMOGRAPHY

General Editor

GEORGE C. MYERS, Director,
Center for Demographic Studies, Duke University

1. Joseph J. Spengler, *Facing Zero Population Growth*
2. Joseph J. Spengler, *France Faces Depopulation* (Revised and Enlarged Edition)

Forthcoming titles to be announced

Facing Zero Population Growth:

Reactions and Interpretations, Past and Present

Joseph J. Spengler

Duke University Press
Durham, N. C.   1978

Printed in the United States of America
by Kingsport Press

To *Dorothy Kress Spengler,*
My wife, companion, and co-worker for fifty years

Contents

List of Tables

Preface

The subject of this book has been a source of interest to me since the 1930's when it became probable that in economically developed countries the birth rate would move into the immediate neighborhood of the death rate if not below it. I could not devote full time to the subject, however, until I retired in 1972 and was awarded a generous Ford-Rockefeller population grant that gave me access to essential clerical and research assistance.

The central concern of this study is quite different from that upon which Malthus focused attention 175 years ago. At the time he wrote concern began to be expressed lest population grow too rapidly—a concern still alive in the Western world early in the present century. After World War I concern developed in the Western world lest births be too few to offset deaths—a concern that was revived subsequently to the tapering off of the baby boom that came in the wake of World War II. Today in a number of advanced countries populations are not replacing themselves and population stationarity if not decline is anticipated (e.g., cf. Alfred Sauvy, *Zero Growth*, 1976). Meanwhile, it is commonly assumed that in the underdeveloped world populations will continue to grow, perhaps for a century or longer.

My major concern in this study is with how scholars, especially economists, have interpreted the supposed consequences of cessation of population growth, and how economies can best adjust to the advent of zero population growth. While my main concern is with the present century and the future, attention is devoted in several chapters to the behavior of population growth over the centuries.

While my obligations, listed under "acknowledgments," are many, I could never have completed this study without the daily inspiration of my wife, Dorothy, so creative herself, and the year-round stream of flowers born of this creativity. Not only did she encourage me and make excellent suggestions; she also freed me of many of the tasks that can consume much of a scholar's time. This book, therefore, is her book as well as mine.

Acknowledgments

As noted in the preface the subject of this book has long been a source of concern to me. In the course of its preparation I have drawn upon the rich world of demographic and related economic scholarship—upon the world whose views and outlook I was interested in reporting. The extent of my consultation of this world is evidenced in the footnotes and bibliography. Of especial assistance have been the works of economists whose interest in the population problem both preceded the early 1920's, continued through the 1940's and thereafter. Most outstanding have been the contributions of J. M. Keynes, together with those of commentators on his work (e.g., A. C. Pigou, J. R. Hicks, Roy Harrod) and those continuing his line of inquiry (e.g., Alvin Hansen). Especially useful also have been Simon Kuznets's works on the history of economic growth and E. F. Denison's studies of growth in Western countries. Helpful also have been some of the regional model life tables developed by Ansley J. Coale and Paul Demeny and similar tables developed by the United Nations.

My indebtedness, other than my outstanding obligation to the Ford Foundation and the Rockefeller Foundation for having made possible continual work on this project and its completion, is various. I am indebted for critical suggestions to my friend and colleague, Professor George Myers of Duke University, to my friend Professor William Serow of the University of Virginia, and to the Duke University Press's readers who made many valuable suggestions for improving the manuscript. I am indebted also to Dr. Roger Morefield, Houston Baptist University, for research assistance.

I am especially indebted to Mrs. Virginia Skinner who has prepared many drafts of parts of the manuscript, caught numerous errors, and helped get the notes, bibliography, and index into final shape. I am much indebted as ever to the Duke University Press for its always priceless editorial assistance. For the errors that remain I am, of course, responsible.

I appreciate permission from Princeton University Press to make use of selections from two tables in *Regional Model Life Tables,* by Ansley J. Coale and Paul Demeny; permission from *Lloyd's Bank Review* to quote at length from W. A. B. Hopkin's essay in *Lloyd's Bank Review,* No. 27, 1953; to Macmillan, London and Basingstroke, for permission to quote from R. F. Harrod's *Economic Essays* and A. C. Pigou's *The Economics of Stationary States;* to *Population Studies* and Nathan Keyfitz for permission to quote from his essay on "Individual Mobility in a Stationary Population;" and to Her Majesty's Stationery Office for permission to quote from papers and reports of the British Royal Commission on Population.

Introduction

In the course of the past three millennia man has experienced both non-growth and decline of population as well as increase in his numbers. Of this variability in the growth of populations evidence has been put forward in United Nations reports and in studies such as Colin Clark's *History of Population Growth* (London: Macmillan, 1967). Prior to the seventeenth century periods of population growth were occasionally interrupted by periods of decline or stationarity associated with upsurges of already high mortality. Not until the seventeenth century did sustained growth of numbers set in, and not until the nineteenth century did quite high and essentially continuous growth prevail, mainly as a result of decline in mortality. More than three-fourths of the increase of world population over the millennia has taken place since 1800, and about two-thirds since 1850. This growth has come in the wake of economic and technological progress and increase in man's productive powers, a manifestation of increasing modernization.

Modernization also brought in its wake improvement in man's capacity both to regulate and to augment his numbers. Over the centuries man made some effort to control his numbers, but they were restrained mainly by positive checks. Modernization not only gave rise to increase in man's capacity for economic and demographic growth, but also to increase in his power to regulate population growth and at times to increase in his incentive to do so. Today fertility is in the neighborhood of the replacement level or slightly below it in a number of modern countries, with the result that in some, population will eventually cease to grow if not decline in number.

Zero population growth is not a modern phenomenon. Since ancient times it has occasionally been viewed as a concomitant of man's limited capacity to augment his means of support. It remained for the classical economists and their predecessors to develop theories and models in terms of which alternative zero populations would come into being. They also learned to distinguish between a stationary population and a stationary economy. The metabolism of populations was neglected, however.

Population decline was slow to command attention in modern times until, after the mid–nineteenth century, France faced the prospect of a decline in numbers, given its then low and falling fertility. Today, however, the populations of a number of modern countries appear to be ap-

This study has been supported by a joint Ford Foundation and Rockefeller Foundation Population Study Grant.

proaching a stationary state, perhaps at the risk of eventually undergoing a decrease in size.

This study is concerned with modern man's reaction to limits to economic growth and to population growth under diverse conditions, with his assessment of the economic implications of cessation of population growth, and with problems associated with adjusting economies to cessation of population growth. For purposes of analysis of these implications much use is made of American data and of probable concomitants of cessation of growth of the United States population. The findings may be applicable, of course, to other countries.

In view of the likelihood that populations of advanced countries will become roughly stable at rates of growth in the neighborhood of zero, the first four of the ten chapters constituting this study are devoted to the historical and ideational setting of the present state of demographic affairs. The concepts and preconditions of stationariness of populations and economies are described in the first chapter. In the second chapter it is shown how conditions affecting demand for population have undergone major changes in the course of man's history. In the next two chapters reactions to the slowing of population growth in the course of the past century are reviewed, and the threat of depopulation is touched upon.

Chapters V–VII deal with the genesis of the age structures associated with stable populations experiencing little or no growth or decreasing. The coming into being of such age structures presents problems that have been accentuated by modern and usually institutionalized conceptions of adulthood, together with the presence of a relatively large number of persons over 65. Major attention is focused on adjustments essential to rational economic accommodation to population aging, lest poverty and unemployment come in the wake of a marked increase in the relative number of persons over (say) 55.

Chapter VIII is devoted to interaction between population growth and economic growth. In Chapters IX and X economic problem areas sensitive to the state of population growth are examined along with international implications of cessation of population growth in the present world.

Facing Zero Population Growth

I. Stationary Population; Stationary Economy

Growth cannot be conceived otherwise than as a passage from one stationary state to another.

Nicholas Georgescu-Roegen

In this chapter we describe stationary populations and look at descriptions of stationary economies put forward by various economists. In the chapter that follows we describe how scholarly attitudes toward growth of population have changed over time as modes of production have changed. In later chapters attention is focused upon *interaction* between growth (or nongrowth) of population, on the one hand, and changes in economies and aggregate output, on the other.

Stationariness of population—that is, zero population growth—is a necessary but not immediately a sufficient condition for stationariness of economy. For, as will be noted, other critical components must also remain stationary. The degree to which stationariness of population makes for stationariness of economy depends in the main on the degree to which aggregate economic growth is conditioned by population growth. Prior to the eighteenth century population growth and economic growth were highly correlated. But with technological progress and capital accumulation in the centuries that followed, the degree of correlation declined.

1. Stationary Population

Our concern is not with populations temporarily stationary due to transitory equivalence of births to deaths, but with populations *both* stationary and *stable* in age composition in keeping with equality between the intrinsic death rate and the intrinsic birth rate. Throughout man's history populations have become temporarily stationary but not stable, since age-specific mortality and age-specific fertility have not remained unchanged at levels compatible with zero population growth.

Populations are roughly divisible into two types, those in which mortality has not been brought under effective control, and those in which mortality has passed under increasing though necessarily limited control. For expositive convenience we may draw an arbitrary dividing line at (say) a life expectancy at birth of 30 years and assume that mortality is being controlled directly or indirectly in some significant measure when life expectancy exceeds 30. This dividing line is arbitrary in that increase in life expectancy to 30 years does reflect man-made improvements in man's environment, inasmuch as life expectancy under primitive conditions was lower. Of populations characterized by a life expectancy of 30 or less, one may, with Fourastié,[1] say that among them death is at the center of life, in part because about half of those born alive will die before attaining the age of five. Not much control over the number of live births through infanticide, abortion, or prevention of conception can be exercised in such a population; otherwise live births would fall short of deaths, and the population would diminish. In a high-mortality population, therefore, since death control is not operative, control of births, though usually present, is ruled out as a major regulative force by the resulting likelihood that population would then decline.

With the establishment of direct and indirect control over mortality and the extension of life expectancy at birth beyond 30 years and eventually into the seventies, there is increasing scope for the exercise of control of live births—a kind of control both reflective of current human decision and perhaps in keeping with customs established through past decision. Accordingly, whereas the advent of a stationary or near-stationary population, given a life expectancy of 30 or less, would almost certainly be attributable to persisting and sufficiently high mortality, its advent when life expectancy is appreciably in excess of 30, and especially when it is 70 or more, would have to be the product of voluntary control of numbers.

Table I.1 may serve to illustrate[2] how in a stable population true natural increase varies with changes in the Gross Reproduction Rate (GRR), in life expectancy at birth, and in combinations of the GRR and life expectancy. It also illustrates man's great potential for natural increase. Combining a life expectancy of 30 with a Gross Reproduction Rate of 2.0 would not quite assure a stationary population, since the

Table I.1 Natural Increase Per 1,000 Inhabitants In Model Stable Populations

Life Expectancy	Gross Reproduction Rate					
	4.0	3.0	2.5	2.0	1.5	1.0
20	10.8	0.3	−6.3	−14.4	−24.9	−39.8
30	24.5	14.0	7.4	− 0.9	−11.2	−25.9
40	33.2	22.7	16.1	8.0	− 2.5	−17.3
50	39.5	29.1	22.4	14.3	3.9	−10.9
60.4	44.7	34.2	27.6	19.5	9.0	− 5.7
70.2	48.6	38.1	31.5	23.3	12.9	− 1.8

Source: United Nations, *The Aging of Populations*, Population Study 26, New York, 1956, p. 26.

birth and death rates eventuating in the resulting stable population would be 32.7 and 33.6 per 1,000 inhabitants. A slight increase in the GRR would give rise to a stationary population, and an increase of the GRR to 3 would give rise to a rate of natural increase of 7.4 per thousand, enough to double a population every century and increase it over 500 times in a millennium. Even with a GRR slightly above 2.0 a stable population would double in about three centuries.

Man's potential for population growth has been nicely illustrated by Ryder.[3] Given a life expectancy in which (female) mean age at death is 25, a total fertility rate of 5.41 produces a stationary population, and one of 7.3 a growth rate of 1 percent. Given a mean age at death of 30 years, the two corresponding rates become 4.53 and 6.12; and given one of 35 years, the two rates become 3.92 and 5.31, and a total fertility of 7.14 produces an annual rate of increase of 2 percent. Evidently, as life expectancy rises above 30, fertility must be subjected to increasing control; otherwise population will grow appreciably. Only through increasing control of fertility, therefore, can a population's *true* rate of growth be reduced to zero.

Figures such as we have presented indicate that population elasticity could often greatly exceed the elasticity of the food supply, especially in the short run prior to the incidence of unusually high mortality. They indicate that only recurring extraordinary mortality could have offset usual fertility and held the rate of natural increase to a very low level. They also indicate that, in high-mortality populations free of extraordinary mortality, control of fertility could have contributed notably to population decline and sometimes was employed as a means of keeping the population stationary. They do not support the argument of Carr-Saunders that regulatory mechanisms tended to hold numbers at an optimum density, but suggest rather why control of numbers had support even in classic times.[4]

2. Past Population Growth

Given man's great potential for population growth and the likelihood that the Gross Reproduction Rate may often have been near or above 3.0,[5] it is evident that only periodic upsurges of mortality, together with efforts at regulation of the number of live births and infants, could account for the failure of man's numbers to grow quite rapidly. How great and frequent such upsurges had to be turns on the prevailing level of life expectancy and upon the height of the GRR, both of which were subject to change. Presumably, there was less need for high mortality in Western Europe than elsewhere, since, after the Middle Ages if not earlier, relatively fewer women married in Western Europe than elsewhere and then at a later age,[6] with the result that births apparently did not often exceed 40 per 1,000 inhabitants, whereas elsewhere they usually exceeded 40 and even 45.[7]

With a GRR in excess of 2.5 or perhaps even in excess of 3.0, and hence with births numbering 40 or more per 1,000 population, even a life expectancy several years below 30 might permit considerable natural increase. Life expectancy often approximated if it did not exceed 30, a value reported for the whole Roman Empire, though within that empire life expectancy varied greatly by region and class.[8] By the late eighteenth century, as a result of improved conditions and despite fluctuating mortality, "an average length of life of 35 to 40 years may have been common in various localities among civilized nations."[9]

Population growth has been dominated throughout most of man's history by his capacity to increase his food supply through extension of areas under cultivation and occasionally through increase in output per acre. Most striking in his early history was the "Neolithic revolution, which gradually added agriculture and animal husbandry to the quest for food."[10] Although output per acre and per agriculturalist improved very slowly when it improved at all, the aggregate output of subsistence occasionally increased, notably in parts of Europe and Asia, and allowed the population to increase until it again was abreast of the flow of subsistence.[11] As late as the sixteenth and seventeenth centuries, A. R. Hall concludes, growth of Europe's population was effectively limited by hunger, not disease. At times, of course, epidemic disease could intervene, as in the fourteenth century.[12]

The history of agriculture and yields in England indicates that even though yields long changed slowly when at all, conditions were not static. England's Agricultural Revolution was preceded by "a long period of preparation," facilitated by, among other things, the derigidifying impact of the Black Death. "At the beginning of the eighteenth century land and its cultivation continued its ancient domination of society and the economy," but acreage under cultivation increased and yields rose.[13]

Because the margin of a country's or a region's output above its food requirements was not great in good times and storage facilities often were limited, vulnerability to unfavorable turns of weather, etc., and to localized food shortages or famine was high. War and pestilence could accentuate these conditions as well as contribute greatly to increase in mortality.[14]

Students of the growth of the population of the world (e.g., M. K. Bennett, Colin Clark, Simon Kuznets, researchers at the United Nations) agree that most of the growth since the beginning of the Christian era has taken place since 1650. The rate of growth for the entire period A.D. 1 to 1650 was roughly sufficient to double the world's population. In contrast, in the course of the next three centuries the world's population increased between 400 and 500 percent. Since 1950 it has grown at a rate about four times that experienced between 1800 and 1950.

The rate of population growth varied regionally as well as in time. Europe's population, after growing barely $\frac{1}{4}$ percent per decade between 30 A.D. and 1000, increased about 2 percent per decade over the next three centuries, under the stimulus of technical advances in agriculture.[15] Then, after declining in size about two-fifths by 1400 as a result of the Black Death, it grew about $3\frac{1}{2}$ percent per decade in 1400–1600 and $2\frac{1}{2}$ percent per decade in 1600–1700. The population of Asia (including Asiatic Russia) increased about $\frac{3}{4}$ percent per decade in 1000–1300; then, after increasing only about $7\frac{1}{2}$ percent in 1300–1400, it grew about $1\frac{3}{8}$ percent per decade in 1400–1600 and $3\frac{1}{8}$ percent per decade in 1600–1700. The world's population increased about $1\frac{1}{8}$ percent per decade in 1000–1300, apparently not at all in the fourteenth century, $1\frac{3}{8}$ percent per decade in 1400–1600, and $2\frac{1}{2}$ percent per decade in 1600–1700. Over the next 50 years, the population of Asia may have increased slightly faster than Europe's, which grew about 4 percent per decade.[16]

The 220 years separating 1750 and 1970 are divisible into two periods. During the first, 1750–1930, population grew more rapidly in the then advancing and now developed countries of the world than in those undergoing relatively little if any development. In the former, numbers increased slightly over 8 percent per decade; in the underdeveloped world, about $4\frac{1}{2}$ percent. After 1930, however, the rate of natural increase in the underdeveloped world began to outstrip that in the developed world. Between 1930 and 1970 population grew, in percent per year, about $\frac{15}{16}$ in the developed world compared with nearly $1\frac{3}{4}$ in the underdeveloped world. It is anticipated, moreover, that over the next 30 years the population of the underdeveloped world may increase nearly 2.4 percent, compared with about 0.9 percent in the developed world.[17]

Had population growth not encountered obstacles prior to 1750, it might have proceeded much as it has since then, and particularly as it has proceeded in the underdeveloped world since 1930. Table I.1 serves to illustrate this. For even with a life expectancy at birth of only 30 years and a Gross Reproduction Rate of 2.5—i.e., a birth rate of 40.6 per 1,000—a population will grow 7.4 per 1,000 inhabitants per year, enough to double a population every century or increase it 512 times in a millennium. Even with a rate of increase of 2.5 per 1,000, a population will double in about three centuries. The failure of population to grow significantly before (say) 1700 is traceable, therefore, not to lack of growth potential but to upsurges of mortality to 45 or more per thousand as a result mainly of epidemics and secondarily of periodic shortages of food and famine.

The failure of population to grow at times and hence to be stationary in times past has been the result mainly of unusually high mortality. Fertility has normally been adequate to give rise to considerable population growth. Accordingly, while populations have been temporarily stationary in the past, they have not been *both* stationary and stable at the population replacement level. Even when these populations have been roughly stable, their stability has been at fertility levels that have normally yielded births in excess of deaths. In short, the absence of natural increase in national or regional populations prior to the present century has been attributable to the height of mortality rather than to the lowness of fertility.

The slowing down of population growth in the present century, usually a continuation of a movement under way already in the nineteenth century, is attributable to decline in fertility. Ironically, the nineteenth century witnessed great increases in life expectancy—increases since continued— which both offset declines in fertility when they took place and, by increasing the ratio of surviving young children to parents, accentuated other forces motivating control of births. In developed countries life expectancy at birth rose from levels of 35–40 or less around 1800 to 50 and over by around 1900 and was in the middle or lower 60s around 1940 and in the neighborhood of 70 and over around 1970. In contrast, despite considerable reduction in mortality between the 1930s and the late 1950s, life expectancy in underdeveloped countries in the late 1950s ranged from under 40 in Africa to 50–55 in Latin America.[18]

How soon populations can or will become stationary and stable depends on how long it takes to get fertility to replacement levels, given current mortality. Even should this be accomplished by (say) 2000–2005, births will continue to exceed deaths for roughly another 50–65 years and populations will increase by about 13–45 percent above the levels attained in 2000, which will already be about 25–100 percent above those reported around 1970.[19]

When these possibilities will be realized is uncertain. Estimates vary of the magnitude that will have been attained by the world's population— 3.7 billion in 1971—upon its having become stable at around the zero-growth-rate level. The quite optimistic run roughly from 8.5 to 10.5 billion; the moderately optimistic run higher, perhaps as high as 15 billion; and the less optimistic run still higher.[20] The terminal figure depends of course, upon how fast fertility declines, whether at, above, or below the rate of decline in nineteenth century Europe.[21] This rate will depend increasingly upon the degree to which population growth is believed to thwart realization of material aspirations at household and national or collective levels.

Stationariness of a national population is compatible with stationariness or growth of an economy. In the former case support and mere replacement absorb the entire flow of inputs that a population is willing and able to provide through time. In the latter case the population does better but not sufficiently better to warrant increase in numbers; it provides a flow of inputs sufficient to replace the population and support its members at a level of income growing at a sustainable rate y' (where y denotes average income). In a stationary population with a stationary average income y the final bill of consumables C remains constant at Py, where P denotes a nation's population that by definition is stationary and stable in form. In an economy whose population is stationary and whose average income y is growing at a supposedly constant rate y', the annual bill of consumables C grows at a rate y'. A population is stationary in the latter case because the flow of components of C can be increased no faster than y'; in the former case the flow of components is not subject to increase.

What has been said may be stated as follows: Let C be composed of n distinct components or sets of inputs $c_1, c_2, \ldots, c_n$. When both population and its average income y are stationary and hence C is constant, it is inferable that the flow of c's composing C is constant. When, however, C grows at a rate y', it is inferable that the c's grow at a similar rate.

Suppose now that the aggregate effective demand D_e for the final bill of goods C is in equilibrium with C and that each of the demand components d_i (that is, $d_1, d_2, \ldots, d_n$) is in equilibrium with its counterpart c_i (that is, $c_1, c_2, \ldots, c_n$). This equilibrium will persist so long as total conduct-determining demand D_t remains equivalent to D_e. D_t also may be affected by other forces than those which govern C and D_t when $D_t = D_e$—by whatever activates latent demands, or gives rise to quite new demands which do not immediately displace marginal current demands—with the result that $D_t > D_e$ and C must function as an overall budgetary constraint and, through the price mechanism and its analogues, restore and preserve equilibrium between d_i and c_i.

D_e can grow no faster than C, and C can grow no faster than the sets of inputs c_i composing C. Similarly, D_c, the demand for children and a component of D_e, can grow no faster than D_e unless more inputs are diverted to the production of children or the input cost of children is reduced, for C, D_e, and the flow of inputs c_i are constant. Even if the flow of c_i and hence C grows at rate y', D_c expressed in terms of children cannot increase if the input cost of children increases at rate y'. In short, in the absence of changes in D_c relative to D_e and given that input costs of children grow at the rate y', the number of children and the population will remain constant. Underlying this nongrowth would be man's inability or unwillingness to increase adequately the rate of flow of certain sets of inputs c_i, to replace these inputs by others susceptible of adequate increase, or to economize sufficiently in the use of critical growth-constraining sets of inputs.

Inasmuch as the forces underlying the growth of sets of inputs c_i and hence of C are subject to variation, it is possible for increase in the ratio D_t / D_e to accelerate the growth of D_e in some measure. The budgetary constraint imposed by inability to augment directly or indirectly some sets of inputs c_i will tend, however, to set limits to the rate of growth of C and hence D_e. Slowly growing or nongrowing rates of flow of some sets of inputs may identify potential or actual limitational factors.

Whereas, before the eighteenth century, C and D_e changed slowly, in modern societies they are subject to considerable change originating in changes in both C and D_e, together with interaction between C and D_t. Ultimately, however, the makeup and rate of growth of D_e are governed by a society's capacity to augment C and adjust its composition to that of D_e. So long as the composition of D_e adjusts easily to that of C, equilibrium between C and D_e is attainable. Insofar, however, as rigidity characterizes the composition of D_e, equilibrium may not prove wholly attainable, since modification of C, unlike that of D_e, is subject to environmental constraints not immediately and directly incident upon D_t and D_e. Then some c's cannot be adjusted to their counterpart d's on conditions "acceptable" to the population, and C cannot be made to keep adjusted to D_e; whence D_e must be modified. Under these circumstances the expected costs of children may rise in relation to the benefits expected of them, with the result that fertility is adjusted downward.

The c's of which C is composed consist ultimately of human services, reproducible assets, and components of man's natural environment whose stock is nonaugmentable though flow from this stock may be augmented for a limited period of time, often if not always at rising marginal cost. The c's whose relatively slow growth constrains the growth of C and thus makes for greater disequilibrium between C and D_t include both natural environmental components whose flow is not easily augmented and those human services whose cost is relatively high and rising.

Growing disequilibrium between C and D_t tends to be accompanied by downward pressure upon fertility when inputs (i.e., the c's) that enter largely into the reproduction and rearing of children become increasingly scarce and hence rise in price or in utility to potential parents. For then the aggregate real cost as well as the expected cost of children will rise more rapidly than the cost of goods and services composed predominantly of relatively abundant and hence lower-priced inputs or c's. Most important of the inputs whose steady increase in relative scarcity and cost will tend to depress fertility in the future is time, for time of various sorts often constitutes the most important input into the reproduction and rearing of children, probably the most time-intensive of physical products.

Because of the steadily increasing productivity of human capital, together with increase in the time-intensiveness of recreation, etc., the alternative-use value or cost of time could rise faster than that of most if not all inputs entering into the production of human capital, especially the reproduction, rearing, and education of children. This cost may be rising faster than can be countervailed by rising income, in part because as income rises investment of time in children and the improvement of their quality rises, perhaps faster than income. It is quite possible, therefore, that substitution effects in favor of quality and against numbers, in favor of fewer children of higher quality and against more children of lower quality, or against both quality and quantity of children and in favor of commodities and knowledge, will become stronger. Even so, forecasts to this effect are subject to uncertainty, since family formation is affected not only by anticipated pecuniary costs and returns associated with the reproduction and rearing of children, but also by anticipations of enjoyment associated with children, the importance of which may vary.[22]

In sum, a nation's population can become stationary (or even subject to decline) because of (a) the steadily rising relative cost of time, or (b) the increasing scarcity of elements in man's environment, or (c) both. The rising cost of time could prove the overriding deterrent in advancing and developed high-income countries. Increasing scarcity of elements in man's physical environment is likely to be more important in underdeveloped countries in the near future. International trade, together with tourism, can, however, intensify environmental scarcity in some countries by adding demands of foreign provenance to those originating with the domestic population.

Stationariness could emerge also if D_t should become constant before growth of C was halted by failure of the rate of flow of indispensable c's to rise. Thus increasing emphasis upon leisure might halt the growth of population and average output. D_t is likely to increase in magnitude in the wake of the emergence of new goods and options, together with the generation and diffusion of new tastes and reduction in the cost of complements to leisure. The composition of D_t may also change in the absence of an increase in D_t (e.g., as a result of change in the price structure of the c's and hence in that of components of the final bill of goods). The monetary demand for goods and services rises as the derived demand of entrepreneurs for inputs rises in anticipation of increase in D_e, and as a result the aggregate income of c's rises. Then, however, as Keynes anticipated, not all of the increment in income may be spent upon the increment in output, some of which may temporarily go unsold; this lag, temporary in nature, is not relevant in the context of nongrowth of C in the longer run.

3. Stationary Economy

Discussion of stationary economies has passed through three stages. The classical economists looked upon a stationary economy as a terminal stage of development in a finite world. Writers in the marginal tradition have utilized it as an analytical instrument. While use of the stationary state as an analytical device has continued, there has also developed in recent years a modified classical view. The finiteness of the world is stressed, limits to growth are recognized, and advantages of a stationary or slowly growing economy are noted and contrasted with those of growing steady-state economies (see Section 4 following).

The emergence of the concept of a stationary state may be viewed in terms that are somewhat dialectical, or put more suggestively, in terms of sequential interaction between "growth and form." As growth proceeds, form comes into being and imposes constraint upon growth until growth wins release—an outcome attainable almost only in the social and ideational worlds, and then only within limits.[23] At any moment in time, therefore, how a concept maps upon the underlying world from which it abstracts may be affected by the state of flux in which concept and world currently are situated, together with the values that condition the shaping of concepts and the selection of facts. Only when a concept is given a highly mathematical form is it likely to become stable, and this form will prove unsatisfactory if it maps imperfectly upon the concrete world.

Most if not all concepts of stationary states have one characteristic in common, namely, origin in the eventual nonaugmentability of some element on which the state is dependent, coupled with inability to surmount this limit either through substitution at the producer and / or the consumer level, or through scientific and technical progress capable of removing the limit. If the limit can be removed, the stationary state may prove transformable into what is called a steady state, though not permanently if this state's internal composition changes. It is also possible, in a world subject to increasing entropy, or shrinkage in the flow of the limitational factor, that negative growth will set in.

A. Classical School

Although Adam Smith is usually credited with having first described a stationary state or economy, the concept was implicit in the Physiocratic *Tableau Économique* and the stationary or continuous circular flow embodied therein,[24] a phenomenon of which John Locke, Richard Cantillon, and others seem to have had a glimpse. It was Adam Smith, however, who defined a stationary state, in terms that were descriptive rather than analytical in purpose. His stationary state held no attraction for him; it embodied a pessimism of the sort that some classical critics of the stationary states of Ricardo and Malthus incorrectly associated with these states.[25]

Smith defined and decribed his stationary state as follows:

> In a country which had acquired that full complement of riches which the nature of its soil and climate, and its situation with respect to other countries, allowed it to acquire; which could, therefore, advance no further, and which was not going backwards, both the wages of labour and the profits of stock would probably be very low. In a country fully peopled in proportion to what either its territory could maintain or its stock employ, the competition for employment would necessarily be so great as to reduce the wages of labour to what was barely sufficient to keep up the number of labourers, and, the country being already fully peopled, that number could never be augmented. In a country fully stocked in proportion to all the business it had to transact, as great a quantity of stock would be employed in every particular branch as the nature and extent of the trade would admit. The competition, therefore, would every-where be as great, and consequently the ordinary profit as low as possible.[26]

Smith goes on to say, however, that if a nation's institutions are suboptimal, an economy will cease to grow before it is forced to by physical constraints. Indeed, much of what he has to say of defective institutions points in this direction.

> But perhaps no country has ever yet arrived at this degree of opulence. China seems to have been long stationary, and had probably long ago acquired that full complement of riches which is consistent with the nature of its laws and institutions. But this complement may be much inferior to what, with other laws and institutions, the nature of its soil, climate, and situation might admit of. A country which neglects or despises foreign commerce, and which admits the vessels of foreign nations into one or two of its ports only, cannot transact the same quantity of business which it might do with different laws and institutions. In a country too, where, though the rich or the owners of large capitals enjoy a good deal of security, the poor or the owners of small capitals enjoy scarce any, but are liable, under the pretence of justice, to be pillaged and plundered at any time by the inferior mandarins, the quantity of stock employed in all the different branches of business transacted within it, can never be equal to what the nature and extent of that business might admit. In every different branch, the oppression of the poor must establish the monopoly of the rich, who, by engrossing the whole trade to themselves, will be able to make very large profits. Twelve per cent, accordingly, is said to be the common interest of money in China, and the ordinary profits of stock must be sufficient to afford this large interest.[27]

Although Ricardo did not find a stationary state attractive, he identified what amounts to a range of stationary states running from one extreme at which population is stationary at a kind of minimal subsistence level[28] to another extreme at which population is stationary at a wage level that includes not only subsistence but also additional conventional goods. Profits tended to fall to and below the minimal level at which they encouraged accumulation, though improvements and discoveries might interrupt this decline associated with diminishing returns and the rising real cost of labor. Stimulus to population growth ceased with the descent of the market price of labor to its natural price at which population became stationary. This natural price was not necessarily limited to subsistence or "fixed and constant"; it could rise as wants increased and men became habituated to higher standards of life, with the result that market wages came into balance with a higher and possibly rising natural price of labor, and numbers ceased to grow. Ricardo's analysis thus allowed for a stationary state in which the natural price of labor could notably exceed mere subsistence.[29] "The friends of humanity cannot but wish that in all countries the labouring classes should have a taste for comforts and enjoyments, and that they should be stimulated by all legal means to their exertions to procure them."[30] He suggested, at least by implication, that the advent of a stationary state depended upon the degree to which raw materials and subsistence were imported, or labor-embodied rather than land-embodied goods dominated the standard of life.[31]

It remained for John Stuart Mill to describe the stationary state in ideal terms and to argue as well that further increase in the productive powers of the British and similar economies would call for no greater population to exploit and realize these powers. He thus indicated the need for population to remain stationary in such economies and, while not asserting that average welfare and output would not further increase, asserted that men could be happy in a stationary population such as England's when this stationariness was the result of prudential control.

Mill wrote as follows:

There is room in the world, no doubt, and even in old countries, for a great increase of population, supposing the arts of life to go on improving, and capital to increase. But even if innocuous, I confess I see very little reason for desiring it. The density of population necessary to enable mankind to obtain, in the greatest degree, all the advantages both of co-operation and of social intercourse, has, in all the most populous countries, been attained. A population may be too crowded, though all be amply supplied with food and raiment. It is not good for man to be kept perforce at all times in the presence of his species. A world from which solitude is extirpated is a very poor ideal. Solitude, in the sense of being often alone, is essential to any depth of mediation or of character; and solitude in the presence of natural beauty and grandeur is the cradle of thoughts and aspirations which are not only good for the individual, but which society could ill do without. Nor is there much satisfaction in contemplating the world with nothing left to the spontaneous activity of nature; with every foot of land brought into cultivation, which is capable of growing food for human beings; every flowery waste or natural pasture ploughed up, all quadrupeds or birds which are not domesticated for man's use exterminated as his rivals for food, every hedgerow or superfluous tree rooted out, and scarcely a place left where a wild shrub or flower could grow without being eradicated as a weed in the name of improved agriculture. If the earth must lose that great portion of its pleasantness which it owes to things that the unlimited increase of wealth and population would extirpate from it, for the mere purpose of enabling it to support a larger, but not a better or a happier population, I sincerely hope, for the sake of posterity, that they will be content to be stationary, long before necessity compels them to it.

It is scarcely necessary to remark that a stationary condition of capital and population implies no stationary state of human improvement. There would be as much scope as ever for all kinds of mental culture, and moral and social progress; as much room for improving the Art of Living, and much more likelihood of its being improved, when minds ceased to be engrossed by the art of getting on. Even the industrial arts might be as earnestly and as successfully cultivated, with this sole difference, that instead of serving no purpose but the increase of wealth, industrial improvements would produce their legitimate effect, that of abridging labour. Hitherto [1848] it is questionable if all the mechanical inventions yet made have lightened the day's toil of any human being. They have enabled a greater population to live the same life of drudgery and imprisonment, and an increased number of manufacturers and others to make fortunes. They have increased the comforts of the middle classes. But they have not yet begun to effect those great changes in human destiny, which it is in their nature and in their futurity to accomplish. Only when, in addition to just institutions, the increase of mankind shall be under the deliberate guidance of judicious foresight, can the conquests made from the powers of nature by the intellect and energy of scientific discoverers become the common property of the species, and the means of improving and elevating the universal lot.[32]

The classical school held in effect that if man did not regulate growth of his numbers, it would be regulated by what Dorfman and his associates call the "needed component of *slowest* growth" which "will set the pace for the whole." This "component," Malthus and others held, would be "subsistence" though it would not be so should man prove able to increase his subsistence faster than his numbers. "In point of fact, Malthus based his theory on the assumption that inorganic natural resources— 'land'—were limited and could not grow in effectiveness in a geometric ratio. The zero own-rate of growth of land would set the pace for organic food and for man, so that a stationary population would be reached in a technologically stationary society."[33] It was preferable, the classical school held, that some other limitational factors be substituted for land. What in effect has happened is that in much of the world man has followed this counsel.

B. *Post-Classical*

The concept of stationary state has entered into post-classical economics in two ways. Most post-classical users of the concept of "stationary state" had different objectives in view. Whereas the classical writers made the stationary state the terminus of forces of change become spent, the post-classical writers employed it as a methodological abstraction or fiction. Best known was J. B. Clark's static or stationary state.[34] He used the "static state" to analyze distribution, but he failed to specify all the essential conditions; they were later identified by Frank Knight in his examination of the role of "uncertainty."[35]

While Alfred Marshall looked upon the "stationary state" as a fictional state in which "the influences exerted by the element of time" are "but little felt" and discussed its significance, he preceded this discussion with an account of increasing returns in terms of materials and / or social enjoyment.

> Taking account of the fact that an increasing density of population generally brings with it access to new social enjoyments we may give a rather broader scope to this statement and say:—An increase of population accompanied by an equal increase in the material sources of enjoyment and aids to production is likely to lead to a more than proportionate increase in the aggregate income of enjoyment of all kinds; provided firstly, an adequate supply of raw produce can be obtained without great difficulty, and secondly there is no such overcrowding as causes physical and moral vigour to be impaired by the want of fresh air and light and of healthy and joyous recreation for the young.

But he adds that importation of food and raw materials, together with conservation of wealth, may not continue to provide an escape from "the pressure of the law of diminishing return" and thus ensure countries situated like England easy access to abundant foreign supplies. "England's foreign supplies of raw produce may at any time be checked by changes in the trade regulations of other countries, and may be almost cut off by a great war, while the naval and military expenditure which would be necessary to make the country fairly secure against this last risk, would appreciably diminish the benefits that she derives from the action of the law of increasing return."[36]

Regarding the fictional stationary state Marshall writes:

> This state obtains its name from the fact that in it the general conditions of production and consumption, of distribution and exchange remain motionless; but yet it is full of movement; for it is a mode of life. The average age of the population may be stationary; though each individual is growing up from youth towards his prime, or downwards to old age. And the same amount of things per head of the population will have been produced in the same ways by the same classes of people for many generations together; and therefore this supply of appliances for production will have had full time to be adjusted to the steady demand.[37]

This state did not correspond to the real world but could be made to approximate more closely the real world and thus, in effect, to become a way station to a steady but growing state of the sort Gustav Cassel put forward.

> The Stationary State has just been taken to be one in which population is stationary. But nearly all its distinctive features may be exhibited in a place where population and wealth are both growing, provided they are growing at about the same rate, and there is no scarcity of land: and provided also the methods of production and the conditions of trade change but little; and above all, where the character of man himself is a constant quantity. For in such a state by far the most important conditions of production and consumption, of exchange and distribution will remain of the same quality, and in the same general relations to one another, though they are all increasing in volume.
>
> This relaxation of the rigid bonds of a purely stationary state brings us one step nearer to the actual conditions of life: and by relaxing them still further we get nearer still. We thus approach by gradual steps towards the difficult problem of the interaction of countless economic causes. In the stationary state all the conditions of production and consumption are reduced to rest: but less violent assumptions are made by what is, not quite accurately, called the *statical* method. By that method we fix our minds on some central point: we suppose it for the time to be reduced to a *stationary* state; and we then study in relation to it the forces that affect the things by which it is surrounded, and any tendency there may be to equilibrium of these forces.[38]

Marshall's approach was continued with elaboration by A. C. Pigou. He identified three degrees of stationary states.

> In every form of economic stationary state, even the least rigorous, the number, the age distribution, the sex distribution and the quality of the units that make up the population, the total amount of work that they

do, and the total stock of capital equipment (as measured in the amount of work waiting that goes to make it) must all be conceived as constant. Of course stationariness in this sense does not mean frozen fixity; individual drops composing the waterfall are continually in movement, though the waterfall itself remains. Wear and tear takes place, but it is always exactly offset by replacement. Moreover, the rates of wear and tear and replacement are constant; there are no jumps involving variations in the aggregate of work done by industries that make capital goods. These general conditions are, however, satisfied by three different arrangements, all of which may claim in a sense to be stationary states. First, the system in industry as a whole may be stationary, while the several industries that compose it are in movement. Secondly, every separate industry may be stationary, while the individual firms in it are in movement. Thirdly, individual firms, as well as individual industries, may be stationary. The characteristics of these three sorts of stationary state must be briefly described.[39]

Pigou's book dealt mainly with the third form:

There remains the third form of stationary state. In it not merely the system of industry and every individual industry stand constant, but also every individual business unit. This form contains all the attributes of the other two with a further attribute added. I shall speak of it as the *thorough-going* stationary state, and shall in this book focus attention on it. It will be found that a study of this simple and highly artificial model enables us to disentangle a number of complex interrelations that are fundamental in the real world.[40]

Of the population in this state Pigou writes:

In order to ensure stationariness it is clearly not enough that the birth-rate and the general death-rate shall be equal. This gives constancy of numbers, but it need not give constancy in age-distribution: and, if the age-distribution of a population varies, this will, in general, entail change both in its power as an instrument of production and in the direction of its choice among different objects of consumption. For example, a population with a large proportion of children and old persons is less productive than one that consists mainly of persons of working age: and, of course, children need different sorts of commodities from people in middle or later life. A stationary state, therefore, requires, not merely constancy in the total number of the population, but also constancy of the numbers in every age group. This entails much more than mere equality of birth-rate and general death-rate. It entails also that the proportion of deaths in each age group is always such as to bring down by the next year the number of those who were living in any age group in the year before to the number who were then living in the next higher age group. But the death-rate of each group depends on conditions which must, for our purpose, be presumed to hold constant: otherwise the state is not stationary. It follows that the structure of the population in respect of age distribution must be such that the number at each age (n) exceeds the number at each age ($n + 1$) in a definite proportion, i.e., by the proportion of those at age n that are due to die in a year. Unless a population is initially of this structure, it *cannot* be frozen into stationariness. A population will necessarily be of this structure provided that, at the time when freezing is attempted, the birth-rate and the death-rate at every age have already remained constant for a period as long as the life of the oldest living person, but not otherwise. Even if it is not of this structure, it is still possible, of course, for it to be held henceforward for ever of a constant structure: but only on condition that the death-rates in the different age groups change from year to year: and a situation in which this happens cannot be called stationary.[41]

Inasmuch as Keynes was much concerned with the impact of longer-run conditions upon current and near-present events, he warned that the "assumptions of the static state" which often underlay "present-day economic theory" imported "into it a large element of unreality." For "regarding the marginal efficiency of capital primarily in terms of the *current* yield of capital equipment" would be "correct only in the static state where there is no changing future to influence the present"; "even the rate of interest is, virtually, a current phenomenon." The link between today and tomorrow must be allowed for.[42] He suggested that we "make our line of division between the theory of stationary equilibrium and the theory of a system in which changing views about the future are capable of influencing the present situation."[43]

Especially significant was the prospective future. For should the state encourage the growth of capital equipment "to approach saturation-point at a rate" which did not disproportionately "burden the standard of life of the present generation," "a properly run community equipped with modern technical resources, of which the population is not increasing rapidly, ought to be able to bring down the marginal efficiency of capital in equilibrium approximately to zero within a single generation; so that we should attain the conditions of a quasi-stationary community where change and progress would result only from changes in technique, taste, population and institutions, with the products of capital selling at a price proportioned to the labour, etc., embodied in them on just the same principles as govern the prices of consumption-goods into which capital-charges enter in an insignificant degree." "Enormous social changes would result" from the "gradual disappearance of a rate of return on accumulated wealth," that is, of "the pure rate of interest apart from any allowance for risk and the like, and not to the gross yield of assets including the return in respect of risk." The disappearance of the rentier did not, however, entail disappearance of room for "enterprise and skill in the estimation of prospective yields about which opinions would differ," possibly accompanied by "eagerness to obtain a yield from doubtful investments" and a resulting "aggregate *negative* net yield" on all investment.[44]

Despite this contingently sanguine prospect, Keynes found the likely future to be disturbing. For the lowness of the average rate of interest under the circumstances prevailing could eventuate in a near-stationary if not contracting economy. The conditions obtaining in the nineteenth-century—"growth of population and of invention, the opening-up of new lands, the state of confidence and the frequency of war . . . , taken in conjunction with the propensity to consume"—had made possible "a schedule of the marginal efficiency of capital which allowed a reasonably satisfactory average level of employment to be compatible with a rate of interest high enough to be psychologically acceptable to wealth-owners." But circumstances had changed. Under prevailing conditions and presumably for the future the schedule of the marginal efficiency of capital implied an average rate of interest "so unacceptable to wealth owners" that it could not result in investment allowing "a reasonable average level of employment."[45] Moreover, given a declining rate of population growth, the "characteristic phase" of the trade cycle would "be lengthened."[46] Current long-term expectations were not highly conducive to confidence insofar as they affected the present through the demand price for durable equipment.[47]

A year after the *General Theory* Keynes returned in greater detail to the population prospect and the possibility that "a change-over from an increasing to a declining population" might "be very disastrous."[48]

While use of the concept of stationary state as an analytical instrument declined with the emergence of growth theory and concern with the steady state,[49] it has been utilized by leading economists. For example, R. M. Goodwin points to the stability of distribution when all net product is consumed, there is no pure profit, operating profit covers interest cost, and all rentier income is consumed. Then income distribution is constant. "It is a striking fact," observes Goodwin,

> that in an unchanging community and many such have existed and some still do, there is no reason why any existing distribution of income should alter. This is, of course, subject to some sort of lower subsistence limit on wages, but otherwise there is no bar to any distribution no matter how extreme. This refers to functional distribution, not distribution by size, though there is usually a close connection between the two.
>
> Not only is distribution arbitrary but so also must be, to a limited extent, prices and the methods of production. . . .[50]

J. E. Meade is interested in contrasting stationary with growing economies under alternative modes of organization. He examines a "stationary economy" in which "land and labour" are used "directly to produce various goods for individual consumption" and [in] which "the underlying conditions are unchanging so that a stationary self-perpetuating equilibrium state is reached."

Investigation of this "horribly unrealistic" society provides training in tools of analysis, and isolates important relationships in the real world. The model also "can provide an example of the basic clash between what is desirable in society on efficiency grounds and what is desirable on distributional grounds; and it provides, therefore, a good introduction to a wide range of problems concerned with the choice of economic policy."[51]

Having assumed a fixed factor, land, in his model, and introduced technical progress, Meade concludes:

> There is, I think, a general conclusion which one can draw. Economic growth is basically due to three components: capital accumulation, population growth, and technical progress. If over a considerable period of years population growth and technical progress make contributions which are not readily changed by economic considerations, then the relationship between capital accumulation and growth of output will tend to bring the rate of economic growth to a steady level which depends upon the rate of population growth and the rate of technical progress and is *independent of the proportion of income saved.*[52]

As Meade's last statement implies, the introduction of technological change greatly complicates the use of a stationary-economy or related model. Thus, as T. K. Rymes points out:

> The notion of capital as a factor of production and the meaning which can be attached to the notion of a production function have been drawn up, until recently, within the context of a stationary state or in a world where, as Keynes assumed, the stock of capital is taken in the short run as part of the environment in which labour works. By a stationary state I shall mean an economy in which output per unit of labor is constant. My concept of a stationary state includes therefore the classical stationary state with zero net accumulation of commodity capital and also a steady-growth state with zero technological progress and a positive rate of growth of net accumulation in forms of commodity capital equal to the rate of growth of the labour input. The classical stationary state is clearly a special case of the steady-state case with the rate of growth of labour set equal to zero. Once technological change is introduced and output per unit of labour is rising, are the traditional notions of capital as an input and the production function affected? To answer such questions, one must have a clear grasp of what capital as a factor of production is in the stationary state.[53]

Rymes concludes that "the intermediate and endogenous nature of the capital input is best understood in the dynamic context of technical change." And he endorses Joan Robinson's conclusion that from the long-run point of view "labour and natural resources are the factors of production in the economy as a whole, while capital goods and the time patterns of production are the means by which the factors are deployed."[54] One may infer from this that limitations leading to stationarity are to be found in both resource scarcity and the exhaustibility of the capacity of technical progress to counterbalance biospheric limitations (e.g., in a slackening of technical progress in particular sectors of economies to which Julius Wolf long ago called attention).[55]

With the increasing importance of actual or prospective rising costs attributable to fixity of resource stocks, increasing entropy, and increasing natural resource scarcity, progress in technology, already very important, becomes more and more critical. For it increases man's capacity to transform labor, capital, and biospheric inputs into output. Accordingly, in controversy respecting prospective scarcity, technological progress, ultimately a joint product of investment in human capital and in the cumulation and application of scientific knowledge, is pitted against constraints present in man's physical environment and subject to intensification by production itself in the form of increasing costs associated with pollution, supposedly a growing concomitant of modern productive processes.[56] A presumption of steady-state theory is, of course, the adequacy of technological progress to continue to surmount limits inherent in man's physical environment and its subjection to contraction. Here we may accept Solow's suggestion and say that an economy is in a steady state when "real output per man (or per man-hour) grows at more or less constant rate," real capital per man grows at a more or less constant rate, the ratio of capital to output shows no systematic trend, and "the rate of profit on capital has a horizontal trend."[57]

4. Emergence of The Steady State Model

Samuelson contributed to the employment of steady state models by distinguishing sharply between static and dynamic models.[58] As has been noted, however, the theory of steady states emerged out of the theory of macroeconomic growth.[59] According to the neo-classical theory of maximal consumption in equilibrium growth, "at maximal consumption per man, the rate of profit is equal to the rate of population growth, which is equal to the general rate of growth."[60]

For purposes of the present discussion, however, it is to be noted that growth models may not map nicely upon actual patterns of growth. Operative mechanisms in an economy are not likely to be such as to generate ideal or steady states, especially within an international setting or one involving intergenerational equity.[61] "It is not easy to bring facts to bear on 'steady states' and 'equilibrium economies,'" especially when theory is "drawn into directions which severely limit its direct empirical applications or usefulness"; for, as Keynes wrote apropos of wage theory, "a scientific theory cannot require the facts to conform to its own assumptions."[62]

5. Sources of Scarcity and Technology

While the classical school built its conception of scarcity and stationarity upon the fixity of an accessible stock of heterogeneous land, it remained for W. S. Jevons to anticipate increasing entropy in the form of exhaustion of easily accessible sources of coal.[63] Jevons put forward in his *The Coal Question* (1865, 1866) what in effect amounts to a theory of a Contractile State. A modern economy, he observed, rested on "economy of power" dependent, at least in England, upon a coal supply that was both shrinking and subject to increasing cost. "Changes here, or in other parts of the world may, even before the failure of our mines, reduce us to a stationary condition. . . ." Even then, as the mines failed, the English economy would contract, since it could not in the long run produce and sell in a highly competitive world products wherewith to import both energy supplies and other essential products. Jevons did not allow for technological progress as did J. S. Mill.[64]

Resource exhaustion, though occasionally referred to in ancient times and before Jevon's time, could hardly be appreciated as important before the growth of per capita consumption moved above one percent per year after the middle of the nineteenth century. After World War I and even earlier it came to be recognized in the United States that both fixity of the stock of some critical natural resources and depletion of stock of exhaustible natural resources would set limits to the augmentation of agricultural output as well as to the long-run availability of various metals and minerals.[65] It remained, however, for Jay Forrester and particularly for Donella H. and Dennis L. Meadows (and associates) to pose the resource problem in their well-publicized report to the Club of Rome, *The Limits to Growth,* a work preceded by Jay W. Forrester's *World Dynamics,* studies subsequently much criticized by writers optimistic respecting world mineral stocks.[66] The Meadows' report, an attempt to demonstrate the importance at a world level of biospheric limits to growth was subjected to two sorts of criticisms: (a) defects in the model and its underlying assumptions, together with neglect of corrective feedbacks and weaknesses in the way the model maps upon the universe it purports to describe; (b) assertion that technical progress can surmount all barriers in the form of limitational factors brought into being. In a subsequent study, also sponsored by the Club of Rome, Mesarovic and Pestel treat the world not as a unity but as a system of interrelated regions subject to limitations in the form of physically nonaugmentable natural resources that technological progress cannot wholly overcome—limitations that are accentuated by population growth. The way out, it is suggested, lies in rationally planned global cooperation on the part of the world's diverse regional communities.[67] At this stage of the debate however, it is not possible in a review such as we have attempted, to undertake anything like a final assessment.

6. Steady State as Objective

While steady-state models may correspond to a Golden Rule, they do not reflect concern respecting biospheric limitations as does a *stationary* steady state when defined as an objective. Such a steady state would come into existence if (a) fertility descended gradually to the replacement level and a stable, stationary population eventuated, and (b) per capita growth of output finally settled at the zero level. The stationary steady state that would result has been described by Daly.

> By "steady state" is meant a constant stock of *physical* wealth (capital), and a constant stock of people (population). Naturally these stocks do not remain constant by themselves. People die, and wealth is physically consumed—that is, worn out, depreciated. Therefore the stocks must be maintained by a rate of inflow (birth, production) equal to the rate of outflow (death, consumption). But this equality may obtain, and stocks remain constant, with a high rate of throughput (equal to both the rate of inflow and the rate of outflow), or with a low rate. Our definition of steady state is not complete until we specify the rates of throughput by which the constant stocks are maintained. For a number of reasons we specify that the rate of throughput should be "as low as possible." For an equilibrium stock the average age at "death" of its members is the reciprocal of the rate of throughput. The faster the water flows through the tank, the less time an average drop spends in the tank. For the population a low rate of throughput (a low birth rate and an equally low consumption) means greater life expectancy or durability of goods and less time sacrificed to production. This means more "leisure" or nonjob time to be divided into consumption time, personal and household maintenance time, culture time, and idleness. This too seems socially desirable, at least within limits.[68]

While this state might long persist, given appropriate demographic and economic behavior, it would undergo some contraction in the long run. For, as Georgescu-Roegen points out, even a steady state consumes low entropy. This makes the "vital question for mankind's future: How long can a given world population . . . be maintained?"[69] This consequence of increasing entropy is recognized by Daly. He writes:

> In sum, the steady state of wealth and population is maintained by an inflow of low-entropy matter-energy (depletion) and an outflow of an

equal quantity of high-entropy matter-energy (pollution). Stocks of wealth and people, like individual organisms, are open systems that feed on low entropy.[70]

Despite conditional long-run advantages associated with a stationary economy, it probably could not be achieved and maintained in the absence of an absolutist state,[71] and even given such a state, a world of diverse national states might militate against the persistence of individual stationary economies. Even granting stability of replacement fertility and a constant annual number of births, maintenance of aggregate output at a stationary level would present very great difficulties. In particular, since some or many of the wants of most families and individuals are unsatisfied, at least under present conditions, the large, unsatisfied fragment of the population would look upon *growth* as a means of decreasing this dissatisfaction, usually under conditions not likely soon to eliminate the dissatisfaction.[72] What may prove possible, however, in particular states is stabilization of population in the neighborhood of the zero growth level and avoidance of such sources of fluctuation in employment and output as are associated with fluctuations in births and secondary fluctuations that echo original fluctuations in births.

Conclusion

It is not possible at this point to anticipate man's prospect, given current international differences in fertility, availability of resources, subjection to biospheric constraints, and capacity for effectively using available resources. While fertility is below the replacement level in many advanced countries, it probably can be elevated to the replacement level through appropriate intervention by the state. Establishment of a stationary steady state probably lies beyond the power of a contemporary political state, given its membership in the present world economy and system of states.

It is possible at this point, however, to identify some factors bearing upon man's future-oriented actions. Of primary importance are individuals' perceptions of their prospects, perceptions issuing out of the options seemingly open to autonomous individuals as well as to groups of individuals acting in concert. For over the past two centuries and especially in (say) the past one hundred years options open to the representative individual, together with his autonomy, have increased. This trend has been favorable to decline in fertility inasmuch as the trend has entailed increase in alternatives to the production and rearing of children. At the same time this trend has been favorable to increase in the output of goods and services per capita inasmuch as increase in the supply of options tends to be accompanied by an offsetting increase in demand for the economic exploitation and fruits of existing and emerging options. Moreover, as some argue, the elasticity of substitution between natural resources and other factors appears to be quite high, and technological change may continue to prove resource-augmenting, with the result that biospheric limits will not become operative in the immediate future.[73]

Given the range of options together with its continuing increase, something like a stationary economy is unlikely to evolve in the absence of growing environmental pressure, though an economy characterized by population growth in the neighborhood of zero and by a somewhat variable increase in average output is likely to emerge and persist in many countries. For the autonomy of individuals, along with the capacity of many to cope with new and old constraints on growth, militates against the transformation of expanding into stationary economies. These same conditions may militate against the achievement and maintenance of a population of optimum size (that is, of a size compatible with the maximization of a designated collective welfare index), or the attainment of an optimum rate of population growth. Indeed, given the difficulties attendant upon achieving optimal steady-state solutions, it is not likely that policies reasonably close to optimal can be both defined and put into effect.[74] Feedback mechanisms, together with their impact, do not appear to be sufficiently incident to produce what are defined as optimum results, particularly if a potential for self-generating waves is present in a society.[75] When such a potential is present, fertility will probably rise or fall at a future date.[76]

II. Attitudes toward Population Growth

From a long-run point of view, labour and natural resources are the factors of production in the economy as a whole.
Joan Robinson, *The Accumulation of Capital*, p. 310

The demand for men, like that for any other commodity, necessarily regulates the production of men.
Adam Smith, *Wealth of Nations I*, viii

In this chapter we review the changes that have taken place in attitudes toward population growth at the collective or national level. These changes underlie policy and changes in policy respecting population. They affect population growth itself insofar as they modify the attitudes and the microeconomic environments of households and hence their propensities to produce children of greater or lesser quality. The probability of a population's becoming stationary may thus be said to depend upon the evolution of attitudes toward population growth.

Having looked at attitudes in general we make use of a sequence of three fictional economic worlds—a two-factor world, a multifactor world, and a "new era" world—to symbolize significant changes in economies and in the collective (as distinguished from intra-household) importance attached to manpower and hence to population. Even though these worlds are abstractions, they seem to map well upon the experience in the West; they thus enable us to see, as from afar, great changes in economic contours, together with their effects upon attitudes toward population. Making use of this fictional sequence requires us to examine situations from the point of view of the railroad contractor in F. Y. Edgeworth's paraphrase of Clerk-Maxwell's comment on the "principle of continuity": "Heterogeneities in the structure of a mound of gravel, which are negligible from the point of view of the railway contractor, may be all important to a worm."[1] We therefore neglect microeconomic sequelae at the household level when examining change at the macrostructural level.

1. Attitudes in General

General attitudes are important not in themselves but in terms of the preferences that they reveal, preferences which in turn affect the behavior of households and the capacity of societies to make use of increments of population.

General attitudes toward population growth have always depended upon (a) current and prospective empirical conditions and (b) man's perceptions and interpretations of these conditions. Population growth has been favored, therefore, by those who have looked upon it as a source of sufficient utility in manpower and other terms to outweigh its cost and therefore warrant incurrence of this cost. Population growth is and has been the product, therefore, of a multitude of decisions, mainly at the hands of households and secondarily at the hands of formulators of decisions governing the social and physical environments of households. These decisions, of course, are not solely the product of a continuing stream of decision-making; they are also a result of decisions, made in the past by earlier decision-makers in response to the economic and other circumstances, which having been found satisfactory, were gradually incorporated into customs and institutions.[2] The impact in the present of such past decisions was much more important, however, before (say) the eighteenth century when the rate of change in custom and institution was very much lower than it is in the age when, as W. E. Smith puts it, "virtually everything is perishable."[3]

Attitudes toward population growth are shaped by the utility such growth is expected to yield and by the costs that this growth entails. The utility associated with this growth is of two sorts, that which is transferable and hence salable (e.g., productive power) and that which is nontransferable and utilizable only within the household (e.g., affection, love, sense of security). Accordingly, while the propensity of the random household to produce children, costs being given, tends to depend upon both sorts of utility, the value set upon population growth outside households depends largely upon the nature of the transferable utility.

Two sets of decisions underlie the maintenance and growth of population—(a) those resulting in the formation of households and the production of children, and (b) those governing the utilization of children as they mature, eventually into adults and full-fledged members of the actual or potential working force of the community. The (a) set of decisions reflects the perceptions that individuals form of the anticipated costs and flow of utility associated with the reproduction of children. While anticipated costs and utility may be underestimated or overestimated and affect reproduction accordingly, disparity between anticipated and realized values diminishes with the accumulation of experience and improvement in information and its use in analysis and decision-making. The (b) set of decisions bears both upon intra- and extra-household behavior. They affect reproduction and population growth indirectly rather than directly; for while they relate *inter alia* to persons already born, they condition the utility derivable from these persons and thus make utility-cost relations more or less attractive and hence more or less conducive to household formation and reproduction.

2. Two-Factor World

Attitudes toward population are dominated by the relative scarcity of manpower and of time at the disposal of individuals. Scarcity of manpower may be viewed as a collective or macroeconomic phenomenon and scarcity of time as an individual or microeconomic phenomenon. If, for the present, we neglect the impact of scarcity of time on individual behavior and the availability of labor time, we may say that the scarcity of undifferentiated manpower is conditioned by the relative abundance of agents of production complementary to manpower. Over the centuries the agents of production have increased in *kind* as well as in relative amounts, and so has man's interpretation of the relative significance to be attached to these agents and manpower. Since our purpose is contrast over time, we may neglect the question of whether the primary factors are two or three in number.

In the essentially two-factor world with which we deal in this section—one in which output and increase therein are imputable almost entirely to land and labor—population and average output grew very slowly, especially in comparison with the multi-factor world that subsequently emerged, or with the still more advanced world that followed. To illustrate, between 1000 and 1700, Europe's population, together with its total product per capita apparently grew not much more than 1.5 percent per decade.[4] Even in relatively advanced England and Wales, between 1695–1715 and 1765–1785, population grew about 3 percent per decade and product per capita, 1.9 percent per decade. In Great Britain, a good example of the multi-factor world that thereafter emerged, product per capita rose 12.7 percent per decade over the first half of the period 1801–1924 and 11.1 percent over the second half. As we note later, with the gradual transformation of multi-factor economies into economies fully representative of a new epoch, the rate of growth per decade of per capita product rose notably.[5] In what follows we shall infer that whereas the replacement of a two-factor by multi-factor economies resulted in a relative increase in the aggregate demand for manpower, the arrival of this "new era" seems likely to result in a decline in the relative importance of manpower and population.

It is not inaccurate to say that macroeconomic attitudes toward manpower and hence population were shaped by the essentially two-factor character of pre-1750 economies. For the prevailing theory of production, such as it was, mapped nicely upon what appeared to be a world in which production was dominated by land and labor—by inputs which, though recognizably variable in quality, could be treated as homogeneous for purposes of analysis and exposition. It is true, of course, that something like an explicit two-factor theory of production, in which output was largely imputed to land and labor, did not receive quite full expression until at the hands of the mercantilists, though the predominance of land and labor had long been noted.

As E. A. J. Johnson has nicely shown, English mercantilists stressed the overriding importance of land and labor (inclusive of "ingenious labour"). Counterparts in France and elsewhere expressed somewhat similar views. In effect these theories were sophisticated developments of earlier opinions which made output flow from combining labor with the bounty of Nature.[6] While it was recognized that land as well as labor varied in quality, there existed as yet no theory of human capital to translate differences in earning power into terms of investment nor a corresponding theory of rent.[7]

In literature relating to economic matters in medieval and earlier classic times one finds not so much a two-factor theory of production as descriptions of economic activities that put overriding emphasis upon land and manpower.[8] It has been held, moreover, that a shortage of manpower developed within the Roman Empire as early as the late second century, with the result that cultivation of land and the production of services began to suffer.[9] With the development of cities and trade in Europe after the tenth century, attention was drawn to the importance of factors besides land and labor, but this did not inspire a rejection of the essentially two-factor view of the economic world.

It is not strange that pre–nineteenth century economic discussion tended to run in terms of land and labor. For before the nineteenth century and in less-developed countries after 1800 the agents of production complementary to labor consisted almost entirely of land and investment in land and its improvement that was not sharply distinguished from land as such. Often there flowed to land (or its owners) in the neighborhood of half the net national product. The size of this share was conditioned, however, by the alternatives available to potential cultivators.[10] With the growth and spread of the industrial revolution and the investment and labor alternatives that is provided, the rental share fell. About a century later (i.e., in 1910), Alfred Marshall remarked that the then stage of social history was no longer one "in which the special features of the income yielded by the ownership of land" "dominated human relations." He added, however, that "perhaps they may again assert a pre-eminence."[11] That the contribution of land to the national income had become very low in many countries was revealed by Olson's study 38 years later.[12]

Statistical data relating to occupational composition lend support to the view that the economic world was essentially a two-factor one before the rise and spread of the industrial revolution. These data indicate that 70 or more percent of the labor force were engaged in agriculture during early stages of development of presently advanced countries and that this condition remains characteristic of many underdeveloped countries.[13] Moreover, since the proportion of the population reported in agriculture was roughly correlated with the proportion living outside urban centers in the past, one may infer from the smallness of the urban population that the fraction engaged in agriculture was very large and that therefore land and labor were the overriding factors of production.[14]

Conditions essential to urban growth and hence to the expansion of nonagricultural employment must have developed very slowly. As late as 1920, 71 percent of the population of the world's "more developed regions" still lived in rural areas and small towns (i.e., localities smaller than 20,000) compared with 94 percent in "less developed regions."[15] In 1815, of the nineteen countries of Europe (then the most urban continent) for which data are given, only two (Britain and the Netherlands) had over 20 percent of their population living in places of over 5,000, and ten had only 8 percent or less in such places.[16] Prior to modern times very large cities were capital cities, situated on waterways and deriving basic support in considerable measure from tax and ecclesiastical revenues. As late as the eleventh century, Bennett conjectures, even in Europe town-dwellers—individuals who got their food from agriculturalists—could not have "constituted more than 15 percent of the total population"; for the world as a whole, perhaps 10 percent.[17] These conjectures are in keeping with the apparent lowness of output per capita.[18]

The urban and hence nonagricultural fraction of the population trended upward very slowly, often subject to interruption and even reversal and always subject to limits imposed by the slowness with which agricultural output increased over time though individual towns might surmount these limits in varying degree.[19] Writing in the first century B.C., M. T. Varro, a famous and apparently observant Roman author, classified economic systems into those dependent upon hunting, fishing, and gathering, those engaged in pastoral activities (herding, domestication of animals), and those engaged in agriculture. "For Varro, the agricultural economy was the highest conceivable form of economic civilization and urban crafts appeared as a superstructure of agriculture. This concept was in harmony with the economic patterns known at that time. Not until the end of the eighteenth century did the urban crafts and trades reach such importance that it became necessary to extend Varro's classification by adding industry and trade as an economic stage succeeding agriculture."[20]

Urban life did, however, develop after Varro's time, in considerable measure because of increasing political stability in the West, only to contract with the disappearance of this stability.[21] Upon the re-emergence of considerable political stability in and after the tenth century, urban life again began to expand.[22] Yet, even in the age of Regionalism which arose and developed between (say) 1100 and its collapse after 1348 under the impact of the Black Death, the urban fraction of the population of most regions apparently did not exceed, if it equaled, 10 percent, though in at least four regions it approached or possibly exceeded one-fifth. Moreover, with the exception of a few places in a small number of regions, city size remained very small.[23] From the lowness of the urban share and slowness with which it grew when it did grow, therefore, one may infer that before the modern period nonagricultural employment grew very slowly, in part because cultivators did not produce a large surplus for exchange with and support of nonagricultural activities in cities. Until the present century, however, a considerable amount of nonagricultural activity, only some of which was complementary to agricultural activity, was undertaken in rural areas, on estates and villas in Roman and medieval times and in villages.[24]

So long as economies were essentially two-factor in character, the relative scarcity of manpower was conditioned by (a) the relative abundance of cultivable and suitably situated land in need of exploitation and (b) the employability of labor in activities virtually independent of inputs of land and "physical capital." The demand for category (a), given demand for produce, tended to increase both as more suitable land became available and as the elasticity of substitution of labor for land was such as to allow increase in labor–land coefficients and the intensity of cultivation. Category (b) is a heterogeneous category, in that even in a predominantly two-factor world many engaged in nonagricultural activities made use of small amounts of physical capital, and a few might use more. Even so, the average amount of *productive* capital used by most nonagricultural workers was small and remained small until modern times. Most of the "wealth" accumulated was incorporated in and with land or assumed *unproductive forms,* and hence did not answer to the conventional description of physical capital. Accordingly, the assumption that manpower not included in (a) may be placed in (b) does not deviate greatly from what was reality. Nor does the corollary that, so long as nonagricultural capital played a very minor role, the demand for labor could increase very slowly as a result of increase in nonlanded inputs complementary to labor. With the change in this condition and the advent of a multi-factor world characterized by a relatively high or rising increase in nonlanded complements to manpower, growth of the demand for manpower was emancipated from constraints imposed by the slow growth of (a).

Category (a) responded positively not only to increase in accessible land but also to increase in the substitutability of labor for land. Increase in substitutability could be facilitated by change in methods of production,[25] or by improvements in the quality of land (e.g., clearing, drainage, irrigation, and so forth) that required more labor, at least temporarily. Increase in (a) due to great increases in output of the sort associated with a "green revolution" has, however, been an essentially recent phenomenon.

The relative importance of category (a) was susceptible of decrease in particular countries as a result of heavy food imports (e.g., in modern England and Wales, in Solon's Athens, in Rome when dependent on Egypt), or of the substitution of inputs for labor as well as for land, a process that became important only in modern times.[26] Labor engaged in agriculture has often been underemployed both because of seasonal variation in the need for it, and because labor engaged in agriculture preferred leisure to work, given the current terms of sale of produce and the lack of sufficiently attractive nonagricultural employment. Such employment became more available as towns emerged.[27] As Adam Smith implied, abundance of food stimulated population growth and thus enlarged the demand for produce.[28]

What may be called "aggregate demand for labor" in an essentially two-factor world grew mainly because of growth of population and growth of what we have called category (b), nonagricultural employment involving mainly labor and only small amounts of nonlabor inputs. For, while increase in available land could, given demand for produce, augment the amount of labor required for its cultivation, the overriding sequence was increase-of-population → increase-of-land-required → increase-of-population-required. Growth of (b) usually amounted to an increase in the *per capita* amount of labor required, with the result that demand for agricultural labor-time eventually rose, and with it the requirement of land and hence of labor complementary to this additional requirement of land. Of course, were (b) to increase rapidly and notably, there could be a diversion of manpower from agriculture, with the result that population capacity would diminish and with it population in the longer run.

Category (b) could not grow more rapidly than the total population unless output per agriculturalist increased and gave rise to a surplus of produce for the support of (b), and this surplus could be made available to population concentrations, especially towns and cities. Such concentrations were conditioned also by the degree of political stability and the quality of transport.[29] Essential to the growth of nonagricultural employment, therefore, was a combination of economical transport, fertile soil, and rising output per agriculturalist. The urban centers that resulted could supply products, the prospect of which stimulated agriculturalists to cultivate more effectively, and, with the improvement of agricultural methods, become sources of equipment and other essentials required in agriculture, though not of fertilizer and oil made critical by modernization of agriculture in recent decades.[30]

3. Multi-Factor World

It may be argued that, with the growth and spread of the industrial revolution and the development of a multi-factor world and hence of more factors complementary to manpower as well as substitutive for it, "aggregate demand" for manpower and hence population grew more rapidly than in the earlier two-factor world. The development of a multi-factor world is reflected in the declining importance of land in national inventories of wealth[31] and the increasing importance of inputs difficult to define appropriately in a world of technical change[32] and bearing sometimes a complementary and sometimes a substitutive relation to manpower.

Movement out of a predominantly two-factor world into a multi-factor one presupposed a sufficiently rapid growth of the food supply to meet the requirements of those parts of Europe undergoing modernization. This was met through increase in domestic agricultural production and in importation from abroad. For example, when imports into England, mainly from the Baltic area in the late 1700s, rose from a small fraction of consumption in the late eighteenth century to about one-half of total consumption by the early 1870s, over 30 percent of all grain consumed was imported.[33] In and after the 1930s Europe absorbed the major share of world food exports, with the United Kingdom accounting for a large fraction.[34]

This trend was in keeping with Adam Smith's expectations as well as with those of mercantilists who found solutions for possible domestic food shortages in the exportation of "wrought" goods to countries capable of supplying food and raw materials to countries lacking them. Adam Smith had assumed that increase in size of a country's population would give release to increasing return and thus serve to augment average output so long as limitation of natural resources (especially agricultural land) and decreasing return in extractive industry did not offset the increasing return outside extractive industry.[35] There thus lurked in Smith's model awareness of the possible advent of that classical stationary state which Ricardo and J. S. Mill later made explicit.

Awareness of the eventual advent of a stationary state was present in Alfred Marshall's observation in 1910 that imports had enabled Britain to escape diminishing returns and continue to give release to increasing returns. For at that time Britain was importing heavily from the Western Hemisphere and Australia where it invested much capital, and he pointed out that a country could almost surmount limitations imposed by a shortage of land and natural resources by drawing upon foreign sources. Indeed, it could virtually suspend "the tendency to Diminishing Return" by the "opening out of new countries, aided by low transport charges on land and sea." Even so, he recognized, as had Malthus nearly a century earlier, that this solution was of limited applicability.[36] His argument ran in full as follows:

> There have been stages in social history in which the special features of the income yielded by the ownership of land have dominated human relations: and perhaps they may again assert a pre-eminence. But in the present age, the opening out of new countries, aided by low transport

charges on land and sea, has almost suspended the tendency to Diminishing Return, in that sense in which the term was used by Malthus and Ricardo, when the English labourers' weekly wages were often less than the price of half a bushel of good wheat. And yet, if the growth of population should continue for very long even at a quarter of its present rate, the aggregate rental values of land for all its uses (assumed to be as free as now from restraint by public authority) may again exceed the aggregate of incomes derived from all other forms of material property; even though that may then embody twenty times as much labour as now.[37]

Marshall would probably have agreed with Joan Robinson's observation 60 years later that

"there was an enormous difference between the population explosion of the nineteenth century and that which is taking place today. Development of the New World, revolutionary improvements in transport and in manufactures to trade for agricultural products, provided an ample supply of food. This is a piece of history that will not repeat itself.[38]

Writing about the same time as Marshall, Warren S. Thompson, destined to become one of the best known of the students of population writing between 1910 and 1960, was less optimistic than Marshall. For he found both much evidence of decreasing return uncounteracted by improvement in technology in agriculture and but limited manifestations of increasing return outside agriculture. Whence he concluded that the capacity of even modern land-short countries to import enough food and raw materials on suitable terms was limited, and their numbers would have to be controlled.[39]

Writing six years after Marshall, during World War I and hence favorably to German expansion, Paul Mombert found population growth desirable, on grounds of increasing returns, so long as Germany's *Nahrungsspielraum* remained adequate to permit avoidance of too marked diminishing returns in agriculture. Whence he favored population growth and some economic policies conducive thereto, in part because he believed power and plenty to be closely associated.[40] However, writing after the war and Germany's defeat, Mombert was less optimistic in his outstanding *Bevölkerungslehre*.[41] Herein he developed his concept of *Nahrungsspielraum* more fully and discussed an issue long of concern in Germany, namely, how dependent might an industrializing state with safety become on foreign sources for food, raw materials, and markets. A solution likely to be satisfying in the longer run, he noted, was becoming ever more difficult of realization, given the spread of industrialization, intensification of competition among industrial countries, and the prospective worsening of the terms of trade between industrial products and food and raw materials, particularly should raw-material-supplying countries join together and price their materials monopolistically (as has recently taken place in oil-supplying countries). Not even technological progress offered a way out, since it tended to produce technological unemployment and increase the probability of socialism though not the likelihood of a solution of the unemployment problem.[42]

Mombert's work may have reflected Julius Wolf's finding in 1912 that, contrary to the belief in exponential progress reflected in such works as Henry Adams's,[43] technico-economic progress was subject to retardation on four grounds.[44] Mombert's later work may also have reflected the increasing concern that population was growing too rapidly, a concern expressed by J. M. Keynes and others as a result of World War I.[45] It underestimated the rate at which world population would grow, however, together with the demand for energy, minerals, and food products.

The grounds for concern expressed by Marshall, Mombert, and other early twentieth century authors were not stressed in the nineteenth century after the initial alarm about the adequacy of food-supply growth to match population growth temporarily abated; for numbers were growing slowly in the then non-European underdeveloped world, and industrial raw materials were just coming into their own. It was not yet well recognized that industrial raw materials were subject to growth limitations that might eventually constrain industrial growth on the part of countries, especially if they were dependent on foreign sources for an important part of their food and related agricultural needs. There was no concern therefore that such increase in the demand for labor and primary products as was accompanying a shift from a two-factor to a multi-factor world would be checked by fear of excessive population growth.[46]

The replacement of two-factor by multi-factor economies increased the demand for manpower, both because agents of production complementary to labor increased and because there was a considerable increase in the use of manpower in ways that were not subject to the test of the market and hence presumably were not very productive, adding to the use rather than to the supply of goods and services, especially those that were relatively labor-oriented. What we earlier called category (b) manpower—that is, use of manpower in ways involving relatively little use of complementary nonlabor inputs—became subdivided as a two-factor world gave way to a multi-factor world, into (b_1) which replaces old (b) and (b_2) which includes all labor that is used jointly with considerable though variable amounts of capital complementary to manpower. Much of the increase in (b_1) took place in various service occupations, among them the military, though in time even some of these became dependent on complementary capital inputs, albeit less so than (b_2) labor. The increase in (b_2) took place mainly in manufactures, mining and quarrying, building, and transport.

We may use the experience of Britain, the most industrially advanced country of Europe in 1801, to illustrate changes in occupational structure, even though Britain's then stage of development corresponded to that attained by many European countries only much later.[47] Between 1801 and 1901 employment in Britain increased nearly 250 percent. Meanwhile, employment in primary industry, after having increased about 23 percent in 1801–1851, thereafter declined steadily. Services of all sorts that correspond roughly to category (b_1) increased about 300 percent, while enrollment in category (b_2) employments (i.e., roughly all employment except that in primary industry and services) increased 486 percent. In a two-factor world there would have been very limited opportunity for increase in (b_2) or even in (b_1) employment. It is inferable, therefore, that adjustment of economies to a multi-factor world greatly increased employment opportunities and the demand for manpower and hence for population.

With the rise of imperialism and the broadening of the scale on which warfare was planned, the demand for manpower for military and imperialistic purposes rose. In reality, of course, the demand for population to be situated in territory taken over by European powers proved negligible; for while many persons left Europe, few went to lands under immediate European control.[48] Military demands for manpower did, however, rise with the "democratization" of military service and warfare and increase in the capacity of states to mobilize manpower and put it to military use. In Napoleon's France as many as 5 percent of the population were put under arms, compared with around 1 percent in and before the eighteenth century, and thereafter this fraction rose to 10 percent or more.[49]

It should be noted that availability of abundant military manpower, together with increase in luxury, has made for waste of such manpower, and may continue to do so. For example, it is said that never more than one American in twenty of those in Viet Nam was engaged at the front. Not so high but still wasteful ratios characterized the war in Korea. Lavishness of supply—Allied planning in World War II called for $3\frac{1}{2}$ times as many tons per division per day as did the Germans—and wastefulness in in the use of supplies entailed unproductive use of manpower as well. In contrast the Russians lived and progressed on very little, as did the North Koreans and North Vietnamese in their wars.[50]

While the "democratization" of military service under both monarchic and republic rule contributed to the widening incidence of conscription, this trend was accentuated by increase in the militarily utilizable and mobilizable fraction of the population. Motivation was supplied by the emergence of combinations of powers viewed as threatening one another. As a result of these changing circumstances, publicists and politicians in particular stressed the importance of population growth. This outcome is

well exemplified in Franco-German relations and policy, especially between 1850 and 1914.[51] It is exemplified also in German literature, during
World War I and even thereafter, with its emphasis upon the need to enlarge Germany's *Nahrungsspielraum*. Reference has already been made to
Mombert's *Bevölkerungspolitik,* in which population growth and seizure
of territory of Germany's enemies are advocated. Otto Prange advocated
seizure of Russian soil in particular.[52]

By way of conclusion to this section it may be said that the changes
underway in the developed world sufficed to keep the "demand" for manpower abreast of its supply, which grew at a slowly rising rate—one in
excess of that experienced in the underdeveloped world—until 1900–1910.
The rate of natural increase returned to its 1900–1910 level after declining
in 1910–1920 and again in 1930–1950, but it will descend below this level
as decline in the Net Reproduction Rate becomes reflected in the rate of
natural increase.

Increase in factors complementary to manpower, together with the expansion of new sources of demand for manpower, account for the growth
in demand for labor. It has been noted that in Britain what we called (b_1)
and (b_2) employment expanded enough to absorb the increase in manpower outside primary industry. In the United States between 1820 and
1900 federal civilian employment increased about four times as fast as the
labor force. The ratio of federal military personnel to the labor force, however, changed very little.[53] In the present century the composition of the
American labor force changed much more rapidly, especially in recent
decades. Between 1900 and 1960 the fraction of the labor force engaged
in civilian government rose from 3.8 to 11.7 percent; that in the armed
forces, from about 0.4 to about 3.8 percent.[54]

These trends remain in force. Between 1960 and 1971 civilian governmental employment increased 50 percent, compared with a 21 percent
increase in the labor force. Underlying these changes have been a steady
increase in governmental expenditure and decrease in the subordination of
gross national expenditure to the test of the market. The fraction of gross
national expenditure represented by government expenditures rose from
about 10 percent in 1929 to 24.5 in 1955 and 32.3 in 1971, with much
of the increase since 1955 related to "health" and "welfare."[55] Between
1959 and 1971 increase in purchases by state and local governments generated about 35 percent of the increase in available employment; of the
increase over three-quarters were added to state and local payrolls and
the remainder primarily in the private sector.[56] The importance of military
expenditure is reflected in the fact that in 1965–1970 the fraction of total
public and private employment attributable to Department of Defense
military expenditure varied between 8.3 and 9.8 percent.[57]

Changes in the wake of the "progress" that accompanied the transformation of two-factor into multi-factor economies also brought into being new uses of manpower comparable to those generated by military and other expenditures upon the maintenance of internal peace and external security. The new uses drew manpower into intermediate activities associated with rising costs of urbanization and modernization—into activities that reduced the ratio of Net National Product to Gross National Product,[58] thereby facilitating consumption. Decrease in hours of work also checked growth of Net National Product, but this has been partly offset recently by increasing entry of females into the labor force (even though their number has been counterbalanced in part by the earlier retirement of males).[59]

4. New Era

What Kuznets calls a new epoch gradually emerged out of what we have called the multi-factor age that succeeded the two-factor age, and it can give rise to a lag in the growth of demand for labor or population relative to the growth of its supply. Kuznets finds that this new epoch was already taking form in the nineteenth century; for what he calls "a new economic epoch" reflects "the emergence of a new group of factors large enough to dominate growth over a long period."[60] This new epoch did not immediately answer to the description of what we shall call a "new era" in respect to growth of the aggregate demand for manpower. This era did, however, become manifest after 1940, in a postwar upsurge in the rate of growth per capita,[61] together with a corresponding decline in the relative importance of manpower and conventional capital.

Kuznets estimates that of past increase in Net National Product (NNP) per capita, about four-fifths is traceable to growth of "productivity," that is, of "output per unit of input—input measured within the accepted framework of national economic accounting, and limited to manhours of labor and to material capital (nonreproducible and reproducible), the latter measured at original or, preferably, reproduction cost)."[62] "Productivity" flows from "improvements in quality of labor and capital—improvements not caused by an extra input of resources." These " 'costless' improvements are connected with the tremendous increase in the stock of useful knowledge, much of it traceable to growth of science viewed as a social institution devoted to the production of new tested and hence potentially useful knowledge."[63] Even though the contribution of "productivity" is reduced, perhaps as much as 30 percent by allowance for costs associated with increase in urbanization and modernization, "productivity" still accounts for 56 or more percent of the increase in NNP per capita.[64]

The trends to which Kuznets draws attention will be intensified if automation and the robotization of labor continue to increase. For, as H. A. Simon suggests, machines will be capable, within twenty years, of doing any work that a man can do. Economically, men will retain their greatest comparative advantage in jobs that require flexible manipulation of those parts of the environment that are relatively rough—some forms of manual work, control of some kinds of machinery (e.g., operating earth-moving equipment), some kinds of nonprogrammed problem solving, and some kinds of service activities where face-to-face human interaction is of the essence. Man will be somewhat less involved in performing day-to-day work of the organization, and somewhat more involved in maintaining the system that performs the work.[65]

The genuinely automatic factory—the workerless factory that can produce output and perhaps also, within limits, maintain and repair itself —will be technically feasible long before our twenty-five years have elapsed.[66]

We may expect (other things being equal) automation of thinking and symbol-manipulating functions to proceed more rapidly than the automation of the more complex eye-brain-hand sequences.[67]

It is evident, in view of what has been said, that in the wake of the "new era" several demand-oriented problems will emerge. (a) The aggregate demand for output may or may not keep pace with potential increase in output. (b) Even though demand does keep pace with output, the composition of output and hence the structure of inputs utilized may change in such ways that some categories of inputs will lose much of their value; for ultimately the demand for any set of inputs derives from the aggregate demand for output. Among the inputs, demand for which may sink to levels below the costs of their production and use, are the services of individuals with irremediable deficiencies either of genetic or early environmental origin. (c) As has been noted, the relative cost of human capital under "new-era" conditions will continue to rise until its derived value no longer warrants its increase. This outcome is parallel to that described under (b), though it relates to what may be called supra-marginal human inputs. The likelihood of outcomes (b) and (c) is conditioned by that of (a), which depends in part on the potlatch propensity of societies, that is, upon the propensity to destroy (e.g., in war-related activities) rather than consume product. Demand-oriented concomitants of zero population growth under "modern-era" conditions are examined in later chapters.

At the macroeconomic level a major outcome of "new-era" conditions may be a decline in the relative importance of "labor" as an aggregate. For, under the new conditions, while the relative importance of human complements to new conditions of production has increased, that of forms of labor replaceable in considerable part has diminished. There is less public concern, therefore, when a population is growing slowly if at all in the long run, less public attention directed to preventing the decline of institutions favorable to fertility,[68] and less questioning of what may be called the structure and orientation of values not only regnant under "new era" conditions but also unfavorable to population growth. It is possible, of course, that should the military security of so-called free nations be perceived to be threatened by growth of modern "non-free" nations in relative military power, there will emerge concern at the low rate of population growth and the resulting relatively small size of the cohorts of prime military age. Even so, countervailing action may not prove very effective, since 17 or more years must elapse before the relative number in the age groups 16–29 can begin to increase.

5. The Prospect

Four conditions may affect future attitudes toward population growth. First, while the integration of family assistance into national welfare legislation has often eased the direct burden of reproducing and rearing children,[69] the net reproduction rate began to decline in the developed world after the temporary upsurge of natality after World War II.[70] Currently net reproduction is below the replacement level in Northern America and most European developed countries. It is possible, therefore, that it will be inferred that short of greater governmental intervention deaths will eventually exceed births and give rise to disadvantages associated with negative population growth. Second, while there is concern in some countries that their populations are too large, greater attention will be directed to disadvantages supposedly associated with the absence of population growth.[71]

Third, and currently of most concern, will be growing awareness of increasing international demographic imbalance with continuing high rates of population growth in the low-income underdeveloped world and low rates in the developed world. For in the underdeveloped world it is estimated that fertility, though expected to decline, will remain high enough in the 1990s to sustain a 2-percent-per-year rate of natural increase at that time compared with about 0.8 percent in the developed world.[72] Accordingly, the fraction of the world's population living in the underdeveloped world will constitute about 78 percent of the world's population by the close of the century; this fraction compares with about 65 percent in 1900 and about 70 percent in 1965.[73]

Undoubtedly policies respecting rapidly growing underdeveloped-country population will be reexamined by advanced countries because this growth will result in increasing pressure upon world natural resources and world markets for manufactures as industrialization proceeds apace and income rises. Even the United States will feel the pressure if, finding its market for nonagricultural exports limited, it must put greater reliance upon agricultural exports.[74]

Fourth, and of growing concern, are implications of the fact that natural resources, biospheric elements, and so on not only are ultimately limited in utilizable amount but also are subject to depletion through consumption and misuse of man's environment. This concern is evident in the growing fear that some of man's energy sources (e.g., oil) are subject to exhaustion; it is evident also in man's increasing concern with his immediate environments, with programs designed to rationalize global ecology, and with the need to reduce pressure upon his relevant environments.[75] It begins to appear probable that this fourth source of concern will outweigh the others as a determinant of attitudes toward population growth and policy, even though growth of per capita consumption may outweigh population growth as a resource of exhaustion.

Even should constraints arising from limits to the availability of natural resources and biospheric elements not impede population growth as expected, other constraints might eventuate in cessation of population growth. Should this come about for whatever reason, a stationary state could then come into being. The case for this possibility has been most effectively presented by R. O. Hieser, who points to implications of the assumption that investment determines the level of activity. "With zero population growth, the rate of economic growth" and the rate of profit "would tend to be zero," thus eliminating outlets and incentives to invest should technical progress be "neutral" or eventually nullified by a shift of labor into leisure. This possible outcome, of course, lies in the less immediate future.[76]

III. Emerging Concern over the Prospect of a Stationary Population: General Considerations

> *I do not depart from the old Malthusian conclusion. I only wish to warn you that the chaining up of one devil may, if we are careless, only serve to loose another still fiercer and more intractable.*
>
> J. M. Keynes, *Eugenics Review*, 1937

The decade succeeding the close of World War I and the signing of the Treaty of Versailles witnessed, on the one hand, continuing concern lest numbers increase too rapidly and on the other an emerging awareness that in some countries population growth might be destined to cease around or soon after the middle of the twentieth century. This concern was focused upon the Western World rather than upon the so-called Underdeveloped World, a world that did not command much attention at the hands of demographers until in and after the late 1930s when consequences of spreading death control and an emerging imbalance between births and deaths began to become apparent.

In this chapter I shall review the switchover from concern at impending population pressure to concern lest population cease to grow. How this change was responded to by economists will be dealt with in the following chapter. In the present chapter discussion of the response will be limited to noneconomic considerations and emergence of the belief that depopulation would result in the absence of family allowances and complementary measures designed to reduce costs of children incident upon families.

1. Concern at Population Pressures

That population had been growing notably in the West despite declines in fertility was well known (see Chap. I above). Furthermore, such growth had not become a matter of concern, eased as its impact was by net emigration abroad, by concomitants of what J. M. Keynes called "that extraordinary episode in the economic progress of man" which came to an end in August 1914, and by obliviousness to the forces that "were to play the serpent to this paradise" and bring about World War I, the most dislocating war in Western history—truly a modern Peloponnesian War.

Search for the causes of this war drew attention to hitherto largely neglected population factors as well as to other conditions that had contributed to the formation of two opposed groups of European powers seeking enlarged places in the sun—among them France, long alarmed at political and military implications of her slow rate of population growth. That population pressure had helped trigger World War I was given wide publicity in 1919 by J. M. Keynes who conjectured that Malthus's devil might be loose again after having been "chained up and out of sight" for half a century. Keynes pointed in particular to the impact of population growth in Austria, Hungary, Germany, and European Russia. He pointed especially to the rise of Bolshevism in Russia.

> The great events of history are often due to secular changes in the growth of population and other fundamental economic causes, which, escaping by their gradual character the notice of contemporary observers, are attributed to the follies of statesmen or the fanaticism of atheists. Thus the extraordinary occurrences of the past two years in Russia, that vast upheaval of society, which has overturned what seemed most stable— religion, the basis of property, the ownership of land, as well as forms of government and the hierarchy of classes—may owe more to the deep influences of expanding numbers than to Lenin or to Nicholas; and the disruptive powers of excessive national fecundity may have played a greater part in bursting the bonds of convention than either the power of ideas or the errors of autocracy.[1]

More important than that which growing population pressure had helped to bring about was what it threatened to bring about if numbers continued to multiply, e.g., rise in the cost of imported produce should it remain available at all. Keynes observed, even as Malthus had anticipated a century earlier,[2] and as Sir William Crookes had warned at the opening of a then supposedly promising twentieth century,[3] that Europe could not escape the impact of the Ricardian Law of Diminishing Returns, a law that operated abroad as well as in the United Kingdom and on the Continent. For population growth abroad, especially in the United States, threatened to absorb what had been an exportable surplus of foodstuffs, available at low prices and easily purchasable with returns on capital previously invested in America and other granary-lands. Keynes must have inferred from the slowness with which yields had been increasing that this slow rate of progress would not be accelerated; he did not, therefore, foresee the upsurge of yields in and after the 1930s, an upsurge that would slow the advent of food shortages. Presumably the exportable surplus of Russia and Roumania was similarly threatened already in 1914.

> In short, Europe's claim on the resources of the New World was becoming precarious; the law of diminishing returns was at last reasserting itself, and was making it necessary year by year for Europe to offer a

greater quantity of other commodities to obtain the same amount of bread; and Europe, therefore, could by no means afford the disorganisation of any of her principal sources of supply.

Much else might be said in an attempt to portray the economic peculiarities of the Europe of 1914. I have selected for emphasis the three or four greatest factors of instability—the instability of an excessive population dependent for its livelihood on a complicated and artificial organisation, the psychological instability of the labouring and capitalist classes, and the instability of Europe's claim, coupled with the completeness of her dependence, on the food supplies of the New World.

The war had so shaken this system as to endanger the life of Europe altogether. A great part of the continent was sick and dying; its population was greatly in excess of the numbers for which a livelihood was available; its organisation was destroyed, its transport system ruptured, and its food supplies terribly impaired.[4]

A warning of impending scarcity was present as well in Keynes's preface to the Roumanian edition of *The Economic Consequences.*

Roumania has great opportunities. But there are those who would tempt her into false and frivolous paths. Let no thoughts of excessive empire or militarist predominance divert her from the pursuits of civilisation and of happiness. Let her avoid not less, the indulgences of extravagant government—extravagant beyond the amount of the immediately available resources. There have been times when it might be argued by light-minded persons that we had a sufficient margin of safety to permit us to indulge in such vain amusements. But it is not so now. The whole of Europe, and especially Central and Eastern Europe, stands on the edge of great dangers and great misfortunes. We must each of us individually be very clear on which side we are going to throw our influence.[5]

Such scarcity underlay in part Keynes's condemnation of the behavior of French representatives at the Peace Conference in Paris and the unreality of the Treaty of Versailles,[6] a condemnation subsequently supported by studies of the capacity of various countries to pay war debts in keeping with the provisions of this treaty.[7]

By way of evidence of increasing population pressure in Europe Keynes pointed to a worsening of the terms of trade, thereby precipitating inquiry into the degree to which changes in the terms of trade could serve as indicators of changes in population pressure.[8] "Up to about 1900 a unit of labour applied to industry yielded year by year a purchasing power over an increasing quantity of food. It is possible that about the year 1900 this process began to be reversed and a diminishing yield of nature to man's efforts was beginning to reassert itself."[9] This upward movement of cereal costs was partly hidden, however, by a rising inflow of substitutes in the form of oilseeds from Africa.

Sir William Beveridge replied to Keynes's argument in his presidential address, declaring that he could find "no ground for Malthusian pessimism, no shadow of over-population before the War," and even less in "the world of white men," and adding that birth control (which had become increasingly effective since 1880) did not as such provide a solution to postwar problems.[10] In his comment accompanying Beveridge's article Keynes provided additional statistical evidence to the effect that the terms of trade had worsened since 1900 and that the rising cost of cereals had not been countervailed by a rising volume of exports.[11] Of greater concern to Keynes was the way in which Beveridge's argument was seized upon by a wide variety of publicists as well as the popular press to deny the presence or threat of overpopulation in Britain and to assert that the argument of Malthus had been demolished. "Sir William Beveridge has given to ignorance and prejudice the shelter of his name."[12]

As a result of Keynes's writings, together with inquiries prompted by the view that population pressure was a cause of war (e.g., World War I)[13] and by recognition that population capacity even in the United States was limited,[14] an extensive literature, both technical and popular, came into being after the war. Malthus's geometrical ratio was rediscovered, along with some of its age-old implications and some of the earlier criticisms of this ratio.[15] Concern was expressed that some countries (especially Japan) faced a lowering of living standards, inasmuch as migration, industrialization, and agricultural development could not counterbalance current rates of natural increase.[16] Respecting countries less subject to population pressure than Japan, concern was expressed that current natural increase threatened to carry many a country's numbers beyond a magnitude that later became viewed as optimum for that country—albeit a dynamic magnitude difficult to define.[17]

2. New Forecasts; Revisionism

Even as concern was increasing in regard to implications of continuing population growth at current rates, demographers, equipped with sharpened tools, were providing more accurate estimates of the current and the prospective course of natural increase in Western countries—among them estimates that revealed numbers to be increasing less rapidly over time than cruder measures implied. That natural increase was low and sometimes negative as in France had become well known before World War I. It was also known that natality and fertility had been declining in the West and could decline, possibly to the level of crude mortality.[18] Refined measures furthermore had revealed the importance of changes in age and marital composition.[19] These measures had not, however, explicitly revealed how rapidly populations were growing and would grow should age-specific fertility and mortality remain unchanged. The answer to this question was provided by R. R. Kuczynski in the form of Gross and Net Reproduction Rates,[20] and by L. I. Dublin and A. J. Lotka with their yet more refined "true rate of natural increase."[21]

The work of Kuczynski, together with that of Dublin and Lotka, probably did more initially than other inquiries to draw attention to the fact that *crude* rates of natural increase currently exceeded *"true"* rates and that in some countries the *"true"* or intrinsic rate was moving toward zero or had already passed below it. Accordingly, concern shifted from effects of continuing population growth to concern that numbers would eventually decline even as would have occurred in France in the absence of net inmigration. Kuczynski found that whereas births exceeded deaths by 48 percent in Western and Northern Europe in 1926 and made possible an increase of 6.2 per thousand (i.e., 19.2 births minus 13 deaths per thousand inhabitants), the long-run rate of growth was negative. For given current age-specific mortality and fertility, "100 mothers gave birth to 93 future mothers only," and thus the population was declining about 7 percent per generation. Net reproduction was below the replacement level in Sweden, France, Germany, and England and Wales, and moving in that direction in other countries.[22] Dublin and Lotka showed that in the mid-1920s and again in the mid-1940s the true rate of natural increase in the United States, while still positive, was about 50 percent lower than the crude rate because the abnormal but transient age structure of the American population was temporarily exaggerating births and understating deaths.[23]

Awareness of what appeared to be the population prospect in the United States was greatly increased by President Herbert Hoover's Research Committee on Social Trends, established in 1929. In 1933 the Committee issued its report, entitled *Recent Social Trends in the United States,* and it was accompanied by a number of monographs, among them *Population Trends In the United States,* by W. S. Thompson and P. K. Whelpton.[24] Thompson and Whelpton presented a number of projections of the population to 1980, based on diverse assumptions respecting expectation of life, fertility, and immigration in 1930–1980. Of the ten projections, six anticipated that the country's population would begin to decline before 1980, two that it would still be growing at a low but declining rate as of 1980, and two (based on "high" birth rates and immigration) that it would still be growing somewhat less than 1 percent per year.[25] The authors conjectured that by 1970 "the population will be almost at its maximum with about 155,000,000 persons,"[26] or about 47 million less than the maximum anticipated as of 1980, therewith joining the many who have failed in their forecasts of future population.[27]

The first of the revisions of these estimates by Thompson and Whelpton appeared in 1938 in one of the series of studies appearing under the auspices of the National Resources Committee set up early in the administration of President F. D. Roosevelt. What the authors now considered the likely near maximum population as of 1980 approximated 158 million, given 100,000 immigration per year, and 153 million, given no immigration.[28] Further revisions made in light of the Census of 1940 put the most likely points of leveling off near 1990 or slightly later and the peak population within a range just over 160 and under 170 million.[29] In short, the 1930s and 1940s witnessed the production of a series of estimates that indicated a leveling off of the population of the United States in this century at totals much below those that subsequently seemed likely to come into being.[30]

Comparable demographic prospects confronted the countries of Northern and Western Europe as well as a number of countries in Southern and Eastern Europe—a number likely to grow, given the decline in fertility.[31] In these countries as in the United States stationary or declining populations were in the offing.

Grounds for easy acceptance of these prognoses had already been established both by the continuing decline of natality and by more refined calculations. Fertility tables dated from 1884.[32] Edwin Cannan in 1895 forecast that the population of England and Wales, numbering about 29 million in 1895, would become nearly stationary by the 1940s and completely stationary by 1995 at about 37.4 million. Six years later he estimated that births per marriage were likely to descend to the long-run replacement level by 1916. In 1932 Cannan wrote of his 1895 forecast as follows:

> But I had noticed that the old rapid increase in the annual number of births seemed to have come to an end, and working on the ages of the people as recorded in successive censuses, I put before Section F of the British Association in 1895 a paper in which I estimated the number of persons who would be living at each census up to that of 1951 on the assumptions that migration, mortality, and, not the rate, but the absolute number of births, remained stationary. I found that on these hypotheses the population of England and Wales would stop increasing during the present century, and would have only a trifling increase after 1941. The paper suggested that this was, at any rate, not improbable.[33]

And to his 1901 forecast he referred in these terms:

> . . . using a method of weighting the annual numbers of marriages by their proximity to the births recorded for each year—a method which seems to have been beneath the notice of the mathematical statisticians of that period—I was able to show, I think conclusively, that the number of children resulting from each marriage was falling steadily and rapidly, and insisted with more emphasis than before on the "considerable proba-

bility of the disappearance of the natural increase of population—excess of births over deaths—in Great Britain within the present century."[34]

Unlike French authors who were greatly disturbed at the actual and prospective course of population growth in France,[35] Cannan was not disturbed at the prospective cessation of British population growth. "So far as Britain alone is concerned," he wrote in 1901, "I cannot see that there is much reason for lamenting the fact. The island is already tolerably full. With another ten millions or so it would be as full as any reasonable person can desire to see it."[36] He pointed out, however, that "the British dominions beyond the seas will have to rely on their own natural increase and the immigration of foreigners." There was little hope, however, "of the colonies peopling themselves, and unless the British race within the Empire can succeed, as it has done outside the Empire, in engrafting into itself foreign elements, a continuance of the decline of natality at home will cause it to become one of the little nations or at any rate to fall with the French into the second class." For it was already outnumbered by the Russians, by the Germans, and by the white population of the United States which was fed by non-English immigrants and their offspring.[37]

Cannan's remarks about the dearth of Britain's emigrants to her overseas dominions must have produced responding notes in Australia and New Zealand, as well as in Canada, whence many foreign-born inhabitants moved to the United States while French-Canadians multiplied in Quebec. In Australia in particular the importance of immigration from Britain had been appreciated since the Napoleonic wars and had been set in a theoretical context. Its importance was accentuated, of course, after 1850 when concern arose respecting nonwhite immigration and eventually ripened into fear of the country's being swamped by the "lower races" should they be allowed free entry. There was concern at Australia's low rate of population growth, a concern highlighted at the turn of the century when T. A. Coghlan first called attention to the decline in the birth rate and inspired a number of studies bearing upon causes of the decline and questions of policy. One later outcome was Australia's well developed post-1945 immigration policy.[38]

Implications of studies of trends in both crude natural increase and net reproduction were reenforced in the 1920s by the independent discovery or rediscovery of the so-called logistic law of population growth, first put forward by P. F. Verhulst in 1838. This theory implied that the rate of natural increase of a population in a finite environment would steadily approach zero and that the population itself would approach an upper asymptotic limit. The actual limit could be determined by fitting an appropriate logistic curve to past growth, given the nonoccurrence of fundamental changes in a population's social and / or physical environment. Raymond Pearl, together with his associate L. J. Reed, popularized the use of this curve in the 1920s. The upper limit of the population of the United States, for example, was put at about 197.3 million to be reached around 2060 and that of the world at about 2,646 million to be closely approached by A.D. 2100. Upper limits were computed for many other countries as well. Of course, should fundamental changes take place in a population's environment, the upper asymptotic value would be increased (as had happened in the case of Germany) or reduced. Of major import for the present discussion, however, is not the tenability of logistic theory and forecasting but the fact that the considerable literature relating to the logistic, together with the accuracy of fits of the curves in a number of instances, made for awareness of the advent of cessation of population growth and stationary populations.[39] As a result, empirical projections based on supposed trends in age-specific mortality and fertility were made in a number of countries. They revealed both how it was likely that national populations would grow and how their age composition would change.

As Cannan's work suggests, even had refined measures and models of the logistic sort not been developed, the continuing downward movement of crude natality and its approach toward crude mortality would have suggested that stationary populations might be in the offing. Of this we have evidence in natality studies, especially in Germany and France.[40] It may be said, therefore, that in the 1930s the advent of a stationary if not declining population was expected in many of the Western countries and led to a variety of governmental reactions.

3. Political Response

Reaction of nations to the discovery that their populations might cease to grow and even decline led to a variety of responses. Here reference will be made only to essentially political responses, since economic interpretations are dealt with in the next chapter. These responses were conditioned in part by the nature of a country's political system and in some measure by an atmosphere of concern that European civilization was in a state of decline and could collapse as had the Roman.[41] For example, in his account of the prospective decline of "Civilization" and his forecast of the ascendancy of Caesarism, Oswald Spengler referred to depopulation as an index of decline.[42] Corrado Gini, writing shortly before World War I, had put forward a biological theory of the rise and fall of civilization.[43] He found in "the slow exhaustion of the reproductive powers of human populations," after an initial upsurge of these powers, the biological source of the decline of nations. "The rise of new races or nations is apparently to be considered as a phenomenon of crossbreeding."[44] He attributed what he called the renewal of the Italian nation, then supposedly under way, to the "amalgamation of the racial stocks of the several regions" constituting Italy, an amalgamation traceable to the increase of mobility within Italy, a movement accentuated after World War I.

Political responses focused on the impact of decline in natality and natural increase upon a country's international standing. Particular concern was expressed respecting the significance of these population trends for a country's relative political and military standing, a standing long believed to rest upon numbers as well as upon wealth and territory.[45] The heavy population losses associated with World War I, together with the resulting redistribution of political power, had directed attention again to the supposed dependence of a people's as well as of a country's standing and security upon the size of its population. Kuczynski in 1929 put the issue in terms of people as follows:

> The Anglo-Saxons, the Germans, the Scandinavians, and the French will very likely retrogress in the course of this century; and since the Slavs and some other races will continue to grow, the proportion of the Teutonic and the French race will diminish even more quickly than their absolute numbers. It is hard to see how this process might effectively be stopped. But it will be accelerated if the birth-restriction movement should continue to be most successful among those nations which no longer reproduce themselves.[46]

The role attributed to manpower prior to World War II as well as at its close was well described by Robert Strausz-Hupé at the close of World War II.[47] Representative is his conclusion, a conclusion quite in keeping with military interpretations before and after World War I. "The dangers of population decline were upon the nations of Europe before they were recognized. The United States has fair warning, and the remedy lies at hand in its own tradition."[48] Notestein emphasized not only the magnitude of the demographic changes under way but also the ascendancy of the Soviet Union to the status of "the major power of the Eurasian continent."[49] It was pointed out in *Life* magazine that by 1970 the Soviet Union might have as many men of military age as the United States, Britain, France, and Italy combined.[50]

The British Royal Commission stated that among the "imponderable considerations that must enter into the question of the desirable trend of population are the effects on the security and influence of Great Britain." The Commission pointed to Britain's role as "the centre of a Commonwealth spread throughout the world" and to "association or alliance with other States" by which "the British Commonwealth is likely to be important" in averting war and in the eventuality of war. Population decline would adversely affect the peopling of the Commonwealth as well as its strength, together with "the maintenance and extension of Western values and culture" and the "prestige and influence of the West." Accordingly, "a replacement size of family is desirable in Great Britain at the present time."[51]

As a result of political and military as well as other population-related concerns, pronatalist measures, long associated with France, began to find favor outside France and to be strengthened in France, especially in the 1930s and after World War II. Indeed, according to *Life,* "without exception every country in the Western world is dedicated in varying degrees to the policy of 'more babies.' "[52] A variety of economic measures and forms of preferential treatment were devised to augment the utility of children and / or decrease their cost, and thus elevate the benefit–cost ratio of children. Prior to World War II, regimes with territorial expansion in view introduced populationist programs intended above all to stimulate natality and natural increase.[53] France, long concerned at her low rate of population growth, finally introduced a more effective birth-stimulating program on the eve of World War II.[54]

The 1930s witnessed the development of a very systematic program in Sweden, under the leadership of Alva and Gunnar Myrdal, whose *Kris i befolkningsfrågan* appeared in 1934. The following year the Swedish Government established the Swedish Population Commission, which issued 16 papers and a final report in 1935–1938. These papers were focused upon social and socioeconomic policy rather than upon the economic consequences of the advent of a stationary or declining population, even though the establishment of the Commission was the result of alarm at the prospect of a rapidly declining population.[55] The aim of the Swedish program was not narrowly pronatalist and family-assisting, but the creation of a democratic economy and economic environment in which lifetime economic security and population maintenance could be combined, and in such wise as not to penalize parents or to encourage unduly natality on the part of those without a desire for children or not capable of producing genuinely desirable births.[56]

The British Royal Commission on Population was established in March, 1944, and issued its report in 1949. It dealt more extensively with the population problem than did the Swedish Commission, dealing not only with population trends in Britain and their relation to the family but also with the economic and political implications of population trends.[57]

The Commission concluded its report as follows:

We have now completed our survey of the trend of population, past and present, its causes and probable consequences, and have outlined what we think should be done to meet the two different sets of problems that arise; first, the adjustment of social and economic arrangements to changes that have actually occurred or are in progress in the numbers and age distribution of the population, and second, the continuing implications for our society of the revolutionary change that has taken place over the past 100 years in the conditions of population growth. These latter form the crux of our inquiry, and in concluding this report, we want to emphasise what we regard as the fundamental implication.

It is that a community like ours in which birth control is generally accepted can only prosper or, in the long run, survive, if its members think it worth while to have families large enough to replace themselves. This is not a question only, or even mainly, of total numbers; it is possible to hold widely different views about the desirable size of population in relation to national resources and responsibilities and yet for the reasons we discuss in Part II to agree that if over a long period parents have families too small to replace themselves, the community concerned must undergo a slow process of weakening. Our inquiry has convinced us that the relation between the trend of family size and community outlook and policies is peculiarly close, and underlying all our recommendations is our concern to have this fact recognised so that in all relevant branches of policy and administration the population factor will be taken into account.[58]

In its report to the Commission, the Economics Committee concluded *inter alia:*

Third, measures which were successfully directed to easing the lot of parents and to making better provision for children would contribute directly to improving the standard of life. Indeed they would remedy what is one of the main causes of poverty and malnutrition under our present arrangements. For, as the evidence of social surveys confirms, much of our poverty is concentrated in homes where the family income has to maintain a large number of young children. Moreover, the proportion of our children who are brought up in such households is, of course, much larger than the proportion of the households.

To the issues of population policy, however, three other considerations are relevant. First, a sub-replacement birth-rate will encourage immigration and so reduce the proportion of home-bred stock in the population. Second, intervention to raise the birth-rate is not likely to have quick results. Third, measures to aid parents and to improve the care of children will strike at one of the main causes of poverty and malnutrition.

We conclude accordingly that in Great Britain at the present day the case for reasonable and well-considered measures to mitigate the burden of parenthood is fully made out on economic and social grounds.[59]

The case for assistance to families was effectively put by Roy Harrod in the memorandum he submitted to the Royal Commission in 1944.[60] Harrod pointed out that prompt action was required, and that the remedies devised should be adequate in scale. He indicated also that these remedies should not penalize better-to-do parents and thus conduce to relative infertility among the "better stocks." He recommended "an endowment to be paid to all out of public funds" and that should "consist of a flat rate for every child after the first."[61]

The widespread decline in natality, together with what was perceived as a threat of population decline, prompted the adoption of family allowances and related measures. These allowances, initially introduced in the public services in some European countries as well as in Australia, New Zealand, and later Canada, originally had as their main purpose a closer adjustment of family income to family living costs. After World War II, however, countries concerned about population growth found in the family-allowance principle an important means suited both to increase natality[62] and to strengthen income redistribution policies.

The success of pronatalist programs has turned on the degree to which they have strengthened incentives to marriage (especially at younger ages) and natality, and weakened disincentives. They may produce these effects both by strengthening incentives already embedded in a society's institutional structure and internalized in many of a society's members and by introducing new incentives such as cash or material rewards, the impact of which may be transitory.[63] Illustrative of this transitoriness may have been Germany's success in the 1930s in pushing up the number of marriages and births through a system of marriage loans and a campaign against abortion. This campaign, however, led to greater care in the avoidance of conception and a consequent arrest of the upward trend of births. "Only a deep-rooted improvement in general economic conditions and in the distribution of income can be expected to produce an enduring increase in fertility."[64]

Illustrative of a successful pronatalist program has been the one initiated in France on the eve of World War II. This program was an outcome of decades of alarm in France at the lowness of French fertility (often below the replacement level), together with the failure of measures introduced prior to the launching of a comprehensive program in 1939. Not only was a comprehensive program introduced; provision was made also for continuous surveillance and inquiry into French and foreign population movements and policy through the establishment of the fine journal *Population,* under the auspices and with support of a governmental ministry aided by an able body of demographic scholars.[65] The striking success of France's demographic and economic policy, together with its emphasis upon the role of the family and the population factor, is evident in the fact that fertility moved above the replacement level as well as above fertility levels in advanced European countries and has remained there.[66]

It was not so much the prospective advent of a stationary population after World War II that aroused concern in various countries and prompted governmental action, as it was fear that intrinsic and later crude natural increase would become negative. There was no basis for assuming that the Net Reproduction Rate would decline to 1.0 and then level off. Indeed, should anticipated effects of decline in natural increase prove as unfavorable as some authors anticipated, natality-depressive forces could become somewhat cumulative until arrested.

The populationist response after World War II was less influenced by political consideration than had been prewar views respecting the significance of population trends in and before the 1930s, especially in Germany, France, and Italy. For, so long as war was explicitly recognized as an instrument of international policy, population was viewed as an important political means. During World War I, for example, Otto Prange observed that since the Russians needed "strong, intelligent, faithful leading" and Germany as a nation had "an excess of intelligence," it would benefit both countries if ten million Germans flowed into Russia.[67]

In contrast with somewhat militarily oriented prewar populationism, postwar measures designed to strengthen the family and favor natality have become components of comprehensive welfare programs. These measures thus reflect the increasing concern of governments for the general welfare of the population, including that of families and children.[68] They may also reflect some concern lest a state's population become stationary when still of suboptimum size.[69]

IV. Emerging Concern over the Prospect of a Stationary or Declining Population: Economic Considerations

Western nations are constant only in pursuit of convenience.
George F. Will, *Durham Morning Herald*, June 5, 1977, p. 4D

In this chapter I examine early interpretations of the probable economic impact of the advent of a near-stationary or declining population. Major emphasis is placed upon general reactions to the supposed or macro-economic effects of this population trend, particularly those popularized by J. M. Keynes and A. H. Hansen. Minor emphasis is placed upon reactions to other effects, not because they are unimportant, but because they commanded less attention initially.

1. Adverse Economic Anticipations

Two conditions contributed jointly to the belief that continuing decline in natural increase and the advent of a stationary population would give rise to a number of economic problems: (a) The coincidence in time of the Great Depression that came into being after 1929 and continuation of the decline in natural increase long under way suggested the possibility that the two phenomena might be connected. (b) Of greater importance than (a) was emergence of doubt lest the economic system be less capable of adjusting automatically to exogenous change than economists had long held to be true of economic systems in the long run.

As noted earlier, J. M. Keynes as well as others (Marxist and non-Marxist) questioned whether under existing institutional and related conditions (e.g., distribution of income), the economic system had "an inherent tendency towards self-adjustment, if it is not interfered with and if the action of change and chance is not too rapid." Keynes questioned in particular the adequacy of the supposed tendency of the rate of interest to adjust itself "more or less automatically, so as to encourage just the right amount of capital goods to keep our incomes at the maximum level that our energies and our organization and our knowledge of how to produce efficiently are capable of providing"—whence, since investment supposedly was the key equilibrating variable, maintenance of desirable equilibrium would depend upon the adequacy of investment outlets, mainly population growth, together with territorial expansion and technological progress. Keynes and his followers were not yet in a position, however, to conclude that the overriding equilibrating agent in the long run would be population growth, cessation of which could finally eventuate in a stationary state. Keynes pointed out, however, that those concerned respecting full employment, especially economists, had arrived "at one of those uncommon junctures of human affairs where we can be saved by the solution of an intellectual problem, and in no other way."[1]

That the economy was self-adjusting in the longer run and could therefore accommodate a declining rate of population growth, especially an orderly decline, was supported in several ways. (i) Not only would such savings or capital as was forthcoming be absorbed, a conclusion supported by Paul Douglas—who estimated the elasticity of demand for capital to be in the neighborhood of -1.33, an estimate supported by F. H. Knight—, savings would also decline as the interest rate fell. Indeed, should (as was unlikely) the rate of return on capital fall to or below 3 percent, saving might decline to or below zero, since, according to Gustav Cassel, at an interest rate near or below 3 percent dissaving was more attractive than saving, given current life expectancy.[2] (ii) Given flexible wages and the fact that the elasticity of demand for labor fell between -3 and -4—a range estimated empirically by Douglas and inferred deductively by A. C. Pigou[3]—downward adjustment of wage rates could eliminate most unemployment. According to Pigou, the "elasticity of demand in terms of wage-goods for labour as a whole" was not less than -3 in times of depression and even in a short period was not less than -2.[4] Moreover, he put the "elasticity of the money demand for labour in times of deep depression at not less numerically than -1.5." It followed that "an all-around cut of 10 percent in money rates of wages would lead, *other things being equal,* to a more than 19 percent expansion in the aggregate volume of labour demanded."[5] It was not likely that monetary factors would greatly modify the assumption of *ceteris paribus.*[6] In sum, while Douglas and Pigou were not dealing with the impact of a stationary population, their analyses suggested that economies could absorb this impact. Douglas even pointed out that labor would benefit from slow or zero growth of the labor force, since "the factor which increases least will secure the greater share of the benefits."[7] Douglas also indicated, as had earlier writers (e.g., Cantillon), that labor as a class stood to benefit from the purchase of articles in which much labor and little capital was embodied, a concomitant, as A. H. Hansen later implied, of the advent of a stationary population and increasing emphasis upon services.[8]

Population movements, among them the advent of a stationary population, were not looked upon as major sources of intractable problems. Even Hansen, who later played a major role in stressing the impact of a declining rate of natural increase, when writing in 1931 did not yet find

in the decline in the rate of population growth a source of increasing unemployment. "The slowing-down of population growth in western Europe
and in the United States is working in the direction of economic stabilization." Moreover, should international fertility differences diminish, there
would be less international political instability, and this in turn would increase the economic stability of the world economy.[9] Hansen did, however, point to "institutional" barriers in the way of absorbing the technologically unemployed.[10] J. M. Clark noted that decline in population
growth would reduce the demand for housing and similar capital, that
such spending could produce secondary (or multiplier) effects,[11] and that
persisting underemployment was quite possible. But he found in a slack-
ened growth of population a possible source of stabilization of the production of capital equipment.[12]

While Pigou did not directly examine the effect of decline in the rate
of population growth upon employment, his inquiry into this part played
by "important factors of a non-monetary character" in the causation of
"unemployment" led him to emphasize the very important though not
exclusive role played by labor mobility and wage flexibility. He did, however, recognize that the impending decline in the rate of population growth
would make more difficult the avoidance of "particular" employment.
"The more rapidly the population of working age is expanding, the more
easy it is for given relative variations in demand to be met by deflections
in the flow of new recruits, in such wise that no question of unemployment can rise."[13]

The views presented suggest that economists with confidence in the self-
adjusting capacity of an economy expected that the advent of a very
slowly growing or stationary population would present problems, but not
problems that would call for a great deal of intervention by the state.
For economies could and would adjust to the new demographic conditions.
Those of this opinion presumably assumed that the decline in natural increase would come to a halt and eventually give rise to a stationary population. They did not assume that the decline would prove cumulative in
character in that its adverse economic effects would reinforce the conditions making for decline in fertility, and that the resulting accentuation
of the decline would in turn intensify adverse economic defects. Such
fear of depopulation as was expressed was based mainly upon the assumption that under existing economic conditions disincentives to fertility
would outweigh incentives thereto.[14] Concern was occasionally expressed
that some financial institutions could not survive should savings be exceeded by dissavings associated with an emerging excess of deaths over
births.

Confidence in the self-adjusting powers of the economy was already
declining in the 1920s, even among those who believed the capitalistic

system to be superior to alternative systems. J. M. Keynes was among those of this opinion and became their most articulate spokesman, initially in articles and tracts and eventually in *The General Theory of Employment, Interest and Money* (1936),[15] a work not only revolutionary in impact but also reflecting *inter alia* a shift in emphasis from long-term to the near-term or present concerns.[16] It was the supposed incapacity of the economy to adjust appropriately and rapidly to the slowing down of population growth that led Keynes and later A. H. Hansen to find in this decline an important source of unemployment. It probably was the devolution of political power in and after the second half of the nineteenth century that played a major role in the shifting of emphasis to near-term concerns, and hence to decline in confidence in the adequacy of long-run adjustments.

2. The Keynesian Revolution

Keynes's interpretation of the impact of a declining rate of population growth was foreshadowed in 1930 in his famous *Treatise On Money*. Therein he drew attention to the stickiness of wages and interest rates and to demographic and other changes requiring reductions in the natural rate of interest and hence in the market rate of interest. He pointed to Great Britain as "an old country with a higher standard of working-class life than exists in most other parts of the world," with a population that "will soon cease to grow," and with "habits and institutions" that were keeping her "thrifty" and "saving some 10 percent" of Britain's income—a country which therefore was not likely, "under a régime of laissez-faire" and its external relations, soon to experience a sufficient fall in "the natural-rate of interest" (i.e., "the rate at which savings and investment are exactly balanced"). Consequently, Britain must invest a larger proportion of its current savings abroad and increase its exports relative to its imports, an objective difficult to realize in the face of foreign tariff walls, high British wages, and Britain's loss of her former "special advantages in manufacture." It might be necessary, therefore, to depart from laissez-faire and achieve equilibrium between savings and investment by "such a device as differential terms for home investment relatively to foreign investment" or "differential terms for home-produced goods relatively to foreign-produced goods," preferably "differential rates for home and foreign lending."[17]

Keynes's focus in the *Treatise* was primarily on monetary and closely related phenomena, with demographic and related real phenomena entering the discussion only in their roles as determinants of the "natural-rate" of interest. His analysis, however, assumed a form that gave direction to his later approach to demographic and related phenomena in his *General*

Theory and to his lack of confidence that economies would readily respond and adjust as their elasticities (e.g., as determined by Douglas and Pigou) indicated they could. He pointed out in the *Treatise* that "the long-term rate of interest" was "nearly 50 percent higher" in 1930 than 20 years earlier, having failed to adjust, after the postwar repair of damage and restoration of required "working capital," to the decline in the need for savings at former levels.

> The population of the industrial countries is not increasing as fast as formerly, and is a good deal better equipped per head than it was with housing, transport and machines. On the other hand, the volume of lending to the less advanced parts of the world is not markedly large—indeed the contrary, since Russia, China and India, which include within their borders a substantial proportion of the population of the world, are able, for one reason or another, to borrow next to nothing on international markets, whilst the United States has converted itself from a borrowing to a lending country.[18]

As a result "there has now developed, somewhat suddenly, an unusually wide gap between the ideas of borrowers and those of lenders, that is between the natural-rate of interest and the market-rate."[19] This gap Keynes connected immediately with "the general return to the Gold Standard, and the Settlement of Reparations and the War Debts."[20] He predicted that "economic historians of the future" might present "the slump of 1930 . . . as the death struggle of the war rates of interest and the re-emergence of the pre-war rates."[21]

In the *General Theory* he emphasized the direct and indirect intensification of disequilibrium between savings and investment by decline in population growth, together with the stickiness of interest and wage rates and related phenomena that prevented appropriate adjustment by the economy and hence made corrective intervention by the state necessary if unemployment consequent upon imbalance between savings and investment were to be eliminated.[22] A year later he brought his new views to bear specifically upon population decline. Between 1860 and 1913, he estimated, the increased demand for British capital "was primarily attributable to the increasing population and to the rising standard of life, and only in a minor degree to technical changes of a kind which called for an increasing capitalization per unit of consumption. . . . It follows that a stationary population with the same improvement in the standard and the same lengthening of the period of production would have required an increase in the stock of capital of only a little more than half of the increase which actually occurred."[23] Meanwhile, it was possible that "the increase in average incomes, the decline in the size of families, and a number of other institutional and social influences may have raised the proportion of the national income which tends to be saved in conditions of full employment."[24] This proportion Keynes put at "between 8 percent and 15 percent of the income each year," or enough to increase "the stock of capital . . . between 2 and 4 percent per annum."[25] Yet "the demands of inventions and improvements which increase output per head and permit a higher standard of life" would absorb only about half of this— that is, about 1 percent per annum cumulative if savings approximated 8 percent—"assuming conditions of full employment and a stationary population" and "improvements . . . in the future as in the recent past."[26]

It follows, Keynes concludes,

> that to ensure equilibrium conditions of prosperity over a period of years it will be essential, *either* that we alter our institutions and the distribution of wealth in a way which causes a smaller proportion of income to be saved, *or* that we reduce the rate of interest sufficiently to make profitable very large changes in technique or in the direction of consumption which involve a much larger use of capital in proportion to output. Or, . . . we could pursue both policies to a certain extent.[27]

Should this not be done, "effective demand" would be inadequate, and unemployment would result and prevent realization of "the rising standard of life" that a stationary population could "facilitate."

Chaining up the "new devil of unemployment," "of Unemployed Resources," should he escape through a "breakdown of effective demand" consequent upon population decline and stationarity, entailed: (a) policies of gradually "increasing consumption by a more equal distribution of incomes and of forcing down the rate of interest so as to make profitable a substantial change in length of the period of production," and (b) gradually evolving an "attitude towards accumulation, so that it shall be appropriate to the circumstances of a stationary or declining population." Otherwise "a chronic tendency towards underemployment of resources must in the end sap and destroy that form of society." Of course, should population decline "too rapidly," "many severe problems" would emerge —problems preventable through measures taken "in the threat of that event."[28]

The paper in the *Eugenics Review* just summarized telescoped Keynes's more elaborate thesis as developed in the *General Theory*.

What would happen, Keynes asked, if with the "marginal efficiency" of a society's capital at zero but with its monetary system one that prevented its rate of interest sinking below zero, additional investment were undertaken? Under "conditions of *laissez-faire*" this society would become "one in which employment is low enough and the standard of life sufficiently miserable to bring savings to zero." For with the marginal efficiency of capital at zero, unemployment must increase sufficiently to ensure zero saving unless, as was most unlikely, the "aggregate desire on the part of the public to make provision for the future, even with full employment," had been satiated "to the full" and "no bonus is obtainable in the form of interest."[29] In short, the rate of interest must fall as fast as the marginal efficiency of capital is reduced by accumulation other than that in the form of economically fruitless assets (e.g., pyramids, cathedrals). It was essential, therefore, for the state to bring down the marginal efficiency of capital and the rate of interest to zero within a generation. Then "we should attain the conditions of a quasi-stationary community where change and progress would result only from changes in technique, taste, population and institutions, with the products of capital selling at a price proportioned to the labour, etc., embodied in them on just the same principles as govern the prices of consumption-goods into which the capital-charges enter in an insignificant degree."[30] The "rentier would disappear" but not the enterpriser.

Writing as he did before World War II and its aftermath, Keynes envisioned imbalance between the marginal efficiency of capital and the interest rate as arising out of decline and disappearance of population growth, together with declines in invention, the opening up of new lands, and war, as sources of demand for capital; whence the marginal efficiency of capital would continue to fall below both the level of interest ruling in the late nineteenth century and that acceptable to wealth-owners.[31] Hence there was need for efforts by the state to modify appropriately the inducement to save and that to invest.[32]

Presumably because of the context in which he put his analysis, Keynes did not directly and explicitly connect his account of "expectations" with population movements. But he did show how "expectations" were related to interest and the marginal efficiency of capital, together with money wages, and thus helped determine output and employment.[33] J. R. Hicks, in his review of the General Theory, made up this deficiency, however. He emphasized the relation of "expectations" to "population," Keynes's "strongest card."

> Expectation of a continually expanding market, made possibly by increasing population, is a fine thing for keeping up the spirits of entrepreneurs. With increasing population investment can go roaring ahead, even if invention is rather stupid; increasing population is therefore actually favorable to employment. It is actually easier to employ an expanding population than a contracting one, whatever arithmetic would suggest—at least this is so when the expansion or contraction is expected, as we may assume generally to be the case.
>
> Consider the situation which is likely to arise when the population of this country is declining, and the populations of most of those countries with which she is in close trading connections are stationary or tending to decline. . . . In these circumstances, the incentive to construct houses,

ships, factories, all sorts of capital equipment will be depressed by the anticipation that capital is wearing out and population dying off at convergent rates. Investment will proceed only with great difficulty, and employment will be low, in spite of the fact that population may have already declined in the past. It is true that in a community with perfect confidence, the situation could be rationally met. With so little of a future to look forward to, most people would spend all, or even more than all, of their incomes, and a high degree of total employment could be reached, with nearly all labour in the consumption trades. But this will hardly be considered a likely state of affairs. For capital will still retain its value as a reserve against unforeseen emergencies, and this need for it will hardly decline.

. . . [T]he dangers he diagnoses . . . are, indeed, one aspect—perhaps the most important economic aspect—of that problem of adapting to less progressive conditions the institutions of a traditionally expansive civilisation, which already vexes us on many sides.[34]

Inasmuch as Hicks's analytical approach was fundamentally more dynamic than Keynes's, he viewed the future as possibly less peril-ridden than did Keynes. Hicks doubted whether the "concept of a stationary state" was analytically useful even "as a special case," for he suspected "the system of economic relations" to have the "form of a progressive economy." He could not "deduce imminent peril" from the "approaching fall in population," despite its importance, since the future trend of innovation was "so difficult to forecast." He noted that "one cannot repress the thought that perhaps the whole Industrial Revolution of the last two hundred years has been nothing else but a vast secular boom, largely induced by the unparalleled rise in population. If this is so, it would help to explain why, as the wisest hold, it has been such a disappointing episode in human history."[35]

3. Hansen's Approach

Of the economists who supported Keynes's treatment of population, A. H. Hansen was most influential, being accredited with developing more fully and explicitly "the concept of secular stagnation, which pervades Keynes's *General Theory*."[36] Extension of emphasis from implications of the population prospect to implications of a syndrome of forces generative of secular stagnation in some instances raised a broader issue, namely, the fundamental source of stagnation and the degree to which the slowing of population growth was governed by other forces included in the syndrome and interpretable in Marxian and related terms, as well as in those of more inclusive non-Marxian terms. For example, Steindl found in the slowing-down of capital formation the immediate explanation of the decline in population growth and stagnation of the economy.[37] Schumpeter, probably the most learned economist of his generation, discounted the importance attached to the role of population decline in assessments of capitalism's future. For capitalism was by nature a nonstationary "form" of "economic change." The evolutionary character of the capitalist system and process was not "due to a quasi-automatic increase in population and capital or to the vagaries of monetary systems of which exactly the same thing holds true. The fundamental impulse that sets and keeps the capitalist engine in motion comes from the new consumers' goods, the new methods of production or transportation, the new markets, the new forms of industrial organization that capitalist enterprise creates."[38] Schumpeter therefore assigned a quite secondary role to population growth and decline as a member of the complex of interrelated causative agents responsible for the emergence and the prospective "vanishing of investment opportunity."[39] He traced the probable collapse of the capitalist system to the hostility of the social environment created by and embracing capitalism,[40] together with resulting "legislative, administrative and judicial practice born of that hostility." Capitalism had undermined the position of its creators, decomposed the "motive forces" of capitalism, and destroyed the extra-capitalist props of the system, among them "the bourgeois family" and its values which in the past had conduced to population growth.[41] In sum, population decline, though unfavorable to savings and economic development, was not the cause but an element in the evolutionary process bringing an end to capitalism and capitalist development as well as to population growth.[42]

Hansen's approach somewhat paralleled that of Keynes. In his presidential address to the American Economic Association,[43] he said that underemployment constituted "the essence of secular stagnation—sick recoveries [from trade-cycle downswings] which die in their infancy and depressions which feed on themselves and leave a hard and seemingly immovable core of unemployment."[44] Underlying persisting unemployment was inadequate investment or capital formation traceable to decline in population growth, which in the last half of the nineteenth century "was responsible for about forty percent of the total volume of capital formation in western Europe and about sixty percent in the capital formation in the United States."[45] Not only would capital-widening associated with increase in final output decline in the future as population growth declined but also capital-deepening associated with cost-reducing changes in technique as well as with interest-rate reduction and change in composition of output.[46] Given the political state of the world and the degree of settlement in the developed world, "the outlets for new investment" were "rapidly narrowing down to those created by the progress of technology" associated with "the further progress of science," invention and innovation, together with the development of industries.[47] Yet "current institutional developments" were restricting remaining outlets for investment. Especially unfavorable were "the growing power of trade unions and trade associations, the development of monopolistic competition, of rivalry for the market through expensive persuasion and advertising, instead of through price competition, . . . [and] the tendency to block the advance of technical progress by the shelving of patents."[48]

Hansen pointed out that "with a stationary population we could maintain as rapid a rise in per capita real income as that experienced in the past, by making annually only half the volume of new investment to which we have been accustomed," and that therefore "a volume of investment adequate to provide full employment could give us an annual percentage increase in per capita output greatly in excess of any hitherto attained."[49] Even so, maintaining full employment would not prove easy in the absence of technological progress and the development of new industries. Tax relief and pubic investment, together with other governmental activities, while attractive in theory, were not very attractive under a political democracy with power distributed as in the United States. "The great transition, incident to a rapid decline in population growth and its impact upon capital formation and the workability of a system of free enterprise," therefore called "for high scientific adventure along all the fronts represented by the social science disciplines."[50]

Two years later Hansen described what he believed to be suitable fiscal policies, together with investment incentives which, carried out within the framework of a "dual" or mixed economy, might assure full use of resources.[51] Ten years later Hansen wrote: "There is no danger of a return to the income level of 1939. But there is the danger that we may not achieve on a sustained basis, our growth potential."[52] He noted the investment-stimulating impact of the population upsurge of the 1940s, but indicated that "a decline in the rate of growth to less than 9 million could not fail to chill the outlook for investment," particularly given its expression in terms of expectations and the acceleration principle.[53]

4. Reactions to Keynes–Hansen Views

While there was general agreement that a slowing down and eventual cessation of population growth could intensify some economic problems, the macroeconomic views of Keynes and Hansen gave rise to a variety of responses ranging from approval to disapproval. As we note in the next section, attention was devoted to some likely effects of population decline prior to the appearance of Keynes's *General Theory* and the thesis embodied therein.

Critical response to Keynes's views assumed various forms—that his theoretical apparatus and hence his interpretation were imperfect, that the economic system was much more homeostatic than Keynes portrayed it, and (though Keynes would agree) that a slowing down of population growth brought with it many advantages, particularly when populations became stable at stationary levels.

Illustrative of critiques of Keynes's analytical apparatus are some of the essays included in Lekachman's symposium[54] or cited in the bibliography to the essays on the business cycle assembled by Haberler and his committee.[55] Representative of the attacks on Keynes's portrayal of the economic system is George Terborgh's *The Bogey of Economic Maturity*.[56] Some economists, while not critical of Keynes's thesis as such, apparently believed it easier than Keynes suggested to maintain balance between savings and investment.[57]

Harrod, who put forward a theory alternative to Keynes, made the maximum rate of growth dependent upon population growth and unemployment dependent upon deviation of the warranted rate of growth from the natural rate.

> Alongside the concept of warranted rate of growth we may introduce another, to be called the natural rate of growth. This is the maximum rate of growth allowed by the increase of population, accumulation of capital, technological improvement and the work / leisure preference schedule, supposing that there is always full employment in some sense.
>
> There is no inherent tendency for these two rates to coincide. Indeed, there is no unique warranted rate; the value of the warranted rate depends upon the phase of the trade cycle and the level of activity.
>
> Consideration may be given to that warranted rate which would obtain in conditions of full employment; this may be regarded as the warranted rate "proper" to the economy. *Prima facie* it might be supposed healthier to have the "proper" warranted rate above than below the natural rate. But this is very doubtful.
>
> The system cannot advance more quickly than the natural rate allows. If the proper warranted rate is above this, there will be a chronic tendency to depression; the depressions drag down the warranted rate below its proper level, and so keep its average value over a term of years down to the natural rate. But this reduction of the warranted rate is only achieved by having chronic unemployment.[58]

> . . . The feeling is justified to the extent that higher propensity to save does, in fact, *warrant* a higher rate of growth. Trouble arises if the rate of growth which it warrants is greater than that which the increase of population and the increase of technical capacity render permanently possible. And the fundamental paradox is that the more ambitious the rate *warranted* is, the greater the probability that the actual output will from time to time, and even persistently, fall below that which the productive capacity of the population would allow.[59]

. . . According to the dynamic theory, the tendency of a system to relapse into depression before full employment is reached in the boom suggests that its proper warranted rate exceeds its natural rate. Outside evidence includes the known decline in the growth of population, which involves a decline in the natural rate.[60]

In *The Trade Cycle* Harrod expressed concern that decline in the rate of population growth could lead to imbalance among growth of debt, debt service, and national income and between insurance premiums and disbursements—forms of imbalance for which one might find solutions that did not eventuate in excessive saving. For example, noting that "the prospective needs of children are one cause of saving among the less well-to-do," Harrod proposed "a scheme for insurance against children, preferably compulsory and payable by bachelors also, with premiums in proportion to assessed income." This "might serve the double object of reducing untoward tendency towards over-saving and the calamitous decline of the birth rate."[61]

Harrod apparently endorsed W. B. Reddaway's thesis that special obstacles to full employment are found in wealthy communities, saying that in a "richer world there is a greater proportion of expenditures which can easily be cut down," and thus become destabilizing in effect. Reddaway had argued in effect that a declining population trend reduced the propensity to consume, the relative importance of basic commodities, and the relative number of openings for investment, together with the inducement to invest, a counterweight to the disposition to save "largely for the sake of security against future risks, both known and unknown."[62] A similar view was put forward by A. Loveday when he included among causes of instability associated with declining population growth, increase in the relative importance of luxuries and decrease in the proportion of income spent upon essential products.[63] Underlying this view was a fear manifested already by Quesnay, that the flow of expenditure and hence economic activity would be subject to discontinuity.

The Report of the Economics Committee to the Royal Commission called attention to implications of Britain's experience.

Both these underlying conditions were fundamentally ephemeral; some day the process of opening up new territories must reach an end; sooner or later technological progress must spread throughout the world. In the nineteenth century these inevitabilities were sufficiently remote for it to be reasonable to disregard their implications. Now, however, the industrialisation of agricultural communities has reached a stage which has involved a large curtailment of British export trade; and we have to reckon with the possibility that it may develop in future along lines which may make it increasingly difficult for us to obtain the large-scale imports of primary commodities essential for the accustomed standard of living of our population. These long-run tendencies, combining as they do with special adverse factors, notably the heavy burden of external indebtedness which we have been incurring during the last few years, have an important bearing which we now turn to examine on questions of population policy.[64]

The Committee concluded that on balance cessation of population growth would be advantageous.

> For two reasons, a stationary population is likely to find it easier than one which is growing rapidly to increase its standard of life. First, the resources which a growing population would have to devote to maintaining capital equipment per head become available for raising standards.
>
> Second, the amount of land per head ceases to decline when the population ceases to grow, with the consequence that the difficulty of obtaining a supply of natural products (which may become serious for Britain in her changed international position) will be at least mitigated.
>
> On the other hand, the cessation of growth has the disadvantages (1) that the average age of the population will increase; (2) that there may be some loss of the economies of large-scale production; (3) that the difficulties of maintaining employment will be increased.
>
> If, however, employment policy is only moderately successful, we think that for Great Britain today the balance of economic advantage is strongly in favour of stationary as compared with increasing numbers.
>
> Unless fertility rises, the population will not merely cease to grow but must in time decline. There can be no question as to the necessity of restoring our fertility rates sooner or later to replacement level, since the alternative is national extinction. There is, however, a question whether it is important that the recovery should be effected quickly enough to avert any material decline.
>
> The consequences of a decline of numbers are broadly similar in kind to those of a cessation of growth, but may differ greatly in degree. There will be advantages from the fact that accumulated capital per head of population will increase; but these advantages are likely to be speculative, transient, and double-edged. A smaller population would be advantageous on balance of payment grounds, but it is difficult to forecast whether this advantage would be slight or important. There would also be a gain on the score of amenity.
>
> The offsetting disadvantages of the cessation of the growth of population —in particular, the extra difficulty of maintaining full employment— would acquire some added practical importance if numbers were to decline materially. The burden that might result from an increase in the proportion of dependants to the working population would, however, be less formidable than is often supposed.
>
> Thus while a smaller population would, as such, be on the whole advantageous, the *process* of decline would be difficult. Whether there would be a net gain would depend mainly on the long-term development of our balance of payments position.[65]

Alan Sweezy identified and replied to three types of criticism of the "declining investment opportunity, or 'secular stagnation thesis' ": those based on misinterpretation, on disagreement respecting the magnitude, and on dissatisfaction regarding the impact of population growth upon investment. Sweezy pointed to the importance attached to science and technology by both Keynes and Hansen as well as to uncertainties respecting investment prospects. "We would be rash to count on an outlet for American capital large enough to absorb a large part of our full employment volume of saving."[66] Sweezy went on to show how "in the absence of population growth, new inventions, etc., to 'invest' in raising the standard of living of the existing population" would eventuate in duplicative investment, in a "glut of capital equipment" and "a shortage of labor to operate it."[67] Sweezy did not anticipate such an outcome, however, or another depression like that of 1929–1932, since "social security, health, housing, education, and public works programs" offered "socially valuable spending channels adequate to compensate for any deficiency in private investment expenditure." This anticipation has been borne out in part in that the ratio of public expenditure to national income has approximately quadrupled.[68]

Typical of more recent treatment of the effect of population growth, an autonomous factor parallel to technological progress, upon investment is that of Warren L. Smith, who noted the weakness of investment given a slow pace of population growth and / or technical development. He does not assess the degree of validity attaching to the stagnation thesis, given allowance for the supposed underestimation of the ability of flexible prices and interest rates to facilitate adjustment, but admits the depressive influence of weakness in the demand for capital. At the same time he indicates that "an excessively rapid rate of population growth and an unduly accelerated pace of technological advance" could press aggregate demand to "the limits imposed by the supply of available resources" and generate "secular inflation."[69] This could happen should "employment" become a "political end, an ideologically enshrined objective of public policy" to be achieved speedily, and cause growth to encounter limits imposed by natural resources.[70]

Hans Staudinger expressed concern lest stationarity of population increase risks surrounding investment, especially that in large new industrial units, thereby darkening expectations and slowing down investment. This outcome was not inevitable, however, since public investment could supplement private investment and much economy in the use of labor and raw materials could be attained. While Staudinger did not differ fundamentally, however, with those who stressed the adverse effect of the slowing down of population growth upon private investment, he believed that this effect could be offset.[71]

Hans Neisser pointed out that in some models (e.g., the classical), as in capital-short countries, population growth was not essential to investment. Moreover, even when the stimulus of population growth was required, that needed growth could be foreign rather than domestic, should a country depend upon foreign trade to obtain full utilization of its capital goods industries. What matters for Germany and England "is not so much the growth of their own population as the growth of the population of the world, which by stimulating investment in some parts of the globe would give these countries an opportunity to utilize fully also their capital goods industries." And he added that from "this point of view they would fare best if their population remained constant while that of the rest of the world increased rapidly."

Neisser looked upon imbalance between the flow of savings and investment as temporary, inasmuch as community preferences could and would change as the return to excessive saving did not offset the sacrifice involved. He expected that *ceteris paribus* a stationary population would save less than a growing one and that excessive liquidity preference would not become a problem. The outcome depended on the feedback and adjustment mechanisms operative in an economy; if they worked, a stationary population would function as effectively as a growing one.[72]

Neisser noted, of course, that more economic friction would be encountered in a stationary population, that the composition of consumer demand would be more subject to change, that investment would not be less risky, that the distribution of profits would change, and that increase in capital per worker and decline in the interest rate would not be much greater than if the population were growing. Accordingly, he did not anticipate serious problems respecting employment maintenance and income growth.[73] Moreover, continuity of expenditure would be easier to maintain. For "in a stationary population the investment activities of insurance companies, social security funds and savings banks would be considerably reduced, because their outgo could come close to their intake."[74]

Early discussion of the relationship between population growth and investment failed to distinguish sharply between percentage and absolute rates of growth. For while a falling percentage rate of increase indicated a later drop in absolute growth, change in the absolute rate could be more significant. It was essential, therefore, to determine which rate was more relevant in a given situation,[75] particularly if acceleration was involved.[76]

While trade-cycle theorists were inclined to treat population growth as an exogenous factor, thus playing down the response of marriage and birth rates to phases of the cycle, several drew attention to the impact of population movements. In Germany August Lösch found that the timing and the form of business cycles had been determined primarily by waves in the labor supply.[77] James Duesenberry noted that population growth contributed to stability, especially before World War I, by increasing "the rate at which the personal-savings ratio declines when income falls" and by reducing the "rate at which the demand for housing falls as income falls."[78] Variability in fertility, together with its impact on variability in the rate of growth of significant categories of the population, received greater attention, however, as the role of exogenous factors began to command greater attention.[79]

The impact of population aging on institutional arrangements for the support of the aged received less analytical attention at first, even though new institutional measures were widely considered. The fundamental problem was, however, well put already by W. A. B. Hopkin in 1953.[80] He observed *inter alia:*

> . . . There is no doubt that in considering the provisions via the pensions system and in other ways for the maintenance of old people we ought always to work out the costs and benefits of any proposed measure that will accrue in the future, as well as those that will appear immediately. As a general principle it would seem reasonable to avoid as far as possible arrangements which will tend to lower the ratio of "producers" (adjusted for levels of productivity) to "consumers" (adjusted for levels of expenditure). This is the fundamental principle; though in its application we must always take account of the fact that a great part of the consumption of the old is financed from public funds via old age pensions. These funds have to be raised by taxation of one kind and another, and must involve some economic loss through the effects of taxation on incentive and in other ways. Thus a rise in the consumption standards of the old financed in this way is likely, besides involving a compulsory transfer of equal amounts from younger people, to do some damage to the productive effort of the country.
>
> What seems to be wrong with our present arrangements is not that the pension is conditional on retirement, but that retirement with a pension is available to, and often compulsory upon, people very many of whom would be quite capable of staying at work for some time longer. There is evidence that lack of income has in the past been the chief cause impelling people to continue work beyond normal retiring age; and while it would be inhuman to use poverty as a weapon to force people genuinely beyond working to carry on, there is no sense in arrangements which provide a gratuitous income to those who are perfectly able to contribute to the social effort. In recent years a good deal of evidence has been accumulated to show that it is rather the exception than the rule for a man to be genuinely past work at 65.
>
> If the pension age were raised tomorrow, millions of contributors would feel that they have been cheated of their rights and there would be a tremendous outcry. This is a dangerous state of affairs, since it can be predicted with considerable confidence that sooner or later a government will feel compelled to raise the pension age. Unless this change is to be delayed far beyond the desirable time, and then to be made with the maxi-

mum of consequential resentment and anger, it is necessary that the principle should be publicly established that the age at which retirement pension may be claimed is variable, and will probably be raised as time goes on. A government which made such an announcement would obtain no immediate credit and probably some immediate odium, but it would earn the gratitude of its successors by establishing the conditions in which the pension arrangements could subsequently be adjusted to changes in the demographic and economic circumstances of the country.[81]

5. Population Decline

Whereas most of the literature relating to population trends in and after the 1930s dealt with decline in the rate of population growth, W. B. Reddaway in 1939 dealt with consequences of decline in numbers and its concomitants. He pointed out that even though the population total would not begin immediately to decline and then would proceed slowly "for a considerable number of years . . . failing a powerful and deliberate 'population policy,' " analysis of the consequences of population decline and population aging was "already important."[82] These consequences he examined under four heads—unemployment, income size and distribution, public finance, and international trade.

Reddaway divides unemployment into particular and general, and then states that absence of population growth makes more interoccupational shifts and adjustments necessary. "The advent of a stationary or declining population will aggravate the effects of changes in technique, demand, or industrial location in throwing people out of their old jobs." He then shows that adjustments are more difficult in a stationary or declining population because relatively more workers are older, new industries are less likely to be started, and fear of industry contraction, together with trade union opposition to expansion, slows the development of opportunity for those needing to transfer to new employments. The incidence of the resulting unemployment tends to be heavier on older workers. Of the means to the easing of particular unemployment "the most important thing is to avoid general unemployment." This is to be accomplished through sustaining the demand not only for consumption goods but also for capital goods when production generates "income without adding to the supply of goods to be bought out of these incomes."[83] For while a falling population could be prejudicial to capital outlay, other forces could sustain the need for capital (e.g., rising average income and living standards, changes in techniques, increase in family–population ratio, improved living accommodations, possibly lower rates of interest).[84] Reddaway describes a variety of measures, however, that might be used to encourage investment, discourage saving, and stimulate consumption.[85]

Reddaway concludes that while the advent of a stationary or declining population may exercise a slightly unfavorable effect upon "particular employment," scale of production, and international trade, this effect will be more than offset by greater capital supply and a slight improvement in age composition; whence increase in real national income per person employed will result. Return per unit of capital will fall, but only slightly, mainly because demand will probably shift toward goods produced mainly by capital. It is likely also that income distribution will become less unequal.[86]

Public financial problems will be intensified because "a falling population increases the risks of prolonged depressions," and the slump will confront "the government with an irresistible demand for more expenditure at a time of rapidly falling revenue." Moreover, because of the age structure the number of old-age pensioners will be relatively high in comparison with the workers who in effect finance pensioners, particularly when population begins to decline. With a relatively smaller working population, moreover, the burden of relatively fixed public costs such as defense and social services incident on this population will be greater. There will be little or no offsets to these increases in public expenditure. Reduction in the relative number of children is not likely to reduce pressure on the budget, since parents bear most of these costs. Moreover, while a decline in population will increase the importance of inheritance and estate taxation as a source of revenue, the revenue derivable from death taxes is limited.[87] In sum, Reddaway anticipates that population decline will be accompanied by growth in the ratio of public expenditures to national income and hence in the burdensomeness of taxes.

Reddaway noted that while a falling population was likely to reduce the volume of international trade, it could improve the terms, though only temporarily if economic developments in the world at large reduced Britain's comparative advantage in their current exports.[88] Political developments in the form of trade restrictions were also likely, particularly in reaction to slumps, unemployment, and fear for economic security.[89] Great Britain needed, therefore, to seek with all her power, "to prevent this gradual throttling of world trade."[90]

Reddaway was essentially optimistic respecting desired modifiability of population trends and the adjustability of an economy to population changes. He also observed "that the economic importance of population changes is often grossly exaggerated." "If we can show sufficient social resourcefulness and adaptability to solve various problems of adjustment, then they will give us a good reward; if we cannot, then they will prove a curse instead of a blessing."[91] "The change from an increasing to a more or less constant population is economically not unwelcome, or at least its consequences do not justify active steps to raise the birth-rate."[92] Given too high a rate of population decline or too sustained a decline, however, a positive pronatalist population policy would be in order. Among its possible components Reddaway mentioned family allowances, increased income-tax allowances, improved maternity services, creches and nursery schools, housing assistance, marriage loans, cheapening of education, and increase of social security, together with measures of coercion (e.g., heavy taxation of bachelors, occupational restrictions, restrictions on women's employment, restrictions on the sale of contraceptives) and propaganda.[93]

Since 1945 the issues that animated Keynes and Hansen have declined in public concern, though they could reanimate it should fertility remain below the replacement level and an absolute decline in population become likely in several or more countries. Perhaps contributive to this decline in concern was the temporary upsurge in natality after World War II, an upsurge remindful of the temporary post-1918 upsurge. Mainly responsible, however, has been assumption by the state of responsibility for a variety of the costs of population maintenance, together with a great increase in the ratio of public expenditure to the Gross National Product— an increase that came in the wake of the Great Depression, World War II, and international readjustment to the results of this war.

Perhaps illustrative is the report *Towards A Population Policy* for the United Kingdom (1970).[94] In the chapter on "Demography and Economics" attention is focused not so much upon macroeconomic aspects of population trends as upon microeconomic aspects, upon connections both between particular population phenomena and changes and modes of economic behavior and between economic phenomena and demographic phenomena.[95] The impact of population trends upon investment and employment is disregarded rather than ruled out in this report, since attention is confined to natural increase, contraception, family planning, and genetics together with "demography and economics."

That cessation of population growth could intensify some economic problems, at least until the economy had become adjusted to something like zero population growth, has not been wholly neglected as a result of the absorption of the impact of population growth trends into a more inclusive theory of economic growth. For example, diminution in the rate of population growth might so reduce the profit rate that "above-equilibrium unemployment" could develop and even activate a tendency for disinvestment. In such case, E. S. Phelps indicates, monetary and fiscal policy would be called for—policy involving "a good deal more flexibility and innovativeness on the part of the Federal government towards the use of its monetary and fiscal policy instruments than have been demonstrated so far."[96] His argument is set within the framework of modern economic growth theory resting upon assumptions of constant growth of population and technological progress, together with constant returns to scale. He indicates, however, that should population growth slow down, technological progress and cultural innovation would be lowered.

Today, however, unlike in the 1930s, concern respecting the emergence of diminishing returns consequent upon natural resource limitations tends to override emphasis upon population growth as an employment-stabilizing agent. Such limitations are noted by Robert Dorfman in his comment upon Phelps's paper.[97] It has been well expressed by A. J. Coale:

> A continued secular economic boom could gain partial support from a continued baby boom. But after a century this trend would produce about a billion Americans, and after two centuries some six billion. There must be a better way to stimulate employment.[98]

Conclusion and Prospect

In recent years published concern respecting the possible consequences of cessation of population growth or of population decline diminished somewhat even though the postwar upsurge of natality eventually gave place to fertility levels that now fall short of population replacement in a number of advanced countries. This diminution in concern apparently reflects both temporary shifts in scholarly interests and the fact that diminution in the size of particular cohorts may be slow to make itself felt. In time, however, problems currently engaging the interests of scholars and / or the state will give way to new problems, among which the impact of changing population trends will be paramount. Then studies bearing upon the significance of those trends will become prominent as they did several decades ago.

Illustrative is the probable influence of a continuation of U.S. fertility below the replacement level based on the assumption that after 1973 fertility had begun to move toward and below replacement, perhaps to 1.7, a movement only partially offset by annual net immigration of 400,000.[99] Then while the five cohorts constituting the age group 0–4 will continue the decline already in effect in the 1960s, the 10 cohorts making up the 25–34 age group will continue to increase until 1990. Meanwhile the age group 45–54 will not begin to decline in size until after 2010, and the age group 65 and over until after 2035. As the number of cohorts subject to decline begins to increase, however, the prospect will intensify political as well as scholarly interest in implications of the advent of a stationary or declining population.

Sensitivity to decline in size of age group, at the practical as distinguished from the scholarly level, is mainly a function of the impact of such decline upon particular sets of interests. For example, sensitivity to decline in natality and the number of children under 5 is likely to be greatest among those supplying goods and services oriented to members of this age group. Similarly, sensitivity will be high on the part of educators to decline in the absolute size of cohorts falling within the range (say) 5 to 18 years.

For example, in the fall of 1976 a small decline in college and school enrollment was anticipated because of an earlier decline in the birth rate no longer offset by increase in enrollment rates by age. Industrialists will be sensitive to decline in the number of those within age groups newly entering the labor force, for example, those aged 20–29 years or 25–34 years. For example, in Japan, according to the White Paper on Labor issued in 1975, the relative availability of workers in their twenties—32 percent of all employed in Japanese enterprises—was shrinking, in part owing to an earlier decline in births. As a result industrial labor policies were found in need of change—especially change suited to increase greater participation of older workers in the labor force and to adjust promotion patterns to the emerging age as well as to the educational structure of the labor force.[100]

Presumably as decline in the number of births and eventually of persons of school and working age[101] begins to have an impact upon the economy in particular countries, adjustments to these impacts will be made even though the aggregate population continues to grow—particularly in countries which do not attract immigrants with the required skills, and so forth. Concern respecting the supposedly adverse impact of decline in population will become manifest long before total population decline is in the immediate offing—indeed, not many years after the absolute number of births begins to decline.

In chapters that follow we shall attempt to assess the impact of the advent of a stationary population, though not entirely in keeping with the sample of authors whose work we have reviewed. Of course, should fertility continue below rather than at the replacement level, the findings of authors such as Reddaway will become pertinent, particularly since the state now assumes financial responsibility for the support of the retired population in much greater degree than formerly.

V. Age Composition

All the world's a stage,/And all the men and women merely players./They have their exits and their entrances;/And one man in his time plays many parts,/His acts being seven ages.

Shakespeare

Age composition is, for two reasons, the economically and socially most significant aspect of a stationary population. (1) The economic, political, and other behavior of the representative individual changes with age both (a) because his mental and physical faculties improve with age up to a point only eventually to deteriorate at rates that vary with faculty and individual, and (b) because "capital" embodied in his person—concrete knowledge, learning skill, etc.—accumulates with training and experience up to a point only eventually to waste away as a result of nonreplacement and / or nonreplaceability. (2) Age composition is one among a number of collective or group characteristics that give shape to the physical, ideational, and (perhaps) ideological environment within which behavior takes place and shape. Time preference and expectations at the individual level also vary with age and affect economic and political behavior accordingly. Given population decline, the significance of age structure increases.

Although irregularities etched into a population's age structure or pyramid reflect the impact of a country's history upon its fertility and mortality in the past, together with echoes of earlier impacts, the impact of events in the distant past[1] finally disappears from age structures. For a property of human populations is "weak ergodicity, . . . the progressive forgetting of the past. . . . The time structure of the birth sequence of a human population and its age structure at a given moment are dominated by the recent history of fertility and mortality to which the population has been subject. It is not necessary to know anything about the history of a population more than two centuries ago to account for the recent sequence of births or the present age composition."[2]

As will be indicated more fully later, the advent of a stationary population is accompanied by structural and processive changes which reflect as well as modify changes in the parameters of populations.[3] In keeping with contemporary and prospective life expectancy we shall confine our remarks to stable populations associated with life expectancies of 70 to 75 years and fertility rates supportive of stable populations growing +1, 0, or −1 percent per year.

Two structural changes may be noted. First, while an increase in life

expectancy from 70 to 75 years would increase the mean age of a population only about 3–4 percent, it would augment the fraction over 65 by about
one-seventh. The impact of fertility differences is much greater; the percentage over 65 is slightly over twice as high, given a −1 percent rate of
growth instead of a +1 percent rate of growth, and about one-third higher
given a −1 rather than a 0 percent growth rate. Second, while a population
that is declining 1 percent per year may include about the same percent
of persons of working age (15–64) as a stationary population, the ratio of
those aged 40–64 to those aged 15–39 is appreciably higher when the
growth rate is negative than when it is zero or positive. The advent of a
negative rate of growth may therefore have profound effects.

Whereas age-structural changes affect economically oriented behavior
somewhat under the influence of age-affected motivation and capacity,
processive changes condition the flexibility of a society and its economy.
What Ryder calls metabolism, the gross and net rate of change in a population of working age (15–64), is nearly the same in populations with life
expectancy in the lower 70s and growing between −1 and +1 percent.
When such a population is stationary, additions to the working-age population equal the departures, whereas when it is declining, departures exceed
additions, and when it is increasing, additions exceed departures. Ryder
suggests that low and balanced metabolism tends to promote stability,
whereas high metabolism and working-age population growth conduces
to flexibility by requiring not only the filling of vacated roles but the development of roles for net additions to the working-age population.

This and the two following chapters deal mainly with age-structural
change. Interaction between environmental change and fertility is not
stressed, though fertility rates may function as cause and effect over time.
This chapter deals with the evolution of age structure; the two that follow,
with the significance of differences in age structure.

1. Evolution of Age Structures

A population's age structure is governed by the behavior of its age-
specific mortality and fertility, particularly the latter. This structure will
assume a stable, unchanging form if age-specific mortality and fertility do
not change over a sufficient period of time. "A population whose mortality
and fertility remain invariable tends to become the stable population corresponding to such levels of mortality and fertility." The constant rate of
population growth (whether positive, negative, or zero) characteristic of
this stable population depends upon the sets of age-specific fertility and
mortality rates underlying this population.[4] If age-specific fertility and / or
age-specific mortality vary over time, the crude rate of natural increase
will vary and the age structure of the population will be less regular in

form. For example, the heavy mortality associated with war, famine, or virulent epidemics gives rise to indentations or hollows in the segments of the age structure most vulnerable to these events. Similarly, an upsurge of natality after a war or great economic depression will give rise to abnormally large cohorts, which thereafter move through a population as a pig swallowed by a large serpent moves through its body. In other words, great upsurges in births give rise to a series of echo effects every 20 or more years, but with each smaller than its predecessor until the echo effect disappears. An upsurge of mortality has an effect insofar as it affects subsequent natality and mortality.[5]

Change in the Gross Reproduction Rate (GRR) modifies age structure in much greater measure than does change in expectation of life at birth.[6] Three stable populations are presented in Table V.1, each based upon the same life expectancy, 70.2 years, but combined with the Gross Reproduction Rate indicated in the first column. Declines of 0.5 and 1.0 point in

Table V.1. Gross Reproduction and Age Structure

	Percentage of Stable Population			Natural Increase Percent
GRR	0–14 years	15–59 years	60 years and over	
2.0	36.8	54.7	8.5	2.33
1.5	29.3	57.7	13.0	1.29
1.0	19.5	58.6	21.9	−0.18

Source: United Nations, *The Aging of Populations and Its Economic and Social Implications*, Population Studies, No. 26, New York, 1956, pp. 26–27.

the initial GRR of 2.0 eventuate not only in reduced natural increase but in marked change in the age structure, especially at the extremes, under 15 and over 59. Thus the fraction of the population under 15 is eventually reduced from 0.368 to 0.195 by a one-point decline in the GRR, while the fraction over 59 is increased from 0.085 to 0.219.

As the rate of natural increase in stable populations rises, the relative number in age groups above 59 begins to decline noticeably, while that in younger age groups begins to increase. Conversely, as the rate of growth declines, the relative number of old persons rises and that of young persons declines. These trends are illustrated in Table V.2, which summarizes the age compositions of stable *male* populations growing at designated rates. Later on, reference will be made again to this table.

In contrast, changes in life expectancy have only a moderate effect upon the age structure within a likely range of change. This is illustrated in Table V.3. The GRR is held constant at 1.5 and combined with the life ex-

Table V.2. Age Structure of Populations Growing at Various Rates (Male, Life Expectancy 73.5 years)

Age Group	Rate of Growth in Stable Population				
	$-\frac{1}{2}\%$	0%	$\frac{1}{2}\%$	1%	2%
0–14	16.99%	19.99%	23.20%	26.60%	33.73%
15–19	5.94	6.64	7.33	7.99	9.14
20–54	45.08	45.62	45.66	45.22	43.07
55–59	6.64	6.09	5.50	4.91	3.76
60–64	6.40	5.72	5.04	4.39	3.20
65–69	5.91	5.15	4.43	3.76	2.61
65 and over	18.95	15.95	13.26	10.89	7.10
20–64	58.12	57.43	56.20	54.52	50.03
20–69	64.13	62.58	60.63	59.28	52.64
18–64	60.50	60.09	59.13	57.72	51.85

Source: A. J. Coale and Paul Demeny, Regional Model Life Tables and Stable Populations (Princeton: Princeton University Press, 1966), p. 168.

pectancies reported in column 1. An increase in life expectancy from 50 to 70.2 years has virtually no effect upon the fraction of the population over 59 years old and only slight effects upon the fractions 0–14 and 15–59 years old. When life expectancy begins to move above 70, the proportion of persons 15–59 begins to decline if the GRR lies between 1.0 and 2.0, while the relative number of aged increases. In a stationary population with a life expectancy of about 76 years, about 25 percent will be 60 and over. But with a life expectancy of 90 and a GRR of about 1.0, over 30 percent will be over 59 and the fraction 15 to 59 will be moving below 50.[7] Should man become immortal, the fraction 60 and over would approach 100 percent provided that the GRR were at or below unity; it would approach only 41.4 percent if the GRR remained at 1.5, and only 9.1 percent if the GRR remained at 3.[8]

The ultimate impact of a change in age-specific fertility or mortality is, as already noted, upon the extreme segments of a population structure, say upon those under 15 or 20 years and those over 55 and over 59. The intermediate segment—say those between 15 or 20 and 54 or 59—is much

Table V.3. Life Expectancy and Age Structure

Life Expectancy (years)	Percentage of Stable Population			Natural Increase Percent
	0–14	15–59	60 and over	
50	27.0	60.0	13.0	3.9
60.4	28.2	58.7	13.1	9.0
70.2	29.3	57.7	13.0	12.9

Source: See under Table V.1.

less sensitive but not insensitive. The ultimate impact is not fully apparent until a population again becomes stable after the change in age-specific fertility or age-specific mortality has been wholly absorbed. As has been implied, while an increase in expectation of life at birth may rejuvenate a population, it does not greatly modify age structure in a modern society with a GRR under 2.0 and a life expectancy much above 50 unless life expectancy moves appreciably above 70 or the GRR is in the neighborhood of 1.0 or lower. It is otherwise with a change in the GRR. For example, with a life expectancy of between 50 and 70.2 years, a decline in the GRR from 2.0 to 1.0—roughly a decline in the birth rate from around 30–31 to around 13 births per 1,000 inhabitants—will be accompanied in a stable population by an increase from around 8.6 to around 21.9 in the percent of the population 60 and over, a decrease of around half in the fraction aged 0–14 years, and an increase of about 6–7 percent in the fraction aged 15 to 59 years.[9] While the impact of change in mortality as a stable population absorbs this change in the course of a century may not be very per-

(1)	(2)	(3)	Col. 3 ÷ Col. 2
0–14	16.99	33.73	1.99
15–59	5.94	9.14	1.54
15–54	51.02	52.21	1.02
20–54	45.08	43.07	0.96
55–64	13.04	6.96	0.53
64+	18.95	7.10	0.37

ceptible, especially after 50 years, that of a corresponding change in the GRR over the course of a century is quite perceptible, initially in the 0–59 segment and later in the over-59 segment.[10]

Comparison of the columns headed —½ and 2 percent, respectively, in Table V.2, and here numbered (2) and (3) serves to illustrate the greater sensitivity to change in the extreme components of an age structure. The comparative stability of the core components of the age structure serves to cushion somewhat changes in the age structure of a population.

2. Prospective Age Structure

In this section we present a sample of stable stationary-population age structures based on somewhat different assumptions with regard to the movement of fertility to the replacement level. We also present several life-table populations which by definition are stable and stationary. Comparison of these populations reveals a marked similarity between the age structures of any two stationary populations based on modern life ex-

pectancy and replacement fertility. Comparison also suggests that, given replacement fertility together with prospective life expectancy, the economic
implications of differences in age structures will be negligible. Should fertility descend below the replacement level, however, the age structure will
become economically less favorable.

Five sample stationary-population age structures are presented in Table
V.4. The two described in columns 2 and 3 are life-table populations for
the white and the total population, respectively, of the United States in
1973 when life expectancy was 72.17 years for the whites and 71.34 years
for the entire population. The figures in column 4 describe the life-table
population for the U.S. population in 1949 when life expectancy was 68
years. The stationary population, attained as of 2050 (see column 5),

Table V.4. Stationary Population

Age Group	Life Table*			Stationary Population (Both Sexes)		
	White	Total				
(1)	1973 (2)	1973 (3)	1949 (4)	2050** (5)	2050ᵃ (6)	2050ᵃᵃ (7)
0–4	6.81	6.88	7.10	6.78	6.69	5.06
5–9	6.79	6.86	7.07	6.77	6.67	5.33
10–14	6.78	6.84	7.05	6.76	6.66	5.63
15–19	6.76	6.82	7.02	6.74	6.64	5.80
20–24	6.72	6.77	6.97	6.71	6.60	5.90
25–29	6.67	6.72	6.91	6.67	6.56	5.99
30–34	6.63	6.67	6.86	6.63	6.53	6.37
35–39	6.58	6.60	6.77	6.57	6.48	6.53
40–44	6.50	6.51	6.64	6.49	6.41	6.59
45–49	6.37	6.37	6.46	6.36⎱	12.40	12.98
50–54	6.17	6.12	6.18	6.17⎰		
55–59	5.88	5.83	5.79	5.88⎱	11.29	13.10
60–64	5.44	5.38	5.25	5.47⎰		
65–69	4.86	4.78	4.57	4.91⎱	9.15	11.02
70–74	4.10	4.01	3.72	4.17⎰		
75 & over	6.91	6.78	5.62	6.92	7.91	9.72
Total %	100.00	100.00	100.00	100.00	100.00	100.00
Median Age (years)	—	—	—	37.2	37.8	42.6
Millions	7.217	7.134	6.800	277	270	227

*Source: U.S. Dept. of Health, Education, and Welfare, *Vital Statistics of the
U.S., 1973*, Vol. 2, Sec. 5, Life Tables, pp. 5–9; ibid., Vol. 37, No. 12, Nov. 16, 1953,
p. 335.

**Source: *Current Population Report P-25*, No. 493, Dec., 1972, p. 26.

ᵃ Ibid., No. 601, Oct., 1975, p. 142. Assumes replacement fertility and zero immigration.

ᵃᵃ Ibid., p. 121. Assumes 400,000 net immigration and fertility declining from
2.0 in 1972 to 1.7 in and after 2015.

rests upon the assumption of fertility at the replacement level of 2.11 children per woman, together with zero immigration, as of 1969. The 277 million total, together with the age structure, would be approximated already by 2037, except for very minor irregularities in age composition remaining to be smoothed out.[11]

The age structure of the stationary population described in column 6 does not differ significantly from that described in column 5. It too is based on the assumption of zero net immigration, together with fertility assumptions that eventuate in a virtually stationary population of about 269 million by 2025. Given these same fertility and mortality assumptions, together with 400,000 immigrants annually, the population would number about 318 million by 2050 but with about the same fraction in the 20–64 age category.[12]

When fertility moves below the replacement level, the median age will move upward along with the fraction of the population over 60 or over 65. Comparison of column 7 with column 6 reveals this upward drift. Implications of data in column 7 will be examined later.

In Table V.5, based on Table V.4, we present a number of critical ratios. The fraction of the stationary population (see columns 2–5) in age groups 20–64, 18–64, and 20–69 does not vary greatly with population, nor, for that matter, does the fraction of the stationary population in age groups 20–54 and 20–59 years. The ratio of the population of so-called

Table V.5. Significant Ratios

Age Group (1)	1973 White (2)	1973 Total (3)	1949 Total (4)	2050 (5)	2050[a] (6)
(1) 0–14	20.38	20.58	21.22	20.01	20.02
(2) 0–14 + ½(15–19)	23.76	23.99	24.73	23.38	23.34
(3) 65–over	15.87	15.57	13.91	16.00	17.06
(4) 20–54	45.64	45.76	46.79	45.60	44.98
(5) 20–59	51.54	51.59	52.58	51.48	[50.15]
(6) 20–64	56.98	56.97	57.83	56.95	56.27
(7) 18–64	59.65	59.65	60.64	59.65	[58.93]
(8) 20–69	61.82	61.75	62.40	61.86	[63.90]
(9) (18–64)/(over 64)	3.78	3.83	4.36	3.73	3.45
(10) (20–64)/(over 64)	3.59	3.97	4.16	3.56	3.30
(11) (20–69)/(over 69)	5.61	5.72	6.68	5.58	[4.95]
(12) (18–64)/(0–17½)*	2.51	2.49	2.45	2.55	2.52
(13) (20–64)/(0–17½)*	2.40	2.37	2.34	2.44	2.41
(14) (20–69)/(0–17½)*	2.60	2.57	2.52	2.64	2.73
(15) (15–19)/(20–64)	0.12	0.12	0.12	0.117	0.118
(16) (15–19)/(59–64)	1.24	1.27	1.34	1.23	[1.20]

* (0–17½) = (0–14) + ½(15–19). Figures in lines 1–8 are in percent; those in lines 9–16 are ratios.
 [a] Percentages in this column are derived from column 6 in Table V.4.

Table V.6. Projection W

Year (1)	Total (2)	0–17 years (3)	18–64 years (4)	65 and over (5)	(4) / (2) 18–64 ——— total (6)	(4) / (5) 18–64 ——— 65 and over (7)
1970	204.8	69.7	114.9	20.2	0.56	5.7
1985	229.2	65.4	138.5	25.3	0.60	5.5
2000	249.0	66.8	154.1	28.1	0.62	5.5
2025	271.4	66.7	162.3	42.4	0.60	3.8
2050	273.2	66.6	162.8	43.8	0.60	3.7

working age 18–64, 20–64, and 20–69 to young dependents (say those under 15 plus one-half of those 15–19) does not vary markedly with population, nor does the ratio of population of working age to old dependents. The percentages in lines 6–8 indicate adequate potential capacity for the support of dependents, and those in line 5 may do so; the ratios in lines 9–14 bear out this relationship. Ratios in lines 15 and 16 will be referred to later.

When fertility declines gradually but with negligible variation as a population's form approaches stability based on replacement-level (or some other constant-level) fertility, the stable age structure of this population is not greatly affected. Tables V.6–V.8 illustrate changes associated with differences in assumptions respecting fertility, given that net immigration remains at the zero level in all instances.[18]

Projection W (Table V.6) is based on the assumption that total fertility drops immediately to the replacement level 2.11 and remains there. The population becomes stationary at about 274 million by 2037, whereas, given immigration at 400,000 per year, the population would number about 312 million by 2037 and 352 million by 2100. The ratio of those aged 18–64 to those over 64 will decline from the present level to 3.7 (see column 7) compared with 3.9 given immigration. The ratio of the

Table V.7. Projection V

Year (1)	Total (2)	0–17 years (5)	18–64 years (4)	65 and over (5)	(4) / (2) 18–64 ——— total (6)	(4) / (5) 18–64 ——— 65 and over (7)
1970	204.8	69.7	114.9	20.2	0.56	5.7
1985	221.4	57.6	138.5	25.3	0.62	5.5
2000	239.5	63.2	148.2	28.1	0.62	5.3
2025	253.7	61.7	149.6	42.4	0.59	3.5
2050	249.8	61.1	150.2	38.5	0.60	3.9

Table V.8. Projection Y

Year (1)	Total (2)	0–17 years (3)	18–64 years (4)	65 and over (5)	(4) / (2) 18–64 ——— total (6)	(4) / (5) 18–64 ——— 65 and over (7)
1970	204.8	69.7	114.9	20.2	0.56	5.7
1985	228.6	64.8	138.5	25.3	0.60	5.5
2000	248.0	65.5	154.4	28.1	0.62	5.5
2025	268.7	65.6	160.7	42.4	0.60	3.8
2050	269.0	65.5	160.5	43.0	0.60	3.7

population supposedly of working age to the total population (see column 6) will approximate 0.6 as it would given immigration.

Projection V (Table V.7), based upon the assumption that total fertility falls to 1.5 by 1980 and then rises to 2.11 and remains there, eventuates in a population that is stationary but not quite stable at 250 million by around 2027. With about 60 percent of the population aged 18 to 64, the ratio of those aged 18–64 to those aged over 64 is destined to settle at 3.7 though still be slightly higher as of 2050 (see column 7). With immigration, Projection V yields about 284 million by 2025 and 296 million by 2050, with a median age of 36.6 years instead of 37.3 years as in a stationary population.

Projection Y (Table V.8) is based upon the assumption that the annual number of births remains fixed at 3,732,000, the number estimated for fiscal year 1970–1971, and that fertility varies as required. The population becomes stationary at about 270 million in 2034. Given immigration, it would number about 289 million. Persons aged 18–64 years constitute 60 percent of the population, about 3.7 times those aged 65 and over.[14]

Projection Z (Table V.9) is based on the unlikely assumption that the population ceases to grow immediately because the number of births equals the "number of deaths minus the number of immigrants, resulting in no

Table V.9. Projection Z

Year (1)	Total (2)	0–17 years (3)	18–64 years (4)	65 and over (5)	(4) / (2) 18–64 ——— total (6)	(4) / (5) 18–64 ——— 65 and over (7)
1970	204.8	69.7	114.9	20.2	0.56	5.7
1985	204.8	41.0	138.5	25.3	0.68	5.5
2000	204.8	41.4	135.3	28.1	0.66	4.8
2025	204.8	50.8	111.6	42.4	0.54	2.7
2050	204.8	57.2	118.8	43.0	0.58	2.8

change in total population." Assuming either no immigration or immigration of 400,000 per year, total fertility would undergo cyclical waves for several centuries, finally settling at the replacement level of 2.11 births per woman given zero immigration, or, given continuous immigration, below 2 births per woman.[15] The age structure varies markedly under the fertility conditions assumed, together with zero immigration. The following figures (in millions) summarize the extent of this variation, together with that in median age and in the ratio of persons 15–19 to those 55–59—a crude index of the ratio of persons newly entering the labor force to those approaching an age when men are likely to withdraw from the labor force (see also last two lines in Table V.5):

Age	1970	1985	2000	2025	2050
Under 5	17.2	10.8	12.1	15.1	14.8
5–14 years	40.7	20.0	22.8	27.8	32.5
15–24 years	36.5	36.7	20.8	25.5	32.2
25–59 years	81.6	101.7	111.5	77.9	87.5
60–64 years	8.7	10.3	9.4	16.0	9.1
65–69 years	6.8	8.6	8.3	15.1	7.8
70 and over years	13.3	16.7	19.8	27.4	20.9
Total (thousands)	204.8	204.8	204.8	204.8	204.8
(15–19)/(55–59)	1.93	1.59	0.89	0.88	1.63
Median Age (years)	27.9	33.8	40.2	39.9	32.9

At this point we may return to the population described in the last column in Table V.4 based on the assumption that fertility is below the replacement level of 2.1, and that despite continuation of net immigration, population is declining as well as somewhat instable in form. More specifically it is assumed that total fertility declines gradually from 2.0 in 1972 to 1.7 in 2015 and thereafter remains at this level. Net immigration is assumed to remain at 400,000 per year. The population peaks at 252 million around the year 2020 and then declines, falling to 226.7 million by 2050.[16]

The most striking characteristic of this population is the more advanced state of its age structure compared with that of prospective stationary populations—a state due to a gradual decline in the number of births. This difference is indicated in the fact that the population's median age is 42.6 years compared with 37.2 and 37.8 years, the medians reported in columns 5 and 6 in Table V.4. This contrast is evident also in the following figures:

Age	Stationary (col. 5)	Declining (col. 7)
0–17.5	23.68	18.92
0–19	27.05	21.82
20–64	56.95	57.44
65 and over	16.00	20.74

While the relative size of the population of working age—here those aged 20–64—is modified only negligibly, the composition of the total dependent population (here those under 20 and over 64) is different. For the ratio of those 65 and over to the total dependent population is 0.487 in the declining population, compared with 0.372 in a stationary population. The ratio of the population 20–64 to that 65 and over is only 2.77, compared with 3.56 in a stationary population. This ratio becomes significant, of course, only if the cost of supporting older dependents is much higher than that of supporting younger dependents. For if dependents are defined as those over 64 and those under 15 plus one-half of those 15–19, the ratio of those 20–64 to dependents so defined is 1.44 in a stationary population and 1.45 in the declining population. If, however, the dependency cost of an older dependent is one-third higher than that of one under 18, the burden per person 20–64 will be about 4 percent higher in the declining population than in the stationary one.[17]

3. Paths to Stationarity

Given the unlikely assumption that a population will gradually approach a stationary or near-stationary level, some paths are preferable on economic and other grounds to other paths, as Coale, Norman Ryder, and others have shown.[18] For example, of the four projections W, V, Y, and Z, Projection Z is the least likely to be approximated. This is fortunate, for even though the age structures that may come into being can be anticipated through computerization,[19] it would be difficult to adjust an economy to a population evolving over time in keeping with the demographic assumptions underlying Projection Z. When a population moves immediately or gradually to the replacement level, little strain is put upon an economy as it adjusts to the resulting age structure; moreover, serious problems do not arise when fertility sinks temporarily below replacement (cf. Projection V) or the number of births remains unchanged and fertility adjusts thereto and the population approaches a stationary level. Continuous immigration at something like a constant numerical level does not significantly modify the age structure in comparison with what it would be given zero immigration.[20]

Selection of an optimum path to replacement-level fertility and eventually a stationary population, given no immigration, must allow for momentum toward population growth when present in a population (e.g., the momentum produced in the U.S. population by the baby boom of 1945–1964)[21]—a momentum present in the U.S. population in 1970 but not in the populations of Western Europe.[22] Norman Ryder generated 3,125 population forecasts in his search for the "demographic optimum projection for the United States," with each projection differing from the others only on the basis of fertility inputs. Attention was focused on the succession of birth sizes (the source *inter alia* of irregularity in age composition when mortality varies little), on changes in fertility determinants (e.g., frequency of zero parity, mean age at first birth, mean birth interval, probability of a mother's having an additional child), and on comparative demographic "costs" of attaining an ultimate stationary population in a shorter or a longer period of time. Ryder's optimum, 278 million, attained in the 2030s, entailed a slight increase in zero parity and in mean age at first birth and a slight decrease in probability of a mother's having an additional child.[23]

Preconditions to an optimal path to a stationary population are easily defined but virtually impossible to establish, given the many factors in which changes modify crude natality and natural increase. Natality tends to vary in the short run with variation in the number of women, especially married women, aged (say) 19–29 years; it is subject to change in the longer run as a result of change in family-size norms, or in conditions affecting power to conform to these norms, and consequent change in the decisions of women respecting timing and number of children. Decisions may thus change sharply, as when fertility rose markedly after 1945 only to fall within two decades.[24] Moreover, echo effects occur when those born in a period of upsurging births or declining births enter the labor force 19 or more years later and (probably) marry. Among the possible consequences, as noted later, are increase or decrease in the total number of births and increase or decrease in access to employment, with the variability in natality as a probable effect.[25] With variability in natality about a trend line confined to within a sufficiently narrow range, age structure will not, however, be greatly modified.

4. The Population Prospect

The population prospect is conditioned by two sets of factors, (a) the demographic and (b) socioeconomic and legal factors that condition the demographic factors.

The demographic factors are three in number, net immigration, mortality, and fertility. While projections usually rest upon the assumption of a net immigration of 400,000 per year, this figure does not include illegal immigration, estimated to be quite high.[26] The contribution to a country's population growth by net foreign immigration depends upon whether the magnitude of the net inflow is subject to changes in regulation designed to keep the inflow within a narrow range and thereby limit its impact upon population growth as well as upon whether native fertility is affected by immigration.[27]

The effect of net immigration upon domestic fertility turns on whether migrants are complementary to or competitive with the domestic population of reproductive age, a relationship that is affected by the impact of the education of immigrants upon their employability; on whether the cultures of the migrants harmonize or conflict with those of the domestic population, together with whether this relationship is further affected by racial differences (e.g., black–white); and on whether the qualitative composition of the immigrants has an expansive effect upon the economy. During the decades of heavy immigration into the United States which ended soon after World War I, the net effect of the immigrant inflow apparently was not generally unfavorable to domestic fertility despite allegations to such effect; moreover, intermarriage of natives with immigrants made fertility higher than it otherwise would have been.[28]

While net immigration may offset a decline in total fertility below the replacement level, it can do so only if it is adequate. For example, with total fertility at 1.7 compared with a 2.1 replacement level, an annual net inflow of 400,000 immigrants will not long suffice to do so. When, however, fertility remains constant at the replacement level, a net immigration of 400,000 can add appreciably to the total population. Thus by 2020 a projection based upon replacement-level fertility would number about 267 and 294 millions, respectively, with net immigration at zero and 400,000 per year net, respectively. By 2050 the corresponding populations would be about 270 and 318 millions, respectively. The net effect of immigration depends, of course, upon whether the total fertility of the domestic population is independent or affected by the amount of net immigration, and upon the age and sex composition and fertility of the immigrants.[29]

Expectation of life at birth and at higher ages, say 50 or 65, is susceptible of some increase. Thus elimination of major cardiovascular-renal disease would increase life expectancy at age 65 by about 10 years—say from 72 to 82 for whites and 66 to 76 for nonwhites. Such elimination is made difficult, however, by the fact that the "causes" of these diseases are partly biological and hence less amenable to control than are "causes" associated with infections and man's environment.[30] Moreover, it is possible that environmental conditions will become worse in many countries.[31] It is questionable, therefore, whether life expectancy at birth can be raised to 90 years, as some anticipate, with the result that 30 or more percent of the population would be 60 and over.[32] Indeed, in a recent projection of the U.S. population the Bureau of the Census has assumed that "average life expectancy at birth will increase from 67.9 for males and 75.7 for females in 1972 to 68.9 for males and 78.0 for females in 2020." Thereafter no marked change is expected.[33]

It is upon changes in fertility, therefore, that change in the population prospect depends in the main, far more so than in the 1920s, 1930s, and 1940s when population projections proved in error because of mistakes in forecasts of trends both in mortality and in fertility.[34] The average number of births *expected* by wives 18 to 25 years old, reported in June, 1973, was 2.3, amounting to about 2.1 per woman of all marital classes and thus serving to replace the population.[35] With the actual rate in the neighborhood of 1.9—half the 1957 rate of 3.8 children per woman—or, as seems possible, settling around 1.7, the population will assume a near stable form, but decline, with the actual outcome depending upon the amount of immigration.[36]

As has already been indicated, the American population is not likely to approach a stationary state until after the first quarter of the next century. Births will not settle to a comparatively constant level until late in the first half of the next century, given that fertility now is settled at or slightly below the replacement level, for the relative number of women of childbearing age remains relatively large and births are affected accordingly.[37]

Even with total fertility given, the size of the population ultimately attained will be affected by the fertility pattern. For example, with fertility at the replacement level and net immigration at 400,000 per year, should cohort fertility proceed along the "most likely" path, the American population would increase from 212 million in 1974 to 318 million in 2050, with median age at 37 years. If, however, a late time pattern should characterize fertility, the population would attain only 299 million by 2050, but with median age at 37. Should fertility vary with cohort size, the population would increase only to 305 million by 2050, but with median age at 38 years. Given zero immigration and fertility at the replacement level, the population would be stationary at 270 million as of 2050, with the median age at 37.8 years. A median age of 42.6 years would also characterize the 227 million population attained in 2050, given total fertility at 1.7 and net immigration at 400,000 per year.[38] It is significant, however, that when fertility is below replacement and a population is declining, median age rises appreciably, and the fraction 55 and over rises until the age structure is stabilized. For example (see columns 6–7 in Table V.4), about 34 percent of the population in column 7 are 55 and over, compared with about 28 percent in column 6.

Projections may not materialize, indeed are not likely to materialize in detail. Many variables affect "the demand for children," while the supply of births is under quite effective control. Not only are birth expectations instable in the short run; longer-run determinants of fertility are subject to change as well. Boone Turchi finds that "aggregate fertility in the United States is now potentially more volatile than at any previous time in the nation's history," having fallen to 1.86 in 1974 compared with about 3.8 in 1957. This sharp drop, due to a reduction of unplanned fertility evident in the reduction during the 1960s in marital fertility,[39] reflects the degree of control that has been established over fertility and its consequent sensitivity to changing circumstances. Expressed expectations therefore are subject to change, more in some than in other social categories, with the result either that the resulting composition of births differs somewhat from that initially expected, or that the total number of births realized exceeds or falls below expectations.[40]

The circumstances surrounding and affecting families may or may not change significantly. The impact of family experience together with family instability may affect fertility negatively, as may sources of change in family-size norms.[41] Given the impact of intergenerational differences in tastes on current decisions regarding consumption and population changes, a consumption-oriented trend over generations may lower fertility and in turn affect current consumption. Moreover, "increased uncertainty with regard to the continuity of the extended family," being equivalent to increased intergenerational discount rates, tends both to increase the rate of population growth and lower "the rate of capital accumulation over generations." Also among factors that may produce a decline in fertility we may include a decrease in unwanted births—a decrease likely to be positively associated with easier access to abortion—together with improvement in the opportunities available to women and hence in the opportunity cost of children.[42] Also to be included is increase in the relative amount of state support of the aged insofar as it reduces the anticipated importance of children as a source of support in old age.[43] Moreover, completion of the transition to a new fertility level may still be underway.[44]

Differences in prospective rates of growth by such categories as race will bring about changes in population composition. For example, the black fraction of the population, 10.5 percent in 1960 and 11.4 percent in 1974, may approximate 12.6–12.7 percent by the year 2000.[45] Members of different social categories may be differentially sensitive to socioeconomic changes affecting fertility. For example, the relative contribution of those with limited education will tend to rise if the conditions motivating reduction in family-size norms—e.g., the assumption that smallness of family size is conducive to the intellectual growth of children—are less effective among those in this category than among those with a year or more of college, or if government subsidization of children allows parents to invest more in one or two children instead of spreading the subsidy over more children.[46] Finally, when egalitarianism militates against the children of a subset of a population, its members may respond by limiting their numbers, should they not determine upon a reproductive struggle.

5. Population Decline

While population decline constitutes one of the possible demographic outcomes facing modern nations, its long-run impact probably would prove

Table V.10. Estimated Projected Population by Age (millions)

Age Group	1975	1980	2000	2010	2025	2040	2050
Under 5	15.8	15.6	14.3	14.0	12.8	12.2	11.5
5–14	37.7	33.8	32.6	29.0	28.2	25.5	24.8
15–17	12.6	12.0	10.4	9.5	8.9	8.1	7.8
18–64	124.8	135.0	157.2	164.5	152.4	142.0	135.6
65 & over	22.3	24.5	30.6	33.2	48.1	50.1	47.0
Total	213.3	220.3	245.1	250.2	250.4	237.9	226.7
Median Age	28.8	30.3	37.0	39.7	41.8	42.9	42.6
Percent 18–64	0.585	0.613	0.641	0.658	0.609	0.596	0.598
(18–64/(64+)	5.6	5.5	5.1	5.0	3.2	2.8	2.9
(18–64)/rest	1.4	1.6	1.8	1.9	1.6	1.5	1.5

Source: Current Population Reports, Series P-25, No. 601, Tables 9, 12.

sufficiently different from that of a stationary population to justify separate treatment. The level of fertility utilized in projections over the past 12 years has been reduced as actual trends have been reinterpreted.[47] Moreover, fertility has moved below the replacement level in a number of modern countries.[48] The possibility of population decline therefore exists in a number of countries, including the United States.

However, given net immigration of 400,000 per year (and perhaps more if illegal immigration is included), numbers will decline more slowly in the U.S. than if the population were closed. Moreover, given the age composition of the immigrant inflow, population decline, initially incident in the very young age groups, will be slower to develop in age groups into which immigrants flow. Table V.10 serves to illustrate this trend in the U.S. It is based upon the assumption that fertility settles at a 1.7 level after moving below 2.0 (with 2.1 required for replacement) and that net immigration continues at 400,000 per year.

The data in Table V.10 indicate that the population 0–17 continues to decline after 1975, whereas the population 18–64 continues to rise until early in the next century, and that number 65 and over continues to rise for about 65 years.[49] Inasmuch as the age groups under 20 begin to decline soon after 1975, it is to be expected that markets and activities oriented to this age group (e.g., educational service) will begin to shrink in the near future. Such shrinkage is already evident in the drop in the U.S. school and college population, a sequel to a steady decline in the total number of births from a peak of 4.35 million in 1960–1961 to just over 3 million currently. However, markets and activities dominated by persons 20–64 should not begin to reflect population decline until early in the following century, to be followed near midcentury by the activities and markets of persons over 64. Aggregate population will peak in 2015–2020, after having continued to age steadily since 1975. The fraction of the population of working age peaks early in the next century and then declines, as does the ratio of persons of working age (i.e., 18–64 years old) to those over 64. Given the demographic conditions summarized in Table V.10, the descent of fertility below the replacement level will not make itself significantly felt until early in the next century.

While this time interval should facilitate adjustment of the economy to the changing age structure and the adoption of policies suited to restore fertility to the replacement level, an awareness of possible disadvantages consequent upon population decline may develop. Expectations relating to investment involving long lead-time may be adversely affected. There may be spill-over effects associated with decline in activities oriented to school and college enrollment. The tendency of some large urban centers to lose population and revenue-generating power (e.g., for municipal retirement systems supported out of current taxes) may have wider fiscal impact.[50]

Although, as we suggest in later chapters, the advent of a stationary population may present problems, these should prove easily soluble given an economy flexible and free of constraints. Because of its unfavorable impact upon the age structure, however, a declining population will present serious problems, the nature of which we touch upon later.

VI. Age Structure and Economic Well-Being: Labor-Force / Population Ratio

The annual labour of every nation is the fund which originally supplies it with all the necessaries and conveniences of life.
Adam Smith, *Wealth of Nations*

In this chapter we examine the impact of changes in age structure upon the economic well-being of both a population as a whole and the population 60 or more years old. In the following chapter we examine the manner in which changes in a population's age structure may affect the functioning of its economy. Our discussion is confined to advanced countries whose populations are approaching a stationary state or characterized by fertility below the replacement level.[1]

The economic well-being of the population in and over the 60s depends upon two conditions: (a) how large a fraction of this population is of working age, and (b) how large a fraction of the population of working age is employed and contributing to the support of unemployed and retired older persons through the medium of pension and social security systems. Conditions (a) and (b) depend in turn upon the degree to which an economy functions effectively and makes a high rate of employment possible, a condition we examine in the latter part of Section 3.

1. Current and Prospective State of Older Population

The relative number of older persons is increasing appreciably.[2] According to a recent Census report the population 65 years and over, 12.4 million in 1950 and 20.1 million in 1970, will approximate 51.6 million by 2030. The number 60 and over, 28.8 million in 1970, will approximate 67 million in 2030. Those 75 and over, 7.6 million in 1970, will approximate 20.7 million by 2030, it is predicted. The percent of the population 65 and over, having risen from 5.4 to 8.1 between 1930 and 1950, and to 9.8 by 1970, is expected to fall within the range 17–21 percent of the population by 2030, appreciably above the highest current European rate, about 14 percent.[3] Of course, since projections of the population under 65 are subject to uncertainty, we cannot at this time foresee with accuracy the fraction that persons 65 and over will comprise of the population in 2030, even though the absolute number 65 and over as of 2030 is approximatable.

Meanwhile, the percent of the male population 65 and over in the labor force, having fallen from 45.8 in 1950 to 26.8 in 1970, is expected to fall to 16.8 by 1990. The corresponding percentage for females, 9.7 in 1950 and 1970, is expected to fall to 7.6 by 1990. This decline can affect adversely the relative income of many persons 65 and over.[4] Between 1900 and 1950 man's work life expectancy rose, but less rapidly than the number of years he spent in retirement and in dependence upon the work of others. Moreover, this trend is continuing. Meanwhile, the work life expectancy of women has been rising. Even so, imbalance between the number of active members of the labor force and the number of retired inactive persons is increasing.[5]

Premature retirement of a man as of a machine amounts to a discarding of *economically useful* human capital and in effect imposes the cost of its support on other human capital. For since individuals, particularly those engaged in both commercial and noncommercial activity, embody human capital which within limits is subject to both accumulation and decumulation, changes in this capital bear upon the whole population's well-being, and need to be taken into account. For example, input of time includes not only time devoted to economic activity as such but also time devoted

Working Age	Total	Working Age (W)	Non–Working Age (N)	W/N
18–64	100	60	40	1.5
18–54	100	50	50	1.0

to the replacement and / or addition to human capital (e.g., retraining, refresher education, improvement in skill).[6] Moreover, human capital may be cumulative in its impact as when "workers with more formal education" (e.g., whites compared with blacks) "gain more specific training" and hence experience less unemployment.[7]

The advent of a stationary population is favorable to the maintenance of a high ratio of the labor force to the population, provided that the age of retirement centers around 65 or above. For illustrative purposes we may utilize the male stationary population figures presented in Table V.2. With working age defined as 18–64 years, about 60 percent of the male stationary population will be of working age, and there will be 1.5 males of working age per male not of working age. If working age is defined as 18–54, the fraction so defined will approximate 50 percent and the ratio of males of working age to males not of working age will be 1 to 1. Diminution of the working-age fraction from 0.6 to 0.5 thus reduces by one-third the ratio of working males to nonworking males. Corresponding ratios for total populations are roughly similar (e.g., see Tables V.5–V.7).

The figures just presented serve to illustrate the gross impact of the

transfer of a considerable fraction of the population of working age—
initially by assumption those 18 to 64 years old—from the labor force to
an inactive role. The gross impact, expressed in terms of reduction of
commercial output, is offset in some measure by the value of the noncommercial output produced by persons who have withdrawn from the
labor force (but not from all utility-creating activity) plus the value as-
signable to the leisure made possible by withdrawal from the labor force.[8]

Decrease in the age of retirement thus increases the ratio of persons of
dependent age to the working population and augments the overhead
cost of pensions and social security systems incident upon the latter. This
may be put in general terms. Let us suppose that everyone in the labor
force L is employed, and that those in retirement R are essentially supported on a pay-as-you-go basis as under Social Security. Let y denote
the average pretax income of members of L; i, the average income provided by members of L to members of R and supplied by a tax t on y
when all L are employed. Then:

$$i = yt \, (L \, / \, R)$$

Should not all but only 95 percent of L be employed the value of i is
reduced 5 percent.

In what follows, emphasis is put mainly upon per capita capacity to
produce commercial output in response to changes in age structure and
in the fraction employed of those of working age. The value assigna-
ble to leisure and to noncommercial output is thus overlooked, even
though it varies inversely with the fraction of total inputs devoted to
commercial output.[9] In this and the following chapter, however, "economic welfare" is implicitly defined in terms of per capita output, a definition in keeping with an economy that produces both commercial output
and demand for this output.

2. Labor-Force / Population Ratio Trend

While this ratio is conditioned by changes in a population's age composition, trends in it are dominated by changes in civilian labor-force
participation ratios, by age and sex categories, together with the circumstances underlying these changes. Since 1890 this ratio has been trending
upward very slightly, with the percent of the population over 13 years
old in the total labor force (i.e., including armed forces) rising from
52.2 in 1890 to 53.5 in 1950, and with the percent of those over 15 in
the labor force moving from 59.9 in 1950 to 61.3 in 1970. This long-run
trend reflects the fact that female labor-force participation has increased
enough since 1890 to more than offset decline in male participation.[10] This
trend reflects a continuously high elasticity of demand for income in

terms of effort, together with many changes, among them the commercialization of output; changes in age structure, hours of work per week, and years spent in educational institutions; increasing entry of women into the labor force; and increase in the number and attractiveness of alternatives to commercial activity, as well as changes in socioeconomic conditions underlying both increase in these alternatives and countervailing improvements in the nature and attractiveness of available employments.

(a) Since the concept of labor force is commercially oriented, transfer of activities from the noncommercial sector of society to the commercial sector whose members are included within the labor force, increases its size. Hence commercialization of activities, much of it reflecting increased specialization, results *ceteris paribus* in increase in the ratio of the labor force to the total population.[11] Over the past 150 years many activities have been transferred from one situs in the economic matrix to another (e.g., today for each worker in food production on the farm there are two support workers off the farm),[12] particularly from the noncommercial to the commercial sector as the farm population has declined and urbanization has progressed.[13] Even so, in 1965 nonmarket activities may have accounted for output amounting in estimated value to 40 or more percent of the estimated value of Gross National Product.[14] Moreover, while it is quite possible that in the future some currently market activities may be transferred to the nonmarket sector, it is also possible that currently nonmarket activities may be commercialized.

(b) While change in the fraction of the population 15–64—from about 40 percent in 1890 when adult immigration was heavy to 38 percent in 1970—exercises some effect on labor-force participation, increase in years spent in school and reduction in hours worked per week and per year have had the most effect upon hours of labor per capita, which declined about 15 percent between 1890 and 1970, according to Gitlow.[15] Although about 5 percent of the labor force hold two or more jobs,[16] overtime adds more hours to the annual total of hours.[17] Weekly hours per worker declined from about 53 in the 1870s to about 40 in the 1970s,[18] with about 98 percent of those employed working five or more days per week.[19] Inasmuch as only 6.7 percent of the nonfarm labor force in 1973 was self-employed compared with 51.4 percent of the farm labor force,[20] further reduction in the number of self-employed will not significantly affect the propensity to retire early.

The recently current male work pattern is represented in Table VI.1, a working life table for males based on data for 1968,[21] at which time civilian male labor force participation was slightly higher than in 1972–1974. Labor-force participation peaks in the age group 30–39, declines steadily, slowly within the age group 40–59, then appreciably and finally rapidly after the age of 64. Even so, 42 percent of those aged 65–69 were

Table VI.1. Working Life for Males, 1968

Year of age	Number living of 100,000 born alive — In population L_x	In labor force — Percent of population w_x	In labor force — Number Lw_x	Accessions to the labor force (per 1,000 in population) 1,000 A_x (In year of age)	Separations from the labor force (per 1,000 in labor force) — Due to all causes 1,000 S_x	Separations — Due to death 1,000 S_x	Separations — Due to retirement 1,000 S_x	Average remaining years — Life $\overset{\circ}{e}_x$	Average remaining years — Labor force participation $\overset{\circ}{ew}_x$ (At beginning of year of age)
16 to 19	385,064.9	58.10	223,723.4	489.7	1.7	1.7	0	52.9	45.3
16	96,499.9	40.69	39,267.5	125.9	1.4	1.4	0	52.9	45.3
17	96,356.1	53.30	51,359.6	112.5	1.6	1.6	0	52.0	44.4
18	96,193.3	64.57	62,113.2	93.4	1.8	1.8	0	51.0	43.4
19	96,015.6	73.93	70,983.0	52.6	1.9	1.9	0	50.1	42.5
20 to 24	477,078.0	86.34	411,933.0	78.6	2.2	2.2	0	49.2	41.5
20	95,831.8	79.20	75,898.6	33.8	2.0	2.0	0	49.2	41.5
21	95,629.6	82.59	78,979.8	41.6	2.2	2.2	0	48.3	40.6
22	95,418.0	86.77	82,789.6	40.8	2.2	2.2	0	47.4	39.7
23	95,203.9	90.86	86,500.4	15.3	2.2	2.2	0	46.5	38.8
24	94,994.6	92.39	87,764.5	16.0	2.2	2.2	0	45.6	37.9
25 to 29	472,092.0	95.01	448,558.1	7.0	2.0	2.0	0	44.7	37.0
25	94,795.0	93.98	89,090.8	5.7	2.1	2.1	0	44.7	37.0
26	94,602.6	94.55	89,450.0	5.2	2.0	2.0	0	43.8	36.0
27	94,416.5	95.07	89,766.1	4.6	1.9	1.9	0	42.9	35.1
28	94,232.3	95.54	90,027.7	4.0	2.0	2.0	0	42.0	34.2
29	94,045.6	95.94	90,223.5	3.2	2.0	2.0	0	41.1	33.2
30 to 34	467,176.0	96.53	450,982.4	0	2.5	2.3	.2	40.2	32.3
30	93,850.8	96.26	90,340.5	.3	2.1	2.1	0	40.2	32.3
31	93,651.8	96.49	90,367.4	1.3	2.2	2.2	0	39.2	31.4
32	93,445.6	96.63	90,296.9	.3	2.3	2.3	0	38.3	30.4
33	93,228.8	96.67	90,123.1	0	2.7	2.4	.3	37.4	29.5
34	92,999.0	96.62	89,854.6	0	3.4	2.5	.9	36.5	28.6
35 to 39	460,955.0	96.25	443,652.7	0	4.4	3.2	1.2	35.6	27.7
35	92,757.6	96.50	89,510.2	0	4.1	2.7	1.4	35.6	27.7
36	92,495.3	96.35	89,121.3	0	4.4	2.9	1.5	34.7	26.8
37	92,213.0	96.22	88,723.6	0	4.4	3.2	1.2	33.8	25.9
38	91,908.7	96.12	88,341.6	0	4.3	3.4	.9	32.9	25.0
39	91,580.4	96.04	87,956.1	0	4.7	3.7	1.0	32.0	24.1
40 to 44	451,925.0	95.63	432,184.9	0	6.5	4.9	1.6	31.1	23.2
40	91,226.6	95.93	87,518.0	0	5.4	4.1	1.3	31.1	23.2
41	90,840.9	95.79	87,012.5	0	6.0	4.4	1.6	30.3	22.4
42	90,421.6	95.63	86,472.0	0	6.4	4.8	1.6	29.4	21.5
43	89,965.8	95.48	85,899.9	0	6.9	5.3	1.6	28.5	20.6
44	89,470.1	95.32	85,282.6	0	7.6	5.8	1.8	27.7	19.8

Age									
45 to 49	438,249.0	94.58	414,507.8	0	10.9	7.7	3.1	26.8	18.9
45	88,933.5	95.13	84,599.6	0	8.6	6.3	2.2	26.8	18.9
46	88,346.9	94.39	83,835.7	0	9.6	6.9	2.7	26.0	18.1
47	87,707.8	94.62	82,990.0	0	10.7	7.6	3.1	25.2	17.2
48	87,010.7	94.31	82,056.0	0	12.0	8.4	3.6	24.4	16.4
49	86,250.0	93.94	81,026.6	0	13.6	9.2	4.4	23.6	15.6
50 to 54	417,188.0	92.49	385,862.1	0	18.4	12.4	6.0	22.8	14.8
50	85,399.0	93.50	79,846.2	0	15.5	10.1	5.4	22.8	14.8
51	84,498.5	92.96	78,547.3	0	16.8	11.1	5.6	22.0	14.1
52	83,521.4	92.45	77,211.8	0	17.4	12.2	5.2	21.2	13.3
53	82,457.3	92.00	75,861.1	0	18.6	13.5	5.1	20.5	12.5
54	81,311.8	91.49	74,395.8	0	24.1	14.6	9.5	19.8	11.7
55 to 59	386,109.0	88.32	341,008.8	0	33.7	19.7	14.0	19.0	11.0
55	80,074.2	90.26	72,272.5	0	25.4	16.1	9.3	19.0	11.0
56	78,747.1	89.82	70,730.9	0	26.4	17.5	8.9	18.3	10.3
57	77,324.0	88.64	68,540.5	0	32.4	19.2	13.2	17.7	9.5
58	75,798.3	87.46	66,296.1	0	40.5	21.0	19.6	17.0	8.8
59	74,165.5	85.17	63,168.8	0	46.0	23.1	23.0	16.3	8.2
60 to 64	342,649.0	75.79	259,677.5	0	94.1	32.5	61.6	15.7	7.5
60	72,445.0	83.49	60,483.3	0	49.6	25.1	24.5	15.7	7.5
61	70,590.1	80.98	57,166.3	0	81.3	27.5	53.8	15.1	6.9
62	68,628.3	74.59	51,189.3	0	89.2	30.6	58.6	14.5	6.4
63	66,568.0	72.16	48,032.8	0	87.3	32.2	55.1	13.9	6.0
64	64,417.7	66.45	42,805.9	0	187.5	35.5	152.0	13.3	5.5
65 to 69	286,774.0	41.93	120,258.4	0	176.3	60.0	116.3	12.8	5.5
65	62,135.7	51.47	31,980.7	0	244.1	41.9	202.2	12.8	5.5
66	59,831.9	45.45	27,193.2	0	155.4	41.8	113.6	12.2	5.9
67	57,448.9	40.96	23,531.4	0	156.5	44.6	111.9	11.7	5.8
68	54,971.3	36.07	19,826.4	0	146.4	49.2	97.2	11.2	5.7
69	52,386.2	33.84	17,726.7	0	145.5	52.1	93.4	10.7	5.5
70 to 74	220,314.0	23.62	52,047.7	0	179.8	86.6	93.2	10.2	5.3
70	49,764.8	29.47	14,666.4	0	205.4	59.5	145.8	10.2	5.3
71	46,960.0	24.92	11,703.0	0	212.8	66.3	146.5	9.8	5.4
72	44,084.3	21.97	9,686.4	0	156.7	70.2	86.4	9.4	5.6
73	41,187.0	21.05	8,667.3	0	136.3	71.8	64.5	9.0	5.6
74	38,318.0	19.11	7,324.1	0	158.2	78.1	80.1	8.6	5.1
75 to 79	151,497.0	15.42	23,363.0	0	169.3	104.1	65.3	8.2	4.9
75	35,635.9	17.82	6,351.0	0	150.3	80.8	69.5	8.2	4.9
76	32,894.6	16.46	5,415.1	0	163.0	85.7	77.3	7.8	4.7
77	30,229.0	15.17	4,585.6	0	172.3	90.9	81.4	7.4	4.4
78	27,633.8	13.88	3,834.9	0	183.7	97.3	86.5	7.1	4.2
79	25,103.7	12.65	3,176.3	0	196.6	104.6	92.0	6.7	3.9
80 to 84	90,429.0	9.42	8,516.1	0	240.4	155.5	84.9	6.3	3.6
80	22,623.3	11.43	2,585.8	0	212.3	113.3	99.0	6.3	3.6
81	20,240.2	10.27	2,078.5	0	228.4	122.5	105.9	6.0	3.4
82	17,955.6	9.11	1,636.1	0	251.0	132.4	118.5	5.7	3.1
83	15,799.4	7.96	1,257.3	0	269.6	142.0	127.6	5.3	2.9
84	13,810.5	6.94	958.2	0	285.8	148.0	137.8	5.0	2.6
85 and over	59,956.0	3.26	1,956.9	—	—	—	—	4.7	2.3

Source: See note 21.

in the labor force, as were 23.62 and 15.42 percent, respectively, of those 70–74 and 75–79. Withdrawal due to retirement has already begun in the middle thirties but does not increase markedly until in and after the late fifties. Comparison of this table with that for 1950 indicates that the man-years of work provided by a stationary male population based on 100,000 births per year had declined only from 4.19 to 4.11 millions, presumably because increase in survivorship among younger men in working ages had offset the trend toward later entry and earlier withdrawal from the labor force.[22]

While continuation of decline in hours worked per year is to be expected, a further reduction to four days a week from the five days and over worked by 98 percent of those employed in May, 1974, is not likely in the near future. For it might entail an objectionable ten-hour day and organizational adjustments not easily made.[23] Thus major emphasis in the near future is likely to be put not *so much on* shortening hours as such as on the "reshuffling of time free of work in order to produce larger blocks of leisure" and thus increase its utility.[24]

Decline in civilian male labor force participation has been selective. It has been continuous among white males 65 years and over since 1948–1949, amounting to 51 percent between 1948–1949 and 1973–1974, compared with a decline of only 11 percent among those 55–64 between 1958–1959 and 1974. Decline among those 35–54 has been slight. Among white females, on the contrary, labor force participation increased in all age groups except among those 65 and over. Turning to nonwhite males, we find marked declines in all age groups, especially among those 16–19 and over 44. In contrast, among nonwhite females labor-force participation has fallen only among those 16–17 and those 65 and over, meanwhile rising in other age groups.[25] Outside the labor force at any time are those who want a job but are not looking for one for various reasons (e.g., ill health, unemployment insurance, belief jobs are not available).[26]

The ratio of the labor force to the population has kept pace roughly with the relative number of those supposedly of dependent age, that is, under 15 and over 64. This ratio approximated 0.42 in 1970 compared with 0.40 between 1930 and 1960. The fraction aged over 65 rose from .041 in 1900 and .046 in 1920 to .081 in 1950 and .099 in 1970. Meanwhile, the fraction under 15 fell from 0.343 in 1900 to 0.269 in 1950, and then rose to 0.283 in 1970. The two fractions combined approximated 0.384 in 1900, then fell gradually to 0.35 in 1950, and thereafter rose to 0.382. In a stationary population about 36 percent of a population will fall within the two categories 0–14 and 65 and over.

Aggregate labor-force participation increased slightly between 1890 and 1950 and again between 1948–1950 and 1972–1974. This increase was due to enough increase in white female labor-force participation to

Table VI.2. Labor Force Participation Rates, 14 Years and Older, by Color and Sex: 1890 to 1950

Year	All			White			Nonwhite		
	Total	Male	Female	Total	Male	Female	Total	Male	Female
1890	52.2	84.3	18.2	51.0	84.0	15.8	63.4	86.7	37.7
1950	54.0	79.4	29.3	53.7	79.7	28.4	56.3	76.8	37.1

Source: Gertrude Bancroft, *The American Labor Force* (New York: Wiley, 1958), pp. 207–8.

offset decline in both white male labor-force participation and total non-white labor-force participation. See Tables VI.2 and VI.3.[27]

Should labor force participation on the part of males continue to decline and not be offset by increased participation on the part of women, the ratio of those in the labor force to the total population will fall below 0.4. Meanwhile, the fraction of the population over 65 will rise much above the current level—indeed close to 0.21 should total fertility settle at 1.7, even with net immigration continuing at 400,000 per year. Inasmuch as male labor-force participation has fallen most among those 55–64 and over 64, increase in the fraction over 54 will reduce male labor-force participation moderately, since in a stationary population about 20 percent of those aged 20–64 are 55–64, compared with about 17 percent when a population is stable and growing about 1.0 percent per year. Fullerton infers that retirement rates at higher ages will be higher than those currently in effect, and that labor-force accession patterns will change as educational patterns change.[28]

(c) The fraction of the female population of working age actually enrolled in the labor force has increased with the commercialization of economic activities.[29] How labor-force participation and fertility interact

Table VI.3. Labor Force Participation Rates, by Sex and Race: 1948 to1974

Year	Civilian and Military			Civilian Labor Force, 16 years and over				
				White		Nonwhite		
	Total	Male	Female	Male	Female	Male	Female	
1948–50	59.6	86.9	33.3	86.4	31.9	86.7	46.5	
1957–58	60.5	85.3	37.0	84.6	35.8	84.2	47.6	
1972–74	61.4	79.5	44.8	79.5	44.2	73.6	49.0	

Source: U.S. Dept. of Labor, Manpower Administration, *Manpower Report of the President*, Washington, April, 1975, pp. 203–9.

depends, however, upon what intervening variables are present.[30] More-over, the pattern of labor force participation by women differs from that of males, being affected by marriage and number of children.[31]

Maintenance of as well as increase in the ratio of the labor force to the population depends on further increase in female labor-force partici-pation. Indeed, given female labor-force participation in 1972 on the part of 66 instead of 44 percent of the female population 16 and over, 16,500,-000 females would have been added to the labor force, increasing it about 18 percent from about 89 million to around 105 million. Under present con-ditions increase in the ratio of the labor force to the population turns mainly if not entirely on increasing female enrollment and preventing continuation of decline in male labor-force participation, which fell from about 87 percent in 1947–1953 to about 79.5 percent in 1972–1974. Be-tween 1973 and 1990, it has been estimated, total labor-force participa-tion will rise only from 44.7 percent to 46.5 percent, with the increase expected to be due to increased participation on the part of women aged 24–64.[32]

While male labor-force projections do not indicate an increase in par-ticipation,[33] female participation has already proved higher than antici-pated.[34] Although facilitation of entry into the labor force on the part of single as well as married women will augment the labor force, it is entry on the part of married women that most needs facilitation[35] and that can contribute most to the labor force, since about 6 million single women and 27 million married women were not in the labor force in 1974.[36] Entry of additional women into the labor force may, however, displace or stimu-late the withdrawal of some males, particularly if women are better edu-cated, work for lower wages, or are favored by removal of discrimination.[37]

D. F. Johnston, projecting fertility at the replacement level, estimated that between 1960 and 2040 labor-force participation would decline moderately among males under 25 and over 54, but remain virtually un-changed among those 25–54. Female labor-force participation would rise in all age groups except among those over 64. Total labor-force partici-pation would change negligibly, with male participation declining only enough to offset increase in female participation.[38]

Presumably rising income and growing job satisfaction (or dissatisfac-tion) will have little effect upon aggregate participation, or participation among those 55–64, since decline in male participation will be offset by increase in female participation. Should the pattern of participation con-tinue as described, the ratio of members of the labor force to those retired will not be a cause for concern with respect to the adequacy of retirement income. However, should fertility continue to decline, the *relative* number of older persons would increase, probably sufficiently to increase the ratio of retired persons to members of the labor force.

3. Constraints; Incentives

The behavior of older persons is subject not only to the incidence of incentives and costs, together with institutional and related constraints, that affect their employment, but also to adverse aspects of aging, a continuous process that increasingly conditions behavior in later years.[39] This process influences an individual's capacities, time horizon, "animal spirits," and so on, and thus eventually constitutes both a constraining element and an important force in an individual's life cycle. In this section we shall examine both barriers and incentives to participation in the labor force on the part of younger as well as older workers, since the economic welfare of older persons depends either upon their access to employment or upon the capacity of *employed* persons to support the pension and social security systems whereon the support of older retirees depends.

We may group under three heads the sources of unemployment or withdrawal from employment, each of which may or does affect the well-being of older persons directly or indirectly: (i) worker disability; (ii) circumstances that make not working more attractive than working; and (iii) institutional constraints upon employment, especially of younger workers.

While an individual's approach to labor-force participation involves decision on his part, such decision tends to reflect his life cycle and that of his cohort (and perhaps those of neighboring cohorts)—the sequence of experiences and decisions he has undergone, as well as decisions made in response to change in opportunities, constraints, the cumulation and decumulation of personal capital, the impact of aging on potential mobility and capacity to work, the accumulation of wealth, and so on. The individual's life-cycle experience may thus condition how he perceives and responds to emerging events (e.g., *unexpected* changes in earning power and changes in the composition of demand that accelerate the depreciation of his personal capital), to the disappearance of job opportunities, to uncertainties respecting personal health and work capacity, and to other changes conditioning employment opportunities. Also relevant, as Weiss points out, are "institutional and social constraints such as forced retirement, standard working day, standard working week and to some extent forced participation at early ages."[40]

(i) Disability (and hence employability) is a function of two variables, (a) the demands of a job and the physical conditions surrounding it and (b) the state of a worker's health, each of which is subject to modification within limits.

A representative occupation makes mental and physical demands upon the individual filling it. These demands, designatable as D, normally do not exceed the capacity C of the person filling it. We may, therefore, define the minimum job requirement ratio as $C/D = 1$ and suppose that in much of an individual's career his $C > D$. In later years, however, C declines, and the ratio falls to and below 1.0. It may be possible, however, to elevate the ratio above 1.0 through appropriate medical treatment and rehabilitation[41] and refresher education that increase C, or by restructuring the job and reducing the value of D. When this is not possible, a reduction in rate of pay in keeping with a worker's reduced performance may enable a person to remain in the labor force. Moreover, given heavier physical demands made on workers by longer workdays under arrangements such as the four-day workweek, it may be possible to divide a week between two older workers and thus allow each a half-week of work. Even given better adaptation of jobs to the capacity of workers, however, C may fall too short of D to permit the *economical* employment of a given worker of normal working age; his or her withdrawal from the labor force, or at least from the occupation in question, may then be indicated. Inasmuch as depreciation of human capital and hence decline in C are eventually correlated with age, labor-force participation eventually declines with age, especially after the fifties. However, given job redesign, along with appropriate worker retraining and replacement of his human-capital loss, withdrawal may normally be averted until he reaches the age of 65.[42] It is essential, of course, that job requirements not be made higher than necessary in order to exclude disadvantaged workers.[43]

(ii) While man's capacity for work may decline with age as his human capital depreciates and he becomes more vulnerable to illness and poor health, especially if he is in a very low income group, poor health (Boskin finds) is not a major cause of retirements, many of which are due to the social security system and excessive taxation of earnings.[44] Aging and illness may therefore impose an increasing burden upon those in the labor force and become responsible for withdrawal from gainful employment.[45] The contribution of poor health to withdrawal from the labor force tends to be exaggerated, however. In 1973 limitations upon activity afflicted about 8.5 percent of those 17–44 years old and 23.3 percent of those 45–64. Days lost from work per employed person were slightly lower among those over 44 than among those 17–44, and accidents per person at work per year were lower among those over 44 than among those 17–44, as was incidence of disability in 1965–1973.[46] Moreover, as Eli Ginzberg remarks, "lack of competence, not poor health, is the cross of the older worker," a lack often associated with inadequate education.[47]

Man's age may be said to assume two forms, chronological age K and biological age B. At time a these two ages become K_a and B_a. Within limits biological aging may proceed more or less rapidly than chronological age or at the same rate. If the two processes proceed at the same rate, $B_a = K_a$; if biological aging is faster, $B_a > K_a$, and if slower, $B_a < K_a$. Capacity to perform is relatively high, therefore, when $K_a > B_a$, and relatively low when $K_a < B_a$. One object of policy then becomes the slowing of biological aging; the other is the accomplishment of a parallel purpose, namely, diminishing the demand made upon man as a biological organism.

Since working and nonworking entail alternate uses of time, there is a trade-off that varies with type of individual and household unit, with changes in options available, and with changes in individual circumstances (e.g., reduction through inflation in value of assets or "permanent income").[48] Trade-off between working and alternatives thereto is more sensitive to changing circumstances among persons in and- beyond the fifties than among younger persons who are under economic pressure to remain in the labor force and who have a greater stock of probable years at their disposal. Preference equilibrium may be described as balance at the margin between perceived and *weighed* advantages of increase in nonwork (or leisure) time and work together with its emoluments. Inasmuch as expressed preference is *ex ante* and often not subject to reversal should it not be confirmed *ex post facto,* one can only infer the persisting strength of this preference from the behavior of those who voluntarily withdraw from the labor force and remain so even when free to return under the *ex ante* conditions.

Degree of preference, if any, of nonwork over work under available income conditions is affected by many factors, among them: family conditions; retirement vs. nonretirement income; conditions surrounding types of work and engaging in it; state of the worker's health and job-filling capacity; level of prospective retirement income in relation to the time, physical, and money costs of "consuming" leisure in retirement; domestic and communal environment; positive nonpecuniary attractions of work— attractions that contribute greatly to the nonwithdrawal of older members of professions from their continued pursuit; and so on.[49] Relevant also are pressures upon the older worker to retire, pressures originating with employers or trade unions, as well as those associated with mobility and other costs of job-changing or with cumulative discouragement at inability to find employment that tends to cause withdrawal from the labor force.[50] Institutional and other conditions that conduce to limitation of employment in various sectors of the economy also generate pressure upon older workers to retire early if they believe themselves in possession of adequate assets. Erosion of assets and living standards by inflation tends, of course, to increase the demand for money income in terms of effort and accentuate the disposition to remain in the labor force.[51]

(iii) Whatever be the contribution of deficiency of aggregate demand to the availability of employment opportunities for older workers, they are likely to be favored by whatever increases the substitutability of one kind of labor for another or for other productive agents, since as a result older as well as younger workers can enter the labor force through a continuous substitution process at the level of consumption and/or at the level of production. Even when such substitution is possible, however, and one kind of labor is directly or indirectly substitutive for another, this kind of labor can become a limitative factor if its technical substitution for another is restricted by one or both of two sources of extra-market interference, government legislation and union-initiated work rules. "With the case of government created institutional limitational factors, statutory law prevents substitution, while in the case of union created institutional limitational work, a work rule agreement between management and labor drawn from collective bargaining prevents the substitution."[52] While it is possible for easy substitution to affect older workers adversely in particular circumstances (e.g., through removal of job-security when an older worker's remuneration is relatively high, his capacity is on the margin of declining, and "early retirement" is available), continuous substitutability attainable through substitution at the producer and/or the consumer level makes possible the continuous expansion of employment.

But such expansion is subject to limits imposed by deficiency of information, by geographical or similar physical impediments or barriers, and (temporarily) by a shortage of complements to labor including a shortage of labor complementary to other types of labor.

As noted earlier the welfare of older persons may be affected adversely by institutional constraints (e.g., uneconomically high minimum wages) which depress employment among others (e.g., among teenagers),[53] especially among persons under 25 years of age.[54] Not only are the unemployed young workers unable to contribute to pension and security funds as well as generate demand for the products of older workers, their inability to find work may discourage search for jobs by other unemployed.[55] Moreover, the presence of unemployment in an economy may limit types of demand and hence the jobs available for older workers and thereby contribute to their unemployment, particularly if the economy is inflexible and dominated by union power.[56] Furthermore, unemployment can subject older workers to pressure to withdraw from the labor force, and it may eventuate in asset-eroding inflationary monetary and fiscal policies.[57]

The findings of Feldstein and others suggest that, given a flexible economy, there would be less unemployment in general and among older workers, and hence a greater flow of funds into pensions and social security systems. Feldstein traces much unemployment to "failure in the development and use of our nation's manpower." "Macroeconomic policy is unlikely to lower the permanent rate of unemployment much below the 4.5 percent that has prevailed during the post-war period. Nevertheless, a series of specific proposals could reduce the unemployment rate for

those seeking permanent full-time employment to a level significantly below three percent and perhaps closer to two percent."[58]

Feldstein's conclusion is borne out by Canadian experience. There also
"either changes in the level of benefits relative to wages or in the nature
and enforcement of eligibility rules" can affect "reported unemployment
rates by altering workers' work/leisure tradeoff and job-search behavior."
Study of the period 1953–1972 suggests "that changes in the unemployment insurance scheme have substantially increased the unemployment
rate in recent years."[59]

Feldstein calls attention in particular to the absence of hard-core unemployment and to the presence of high unemployment among youth as a
result of "slow absorption of new entrants," "low job attachment among
those at work," the tendency of young men and women to quit jobs,
especially those seasonal in character, and "the hard economic reality that
firms cannot afford" to offer useful "on-the-job training to a broad class
of young employees" under current minimum wage laws. Turning to
older workers, Feldman points to cyclical and seasonal variation in the
demand for labor encouraged by our system of employment insurance, to
weak labor-force attachment, to difficulties faced by "persons with very
low skills or other employment disabilities," to "the average of several
months of unemployment among job losers," and to "voluntary non-
employment" fostered by today's welfare rules, "a notorious deterrent to
work for those who are receiving welfare."[60] To unemployment of the sort
described may be added "transitional unemployment among men" whose
wives are working and supporting the family.[61] Institutional explanations
have been put forward by James Coleman and others, who believe that
clustering "youth" (i.e., persons 4–24) so long in bureaucratic institutions
called schools unfits them for responsible adult life,[62] particularly when
they may rely upon others for financial support. Indeed, the labor force
could be increased about 2 percent if years in educational institutions at
every level were decreased by about 25 percent. Public employment programs contribute little in this connection. Alan Fechter concludes "that
in the long run 60 to 90 percent of public employment program funds
would merely displace state and local funds. The short-run displacement
effect ranges from 40 to 50 percent. Apparently public employment programs add considerably fewer jobs than the nominal number of slots they
fund."[63]

The burden of much of what has been said is that whatever weakens the
incentive of persons without employment to search for jobs and accept
them increases unemployment under a given set of conditions. Since unemployment is preferred when unemployment pays, welfare and related
legislation which put a premium upon remaining unemployed produce un-

employment. In a parallel fashion, retirement systems can be so financed as to put a premium on nonsaving and thus discourage capital formation that could be conducive to employment. For example, according to Feldstein, the prospect of receiving Social Security payments depresses personal saving by 30–50 percent and stimulates earlier retirement, since receipt of a pension requires the pensioner to retire from his current job and give up union security.[64] Presumably such measures as Medicare and Medicaid have a similar effect. As yet, however, the Feldstein-Munnell thesis requires further supporting analysis before it may be considered confirmed.[65]

4. Implications for Intergenerational Equity

In this section we deal with the implications of changes in age structure for the preservation of equity or justice between generations or sets of cohorts. We assume with Rawls that "persons in different generations have duties and obligations to one another just as contemporaries do."[66] Maintenance of these duties and obligations is easier when the obligation is reenforced by sentiment as within a nuclear or extended family. Under modern conditions, however, reliance must be put largely upon institutional arrangements,[67] the effectiveness of which is conditioned by a society's age structure and the degree to which uncompensated inflation flourishes.[68] "Intergenerational transfers of income are, in fact, nothing more than an instance of debt finance shifting costs to future generations" writes Browning.[69]

Intergenerational transfers under old-age support systems (e.g., funded or partially funded old-age pensions or benefits under systems such as the American Social Security system) rest essentially upon a pay-as-you-go basis. For retirees are provided with current and continuous claims upon goods and services, that is, with claims upon the current joint product of the labor force and the physical assets at its command—a product that necessarily shrinks with shrinkage in the labor force insofar as assets are not susbstitutable for labor or human capital. The capacity of any retiree-support system to maintain retirees at given levels of support, whether national or subnational or municipal in its basis of support, thus depends on the adequacy of the ratio of the manpower actually supporting the system to the beneficiaries of that system. Should a support system contract in relation to those dependent upon it as a result of change in age structure or decline in a city's population and labor force, current claims on the system could no longer be met as expected if at all.[70]

So long as a labor force grows faster than the number of retired and other persons dependent for support upon this labor force, the potential condition of the latter improves. Thus, as Samuelson put it in 1958: "In a growing population men of twenty outnumber men of forty; and retired men are outnumbered by workers more than in the ratio of the work span to the retirement span. With more workers to support them, the aged live better than in the stationary state—the excess being positive interest on their savings."[71] With both a labor force and its average income growing 1 percent per year, the stream of income available for support of older dependents grows 2 percent per year.[72] Or as Aaron writes:

> . . . if the sum of the rates of growth of per capita wages and of population exceeds the rate of interest, and if the rate of interest equals the marginal rate of time preference and the marginal rate of transformation of present into future goods, then the introduction of some social insurance pensions on a pay as you go basis will improve the welfare position of each person. If saving and, hence, investment and, hence, the rate of growth of income are reduced as the level of social insurance increases, this conclusion does not necessarily follow. If the rate of growth is unaffected, the effective rate of return on premiums paid for such social insurance will exceed the marginal rate of time preference, and consequently, people in the active labour force would willingly forego some current consumption in order to obtain such returns. Individually they are unable to do so; collectively they can.[73]

With the advent of a stable population, these conditions are modified. Each of the age groups constituting a stable population will grow at the same zero or positive rate as the total population, and the ratio of the population of working age to that beyond retirement age becomes constant. Then change in the amount of income per retiree transferred from the aggregate income stream to that for retirees will depend on change in (a) labor-force participation ratio, or in (b) social security or corresponding tax rate, or in (c) taxable income per member of the labor force, or in (d) some combination of (a), (b), and (c). As noted earlier, factor (a) is of critical importance, since a shift of individuals from the labor force to the retiree category simultaneously decreases the number of contributors to the retirement-income stream and increases the number drawing upon this stream.

What has just been said with respect to a collective program may be put in somewhat analogous terms respecting a representative individual funding an annuity. Suppose initially that a white male enters the labor force at age 20 and plans to retire at either age 65, 60, or 55, after having worked 45, 40, or 35 years. His life expectancy at age 65 will be about 13.2 years, whereas at ages 60 and 55 it will be 16.2 and 19.7 years, respectively. Should he retire at age 65, he will have worked about 3.4 years for each year in retirement; whereas should he retire at 60 or 55, the corresponding numbers fall to 2.47 and 1.53, respectively. As a result, the earlier a white male retires, the lower will be his retirement income if it is based on identical annual payments into the system each year he remains in the work force. Or, should he set a target retirement income, the smaller number of years he remains in the labor force, the more must he save per year to offset the smallness of the number of years he works and the largeness of the span of time to expects to live in retirement.

Should a prospective annuitant retire at age 55 instead of at age 65 or 69, the cost of a given annuity will be much higher. If based on the A-1949 Ultimate Table, it will be about 30 percent higher at age 55 than at age 65 and about 50 percent higher than at age 69. Given a Flexible Purchase Annuity Contract (FPPA) at current (i.e., July, 1977) dividend scale and settlement option rates, payment of $100 a month into such a contract by a male starting at age 20, would pay him a monthly income of $888 if he retired at 50, $2,319 if he retired at 60, and $3,787 if he retired at 65. If he did not begin his monthly payments until age 25, his monthly annuity would be $576 if he retired at 50, $1,553 if he retired at 60, and $2,556 if he retired at 65. Retiring at 65 instead of 55 makes retirement pay 164 percent higher in the first case, and about 169 percent higher in the second.[74]

Intergenerationally transferred income flows in two directions at any point in time, from those in the labor force: (a) to those in retirement as already discussed and (b) to younger persons not yet in the labor force. Accordingly, the capacity of those in the labor force to sustain flow (a) is conditioned by the size of flow (b). Indeed, T. D. Hogan has estimated that decrease in the cost of youth-related programs between 1972 and the advent of a stationary population would offset the associated increase in the cost of total old-age–related programs.[75] Hogan's forecast depends upon a number of assumptions, some of which may not be realized, among them labor-force participation. Turning to the total (i.e., private plus public) costs of dependency, we may infer from Robert Clark's forth-coming studies that public and out-of-pocket costs of young dependents are less than those of older dependents. However, inclusion of the op-portunity costs of producing and rearing young dependents may increase their total cost even if allowance is made for offsets due to *increase* in edu-cational and similar investment per capita.[76] Over against this cost, how-ever, must be set the value put upon the utility children are expected to yield over time, a return not correspondingly associated with elderly de-pendents.

There are intergenerational transfers of claims to wealth besides the intergenerational transfers of income discussed earlier. Associated with the death or anticipated death of wealth-owners, these wealth transfers are to heirs or other beneficiaries with a generally greater life expectancy than those transferring the claims. The amount of these claims passing each year from older persons to younger persons, thereby offsetting in some measure the flow of support from persons in the labor force to retired persons, may approximate 4–5 or more percent of the national income.[77] There also pass into the hands of enterprise and members of the labor force what may be called floating rents, imputable to government and eleemosynary-institutional property and investment, for the use of which little or no charge is imposed by the state or institution in its capacity as owner and investor.[78] Should estimates of intergenerational transfer of claims allow for such elements as floating rents and property transferred at death or in anticipation of death, the net flow of income from those in the labor force to those in retirement would prove smaller than when these transfers are neglected.

Whereas it is quite evident to the would-be annuitant that the ratio of his yearly income in retirement to his income when in the labor force will depend upon the years he spends in the work force compared with his life expectancy at retirement, this is less evident under the U.S. Social Security System; for retirement benefits are less closely connected with years spent in the work force and age of retirement.[79] Even so, changes in the Social Security System—changes connected in part with changes in age structure—resulted in an increase of from 6 to 30 beneficiaries per 100 contributors between 1950 and 1974, and this ratio is expected to reach 45 to 100 by 2030; it would increase less given a higher fertility rate and/or labor-force participation rate, especially higher labor-force participation on the part of older persons.[80]

In view of the fact that a population's age structure cannot be so modified in the short run as to increase the fraction of working age significantly, deferment of retirement remains the only effective means of increasing the ratio of males in the labor force to the male population. While deferment of retirement on the part of female members of the labor force has a similar effect, this effect may also be supplemented by increase in female labor-force participation. Since, as we have seen, labor-force participation has been declining sharply on the part of older males since 1950 and slightly on the part of older females since 1970, these trends need to be reversed. Such reversal would entail reduction of economic incentives to early retirement under governmental and private retirement systems, modification of conditions of employment in ways suited to make it more attractive, and increase in economic incentives to continuing participation in the labor force.[81]

Conclusion

Our emphasis in this chapter has been upon several somewhat demographic factors affecting the well-being of the population, especially that of retired older persons. Two factors have been emphasized.

The first factor is decline in the ratio of employed members of the labor force to persons permanently retired. Of the sources of this decline, two are of paramount importance. The first is increase in the relative number of persons over 64 years of age, an increase having its origin in the decline in fertility and the prospective advent of a stationary or declining population. The second source is early voluntary retirement from the labor force.

The second factor is the involuntary unemployment of persons of near-retirement age as well as of persons in and below their sixties, among them unemployed younger persons. This unemployment has two effects. First, it reduces the capacity of the population of working age to contribute to the pension and social security funds whereon the support of retired persons depends. Second, insofar as the activities in which younger workers engage complement those of older workers or generate income and hence demand for the products of older workers, unemployment of younger workers depresses employment and income among older workers.

Assurance of the continued economic well-being of older retired persons depends upon at least four conditions: reduction in the trend toward retirement below age 65; avoidance of involuntary unemployment, especially of older workers; maintenance of fertility at or slightly above the replacement level; and elimination of inflexibilities in the economy that reduce the mobility of labor as well as the demand for particular kinds of labor. These inflexibilities originate mainly in governmental controls and wage and price supports, and in price and/or wage supports imposed by trade unions and business oligopolies.

Serow's study suggests that so long as fertility is at or not too far removed from the replacement level, the age structure will be relatively favorable to aggregate labor productivity even though earnings and presumably the productivity of individuals move downward after they pass the early fifties if not sooner. The validity of this finding turns on other conditions than age structure as well, conditions such as occupational composition, the technologies in effect, and so on.[82]

VII. Age Structure and Economic Well-Being: Vertical and Horizontal Mobility

*The demand for final products reflects directly the "utility"
attached to them; the demand for factors of production does so
indirectly, being derived from the demand for the final product.*
Milton Friedman

In the preceding chapter we dealt with the impact of changes in the age
structure of a population upon its employability and welfare. We also dealt
with the impact of policies, institutions, and other factors upon the rate
of employment of older workers. In this chapter we deal with the impact
of age structure upon mobility, together with its significance for economic
well-being.

Attention will be focused upon five age ratios described below—ratios
that, though they vary slightly with sex, carry quite similar implications.

(a) The ratio of those of what may be called age of entry into the
labor force to those of what may be called age of departure
from the labor force.

(b) The ratio of those of age of entry into the labor force to those
of working age and hence (presumably) in the labor force.

(c) The ratio of those of (say) age 50–59 and in the labor force
to those of (say) age 25–34 and in the labor force.

(d) The ratio of those in the relatively low age categories—(say)
18 to 30 or 34—compared with those in the older age categories—(say) over 45 or 50.

(e) The ratio of those of voting age and under (say) 45 to those
of voting age and 45 or more years old—an indicator of the
likely impact of younger versus older voters upon economic and
social policies.

While our discussion is based mainly upon the assumption that the
ratios studied have been stable, note needs to be taken of the effect of
changes in particular ratios. For, given a population long-stationary, the
economy becomes adjusted to the fixity of these ratios, with the result that
adverse effects initially associated with the advent of the ratios in question
are adjusted to or compensated in various ways. Accordingly, given change
in these ratios, the compensatory impact of adjustments and accommodations may be reduced or intensified in comparison with the impact of the
ratios under stationary-population conditions, at least initially until compensatory adjustments have been made. Adverse effects associated with

ratios characteristic of a stationary population will tend to be inversely associated with the flexibility of that population's economy.

Returning now to the five ratios listed above, it is to be noted that they do not bear *directly* upon productivity and dependency as do the ratios treated in the two previous chapters. Thus, ratios (a), (b), and (c) bear upon upward mobility, opportunity, and ease of finding employment. Ratio (d) may affect the capacity of a population for invention and innovation, together with its congeniality to technological and cultural change, invention, innovation, and so on. Ratio (e) bears upon the distribution of political power between the relatively younger and the relatively older electorate, a distribution that may in turn affect the economic security of older members of a population.

Before we examine the ratios in detail, the general impact of stationariness upon ratio values and their implications may be indicated. While the resulting values of ratios (a) and (b) will be favorable to the employment of persons newly entering the labor force, they will be somewhat unfavorable to easy maintenance of optimum interoccupational and interindustrial balance. The value of ratio (c) will be relatively unfavorable to vertical mobility both because so many of those who enter the labor force survive into the fifties and sixties, thus slowing or preventing advancement, and because slowness of growth of population checks the creation of new posts contributive to upward mobility. While the value of ratio (d) may be less favorable to progress in a stationary than in a growing population, somewhat compensatory actions may prove possible if desirable. The value of ratio (e) is favored by a slowing down of population growth and a resulting increase in the relative number of older voters.

1. Ratios (a) and (b)

So long as a population is growing, the number of persons of working age will be growing unless growth has just been resumed after a population has been stationary; then growth of those of working age will not be resumed until those aged 16 or more years begin to grow in number. Given a population that has been stationary or growing slightly, the ratio of those of working age, say those 15–24, to those departing the labor force, say those 60–64, will grow until the population becomes stable under the ruling age-specific mortality conditions. The ratio will be higher, however, accordingly as the rate of population growth is higher. The tables on which Table VII.1 is based rest upon life expectancies at birth of 73.5 years for males and 77.5 for females.[1] The ratios reported in the last line of Table VII.1 indicate how the ratio of persons of working age to the number approaching or going into retirement increases with the rate of population growth. Given other necessary conditions, together with the

Table VII.1. Stable Population Proportions, (15–24):(60–64) by Sex and Growth Rate

	Rate of Population Growth in Percent							
	Male				Female			
Age Composition	−1	0	+1	+2	−1	0	+1	+2
(a) (15–24)	10.72	13.26	15.57	17.39	10.14	12.75	15.15	17.09
(b) (59–64)	7.06	5.72	4.39	3.20	7.06	5.80	4.51	3.32
a ÷ b	1.52	2.32	3.55	5.43	1.44	2.20	3.36	5.15

Source: Coale and Demeny, *Regional Model Life Tables*, pp. 72, 168.

assumption that all persons of working age are in the labor force, over twice as many jobs will have to be supplied as are vacated when a stable population is growing 2 instead of zero percent per year. That is, about as many new jobs must be created as were vacated and filled, and the derived demand for labor must increase correspondingly.

Should the fertility rate underlying the zero rate of population growth rise gradually to that underlying a rate of growth of 1 percent, a change in the number of persons aged 15–24 does not set in until after 14 years have passed, and does not work itself out for many years, nor does realization of ratio of (a) to (b) associated with a population growing 1 percent annually. There is ample forewarning to entrepreneurs, therefore, when the fertility rate changes, to anticipate its slowly evolving impact and accommodate these changes in keeping with market and price-system indications.

Given a stable population of given sex composition that is stationary, together with constant labor-force participation rates by age, we have an expected working life table (see Table VI.1) as of 1968 for that population, be it male, female, or both sexes. While, as has been indicated, most males enter the labor force by age 25, retirement from the labor force, as of 1968 experience, began at very low rates in the thirties, rising among those still in the labor force from about .002 in the forties to .062 in the early sixties and .116 in the late sixties; thereafter the withdrawal rate declined to around .08 in the seventies and early eighties.

Of course, even if the population is stable and stationary, the labor force can be increased provided labor-force participation increases, especially among those 15–24, and retirement from the labor force declines, especially among those over 54 (see Table VI.1). Thus, of the life-table population within the age category 16–64—4.3 million—88.7 percent, or 3.812 million, were in the labor force in 1968. Presumably many of the 487,000 not in the labor force could be enrolled if years spent in educational institutions were reduced by one-fourth. Moreover, the fraction of those 65–84 and in the labor force—about 27 percent—could be increased somewhat.

A stationary population, together with a stationary labor force (e.g., see Table VI.1), is not an unmixed blessing. On the one hand, the number of persons entering the labor force each year relative to the number in it is at or near a minimum, with the result that workers newly entering the labor force are likely to be scarce relative to those remaining in the labor force and hence with relatively good employment prospects. For example, the life-table population described in Table VI.1 is subject to an annual separation rate (due to death and retirement) of approximately 22.1 per 1,000 and hence to an offsetting accession rate of 22.1 per 1,000. Were the population stable but growing 2 percent per year, the accession rate would approximate 42 per 1,000, that is, enough to replace annual separations from the labor force due to death and retirement and also add 2 percent per year to enable the labor force to grow commensurately with the supposed 2 percent rate of population growth.

By way of further illustration, we may turn to a United Nations model male table based on a life expectancy of 70 years and Gross Reproduction Rates of 2.0 and 1.0 (i.e., birth rates of about 30.1 and 13.3 per 1,000), respectively. With the GRR at 2.0 and separations from the labor force (due to death and retirement) at 11.8, the labor force increases about 2.2 percent per year instead of declining .0018 per year when the GRR is just below replacement. In the former case, annual gross entries into the labor force approximate 33.7 males per 1,000 active males, compared with separations of about 11.8. In the latter case, separations (21.1 per 1,000 active males) slightly exceed accessions (19.2 per 1,000 active males). Given a stationary working-age population (15–64) with life expectancy in the 70–75-year range, departures equal additions at approximately 21 per 1,000. If, however, the population is declining 1 percent per year, departures will approximate 43 per 1,000 compared with about 16.5 additions, resulting in a diminution of about 26 per 1,000. Of course, when life expectancy is high, say 75, four-fifths or more of those departing the labor force are retirees at 65; whereas when life expectancy is around 50, about one-half are retirees.[2]

When a population and labor force are stationary, only enough persons enter the labor force to replace those removed by death and retirement, and there is no surplus of entries to operate expanding industries and occupations. The latter can enlarge their complements of manpower only by drawing on members of the labor force made unemployed by labor-saving change or by changes in the demand for labor due to changes in tastes or in income growth and distribution. With current life and work-life expectancies, in the neighborhood of 20 per 1,000 jobs would be vacated each year by death and retirement in a stationary male population, and an equivalent number of males would enter the labor force to fill vacated and newly created jobs. Should progress, together with low elasticity of demand, displace 11 male workers per 1,000 from their jobs each year, there would be available 11 workers per 1,000 per year to fill jobs developing annually in *new* and / or *emerging* lines of activity; the remaining 9 of the gross addition of 20 would be available to fill jobs made vacant by death and retirement. We would then have a *mobile* labor reserve of 11 per 1,000 workers. Accordingly, as we show below, should this reserve prove inadequate owing to job expansion, wages would tend to rise in newly emerging and expanding employments and workers would be attracted from other employments, with the result that in the latter wages would tend to rise and employment shrink until equilibrium was established between new and / or emerging employments and other employments.

Intensification of the problem of maintaining optimum interoccupational balance when a population and its labor force are stationary while its economy is dynamic may be put in more general terms. We may divide labor force L into two categories, I and M, the Immobile and the Mobile. Within the Immobile or I category we may include those not much disposed to transfer out of their current employments; this category is not absolutely fixed, however, since some included therein will transfer if the alternative presented is sufficiently attractive to outweigh the subjective and objective costs of transference. Within the Mobile category in a stationary labor force we include (a) those who, though replacements for individuals withdrawing from the labor force, are newly entering it and hence are not yet strongly attached to any given employment in a given situation; (b) those who are unemployed, having been displaced from employments they have hitherto held; and (c) those who, though employed, are on the margin of transference from their current employment because of dissatisfaction with it or with the conditions surrounding it as compared with perceived alternative prospects, and hence are potentially mobile.[3] When, however, a population is growing, the Mobile category M includes besides a, b, and c, an annual increment l in L due to natural increase or to net immigration. Accordingly, in a stationary population the ratio of M to L is $(a + b + c) / L$; whereas when the population is growing, the ratio becomes $(a + b + c + l) / L$.

When a population is dynamic, it is essential that its occupational composition continually undergo readjustment to changing conditions. Such adjustment may be somewhat easier to achieve if the population and labor force are growing at a steady rate than if they are stationary. How great this advantage may prove is uncertain. If l / L varies, the cost of adjusting the derived demand for labor to this variation may cancel out the advantages associated with l. With l / L in the neighborhood of 1 percent or less this advantage may not be very significant. For example, with the value of a / L in the neighborhood of 2 percent and $(b + c) / L^4$ in the neighborhood of (say) 3 percent, the ratio of M to L in a stationary population would approximate .05, compared with .06 should l / L approximate 1 percent.

The actual *plus* the potential supply of labor—call it S—exceeds significantly the actual supply, estimated to remain around 60 percent of the noninstitutional population over 15 years old.[5] For only 44 percent of females within this age category are in the labor force, compared with 78 percent of the males. Moreover, about one-fifth of the males 55–64 and about 5 percent of those 35 to 54 are not in the labor force. Hours of work per week may also be susceptible of temporary increase now that their number is in the thirties in many lines of activity. Given the availability of a considerable potential supply of labor, it should prove feasible to counterbalance variation in the rate at which the labor force grows and to facilitate the achievement of interoccupational balance when the labor force is stationary.

How much interoccupational and interindustrial mobility is required to preserve optimal balance depends mainly upon the rate of technological progress and the distribution of its incidence. In order to illustrate how much interoccupational mobility is required in a stationary population, we may divide activities in an economy into three sectors, S_m, S_i, and S_e, where S_m designates newly emerging industries or categories of production, S_i designates categories of activities the demand for which is quite inelastic, and S_e denotes categories of activities the demand for which is elastic. Increase in labor requirements originates in S_m and S_e, mainly as a result of technological progress generative of economy in production or conducive to innovation in the form of *distinctly* new forms of goods and services. These labor requirements may be met at least in part out of shrinkage in jobs in S_i as technological progress increases output per worker in the face of an inelastic market; for S_i will not attract persons newly entering the labor force. Should S_m and S_e together require more additional labor than is made available through contraction of employment in S_i, they will have to bid labor away from S_i or from one another, with the result that wage levels will be pushed upward, probably more so than if the labor force were still growing. Of course, if many persons not in the labor force are on the margin of entering it, they will be drawn in under the circumstances described and thus cushion the impact of the increase in demand for labor.[6]

While the advent of a stationary population and the consequent shrinkage in the relative size of the mobile reserve component of the labor force may make more difficult the maintenance of optimum interoccupational balance, this difficulty can be overcome if an economy is flexible, free of man-made monopoly-preserving barriers to interoccupational mobility, and equipped with satisfactory means of gathering and diffusing information bearing upon the supply of jobs and the demand for them in the present and the near future.

In view of what has been said, it may be plausible to infer that it is easier to man industrial and occupational expansion and / or change when the labor force is growing, albeit not at rates too high for easy absorption, than when the labor force is stationary. This condition is complemented also by the fact (see below, Section 3) that a growing population is likely to be more congenial to industrial change and expansion than is a stationary population. Accommodation of transitional labor "shortage" until a new and more stable overall equilibrium employment rate is reached should prove easier with labor-force participation lower than in the past and hence a potential temporary labor reserve in the form of persons withdrawn from the labor force but still on the margin of employment acceptance.

In general, the manpower market will be tighter in a stationary population, with the result that the price of labor relative to the price of capital will tend to be higher than in a growing population, particularly if changes in the composition of demand accentuate the need for greater amounts of job change and mobility, given the inverse relationship between proneness to move and age.

2. Ratio (c)

Nongrowth of population may also increase problems associated with diminution in upward mobility. For given a relatively hierarchical and stable job structure, together with seniority as a determinant of selection, and advancement, increase in the ratio of older to younger members of the labor force will reduce the opportunity for upward mobility available to younger persons. For expositive convenience I present Table VII.2 to illustrate how the ratio of older (e.g., those aged 50–59) to younger per-

Table VII.2. Ratio of Population 50–59 to Population 25–34 in Stable Populations

| | Rate of Population Growth in Percent | | | | | | | |
| | Male | | | | Female | | | |
Age Group	−1	0	+1	+2	−1	0	+1	+2
(a) 25–34	11.77	13.18	14.00	14.25	11.17	12.71	13.67	13.95
(b) 50–59	14.21	12.40	10.26	8.08	13.65	12.18	10.21	8.12
(b) ÷ (a)	1.21	0.94	0.73	0.57	1.22	0.96	0.75	0.58

Source: See under Table VII.1.

Table VII.3. Life Table Populations Contrasted; 1900–1902 and 1973

Age	1900–1902	1973	1973/(1900–1902)
0	100,000 (—)	100,000 (—)	1.00
20	76,376 (100)	96,714 (100)	1.27
40	64,954 (85)	92,889 (96)	1.36
45	61,369 (80)	91,074 (94)	1.48
55	52,491 (67)	83,718 (87)	1.60
65	39,245 (51)	67,459 (70)	1.72
75	21,387 (28)	41,510 (43)	1.94
Total Population	4,823,000	6,840,000	1.42

Source: See under Table V.4.

sons (e.g., those aged 25–34) increases as the rate of growth of a stable male population declines from 2 to −1 percent; and Table VII.3 to illustrate how increase in life-expectancy changed the age structure of the U.S. white male stationary population between 1900–1902 and 1973. With these two age distributions we may contrast a nation's job structure with jobs distributed into three or four categories A, B, C, or A, B, C, D, ranging from the most preferred category A to the least preferred category C or D.

The job structure, categorized according to the comparative attractiveness of jobs, does not change significantly *because* a population ages, and older members of the labor force, equipped with experience and seniority, tend to have preferential access to jobs in category A, or in categories A and B; as a result younger members of the labor force will find themselves with diminished access to preferred positions and hence required to wait longer for a shorter period of stay within preferred positions, should such positions be attained. For example (see Table VII.2), with a stable population growing 2 percent per year, the relative number of persons aged 50–59 and hence likely to occupy preferred positions is only 0.57 as numerous as those aged 25–34 and looking forward to occupying preferred positions. In contrast, given a stationary population, there are nearly as many older as younger persons, with the result that the ratio of preferred positions attainable by younger persons to the number of younger persons actually aspiring to these positions will be smaller.

To illustrate further the increase in the pressure of aspirants upon A-category jobs as the rate of growth of a stable population approaches zero, let us suppose that 30 percent of all jobs fall in the A or most preferred category. Suppose also that aspiration to these jobs is most intense among those 50–64 years of age and secondarily among those aged 35–49. Given a stable male population growing 2 percent per year, about 27 percent will be aged 50–64 compared with about 36 percent if this stable population is stationary.[7] We thus have about one-third more aspirants aged 50–64 years to a given number of A jobs when a population is stationary than when it is growing 2 percent per year. Comparison of the number of males aged 35–64 years with A plus B jobs yields a similar though much less striking difference.

Let us turn now to Table VII.3 and suppose that each member of the two populations entered the labor force at age 20 and that only death removes a member from the labor force. With the stationary population based on 1973 mortality exceeding that based on 1900–1902 mortality by 42 percent (see last line), there were relatively more persons aged over 43 in the former than in the latter population. There was greater pressure of persons aged over 43 on relatively more attractive positions in the later than in the earlier of these two life table stationary populations. There is less opportunity for upward mobility, therefore, in a stationary population based on 1973 mortality than in one based on 1900–1902 mortality. Were the population based on 1973 mortality growing and with it the number of jobs, and hence there were relatively fewer persons aged 43 and more years, the pressure of those 43 and over on preferred jobs would be relatively less.

The way that increase in the relative number of older persons due to the advent of a stationary population slows down upward mobility on the part of younger persons has been admirably represented by Nathan Keyfitz.[8] He writes as follows:

> This paper will set up an equation for the relation between individual mobility and population increase, and apply the equation to determining the age of promotion to a given rank in a stable organization. It will show in what degree the age of promotion depends on the rate of increase of the population under different mortality schedules and other circumstances. The effect will turn out to be numerically substantial—change from the 2% annual increase of the United States a few years ago to its prospective stationary condition implies a delay in reaching the middle positions of the average factory or office of $4\frac{1}{2}$ years.
>
> Whether the hierarchy is planned or not, individuals work their way up through the several ranks. They take unequal lengths of time to do so, and by no means all get to the top. Our results may thus be interpreted in three ways:
>
> (1) As applying to a system of strict seniority, in which every promotion is determined only by time of entry. Because strict seniority schemes are rare, this is the least interesting application.
>
> (2) As applying to an organization in which merit, influence, and other factors determine individual promotion, but in which experience is a factor of some importance. Some kind of age-complementarity must exist in production; old hands generally do different jobs from new recruits. If merit and influence are considered to act at random in relation to seniority, then our results give an average rate of promotion.

(3) As showing the pure effect of population increase on promotion, in abstraction from all other circumstances. From this viewpoint, merit and influence that may be determining for the individual are superimposed on the population factor. A person would move up $4\frac{1}{2}$ years earlier if he lived in a population increasing at 2% per year than if he lived in one that was stationary; he would have this advantage whether he is above or below average in mobility. He may be brilliant and move up fast in a stationary population; our argument shows that he would move up faster in an increasing population. This seems the most valuable of the three interpretations of the results that follow.

Population increase provides a push for an individual that has its effect more or less independently of the other factors working for or against him. An analysis that would fully explain the upward mobility of individuals would have to take into account all of those factors, but such a complete analysis is not the object of this paper, which is confined to mobility in relation to the one factor of population growth.

National populations are structured into smaller organizations, and individuals have their ranks in these rather than in the nation as a whole. All organizations within a country do not grow at the same rate, and the fate of the individual is affected only by the growth of the one he is working in. The advantage to the individual of being in a fast-growing organization is covered by this paper equally with the advantage to all the individuals in all the organizations in a country if that country is growing rapidly.[9]

Keyfitz contrasts populations with different rates of increase, searching for the impact of rate of population growth upon the rate of mobility and the earliness of the age of promotion. He makes three points:

(1) If the population is increasing at the rate of 0.01, a person will pass the gateway represented by $k = 1$, which is to say he crosses into the upper half of the hierarchy, at 38.55 years rather than at 40.86 years of age as he would in a stationary population with the same life table. He saves 2.31 years because the population is increasing at 1% per year rather than stationary.
(2) The effect of a 1% increase becomes smaller as one goes to the higher gateway—for $k = 0.2$, where each person has five others reporting to him the difference between $r = 0$ and $r = 0.01$ is only 1.66 years. Promotion at the top is not as much affected by population growth as promotion at the middle ranks.
(3) Some diminishing returns appear with increasing r. The benefit of going from $r = 0.03$ to $r = 0.04$ at the gateway $k = 1$ is to lower the age by 1.72 years as against 2.31 years by going from $r = 0.00$ to $r = 0.01$.[10]

Keyfitz deals with the effects of both mortality and variation in the number of deaths per year. He finds the impact of mortality on mobility to be less than that of population growth, together with the impact of premature retirement and net migration.[11] Decreasing population, whether due to an excess of deaths or net emigration, slows promotion even more than does cessation of population growth, Keyfitz finds.[12] Variation in the annual number of births produces what may be called cohort effects. Thus

> a person born in a cohort that is small in relation to those before and after him will be advantaged by many people retiring ahead of him, leaving places to which he can be promoted. Even when he is young the effect will reach him, through retirements that have to be filled by people older than himself, for those places he will in turn be a candidate. At the same time he will be followed by many new entrants, and these will require instruction and supervision so that he will be quickly pushed up. The new entrants will have this effect as routine workers in a factory, as students in a university, or clerks in a government office—in relation to supervisors, staff, and administrators respectively. Thus, in this unstable case the member of a small cohort is favoured in two distinct ways: by many retirements above him, and by many entrants below him. Moreover, the benefit is with him throughout life, since as the several cohorts move forward in age and time their relative sizes are approximately preserved.[13]

Slowing down of the rate of vertical mobility and hence of promotion imposes on society the need to offset these adverse effects of the advent of zero population growth and the problems that can emerge later on. For example, conflict will develop between those with preferred positions and those who, though quite able to fill preferred positions, are in effect denied access either to these positions, say by occupational licensure,[14] or to adequate compensation for such denial. The burden of this conflict may be incident upon older workers and conduce to their premature involuntary retirement. Appropriate reactions may assume three forms: (i) increase in the number of distinct essentially autonomous organizations within an economy or population; (ii) decrease in the degree of inequality with which the wage and salary component of the aggregate income of a representative organization is distributed to its wage and salaried personnel; (iii) modification of an organization's technological and personnel structure in ways suited to produce an equalizing effect similar to that discussed under (ii).

The value attached to upward mobility in any particular organization turns mainly upon (a) the relative pecuniary rewards associated with higher as compared with lower ranks in the hierarchically arranged structure and order of ranks characteristic of that organization; and (b) the number of organizations to be found in the economy as a whole, together with the number of accessible positions of comparable order to be found in the society or economy as a whole. Insofar as arbitrariness and imperfection in the pricing of inputs often underlie the level of reward associated with a rank or status level, increasing competition for such status may serve to reduce the level of reward required to attract an occupant to that status or rank. As a result, new exchange ratios between rank and reward may emerge, and reward patterns may adjust downward. For example, the salary of the professor may over time be adjusted downward relative to that of the assistant professor.[15] The age-earnings profile over a representative individual's work life will become less steep if it is freed of all discrimination in favor of older persons and dominated by increase both in complements to labor and in improvements in industrial organization, that is, by factors which tend to elevate the income of *all* workers and so lift the earnings profiles of nearly all members of the labor force in about the same relative measure.[16] In other words, disadvantage in the form of reduction in access to relatively high-status jobs, together with the relative scarcity of individuals newly entering the labor force, will prompt and enable younger workers to seek pecuniary offsets in the form of higher wages or salaries, making age-earnings profiles less steep. The distribution of personal incomes will become somewhat less unequal as a result, at least relative to age. Moreover, insofar as younger persons often tend to become as productive as middle-aged persons after several or more years' experience, the readjustment in earnings structure may coincide more closely with worker performance than do current earnings profiles. Reduction in the gradients of earnings profiles may prove of some advantage to older workers, since they will become under less pressure to retire because of the comparative costliness of their labor.

Technological and related changes in the conduct of productive activities may modify the job structure within organizations by reducing the demands made upon individuals by the "jobs" or "positions" they occupy, with the result that reward structures within organizations are made less unequal and therefore the financial rewards attaching to so-called higher-ranking positions are reduced relative to rewards associated with lower ranks.

The ratio of higher- to lower-ranking positions in an economy as a whole varies with industrial structure. Accordingly, the advent of zero population growth will tend to increase the comparative advantage of types of industrial organization in which this ratio is relatively high, possibly at the cost of some reduction in overall output per head. There may be greater tendency to develop new and smaller-scale firms in place of larger ones, on the ground that greater autonomy and relatively higher rank are realizable when there are more firms.

Both vertical and horizontal mobility may be favored by removing man-made barriers to interoccupational mobility, anticipating likely trends in occupational composition, and improving the flow of information relating to prospective job shrinkage and job expansion in specific occupations, professions, industries, and locations. Policy conducive to mobility consists essentially in identifying and devising countervailants to sources of inflexibility in the economy and barriers to labor mobility that give rise to unemployment or underemployment in the sense of engagement in activities that are less productive than those of which workers are capable. Countervailing action needs, of course, to focus upon removal of incentives conducive to inflexibility and avoidance of job search, and to strength incentives to mobility. When income inequality is under consideration, inequality due to market imperfections needs to be distinguished from inequality due to differences in the willingness of people to bear risks—differences which help to account for greater variability in occupations subject to much greater risk than to others subject to little risk, even when average income is the same in each set of occupations.[17]

3. Ratio (d)

It has been inferred that in a stationary population the ratio of relatively young to relatively old persons may be unfavorable to (i) discovery, invention, and innovation, and (ii) willingness to adopt new methods and products. In Table VII.4 we illustrate how the supposedly innovative and inventive fractions of the population vary with the rate of growth of a stable population. The data there presented indicate that the fraction of a stationary population in what might be called innovative age groups is not quite as large so long as the innovative group is defined as falling within the 20–39 range. Only when the inventive category is defined as made up of those aged 25–39 or 25–44 years is the relative magnitude of this group little-influenced by variation in the rate of growth between zero and 2 percent.

(i) The frequency of inventors and innovators is greatly influenced, of course, by a country's educational and industrial system and by the degree of incentive to invent and innovate. Age structure is only one of many contributive factors. Moreover, years of peak performance vary with the nature of the particular activity in which individuals are engaged, tending

Table VII.4. Age Structure and Rate of Population Growth In Stable Male Population (Percent)

Age Category	Annual Rate of Population Growth (Percent)						
	-1	$-\frac{1}{2}$	0	$\frac{1}{2}$	1	$1\frac{1}{2}$	2
20–34	17.26	18.61	19.80	20.80	21.58	22.12	22.40
25–39	18.08	19.01	19.73	20.22	20.45	20.22	20.53
20–39	23.57	25.08	26.35	27.35	28.03	28.18	28.78
25–44	24.67	25.60	26.24	26.57	26.55	26.57	26.32

Source: Coale and Demeny, *Regional Model Life Tables*, p. 168.

to be lower in fields such as mathematics and physics and higher in fields wherein cumulation[18] of knowledge and experience is an important contributive factor.

Alan Sweezy and Aaron Owens point out, on the basis of Owens's study of the ages at which Nobel Prize winners did their prize-winning work, that "the relative per capita probability of Nobel-quality work in physics has a broad maximum from zero to 1.5 percent growth but falls off rapidly for growth rates less than −0.5 percent and more than 2.0 percent per year. Clearly there is no justification here for fears that slow or zero population growth would have a stultifying effect on scientific creative activity."[19]

The authors add that

there is a strong presumption, however, that youth is more important in physics than in most other fields. The average ages of Nobel Prize–winning work in physics (36), chemistry (38), and medicine and physiology (41) indicate a progression from younger to older as the research becomes more applied. Similarly, among the physicists the experimentalists are five years older than their theoretical colleagues. It seems likely that theoretical brilliance is less and empirical experience more of a factor in the success of businessmen and politicians than of scientists. There are some areas, notably athletics, in which youth has a clear advantage. But over the whole range of creative activities fears that a stationary population will bring stagnation seem unjustified.[20]

(ii) Data in Table VII.5 indicate that the proportion of the population 20–64 under 35 years of age varies appreciably with the rate of growth of a stable population. Harvey Leibenstein puts the matter this way:

The rate at which a population transmits acquired characteristics to subsequent generations will depend in part on the growth rate of the population and its age structure. This is readily seen if we assume that all quality improvements take place among the lower age groups and not the higher ones. For example, nurture and schooling improvements are, for

Table VII.5. Age Structure and Rate of Population Growth In Male Stable Population (Percent)

Age Category	Annual Rate of Population Growth (Percent)			
	−1	0	1	2
(a) 20–64	58.28	57.42	54.52	50.03
(b) 20–29	11.24	13.22	14.77	15.69
(c) 20–34	17.26	19.80	21.58	22.40
b ÷ a	0.193	0.233	0.270	0.314
c ÷ a	0.296	0.345	0.395	0.448

Source: Coale and Demeny, *Regional Model Life Tables*, p. 168.

the most part, likely to enter the system during early ages. To the extent that entrants into the work force are of higher quality (i.e., higher education and acquired skills, etc.) than those that leave through retirement or death, the average quality of the labor force improves more rapidly if the rate of population growth is higher (other things equal) rather than lower.[21]

Leibenstein thus visualizes what he calls a "replacement effect." "We visualize an economic quality replacement effect in the sense that those who enter the economically active population have a higher productive capacity than those who leave, and hence they increase the average quality of the labor force."[22] Later he adds that his "replacement-effect type of argument" implies

that the more rapidly growing population has a positive aspect which counteracts the negative aspects of rapid growth, and that this aspect is less significant in the slow-growing population.

Whether or not the replacement effect is of interest depends on the acceptability of the assumptions, especially with respect to the assumptions: (a) that the costs of education are consumption costs rather than investment costs, and (b) that the level of education per person provided for later entrants (rather than earlier entrants) is unaffected (or less than proportionately reduced) by positive rates of population growth.[23]

The upshot of what may be said respecting the advent of the type of age structure associated with a stationary population may be put thus: While the potential for invention and innovation in the broad sense of the terms will not be much if at all affected by the age structure as such, the decline in the relative number of persons in the younger age groups—say under 40—may make the preponderant point of view of industrial and political leadership, together with that of the adult population as a whole, less congenial to change unless change gives promise of substantial returns in the shorter run. For discount rates rise with age, and presumably what some have called "animal spirit" becomes less buoyant. Prospective payoffs that will conduce to change when decision-makers are younger prove less and less adequate as decision-makers become older. Moreover, this tendency will be strengthened as the comparative political power of older persons increases (see next section).

Within social organizations, and on directorships, of course, arbitrary arrangements may be made to assure disproportionately large representation to younger persons—say persons under 50—in order to assure effective representation of young persons as a countervailant to the prospect of excessive conservatism of older decision-makers. Conceivably also the reestablishment of the multigeneration family and similar multigeneration organizations may extend the animating and effective planning horizon of decision-makers, and outweigh the shortening of the planning horizon of the representative individual and of the number of years remaining to him in the course of which he can recoup losses due to mistaken decision. We shall return to this subject when discussing the impact of population aging upon investment.[24] Here it may be added, however, that if discretionary or uncommitted incomes are higher in a stationary population, thus reducing the psychological and economic burden of risk- and uncertainty-bearing, the adversity of the age factor to risk-bearing is reduced.

4. Ratio (e)

As an individual ages, the composition of his tastes changes, as does his outlook upon life and the future. This change reflects change in an individual's physical state, together with decrease in the number of years remaining to him for achieving whatever he seeks in life. Presumably conclusions based upon present life expectancies will hold for the future in advanced countries. In the United States, by 1973 about 82 percent of white females survived to age 65, as did about 67 percent of white males. Moreover, while elimination of one-half of all major causes of mortality would add an average of 7.17 years to the life of a male aged 65, raising his expectancy to 20.30 years, and 7.57 to that of a female aged 65, raising her expectancy to 24.72 years, such elimination is not to be expected. Indeed, "a reduction of as much as one fourth in the number of deaths from any one cause" would "require a major breakthrough in research."[25] Accordingly, while life expectancy rose 25 years among white females between 1900 and 1973, and while older persons have shared in life extension in recent years, prospective gains at higher ages remain quite limited, as presumably does the prospect of greatly slowing the aging process. This process, therefore, will continue to reduce the capacity of the individual to exploit his time as effectively in his later as in his earlier years. His tastes, aspirations, and decision-oriented time horizon are affected accordingly.

Because of changes concomitant with the aging of the individual, his political outlook, together with what he expects of the state, is likely to change as he ages. Moreover, as a population ages, a larger fraction of its members fall within older age groups. Aging of a population therefore changes the composition of its political outlook. This change becomes more significant when the majority of the population passes a critical age level, particularly if seniority rules favor older persons and the outlook of older voters evolves into a consensus of sorts.

As the rate of population growth declines, the fraction of the population below a critical age—let us call it 45—decreases. This is illustrated for stable populations in Table VII.6. As the rate of population growth approaches zero, the relative number of persons over 44 years of age ap-

Table VII.6. Rate of Population Growth and Percent of Population 18 and Over, That Is, 45 and Over

Age Group	Rate of Population Growth (Percent)							
	Male				Female			
	−1	0	1	2	−1	0	1	2
18–44	32.24	35.51	37.34	37.54	30.52	35.22	36.48	37.03
Over 44	50.36	40.50	31.27	23.24	52.96	42.76	33.07	24.57
Percent over 44	61.0	53.3	45.6	38.2	63.4	54.8	47.5	39.9

Source: Coale and Demeny, Regional Model Life Tables, pp. 72, 168.

proaches one-half of those 18 and over and rises above it. In the United States, with fertility at the replacement level, the fraction of the population 18 and over that is 45 and over will remain in the neighborhood of 0.45 until in the early 1990s. Thereafter it will rise slowly to nearly 0.51 by the year 2010 and to about 0.524 in 2050.[26] Given zero immigration, those 45 and over will constitute slightly over half of the population 18 and over by 2010; by 2050 the fraction may approximate 0.536.

What is the critical year, the year when an individual's interests become identified with the older half of the population of voting age, 18 and over? While there is no such year, I have selected age 45 as the year dividing those with predominantly age-oriented interests from those with youth-oriented interests. If this selection be valid, persons under 45 will have greater political power than older persons until early in the next century. This preponderance of power will serve to limit wage and salary taxation for the purpose of financing age-connected programs such as Social Security, Medicare, and Medicaid. This in turn will set limits to the introduction of "early retirement," particularly as it is realized that the sustainability of social security systems is contingent upon maintenance of a sufficiently high contributor–beneficiary ratio.

Conclusion

The behavior of an economy will reflect the advent of an age structure characteristic of a stationary population. The values associated with ratios (a) and (b) will be conducive to the easy employment of young people newly entering the labor force and hence to the avoidance of teen-ager unemployment sometimes associated with population growth, especially 16–20 years after a baby boom. Since ratio (c) is unfavorable to upward mobility, some adjustment of earning profiles in ways suited to compensate for diminished upward mobility may be expected. The values likely to be associated with ratio (d) will make stationary populations less favorable to change, and this tendency will be reenforced as the balance of political power passes into the hands of those in older age groups, especially those in the fifties and over. The response of an economy to the advent of ratios such as have been selected will be conditioned by the institutional structure of an economy, its flexibility, and resort to compensatory measures.

A population can adjust gradually to the age parameters of a stationary population and learn both to cushion its adverse impact and to derive advantage from its favorable impact; for these parameters come into existence gradually. Perhaps significant responses to the impact of adverse changes may result. For example, as Keyfitz has shown, upward mobility is slowed. As a result there may be an increase in *entrepreneurial* activity and intensity of the search for relatively small but potentially profitable economic opportunities and niches to which large corporations and conglomerates are insensitive. After all, it may be more attractive to be first in Peoria than fiftieth in New York City. One outcome would be increase in the aggregate input of *enterprise,* an aggregate somewhat limited by the ascendancy of large corporate and conglomerate pyramids insensitive to lesser opportunities. Another outcome will be much greater sensitivity to the actual wants of consumers, many of which may be going unsatisfied at present.

Within limits new age parameters may compel populations to reduce or partly solve problems that have troubled societies in the past. Illustrative is an observation by John P. Lewis respecting the impact of population aging upon actions respecting circumstances affecting consumers adversely: "Even more than Ralph Nader, an aging electorate may make something of the sort [a Department of Consumer Protection] increasingly feasible politically."[27] Indeed, it is already seeking to protect itself against the inflation-generating activity of the American Congress.

VIII. Population Growth and Output Growth

The simplest things, which only fifty years ago one could do without difficulty, cannot get done anymore.
E. F. Schumacher, *Small Is Beautiful,* p. 65

Schumpeter, finding no unique relation between "variations in population" and "variations in the flow of commodities," treated population growth as "an environmental change conditioning certain phenomena," though admitting that this mode of treatment would be inadequate for some purposes. In this chapter we treat the direct impact of population growth upon the growth of aggregate and per capita output, together with some but not all concomitants of this impact on costs, prospects, and returns. While our emphasis will be upon the lines of causation running from increase in population to increase in output, we cannot wholly disregard the fact that population growth is not an exogenous factor, inasmuch as population growth may be facilitated by growth of output as the two forms of growth interact through time. When, however, changes under consideration are short-run, population growth, being a time-oriented process, is of too little magnitude to be significant other than as a part of the environment[1] and as a prospective element in man's anticipations.

Determination of the contribution of population growth to aggregate growth is difficult. We may, of course, describe the rate of growth of aggregate output as approximating the sum of the rate of growth of the labor force and the rate of growth of output per member of the labor force. What we need to know, however, is the distinct contribution of each of the sources of increase in output per member of the labor force and the nature of the impact of population growth upon each of these sources. It has been recognized, particularly since P. H. Douglas effectively introduced the production function into the tool bag of the economist, that output is the product of multifactor input and that increase in "labor" and "capital" inputs—neither usually well-defined in the past—does not adequately account for increase in output. There remains to be explained a large "Unexplained Residual" sometimes described as "The Measure of Our Ignorance."[2] This need began to be stressed soon after Douglas quantified the production function.[3]

Determination of the precise contribution of the inputs responsible for output presents problems both in the realm of conceptualization and in that of quantification and measurement, in part because of the degree of correlation between the outputs associated with some inputs and because of the fact that the supply of some inputs is modified by their owners in the light of rewards associated with the supply of these inputs. Thus the supply of some "labor" inputs may respond negatively to increase in their "rewards," whereas the supply of other inputs may respond positively if only because the margin of their supply is thereby made extensible.[4] Difficulties are further accentuated when the determination at issue is not merely current input contributions but also the impact of population growth upon the supply and behavior of diverse inputs over time. For this impact is conditioned by the fact that an economy and its relevant operations constitute an interrelated whole.

It is helpful to keep in mind a distinction Milton Friedman has made between two sets of effects of population, between (1) effects "which tend to offset some unfavorable effects of population growth" and (2) effects which "are favorable in the sense that they are reasons why population growth would on net mean a higher rate of growth in per capita output than otherwise."[5] In the former category Friedman includes such conditions as the "need for the reshuffling of the economy to adapt to the new conditions associated with population growth," the need to invest more in human capital and offset greater pressure on the supply of savings, and adaptive changes in tastes. In the second category Friedman places various effects that belong within the category of "external economies." "Classical 'external economies' are the only category of effects we have yet found that can render population growth positively favorable to per capita output." But Friedman points out that economies are not closed, that "an extension of the market giving rise to external economies can be achieved through more extensive international trade as well as through a growth in the national market. And external economies produced in this way are likely to give rise to none of the unfavorable effects accompanying external economies produced by population growth."[6]

Friedman's emphasis upon external economies calls attention to size of state as well as to size of population. For since, as Kuznets observes, "the individual country is the locus of decisions on changes in social, political, and economic conditions,"[7] the actions of individual countries may limit the access of particular countries to external economies through the medium of external trade. Insofar as this is the case, some enlargement of a country in area as well as population may be essential to full realization of external economies. We touch upon this matter later in this chapter.

The impact of population growth upon economic growth may be examined at three levels or from three points of view. (1) Population growth conditions economic growth through its distinct effects upon the aggregate stock of manpower and upon the performance of individual units of manpower over selected periods of time. This distinction as to periods of time is essential if we are to allow for the fact that the consumption of present generations not only conditions favorably that of future generations but can condition the state of future generations unfavorably insofar as the availability of natural resources (e.g., energy, raw materials) is subject to depletion, exhaustion, and rising costs over time. (2) Population growth affects aggregate economic growth both as a result of sheer increase in numbers and as a result of pertinent changes in the age structure. (3) Population growth may directly or indirectly affect output per capita or per worker through its immediate effects upon capital formation per capita, improvement in methods, and so on.

The effect of increase in a population's size assumes several forms. (a) Population growth absorbs inputs that might otherwise be devoted to increasing output per head. (b) Population growth may stimulate asset formation, though not necessarily enough to increase assets per head as much as otherwise might have been possible.[8] (c) Population growth may intensify or affect adversely various forces that contribute to increase in output per unit of input and per capita.

Illustrative of these forces are five stressed by Denison, in some instances with the support of Kelley, Kuznets, and others.[9] Briefly, these five forces include advances in knowledge, degree to which resources are optimally distributed, degree to which obstacles are deliberately put in the way of growth, market expansion, and changes in resource utilization. These forces, whose possible response to population growth we refer to later, are discussed as follows:

1. One major force consists of "advances in technological and managerial knowledge, including business organization"—advances distinguishable from their actual application inasmuch as the average of actual practice lags in verying degree behind the best known practice.[10]

Writing in a similar vein, Kuznets stresses "the increasing stock of tested, useful knowledge," a stock to which increments of population may add within a country and possibly even beyond its borders, by adding to "the number of creators of new knowledge"—and proportionately more if there should be increasing returns "on output of new knowledge, per head of knowledge-creator and hence per head of population."[11]

Kelley presents data and results "consistent with the hypothesis that population exerted a positive stimulus to the rate of economic progress," though some evidence indicates "that this impact may have diminished over time and is possibly insignificant today."[12] "An expanding population base may have stimulated the rate of per capita inventive activity" and accelerated the rate at which technology was put to use."[13]

2. While there is always "some allocation of resources that would yield a maximum national product," this optimum distribution of resources among uses is never achieved for a variety of reasons, among them imperfect mobility of resources when responding to changes in what is the optimum distribution, to legal and institutional barriers to movements toward a current optimum, and to disparity between earnings preferences and preference for alternatives to greater earnings.[14]

3. Denison adds that "obstacles may be deliberately imposed by governments, business, or labor unions against the most efficient utilization of resources in the uses to which they are put."[15] These obstacles *ceteris paribus* may be reenforced in greater measure in a nongrowing than in a growing population.[16]

4. "Enlargement of markets makes possible the reduction of unit costs by greater specialization and thus increases output per unit of input. The size of these gains depends upon the distribution of increased expenditures among products as per capita expenditures rise, and shifting consumption patterns have a great deal to do with observed differences" in national growth rates.[17]

In this connection Kelley calls attention to the diversity of external economies and scale effects that may have been, and may possibly still be, associated with the enlargement of the American population. He interprets the impact of population size on rates of economic progress "to include both the traditional scale economies and the scale effects of utilizing the relatively large indivisible capital outlays dictated by industrial and transport technology." Associated with these economies are not only "the advantages of increasing specialization in production" but also "Kuznets' hypothesis that population size exerts increasing returns to scale on the pace of inventive and innovative activity," an hypothesis for which Kelley has found some historical support.[18]

5. Changes in the extent to which a nation and its economy utilizes its available resources constitute a factor to which Kuznets also attaches importance.[19]

Besides forces such as these five and those listed earlier, there are the demographic conditions associated with the rate of population growth, namely, age structure and relative size of the labor force. All these will now be examined, together with their response to change in population size. Of overriding concern, of course, is not whether in the past population expansion strengthened these forces and thereby accelerated economic progress, but whether the favorable impact of population expansion is spent in countries such as the United States or accompanied by more than offsetting costs.

1. Population Growth and Output Per Capita

We shall assemble the determinants of output per capita into nine categories and then inquire into how population growth affects the income-augmenting power of each of these nine sets of determinants. These categories are:

(1) Age structure
(2) Labor-force participation
(3) Hours of work
(4) External economies and economies of scale
(5) Utilizable physical assets per head
(6) Human capital per capita
(7) State of technology
(8) Organization and direction of economy
(9) Dynamism of economy

(1)–(3) *Age Structure, Labor-Force Participation, Hours of Work.* As we have shown in previous chapters, the age structure of a near-stationary stable population is potentially more favorable to economic growth per capita *ceteris paribus* than is a growing stable population. Whether this potential is realized, however, depends upon whether labor-force participation rates and hours of work per year remain unchanged or decline very little. When a population is stationary, of course, fertility is relatively low by implication (perhaps as a result of the desire of many women to be enrolled in the labor force), and female participation in the labor force tends to increase as it has in the United States. This increase may, however, be offset by reduction in male labor-force participation, should males find the terms of employment slightly less attractive as a result of female competition. Indeed, the fraction of the combined male and female population 14 and older and enrolled in the labor force fluctuated only negligibly between 1890 and 1950.[20] Moreover, as Galloway points out, if the constancy of this fraction is the product of compensatory offsets in the short and the long run, then this constancy arises not so much from the bisexual character of the labor force and the substitution of females for males (especially young and old males) as from positive and negative correlations among sectors and the operation of "the laws of chance."[21] More generally, "variations in the size of the aggregate labor force in the United States are responsive to changes in the general levels of economic activity."[22]

Contributive to increase in labor-force participation on the part of women, particularly married women, has been reduction in the number of hours worked per week.[23] Even so, about 42 percent of the *total* population was in the labor force in 1970 even as in 1950. Moreover, despite a greater tendency to earlier retirement now than formerly, the fraction of the population 16 years and over in the labor force approximated 59.2 percent in 1960 and 60.3 in 1970; it is expected to rise slightly, to 61.3 in 1985 and 61.5 in 1990, when the age structure will still be reflecting the baby boom.[24] Also contributive to hours worked per worker per year is multiple–job holding ("moonlighting"), sometimes associated with family size. While persons with two jobs or more comprised roughly 4.5–5 percent of the employed population in 1956–1974, this fraction could fall if in the future relative earnings on less well-paying jobs rose.[25]

(4) *External Economies and Economies of Scale.* Since the time of Adam Smith a part of the increase in output per unit of input has been attributed to external economies and economies of scale. Smith, of course, looked upon division of labor as a source both of specialization and of learning experience whence might and did flow improvements in methods of production. Whereas Smith found limits to output and to progress in division of labor in agriculture, J. S. Mill did not believe that the fruits of what he called "cooperation" would justify population growth beyond what amounted to size of optimum magnitude.[26] Perhaps the most optimistic of the twentieth century economists who have stressed increasing returns have been Allyn Young and Colin Clark.

Allyn Young inquired into conditions favorable and unfavorable to division of labor, internal and external economies, and elasticity and reciprocity of demand and progress. Increase in supply of one commodity amounted to demand for others, the supply of which increased as a result. "The rate at which any one industry grows is conditioned by the rate at which other industries grow, but since the elasticities of demand and of supply will differ for different products, some industries will grow faster than others."[27] Obstacles to progress were of two sorts, the resistance of human material to change (e.g., resistance to learning or acquiring new trades) and the slowness with which capital equipment was formed and shaped. Emerging inelasticity of demand, "natural scarcities, limitations or inelasticities of supply," and obstacles in the way of improvement in methods of production slowed progress, whereas the discovery of new natural resources, new uses, and new knowledge accelerated it.

Population growth was favorable but not essential. "Even with a stationary population and in the absence of new discoveries in pure or applied science there are no limits to the process of expansion except the limits beyond which demand is not elastic and returns do not increase." Under "most circumstances," however, "though not in all, the growth of population still has to be counted a factor making for a larger *per capita* product—although even that cautious statement needs to be interpreted and qualified. But just as there may be population growth with no increase of the average *per capita* product, so also, as I have tried to suggest, markets may grow and increasing returns may be secured while the population remains stationary."[28]

Clark, who had worked with Young and later edited G. T. Jones's *Increasing Return* (Cambridge, 1933), still later dealt with increasing returns in his *Conditions of Economic Progress* (London, 1940, 1957) and stressed the evidence of "increasing returns" in the manufacturing sector as the market for manufactures was enlarged. His analysis of economics of scale in a number of countries led him to conclude that "for any increase in the scale of manufacture, all other things being equal, productivity tends to rise by a factor of the one-sixth power of the increase, not the square root."[29] This differs somewhat from Verdoorn's generalization, perhaps reflecting a learning effect, that product per man hour of labor input "tended to grow at the square root of the rate of growth of total product," a relationship which, though Clark found it approximated in "an Anglo-American industry comparison," overstated "the true effect of a change of scale of production, as distinguished from technical changes, or from the institutional and external factors which affect different industries or different countries."[30] Yet another study suggested that "Verdoorn's square root law" might be "true for individual industries" though not for "manufacture as a whole."[31] Of course, as Hahn and Matthews point out, economies of scale can "bring about steady growth in income per head so long as population is growing" even in the absence of technical progress, provided that an uncompensated tendency to diminishing returns is not in existence.[32]

In 1966 N. Kaldor, on the basis of data drawn from twelve countries, "claimed to have confirmed Verdoorn's law for industry." Moreover, he "concluded that the potential growth of industrial productivity is limited by the supply of labour, arguing that when industry suffers from a shortage of labour it is unable to exploit economies of scale and productivity is thereby harmed."[33] Rowthorn concludes from his statistical analysis "that there is no empirical evidence that Kaldor's law has operated during the post-war period in manufacturing." Results purporting to confirm Kaldor's law "are based upon a small sample of countries in such a way that the extreme observations in one special case—Japan—account for the bulk of the observed correlation between productivity growth and employment growth."[34] In a subsequent exchange of views bearing upon exogenous components of demand and the availability of labor, the authors do not effectively focus attention upon the technological and related conditions that might make output behave in keeping with the "Verdoorn Law."[35]

Perhaps most extensive of the quantitative inquiries into the effects of economies of scale have been E. F. Denison's two studies.[36] These economies are associated with increase in the size of markets as a result of growth of a country's domestic economy and improvement in its market structure, perhaps reenforced by extension of markets external to a country.[37] Denison describes these economies and their impact as follows:

> Growth of an economy automatically means growth in the average size of the local, regional, and national markets for end products that business serves. Growth of markets brings opportunities for greater specialization—both among and within industries, firms, and establishments —and opportunities for establishments and firms within the economy to become larger without impairing the competitive pressures on firms that stimulate efficiency. Longer production runs for individual products become possible. So, in almost all industries including wholesale and retail trade, do larger transactions in buying, selling, and shipping. This is important, because the length of runs and the size of the transactions in which business deals are major determinants of unit costs. Larger regional and local markets permit greater geographic specialization and less transporting of products. The opportunities for greater specialization, bigger units, longer runs, and larger transactions provide clear reason to expect increasing returns in the production and distribution of many products, and examples of increasing returns are plentiful.
>
> There are almost no necessary offsets from industries operating under decreasing returns to scale because increasing cost is almost never a necessary concomitant to the growth of demand for a product. Although individual establishments and firms can become too large for efficiency, their number can be multiplied without limit. There is no necessity to carry specialization beyond the point at which it is efficient. When land is counted as an input there is no reason to expect decreasing returns to scale for any product unless some very unusual situation is present.
>
> In my opinion, it is clear from general knowledge and many studies that the United States business economy operates under increasing returns to scale, and that the size of the gains is large enough to contribute importantly to the growth of total output. One can go further and quantify this contribution only by arriving at some judgment as to the *size* of the gains from economies of scale realized as the economy grows.[38]

Estimating the net contribution of economies of scale presents difficulties. Denison earlier put at about 10 percent the gains in national income from economies of scale that resulted when the national market in the United States grew. He put the percentage for European countries not much higher.[39] Scale economies raised the growth rate 12–32 percent in the United States and European countries in subperiods of the period 1950–1962.[40] Denison later put at about 13 percent the fraction of the United States growth rate that was attributable to economies of scale.[41]

Of course, whatever be the contribution of economies of scale to increase in output per unit of input, only a fraction of it can be traced to growth of population as such, a fraction that depends on the composition

of output, inasmuch as the scope for economies of scale varies with industry and activity. For example, as Clark points out, increase in the demand for services, governmental and private, "can only be supplied under
conditions of productivity increase much slower than in manufacture or
transport. Productivity increase in the building and construction sector is
also slow."[42] However, Denison estimates that while an increasing shift
to services can slow the growth of productivity, the growth rate in output
per person will be reduced by only 0.12 to 0.14 of a percentage point.[43]

Estimation of the contribution of economies of scale presents difficulties.
Jorgenson and Griliches initially imputed 96.7 percent of the rate of
growth of output to the growth of inputs, leaving only 3.3 percent to be
attributed to change in "total factor productivity," putting at only 0.10
percentage points the increase in output per unit of input.[44] Subsequently
Jorgenson and Christensen prepared new estimates, putting at 0.43, 0.31,
and 0.36, respectively, the fractions of the average annual growth in real
product in 1929–1948, 1948–1967, and 1929–1967, respectively, attributable to increase in factor productivity instead of to real factor input.[45] Denison had attributed about one-fourth of the increase in output
per unit of input in 1929–1969 to economies of scale.[46] Dan Usher denies
the separability of economies of scale from technical change, saying "that
output per head would not have increased at all since 1929 if technical
change had ceased at that time." Technical change not only makes possible
changes with which increase in productivity is associated;[47] it also leads
to increase in the capital stock and may affect labor-force participation.[48]
Moreover, economists underestimate the importance of technological
progress and then attribute to "scale phenomena that which in truth is
the consequence of even greater improvements in the successive generations of capital goods." Whence some economists "lean generally to the
view that constant returns is the conservative view regarding scale proper-
ties of our economy."[49] In any case, given a correct estimate of economies
of scale as a source of growth, there remains the task of discovering the
fraction of this source that can be traced to population growth.

(5) *Utilizable Physical Assets per Head.* A nation's physical assets are
of three sorts: (a) those that are reproducible and hence augmentable as
well as depletable, (b) those that are assumed to be constant (e.g., land
if conserved, some power sources), and (c) those that are depletable
and finally exhaustible (e.g., many mineral and energy sources). Distinction between categories (b) and (c) is not always sharp; for excessive
use of what appear to be fixed and nondepletable physical assets may
partly destroy them, sometimes in ways that make impossible their full
restoration and subsequent use. For example, cultivation or use that is
excessive, neglectful of maintenance of a resource's quality (e.g., fertility

of the soil, topography, water flow), or destructive of fragile ecosystems (especially in the tropics) can deplete even if it does not completely destroy assets that could be treated as fixed under suitable conditions of use. Accordingly, it is essential to determine if population growth contributed to conversion of some supposedly fixed assets into assets subject to partial depletion.

Turning now to the impact of population growth upon aggregate and per capita savings, we find that opinions differ. Inasmuch as population growth absorbs resources that might otherwise have assumed productive forms of human and nonhuman capital, per capita savings and capital formation can be higher in a stationary than in a growing population, particularly if the age structure of the growing population makes for higher per capita output. Population growth may, however, intensify motivation to save and conduce to dynamism, economies of scale, and flexibility. Both Kelley and Kuznets point to ways in which population growth may stimulate savings, though not necessarily in sufficient degree to offset decrease in ability to save and thereby increase savings per capita. Kuznets suggests also that pressure of population upon savings may stimulate capital-saving innovation, and Kelley presents findings which "cast some doubt on the widely applied generalizations relating to the strong negative impact of children on household savings rates."[50]

Modigliani and Brumberg find a growing population favorable to net saving. For such a population will include a disproportionately small number of retired people and hence of dissavers. Moreover, since real income per head will be rising, savers will tend to have larger lifetime incomes than dissavers. They estimate that for rates of growth up to 5 percent in either real income per head or population, each 1 percent of growth would lead to 3–4 percent of aggregate real income being saved. Of course, whether this supposed saving rate increases assets per capita turns on the adequacy and the disposition of this saving.[51]

Clark too stresses the stock of savings rather than per capita savings.

> Population growth, other things being equal, is found to have a positive effect upon savings. This indeed is to be expected, on the grounds, amongst others, that a slow growing population will have a higher proportion of old people, who tend to consume rather than to save capital; that parents of larger families may make more effort to save for them; and, perhaps most important, that with larger families younger men expect less inheritance, and therefore have to make greater efforts to accumulate for themselves.

> In assessing the effect of increasing rates of population growth on the rate of savings, we should bear in mind that, for low income countries, the capital-output ratio is usually of the order of magnitude of 2 or less; and therefore the effect of the increased savings upon the capital stock will also be significant.[52]

Clark does not, of course, allow for the increase in resource consumption (e.g., mineral exhaustion) that is likely to be associated with a heightened rate of population growth, especially after a country has become adequately settled and its resource potential determined.

The potential for output-increasing savings per capita tends to be greater when a population is near-stationary than when it is growing, for population growth absorbs capital or savings that might otherwise be invested in assets designed to increase output. Moreover, some population-oriented investment (e.g., housing) is less conducive to increase in output than is business-oriented investment.[53] Kendrick has found, for example, that provision for growth of population in 1883–1953 annually absorbed 4.5 percent of Gross National Product (GNP). His data suggest that a continuing rate of population growth of 1 percent annually absorbed about 3.2 percent of GNP or about 3.8 percent of national income.[54] Kuznets found that between 1870 and 1949

> when population-sensitive capital formation was increasing more rapidly, other capital formation was increasing less rapidly, and vice versa. It suggests also that there were limits to total capital formation with the result that acceleration (or deceleration) in the population-sensitive components left so much less (or so much more) room for growth of other capital formation. This restraining influence of a limit on total capital formation appears to have been removed in the 1920's, and synchronism has prevailed since then.[55]

Capital limitation in turn sets limits to the amount of population growth realizable through immigration without depressing average output.[56]

One may say roughly that with the ratio of tangible wealth to national income in the neighborhood of 4 to 1 and with a stable population growing 1 percent per year, maintenance of the wealth–population ratio at a constant level would call for an increase of 1 percent in the stock of tangible wealth—that is, for the investment of at least 4 percent of the national income in the maintenance of the wealth–population ratio. Given a stationary population, this 4 percent might be available for increasing productive wealth per capita by 1 percent, provided that wage increases consequent upon cessation of labor-force growth do not slow capital formation and stimulate labor-displacing investment.[57] Our assumed 4-to-1 ratio, even if characteristic of an economy, changes with the composition of output and input and other conditions, and may affect the input-absorbing capacity of population growth accordingly.[58]

The wealth–population ratio, together with the increase in wealth essential to offset a continuing 1 percent per year increase in a roughly stable population, depends upon what is included in the "wealth" category —all wealth or capital, only reproducible capital, or human capital as well. Over time the ratio of physical assets to output or income has fallen because agencies of production besides "capital," "wealth," or "physical assets" have cooperated with labor in producing output. For example, allowance for investment in human capital in the form of education was omitted as a rule. Yet, T. W. Schultz estimated, the capital–income ratio in 1929 and 1957 approximated 6 when investment in education was included,[59] thus implying that *ceteris paribus* a continuing 1 percent per year increase in population would require an annual investment of somewhat less than 6 percent of the national income to maintain the average output level in the face of the population growth. Moreover, since investment in human capital undergoes deterioration as does investment in reproducible physical capital, it needs to be maintained as does reproducible capital.[60] Both forms are subject to obsolescence as well, especially in a dynamic society. Similarly, investment in replacement of human as of physical capital has an improvement bias that reflects a society's growth of knowledge. Only in a static society is mere capital replacement possible; in a dynamic society mere replacement in a physical sense might amount to investment in some actual or prospective obsolescences.[61] Moreover, since humans unlike capital produce children, there can be productive second- or third-generational effects beyond investment in the education of the first generation.

Respecting physical assets in fixed aggregate supply (e.g., land, recreational areas), we may say that continued population growth within a country as well as increase in average income accentuates the relative long-run scarcity of these assets, thereby affecting average output and welfare unfavorably and eventually compelling recourse to the discovery of substitutes, or to reduction of the input of these fixed-supply assets per unit of output, or to importation of the peculiar products of these assets from regions where they remain underutilized.

Respecting physical assets, the stock of which is subject to depletion and eventual exhaustion, response to their growing physical scarcity may be subject to delay. For depletion may not be reflected immediately in costs of production and rising prices that consequently stimulate search for substitutes as well as reduction in their input per unit of output. Depletion may, of course, be reflected in growth of pollutants and the costs of coping with pollutants—costs whose increase is likely to prompt greater economy in the use of some depletable assets, particularly if the costs are made incident upon the purchasers of the resources subject to depletion.[62]

Fixity is not a characteristic of the existing stock of any particular set of physical assets known to man, since more may be discovered and a larger fraction of what is known may become subservient to man's uses. Fixity is characteristic, however, of the stock initially in existence—a stock that therefore is depletable through use. This stock, being subject to depletion, thus differs from the stock of man-made instruments or artifacts, or from the stock of "human capital," in existence at any time; for those stocks, while subject to depreciation, are subject to replacement and augmentation. Of course, the augmentability even of those stocks is limited by the availability of critical components entering into their composition.

While growth of population is responsible for increase in the use of both fixed and depletable physical assets—mainly when the income-elasticity of demand for these assets and products into which they enter is low—growth of average consumption often is much more responsible than growth of population.[63] Moreover, insofar as increase in average income due to slowing of population growth augments average consumption of depletable resources and of output flowing from fixed-supply resources, the capacity of a slowing of population growth to ease the growth of pressure upon these two sets of resources is reduced. Nor does it make less difficult than it might otherwise be the resource problems confronting tomorrow's generations as a result of depletion in the near future. Nor can technical progress continue to counterbalance depletion.[64]

(6) *Human Capital per Capita.* Given a static society and a stationary population, gross investment in human capital serves only to replace the human capital consumed by use, wear, and mortality. When, however, a society is dynamic and in need of "better" human capital though based on a stationary population, gross investment in human capital will exceed that consumed by use, wear, mortality, and obsolescence. When, however, a population is growing, say 1 percent annually, gross investment in human capital must cover both *all* outlay upon the 1 percent added annually to the population base and, as in the previous case, needed "better" human capital. What this will amount to turns on whether say (a) a stationary population *begins* to grow 1 percent annually and hence must wait 18–20 years before this series of annual increments begins to produce, or (b) the population under analysis is already stable and growing 1 percent per year continuously. In these or other cases in which a population is growing, net total investment in human capital will be higher than in a stationary population under otherwise comparable conditions. However, because less investment is required in the last case, more resources per capita remain free to make investment per capita higher either in human capital, or in other forms of capital, or both, with the result that *ceteris paribus* average output can become higher than in the other cases.

In view of what has been said in (5) and (6) respecting physical assets and human capital, in a stationary population a considerable amount of annual income will normally be available for investment beyond what would be available if the population were stable and growing (say) 1 percent per year. While the actual amount depends on circumstances, it may amount to 5 percent or more of the national income. Annual investment of this available amount may in turn make possible a higher annual rate of increase in annual income—perhaps as high as one percentage point—than would be realizable were the population stable and growing 1 percent annually but subject to *ceteris paribus*. This differential advantage would be somewhat less, of course, if relatively more resources had to be invested in retraining and so on, should relatively more older workers be subject to job changes calling for the acquisition of new knowledge —changes somewhat avoidable if less interoccupational mobility is called for in a stationary population.

Investment in human capital is accompanied by side effects that bear upon productivity in varying degrees. For example, since quality of children is inversely related to number of children,[65] greater emphasis upon investment in the education of children makes for reduction in their number, thus substituting human-capital deepening for human-capital widening. Again degree of education is a factor affecting labor-force participation directly and indirectly[66] and through the medium of the impact of education on health and employability if it is not affected adversely by other circumstances (e.g., unionization).[67]

The productivity of investment in human capital in the form of education is conditioned by the "natural ability" of the person subject to education. "Ability is an important determinant of earnings; . . . for the same group of people the effects of education and ability do not increase at the same rate with age."[68] The effect of education continues longer than the effect of ability. Quality of the institutions of higher education "has an important impact on lifetime earnings of those who attend."[69]

Investment in human capital is complementary to investment in technological progress (see below), a partial antidote to natural-resource exhaustion. As Beckman writes: "Positive technical progress is required in order that resource exhaustion should not lead to an eventual inevitable decline of the utility level. The rate of technical change properly weighted with the coefficients of the utility and the elasticities of the production function impose an upper bound upon the permissible rates of exhaustion."[70] Even so, as Lydall observes in his critique of W. Beckerman's *In Defence of Growth* and expression of confidence in technology, should the price mechanism prove inadequate: "The mind boggles at the whole world industrialised up to the American level."[71] At the same time, R. L. Gordon makes a good case for the proposition that "policies designed to increase the weight given to future demands" can speed up mineral exhaustion by discouraging mineral-resource exploitation.[72] However, disregard of the impact of current consumption upon future options may contribute to high current consumption and accelerate exhaustion, as Georgescu-Roegen indicates.[73]

While population growth does not affect the rationale of investment, it does affect what is the appropriate *aggregate* amount of net investment of all sorts and how this aggregate should be divided between human capital and other forms of capital.[74] When a stable population is growing very little if at all, greater investment per person in younger age groups is possible than when a population is growing. At the same time more investment per capita may be necessary when a population is stationary to keep the population dynamic and sufficiently abreast of change to be adequately mobile.

(7) *State of Technology.* Most important of the sources of increase in per capita productivity in modern societies has been technical progress, the application of which has, however, been contingent upon adequate investment in appropriate tangible assets, knowledge, and manpower training. While estimates of the contribution of technical progress differ, they usually are relatively high;[75] indeed, technical experience and education together explain much intercountry difference in productivity.[76] The impact of advances in knowledge and technology differs, of course, from the impact of increases in the total input of factors (i.e., labor, capital, education), in that these advances increase output per unit of input, thus resembling the impact of increase in capital per worker upon output per worker.

Turning now to estimates of the contribution of advances in knowledge and what is not otherwise accounted for, we find Denison putting this contribution at about 62 percent of the increase in output per unit of input in the United States in 1948–1969 and at 31 percent of the annual increase in national income. This contribution, together with that of economies of scale—23 percent of the increase in output per unit of input—thus accounted for 85 percent of the increase in output per unit of input.[77] Earlier the findings of R. Solow (a leader in the revival in the 1950s of the study of the contribution of technological change to growth) suggested that between 1909 and 1949 technological change increased at a rate of about 1.5 percent per year "the output that could be derived from a fixed amount of inputs."[78] As has already been implied, however, estimates of the contribution of advances in knowledge—put at 40 to about 90 percent—to increase in output per capita in the United States, "are extremely rough," given the character of historical statistics and "the complex interactions among the various factors that affect the economic development of a country."[79] But the contribution is high even at the lower end of the range of estimates.

There is little or no evidence that population growth as such contributes to advance in knowledge on balance, though, within limits, increase in density might. Of course, stationarity of the labor force could encourage the development and introduction of labor-saving innovations, and the prospect of market expansion due to population growth could favor cost-reducing innovations not yet profitable.[80] However, the incentive to cut labor costs is always strong in laboristic societies, and there is always incentive in a competitive world to cut product-costs and thus increase security of markets if not also profits. The pressure to advance knowledge, innovate, and adopt improvements in products and methods of production is great within advanced economies inasmuch as firms face competition not only at home but also in the international markets into which they export.

In a sense the character and quality of man's long-run future may be described as dependent upon the course of the race between technological progress and increasing entropy, even given a slackening of the rates of population growth and economic consumption. For, as Georgescu-Roegen points out, even as exponential growth cannot continue without interruption in a finite world, so zero population and capital growth characteristic of a stationary state cannot persist in a world subject to increasing entropy, to exhaustion of its finite sources of energy and critical materials. "The crucial error consists in not seeing that not only growth, but also a zero-growth state, nay, even a declining state which does not converge toward annihilation, cannot exist forever in a finite environment." Given a finite amount of resources in the crust of the earth and limits to the earth's so-called carrying capacity, "a steady state may exist in fact only in an approximated manner and over a finite duration,"[81] with duration dependent on population size and average consumption. Technological progress serves, on the one hand, to increase the fraction of man's biosphere that can be made subservient to his purposes, including in particular his capacity to utilize solar energy and marshal the alchemic potential of energy use. On the other hand, technological progress increases average consumption and hence average resource use, and it may contribute to population growth as well. Technological progress cannot, therefore, long play the critical role it is assigned in either steady-state or potential-growth models; it cannot continually triumph over limitational factors, though it may be directed to the reduction of resource depletion and of production of pollutants.

While the stationary state, though (some believe) less congenial to technological progress than a growing state, is put forward as an attractive alternative to a growing state, it is subject to difficulties as well. Thus, as Georgescu-Roegen points out,

> there are simple reasons against believing that mankind can live in a perpetual stationary state. The structure of such a state remains the same

throughout; it does not contain in itself the seed of the inexorable death of all open macrosystems. On the other hand, a world with a stationary population would, on the contrary, be continually forced to change its technology as well as its mode of life in response to the inevitable decrease of resource accessibility. Even if we beg the issue of how capital may change qualitatively and still remain constant, we would have to assume that the unpredictable decrease in accessibility will be miraculously compensated by the right innovations at the right time. A stationary world may for a while be interlocked with the changing environment through a system of balancing feedbacks analogous to those of a living organism during one phase of its life. But as Bormann reminded us, the miracle cannot last forever; sooner or later the balancing system will collapse. At that time, the stationary state will enter a crisis, which will defeat its alleged purpose and nature.[82]

(8) *Organization and Direction of Economy.* How an economy is organized and directed bears upon the strength of some of the other sources of growth, together with the degree to which inputs, especially of labor, capital, and investment in applied science and technology, are optimally allocated and supplied. Denison put at about 20 percent the fraction of the increase in output of national income per unit of input in 1929–1969 attributable to "improved resource allocation."[83] Absence of barriers to mobility, together with an adequate flow of information relating to the availability and type of jobs[84] and to future natural-resource, economic, and investment prospects,[85] characterizes a well-organized and directed-economy. Given power blocs[86] (e.g., trade unions), monopolies, and premiums on idleness,[87] together with the overpricing of inputs, especially of labor through trade-union and government intervention, tendencies to unemployment and malallocation of inputs and income are strengthened.[88]

When a population and hence the labor force are growing slightly, there should be less need for change in employment than in a stationary situation, since the annual net increment to the labor force can contribute to the approximation of optimum interoccupational and interindustrial balance. Moreover, since the fraction of the labor force under (say) 25 will be somewhat larger, there may be a greater number of employed persons still at the margin of transference to other employments. In 1955 about 10.6 percent of those occupying civilian jobs changed jobs, three-fourths of them (even among those 35 to 54) making radical changes. Denison concludes that the relative number of job changes was "probably sufficient for one purpose for which mobility is needed: to make earnings differentials an effective allocator of the total labor supply among employers, industries, and occupations."[89] Gallaway, having distinguished between "stayers" and "movers," finds the latter responsive to "differences in income levels among industries" and "individuals moving between geographic areas in a highly purposive and intelligent fashion in quest of better economic opportunities."[90] Respecting interoccupational mobility, he finds workers responsive to interoccupational differences in advantages as well as a "substantial amount of opportunity for individuals to move between different occupations."[91] These findings suggest, therefore, that sensitivity to advantages associated with mobility should prove great enough to counterbalance increase in the amount of mobility called for in a stationary population, particularly given the conduciveness of improved education and experience to optimal resource allocation in response to changes in economic conditions.[92] Furthermore, the "possibilities of substitution between different types of labour" may greatly facilitate the approach to a near optimal pattern of labor use.[93] Kuznets infers that a growing labor force will be more mobile and flexible than a stationary one, and that a population which is growing and hence younger will be more responsive to new products and hence to inventiveness and "forward-looking" ventures and investment than will a nongrowing and more stagnant population.[94]

The organization and direction of a country's economy may be somewhat conditioned by the size of a country and nation. Since a nation as a collectivity exercises more control over its own economy than over those with which it trades, it is likely to enjoy freer and probably more competitive trade within its boundaries than across them. Although a nation, if it is relatively small, is less likely than a large one to be composed of heterogeneous, potentially destabilizing, cultural elements, it will probably be less sufficient in terms of natural resources and more dependent upon external trade for raw materials, markets, and the opportunity to realize scale economies and its own differential advantages more fully. Denison concluded, however, respecting the European countries contrasted, that "in the absence of manmade barriers to international specialization of production," differences in "the availability of farmland and mineral resources" though great "would create little difference in national income per person employed under present-day conditions."[95]

E. A. G. Robinson reports, moreover, that the general impression formed by a conference on effects of national size was that "most of the major industrial economies of scale could be achieved by a relatively high-income nation of 50 million; that nations of 10–15 million were probably too small to get all the technical economies available; that the industrial economies of scale beyond a size of 50 million were mainly those that derive from a change in the character of competition and specialization."[96] Of course, superpower status, being largely military in character, may currently call for as much as two hundred million or more population.

Denison points out, in his comparative study of growth in the United States and eight European countries, that it is not the industries serving local and regional markets that are likely to generate marked differences. "If the size of nations creates a difference among countries in gains from economies of scale that are reflected in the growth rates of national income measured in the United States prices, the difference ought to be concentrated in industries that serve national or international markets. These are mainly commodity-producing industries." Denison found, however, that small European countries did "not suffer a great deal more than the large European countries from diseconomies of scale," the absence of which made output per man only about 4 percent higher in the United States than in the large Northwest European countries.[97] On the basis of an international comparison of production establishments, Pryor concludes that size of market is the chief limit to size of establishment, and that the smaller the domestic market, the more important is the size of the foreign market.[98]

(9) *Dynamism of Economy.* Population growth can reenforce the dynamic change. Second, somewhat more weight may be given to the somewhat removed future when currently young but increasingly large increments to the population enter adulthood and the labor force. Third, when a population is growing, the nondiscretionary component of aggregate consumer expenditure, to be discussed later, is relatively larger *ceteris paribus* than when a population is not growing. As a result aggregate demand may be viewed as more stable than when much of aggregate expenditure is nondiscretionary and hence stable in character. As Friedman suggests, however, what Kuznets calls a "climate of belief in the future" supposedly associated with population growth has its origin in conditions other than population growth as such.[99] Most responsible probably is the amount of resources invested in science, research, development, and communication of the results and prospects to the population at large. Kuznets has suggested also that additions to the stock of knowledge are the work of a few exceptionally gifted individuals, of whom there are more in large than in small populations.[100]

Among the characteristics that are associated with the dynamism of an economy is the relative size of its appropriately educated class, together with what may be called the time-horizon of the entrepreneurial and creative classes. While the former condition reflects the amount and character of a society's investment in human capital and technologically oriented science, the latter reflects a society's age structure, in that those in moderately young age groups (say 20–40) tend to be more energetic, innovative, and animated by a longer time-horizon than those who are older (say over 40). Insofar as this is true, a moderately growing population will have an advantage over a stationary one inasmuch as there are relatively fewer persons aged 20--40 years in a stationary population.

2. Is Population Growth Endogenous to an Economy?

In what has gone before, attention has been focused on the impact of population growth upon economic growth, but not upon the response of population growth to economic growth. While there may, of course, be no response, Kelley finds that population growth "may have been quite responsive to economic, environmental, and social change."[101] This has been true in particular of net immigration, since, as a rule, immigrants, together with migrants within a country, move to situations they expect to find more advantageous than those which they plan to leave. Furthermore, insofar as parenthood is voluntary, it is essentially the outcome of the belief that the utility expected of one or more children will outweigh the actual and expected as well as the opportunity costs of additional children within variable limits. Accordingly, as a society undergoes economic, environmental, and social change, actual and anticipated costs and utility at the margin may change, with the result that current and eventually total fertility will move upward or downward.[102] While the economy may in turn adjust to this change in fertility, this adjustment may not further affect fertility, and a new equilibrium between economy and fertility will have been established. Of course, such an equilibrium may prove temporary, since children resemble discretionary goods and services. Indeed, fluctuation in natality and number of births is likely, especially if pronounced, to alter the age structure and produce fluctuation in future natality via echo effects.[103]

3. Size of State; International Setting

The size of a state may influence economies of scale in at least four ways: (a) by its impact on the efficiency of the apparatus of state as such, given the degree of cultural and racial heterogeneity of the underlying population; (b) by its capacity to exercise power within the international network of states; (c) by its provision of a theater within which forms of increasing return can find expression; and (d) by its capacity to supply biospheric elements essential to economic activity. The impact of size under each of these four headings is, of course, conditioned by the multiplicity of a state's goals and the aggregate burden imposed on its apparatus and the underlying economy.

(a) An economy's capacity is conditioned by the organizational structure and decisions of the nation-state to whose sovereignty this economy is subject.[104] Given the degree of cultural and racial heterogeneity of the population, the apparatus of state may be about optimal size, or less than or in excess of this size, for the feedback or regulative mechanisms governing this apparatus may not develop in keeping with the size and number of a state's functions. As we note below, while the populations of a few states appear to be of supra-optimum political size, most are too small.

(b) An economy is subject to international political as well as economic constraints. For every economy is part of "the world economy," which "like the economy of a single country, can be visualized as a system of interdependent processes," with each process generating certain outputs and absorbing "a specific combination of inputs."[105] The autonomy of a nation-state economy is restrained, therefore, by its role within the world economy, not only by the impact of international corporations, agencies, agreements, and monetary and investment policies,[106] but also by constraints incident upon a state's pursuit of domestic policies (e.g., smallness of its multiplier due to external leakage). Furthermore, a small state, lacking the political and military power of a large state, may also be more vulnerable to economic constraints of political origin, such as cartellization and interruption of exchange and the normal flow of imports and exports.[107]

(c) While most states are too small in the absence of freedom of international trade to exploit economies of scale fully, their capacity to do so often may be greater than is commonly supposed; for, as Stigler has found, "there is customarily a fairly wide range of optimum sizes of firms,"[108] a condition that tends to reduce state size required to maximize scale economies. However, Robinson put at around 50 million population the size of a developed economy essential to full economies of scale, and Keesing found that "small countries appeared to experience a comparative disadvantage in most of the important manufacturing industries, uncompensated by a comparative advantage in others."[109] While it is true that decreasing returns may be encountered in small economies,[110] a number of small countries rank among those topmost in average income. Several countries (e.g., Switzerland, Sweden) with 6 and 8 million inhabitants, respectively, have been realizing levels of GNP per capita close to or above that of the United States. Moreover, of the 15 non–oil-rich countries ranking highest in GNP per capita in 1973, 10 had populations of less than 10 million.

(d) As a rule, small countries are less well equipped than large ones with the natural resources or biospheric elements basic to modern economies. For this reason, together with the need of small countries to seek economies of scale through export trade, such countries are more dependent than large countries on international trade; whence the ratio of foreign trade to Gross National Product varies inversely with a country's size.[111] Even so, most large high-income countries are quite dependent on foreign sources for critical and strategic natural resources, even as are some small countries.[112]

Maximization of scale economies at the international level turns on the achievement of international freedom of trade. For in 1973 only 15 of the world's states included 50 or more million inhabitants; 71 numbered less than 10 million, and 40 had populations of 10 to 40 million.[113] Of 125 countries for which GNP is given, only 19 averaged $3,000 or more GNP per capita, 19 averaged between $1,000 and $3,000, 20 averaged $500 to $1,000, 45 averaged $120 to $500, and 22 averaged under $120. Moreover, only 19 countries produced an aggregate GNP in excess of $50 billion, thereby providing a correspondingly large domestic market, but of these only 14 averaged more than $2,000 per capita. Accordingly, internal markets in most countries are not only limited, but, as Chenery shows, not easily expanded through industrialization in the present international setting.[114] Despite obstacles to trade expansion, it can contribute relatively rapidly to the generation of scale economies, whereas population growth can only contribute very slowly and then possibly may result in adverse externalities comparable to those that accompany city growth but less likely to be compensated over time.[115]

Despite the economic and other disadvantages under which very small states operate, their number has greatly increased since World War II, in part because large states have allowed the small states both to exist and to limit the autonomy of large states. Today, for example, a "decisive two-thirds" of the vote dominating "U. N. decision making" is in the hands of a group of diminutive states that altogether pay "only $2\frac{1}{2}$ cents of each U. N. budget dollar." Moreover, the current situation is destined to worsen since the number of "independent" nations, 64 in 1940 and 155 in 1975, could increase to 305. By 1976, 16 of the microstates numbered only 100 to 300 thousand inhabitants, and 16 ranged in size only from 300,000 to 1,000,000. Indeed, 63 of the 155 states ranged in population from 100,000 to 500,000, whereas only 26 numbered 25 or more million.[116]

In light of earlier discussion, increase in population would have but limited effect upon the state of returns in many of the microstates, limited as they are in territorial scope.[117] It is true that national diversity may contribute to world progress by providing "a favorable and desirable milieu for the evolution of new methods and innovations in such areas as material technology and social arrangements.[118] Most of the very small states, however, lack the elements essential to the generation of progress.

Conclusion

Our review of the many factors responsible for increase in output per capita suggests that even if a country is small and its population is stationary or nearly so, it can achieve a level of output per capita on a par with or higher than that achieved by a larger country with a growing population. Population growth is not essential to growth per capita and may even be a deterrent if it absorbs too much of a nation's flow of savings, or adversely affects a nation's terms of trade. A small country may, of course, be more dependent upon international trade than a large country and hence vulnerable to the introduction of barriers to trade. In our modern world, however, large countries with large populations, whether stationary or growing, face similar problems. Moreover, industrialists and trade unions in countries encountering foreign competition tend to act more aggressively against large than small foreign exporters (e.g., against Japan than against Scandinavian countries or Taiwan).

IX. Cessation of Population Growth: Implications, Problem Areas

> *As Professor Knight has repeatedly reminded us in recent years, all human activity is problem-solving.*
> L. M. Lachmann, *Economica*, Feb., 1943, p. 15

In this chapter and the one following we examine in summary fashion implications of cessation of population growth, building somewhat upon what has gone before, but in the main looking at the incidence of population stationarity upon a selected set of problems. This review indicates that the approach of a stationary population is economically advantageous provided that a decline in numbers, now a possibility, is averted and that the behavior of the economy and polity is in keeping with the requirements of zero population growth.

A common set of problems confronts every population's economy. The importance of any one of these problems is likely to be affected by demographic variables and parameters characteristic of the population in question, in particular by rate of population growth, age structure, sources of population growth, migration, and population distribution. Among the more important of the problem areas affected are those relating to employment, allocation of factors of production, the distribution of national income, and international economic relations.

We shall review briefly the impact of stationarity or near stationarity of population upon major economic problem areas and the options available for dealing with these problems. Problem areas are common, of course, to all types of populations. However, the concrete specific problems confronting a stable population growing (say) 3 percent per year will differ from those confronting a stable or near-stable population with a rate of growth in the neighborhood of zero.

Our analysis is focused mainly upon the behavior of economies when a population is roughly stable and stationary, not upon those in transit. Transition problems may arise, however, if a population moves from one stable state to another, say from a state of growth of 1 or 2 percent to a stationary state. How intense these problems prove turns on the degree to which this movement is smooth and along an optimal rather than a suboptimal route.

A. Problem Solving

Coping with economic problems that come in the wake of a slowing down or cessation of population growth in the United States turns mainly on the skill and flexibility of private enterprise, supplemented if necessary by the apparatus of state. The main function of private enterprise, transforming inputs into output, remains unaltered by the rate of population growth or by the advent of a stationary population. For, while there will be changes in the composition and growth of input and output, the objective, transformation of inputs into output compatible with augmentation of utility or serviceability and realization of essential profit, will remain the same.

So long as barriers are not placed in the way of factor mobility by agencies of the state and / or quasi-monopolistic agencies (e.g., trade unions, oligopolistic or monopolistic organizations), entrepreneurs should experience no increase in net difficulty attendant upon the transformation process. For if, as G. J. Stigler observes in another connection, "business is the collection of devices for circumventing barriers to profits," changes associated with population growth and aging are hardly adequate to thwart businessmen.[1] Moreover, as Kirzner demonstrates, the entrepreneur is the key decision-maker in the market, the "decision-maker whose entire role arises out of his alertness to hitherto unnoticed opportunities."[2]

Inasmuch as "countless opportunities are passed up" by "market participants," it is the function of the entrepreneur to overcome this unawareness, to discover information "concerning new sources of resources, new technological opportunities, new possible combinations of product specifications, new patterns of consumer tastes," and to generate relevant production plans.[3] The producer in his capacity as entrepreneur supplies "the talent needed to organize factors of production into a smoothly working team," together with "the resources needed to effectively complete the transactions which his entrepreneurship suggests he enter into."[4] The "kind of 'knowledge' required for entrepreneurship is 'knowing where to look for knowledge' rather than knowledge of substantive market information."[5] Challenges issuing out of the approach of a stationary population may be expected to yield to "the active, alert, searching role of entrepreneurial activity,"[6] even as those associated with population growth have yielded.

What has been said is applicable to large-scale as well as small-scale entrepreneurs. Presumably the large-scale entrepreneur is better equipped with resources than the small-scale entrepreneur to support a new undertaking. Even so, more opportunities will probably continue to be discovered by small-scale entrepreneurs, since there are so many more of them, and they are initially satisfied with exploiting small economic niches that are without much appeal to large operators even if perceived. Of overriding importance, however, is the multiplicity of the searchers for new opportunities.

B. Institutional Structure

While a state's institutional structure changes over time as technological and other conditions change, much less change takes place in the functions that an institutional structure is designed to perform. Moreover, at any given time a range of institutional options is available for the performance of these functions. The overriding problem thus consists in selecting the optimal set of institutional arrangements available, together with their effective use. This problem confronts a population that is roughly stable and stationary, as well as one that is growing regularly or irregularly.

How an institutional structure changes over time may be illustrated with reference to the United States around 1900—specifically with reference to "old age," the last stage of adulthood, the stage marked by increasing withdrawal of older persons from effective participation in communal activities. The importance of this stage has increased over the past hundred years as white life expectancy has risen—from 41.74 and 43.50 years for Massachusetts males and females in 1878–1882 to 68.4 and 76.1 for American males and females in 1973. Table IX.1 has been devised to illustrate the nature of this increase.

Given a population that is stable and stationary, the fraction of the population about to enter or already within the withdrawal category increases with life expectancy, in large part, of course, because fertility is lower in a low-mortality than in a high-mortality stationary population. Table IX.1 serves to illustrate the impact of variation in life expectancy. Let us describe those in the 65–74 group as approaching or entering the withdrawal category, and those 75 and over as consisting almost entirely of persons in the withdrawal category. The fraction 65 and over is over

Table IX.1. Stationary Age Structure; Male and Female

	Male		Female	
(1) Life Expectancy	73.9	39.7	77.5	42.5
(2) All Ages	100.0	100.0	100.0	100.0
(3) 20–64	57.42	57.17	55.94	56.85
(4) 65–74	9.47	4.94	10.21	5.89
(5) 75 & over	6.48	1.77	8.31	2.47
(6) 65 & over	15.95	6.71	18.52	8.36
(7) (5)/(6)	0.41	0.26	0.45	0.30

Source: Coale and Demeny, *Regional Model Life Tables*, pp. 44, 72, 140, 168.

twice as high when life expectancy is at the high levels in Table IX.1 as when it is at the low levels (line 6). Moreover, when life expectancy is at the high level, the fraction of those 65 and over who are in the withdrawal category is $1\frac{1}{2}$ times as high as when life expectancy is at the lower level (line 7). Given the higher life expectancy in Table IX.1, together with a stable rate of population growth of -1.0 percent, the fraction 65 and over becomes 22.2 percent for males and 25.6 percent for females. Of these males about 43 percent are in the 75 and over category, and of the females, nearly 48 percent.

The increase in the proportion of aged, particularly of those who, voluntarily or under pressure (of governments, trade unions, and corporations), withdraw, may present problems to whose solution a commercial, exploitative, and bureaucratic society is badly adapted—particularly an institutionalized society whose decisions are governed by an individual's age rather than by his competence. In 1900, although 90 percent of the males between 55 and 65 and 68.4 percent of those over 65 were still employed, many persons over 64—24 percent of those in the population in Massachusetts in 1900—were dependent on charity, in part because workers, deemed unfit to fill prime jobs after age 45, were then shunted into very low-paying inferior jobs (e.g., sweeper) or dismissed.[7]

To the situation described there was a collective reaction of sorts, a reaction whose form continued that long-characteristic of an agricultural society. For, as Hareven points out:

> The insecurities and vagaries of old age, intensified by unstable employment and recurrent poverty at earlier ages, made collective economic strategies imperative for the family unit. The functions of old people in the late nineteenth and early twentieth century can be better understood within the framework of the family economy. Work careers and family organization were clearly intertwined, and reciprocity among family members along the life course was essential for survival in old age. Exchanges across generations were critical for the survival of old people, particularly in the working class, as an intensifying industrial system was gradually ousting them from their jobs without providing public-welfare mechanisms for their support.[8]

The solution described, such as it was, has become increasingly obsolete both because of the dispersal and / or break-up of the family and because of the increase in the relative number of aged persons. Only 4 percent of the male population of the United States were 65 years and over in 1900 compared with nearly 8.6 percent in 1970 and 16 or more percent in prospect. Moreover, in the nineteenth century a much smaller fraction of those over 64 were over 74 than is true of today's population or will be true of a future stationary population.

While the solution described above no longer is relevant, functions embodied therein need to be replicated. (1) The problems in prospect issue
largely out of the voluntary or enforced withdrawal of an increasing number of older persons from economic and related activities. (2) Since, given
family dispersal, work careers and family organization are no longer inter-
twined, a substitute for reciprocity among family members along the life
course becomes essential insofar as this reciprocity is reduced. (3) Although exchanges across generations are more critical than ever for older
people, these exchanges, no longer being realizable within the family
system, must be sought through a mechanism that guards older persons
and their dependents against real-income–destroying inflation and guaran-
tees them a share in the increase in average income, an increase imputable
in part to public and eleemosynary investment. (4) The mechanism best
suited to accomplish (3) may be a pay-as-you-go income-replacing system
reflecting both increase in money-income and increase in real-income per
member of the labor force. (5) Separate mechanisms are required against
contingencies other than that covered under (4), contingencies formerly
met by the family and / or charitable institutions. In sum, the advent of a
stationary or declining population is likely to call for important institutional changes.

C. Population Growth and Economic Expectations

The state of a nation's population growth, be it positive or negative,
tends to modify the structure of options available to a population, eliminating or reducing some and introducing others. It may also modify the
conspectus of subjective probabilities that individuals attach to the likelihood of realizing various options which they believe to be within reach.
Here relevant is the fact that cessation of population growth may modify
this conspectus, both by decreasing the relative number of younger persons
with longer planning-time horizons and increasing that of older persons
with shorter such horizons and by changing the demographic aspects of
the macroeconomic environment. Population growth therefore is to be
included among the determinants of the system of expectations by which
economic behavior is conditioned, particularly when these expectations
rest upon estimates of less-immediate prospects regarding which information is quite inadequate;[9] it also functions *inter alia* as a stabilizer (e.g.,
serving to sustain the demand for commodities with low income elasticities
and to support a relatively high propensity to consume).[10] The importance
of expectations in general derives from the fact that they mentally connect
the future with the present and help shape the present and through it the
future. Of the several categories of expectations, those of greatest significance (among them some relating to consumption) relate to a future some-

what removed from the present and bear upon the stability of the distribution of politico-economic power as well as upon the degree of confidence that entrepreneurs and potential buyers, especially those in economically critical industries, have in the future availability of adequate sales opportunities together with requisite inputs. Short-term expectations, however important per se and in the literature of expectations, lie outside our concern in this chapter, even though they may slightly influence investment-prompting anticipation relating to distant points in time.[11]

When a population ceases to grow, or decreases, it undergoes structural and processive changes and acquires new parameters—changes that may be accompanied by intensification of some economic problems and reduction of others. The substantive content of these problems varies both with the parametric structure and processive state of the population and with the psychological orientation of a society's major decision-makers. Should the latter condition be of minor import, outcomes will depend on the technical capacity of decision-makers and the market to respond to parametrical change as such. This capacity is subject to impairment, however, if a society's decision-makers undergo psychological reorientation unfavorable to making optimal response to parametrical change. The phenomenon of psychological orientation, essentially mental in character, may be examined under the general head of "expectations concerning the future" because they "affect what we do today,"[12] thereby giving shape to the future; it is important because uncertainty permeates an entrepreneur's interpretation of the validity and meaning of information relating to the future and the likely response thereto of other entrepreneurs.[13] Long-term expectations may even tend in some degree to be self-confirming if potentially realizable.[14]

As will be indicated in the next section, outstanding among the problems commonly associated with the slowing down or cessation of a nation's population growth, or the actual decline in its numbers, is the impact of such a trend upon difficulties connected with decline in the rate of investment. Also of importance, of course, are companion changes in the composition of consumption, the level and structure of employment, socioeconomic mobility and flexibility, the distribution of income, and social security. Most of these problems are somewhat interrelated. While they are assumed to be accentuated by an economy's having attained maturity,[15] coping with them is eased in some instances by advantages supposedly flowing from a low or zero rate of population growth.

While the term "expectations" as used here denotes a state of mind relating to a relatively limited time horizon, it may also refer to a belief respecting the persistence or nonpersistence of current biospheric or institutional conditions that constrain man's decisions and behavior. Illustrative of such belief is expectation concerning the prospective exhaustibility of relevant natural resources, together with the significance of resource depletion, or the future course of innovation in the U.S. Respecting such prospects men differ. For example, Nordhaus and Tobin reject the "tacit assumption of environmentalists that no substitutes are available for natural resources" and assert that "if the past is any guide for the future, there seems to be little reason to worry about the exhaustion of resources which the market already treats as economic goods." Presumably, the elasticity of substitution between natural resources and other factors is sufficiently high, and / or "resource-augmenting technological change" proceeds rapidly enough.[16] Much less optimistic, however, are Daly and Georgescu-Roegen [17] and those who fear the U.S. has lost its initiative in technological innovation.[18] Should one of these assessments take an unequivocally optimistic or a pessimistic turn, investment and other policies would be affected accordingly.

In what follows, the term "expectations" denotes mental states or states of mind, both individual and collective, that modify the response of individual and collective decision-makers in their capacities as purchasers and / or transformers of inputs into output. Expectations respecting tomorrow help shape tomorrow by shaping today's activities upon which tomorrow's activities depend. We may define this impact thus: $R = f (S, E)$ where R denotes decision-maker response, S denotes the concrete set of opportunities to which he is responding, and E denotes expectations that may condition R. Here E, while somewhat influenced by the availability of future markets, does not include ratiocinative behavioral tendencies but mainly outlooks such as great uncertainty, excessive pessimism, or excessive optimism ("animal spirits" Keynes sometimes called it) respecting the longer-run future course of events beyond the decision-maker's control.[19]

Expectations have been looked upon as important though instable determinants of the level of activity in both the short and the long run, particularly because of their bearing upon the making of long-term decisions relating to investment and possibly conducing to over- or under-reaction to change in S.[20] It remained for the advent of a declining rate of population growth, together with the emergence of investment as the supposedly dominant determinant of fullness of employment, to focus attention, especially that of Keynes and Hansen, upon the supposed role of longer-run expectations.

Keynes, in his *General Theory,* as we saw in Chapter IV, was concerned with analyzing the effects of uncertainty and disappointment in a world of which we lack knowledge about the future and its calculable uncertainty.[21] For, while he treated the stock of capital as constant in his main model, he pointed out that during the nineteenth century, the growth of population and of invention, the opening-up of new lands, the state of confidence and the frequency of war . . . seem to have been sufficient in conjunction with the propensity to consume, to establish a schedule of the marginal efficiency of capital which allowed a reasonably satisfactory average level of employment to be compatible with a rate of interest high enough to be psychologically acceptable to wealth owners.[22]

Moreover, a year later he tied business expectations to the population prospect and the demand for capital.

An increasing population has a very important influence on the demand for capital. Not only does the demand for capital—apart from technical changes and an improved standard of life—increase more or less in proportion to population. But, business expectations being based much more on present than on prospective demand, an era of increasing population tends to promote optimism, since demand will in general tend to exceed, rather than fall short of, what was hoped for. Moreover a mistake, resulting in a particular type of capital being in temporary over-supply, is in such conditions rapidly corrected. But in an era of declining population the opposite is true. Demand tends to be below what was expected, and a state of over-supply is less easily corrected. Thus a pessimistic atmosphere may ensue; and, although at long last pessimism may tend to correct itself through its effect on supply, the first result to prosperity of a change-over from an increasing to a declining population may be very disastrous.[23]

Writing much later, Pigou admitted the theoretical possibility that with population near stationary, investment, continuing from year to year, could lead to such "a filling-up of the profitable openings for capital that the rate of interest is only just above nil," with the possibility of a cumulative decline. But Pigou added that all this possibility was "before the war, with its massive destruction of capital assets." Pigou himself, anticipating new openings for profitable investment in the future as in the past due to scientific discovery, did not count upon the emergence of a "stationary state" of any sort, "neither heaven nor hell," though admitting an intermediate "purgatory." He also noted the possibility of a temporary increase in demand for capital due to an error of "optimism," an error easily nipped in the bud by Central Bank policy.[24] Later on J. E. Meade introduced the concepts of "capital glut" and "product glut" in his discussion of economic welfare.[25]

A net effect of Keynes's work was increase in the importance attached to the role of the psychological factor, "expectations." It also drew attention to the degree to which the future is unknowable and to limits to the "capacities of humans (and machines) for imagination and computation."[26] It is possible, however, to study the "ways humans do behave in complex decision-making situations" and infer "consequences of different modes of behavior."[27] For, while "the future is unknowable," it is not "unimaginable." "The world of the market economy is thus a kaleidic world of flux, in which the ceaseless flow of news daily impinges on human choice and the making of decisions."[28] Of course, memories of the past may affect reactions to the events of the present,[29] even as anticipations of concrete future events may modify it through the medium of the present (e.g., anticipation of technical progress).[30] Similarly, anticipation of the future structure of the market and its impact upon the degree of competition in the future may temporarily affect current investment.[31] Producer expectations based upon consumer expectations are somewhat similar in being likely to rest upon transitory conditions.[32]

Changes in the rate of population growth introduce uncertainty through a variety of channels and hence tend to affect expectations respecting the state of economic activity tomorrow in general as well as in specific areas —by the impact of uncertainty respecting the actual course of population growth, population aging, and so on, upon investment, consumption patterns, etc. Response to these changes is conditioned, however, by the character, quality, and number of a society's entrepreneurial decision-makers—a number that may increase if relative reduction in opportunity to rise in economic hierarchies prompts more individuals to become entrepreneurs.

The actual course of future population growth is not a known quantity. Despite improvement in the methodology of population projection, uncertainty does or may characterize current anticipations of the course of population growth even in the near future. Thus while it appears likely in the United States that fertility will remain in the neighborhood of the replacement level, determinants of fertility are subject to change. For example, increase in concern respecting the health[33] or destiny of potential parents' offspring could become a deterrent to reproduction, as could the absence of sufficiently strong microeconomic stimuli to parenthood, together with conditions facilitative of the pursuit, sequentially or simultaneously, of both motherhood and labor-force participation.[34]

Correctly forecasting marital fertility also remains virtually impossible even though crude approximations, especially of shorter-run trends, have been achieved. For family size not only reflects estimates both of direct and opportunity costs of children and of expectations of economic benefits to be derived from them; it also reflects potentially variable family interests that can transcend these estimates of economic costs and benefits. Accordingly, as Blandy observes, we may assume "that parents enjoy children on the whole (at least in anticipation) and that family size will not be reduced very much" without a prior "desire for family size to be less."[35]

Perceptions of net benefits associated with marriage and family formation can therefore change even in the absence of changes in economic costs and / or benefits, with the result that fertility rises or falls accordingly. Thus, even if the value of some benefits associated with parenthood (e.g., support in old age) are depreciated through the state's becoming responsible for their provision (e.g., through the establishment of security for older persons), the value of other benefits (e.g., desire for affection) may increase. For example, the anticipated value of affection to be bestowed on parents in old age may increase as alternative sources of affection, simulated and otherwise, are observed to be falling below expectations.[36]

D. Savings and Investment

Decline in the rate of population growth, age composition and other variable determinants being given, reduces the amount of capital per head required and likely to be demanded, compared with what it would be given a higher or rising rate of population growth. It also makes possible increase in the amount of savings per capita, since a smaller amount of inputs is required to form, develop, and equip increments to the population. Accordingly, imbalance will develop between savings and investment and prevent attainment of "full" employment unless interest rates and other variables respond adequately to bring about a new equilibrium in the form of higher per capita use of capital and / or lower per capita supply of savings. Such a change might, of course, require considerable time, entailing as it does both change in behavior and probably some change in relevant social parameters or institutions; it may be said to involve what post-Keynesians call expansion of "an economic system . . . over *time* in the context of *history*."[37]

Inasmuch as a continuing decline in population growth and investment is unlikely even though investment may fluctuate somewhat from year to year, partly in response to earlier minor fluctuations in the annual number of births, our major concern in this chapter is the impact of transition from one rate of population growth to a lower and relatively stable rate. For then not only are rates of saving and investment likely to be affected; the impact of these effects is likely to be accentuated by the accelerator principle, since the demand for some forms of capital may temporarily shrink or increase faster than demand for the services of this capital.[38] In the longer run, however, after a population, together with its rate of growth, has become stable, savings and investment tend to come into a rough balance, perhaps assisted by growth of government expenditure and capital consumption.

In the 1930s, as remarked earlier, concern arose lest decline in the rate of population growth, together with stagnation of other sources of demand for capital,[39] result in imbalance between savings and investment at a "full" or near-full employment level.[40] For so great had been the demand for capital, especially "population-sensitive" (or "widening" as distinguished from "deepening") capital,[41] that the aggregate demand for capital exceeded the total amount of capital being formed, with the result that requirements for capital other than "population-sensitive" types could not be wholly met.[42]

Will the advent of zero population growth greatly increase the likelihood of imbalance between the demand for savings or capital and the supply of savings or capital? We may symbolize the situation as follows. Let annual gross capital formation C consist of C_r, capital replacement; C_i, increment in capital per capita; and C_p, increment in capital to equip increment in population p. C_r depends on the size of the total stock K of capital or tangible reproducible assets, its age and average life, and the degree to which replacement, usually less pronounced among old than young property owners, is accelerated or postponed. C_i depends on the availability of "net savings" and the urgency of the need for C_p. Total stock K increases by $C_i + C_p$ each year if population is growing. If, however, $C_p = 0$, C_i tends to be somewhat greater than when $C_p > 0$, since some of the inputs that would otherwise have been absorbed by C_p will be released to C_i; moreover, with $C_p = 0$, replacement may accelerate somewhat and thus increase C_r. Indeed, given two similar stable populations, but with one stationary and the other growing 1 percent annually, the per capita capacity of the former to form capital should be appreciably higher *ceteris paribus*.[43] The potentially greater per capita saving capacity supposedly characteristic of a stationary population would not, however, fully materialize should taxation and / or consumption increase, or the gain be consumed in the form of greater leisure.

Data for the period 1952–1968 indicate recent orders of magnitude. Between 1952 and 1968 total reproducible assets increased (in billions of 1958 dollars) from 1,025 to 1,936, of which increase about 44 percent, or 533 billion, was associated with increase in assets per capita, and the balance, 378 billion, with increase in population. Total assets increased about 4 percent per year; per capita assets, about 2.5 percent per year, and population, about 1.5 percent per year. Reproducible assets per capita in 1958 dollars rose from $6,487 in 1952 through $8,757 in 1965 to $9,646 in 1968. Investment per capita associated with the *increase* in population, about $8,770, was close to the 1965 per capita average given above.[44] The composition of national reproducible tangible assets did not change markedly between 1952 and 1968.[45] Data for the period 1952–1968 suggest that if population growth is at or very close to zero, aggregate reproductive tangible assets may increase 2–3.5 percent per year or more if resources released by cessation of population growth are not absorbed by leisure-time activities and consumption embodying little capital.

With C_p at zero instead of positive, equivalence of C to S requires that $(C_i + C_r)$ increase or S decline; otherwise, in keeping with the Keynesian model, an underemployment balance between savings and investment would tend to result. C_r has been increasing as decline in the life-span of capital, together with growth in the stock of capital, has augmented capital consumption (i.e., C_r).[46] While decrease in the rate of growth of the stock of capital will reduce the annual amount of capital consumption, factors (e.g., purposeful obsolescence) that reduce the average economic lifetime of the stock of capital will augment capital consumption.[47] The ratio of capital consumption to gross private investment rose from 0.49 in 1929 to 0.56 in 1973.[48] Government expenditures expressed as a fraction of Gross National Product rose from 8.2 in 1929 to 21.5 in 1973.[49] The ratio of disposable to personal income declined from 0.97 in 1929 to 0.85 in 1973, thus serving to increase the fraction of disposable income that is spent.[50] Contrary to expectation in the 1930s, the ratio of savings to income has not increased as average income has grown, thus serving to constrain investment if Kuznets's impression is valid.[51]

By 1946–1955 net capital formation expressed as a percentage of net national product, slightly over 13 percent in 1869–1908 and 11.7 percent in 1919–1928, had fallen to slightly over 7 percent.[52] Personal saving expressed as percent of disposable income (exclusive of the war period 1941–1946) has varied within a range of 5–8.1 percent; it stood at 5 in 1929 and 6.15 in 1972–1973.[53] Moreover, personal consumption of durable goods plus fixed investment in structures and producers' durable equipment, expressed as percent of Gross National Product, has varied little; it approximated 23 in 1929, 23.9 in 1956, and 22.8 in 1970.[54] The ratio of gross private investment to Gross National Product, 0.157 in 1929, hovered around 15 percent in 1955–1973. Meanwhile, with capital consumption increasing, the ratio of net private investment to net national product declined from about 8.7 percent in 1929 to about 7.8 percent in 1973.[55]

While internal taxation and international economic pressures are likely to depress the rate at which capital is formed, imbalance between the supply of *net* savings and the demand for them can come in the wake of cessation of population growth. Of the three components of C—i.e., C_r, C_p, C_i—C_p will settle at zero (perhaps being replaced by dissaving should population decline), C_r will continue to increase as the stock of capital K increases and the economic lifetime of K falls, and C_i will move downward as individual satiety and other forces generative of demand for more capital per head become weaker. The dominant determinant of this demand, suggest Dorfman, Heisser, and others, will be technical progress and the exploitation of new knowledge, for upon such progress and knowledge will depend growth of capacity for increasing and using capital per head as well as increase in the desire for both consumer and producer durables per head and profit in their production.[56]

Given that technical progress is both autonomous and demand-generated in origin, the role of *autonomous* technical progress in generating new wants and methods is likely to be reenforced by a growing need to overcome resource shortages and biospheric constraints. Even so, the economy will have to be increasingly organized on a pay-as-you-go basis if the shrinkage of investment limits the growth of securities available for retirement and similar funds,[57] and for investment in securities as a means of financing retirement.

Inasmuch as a crude rate of population growth in the neighborhood of zero may be approached gradually, subject to fluctuations originating in echoes of past growth spurts and in current natality variation, the economy can adjust to a state dominated by capital replacement, supplemented by small increase in the aggregate stock of capital. At present and in the near future the supply of capital is generally considered inadequate. For example, the Bureau of Economic Analysis of the Department of Commerce put at over 12 percent the fraction of projected GNP needing to be saved in 1976–1980, in comparison with a current rate of 9.6 percent and a rate of 10.4 percent in the prior decade.[58] Wallich reports total savings as a fraction of Gross Domestic Product in 1961–1973 as ranging between 6.8 and 9.8 percent, lower than in the United Kingdom, and very much lower than in Germany, France, and Japan.[59]

E. Consumption

The impact of changing population growth rates is hard to estimate, given the limitedness of current knowledge respecting consumer behavior.[60] Slowing down of population growth, it is believed, affects a nation's consumption both as an aggregate and as a set of components whose relative importance is modified. Demographic movements may guard an economy against the risk of "a slowly rising national debt to income ratio," as well as make its expenditure less prone to decline. In general, population growth contributes to an economy's long-run stability by introducing "an expansion bias into the system."[61] Moreover, besides producing effects associated with reduction in the importance of investment (see preceding section), slowing down of population growth may increase consumer volatility and instability, modify the rate of growth of demand for new and durable products, and accentuate the influence of changes in population composition, especially in age composition.

Even given a positive rate of growth, the movement of per capita aggregate demand or expenditure as of that of per capita supply remains under the control of per capita growth of aggregate output. The composition of aggregate demand and (hence) supply may be somewhat more prone to change, however, when the rate of population growth is low or zero than when it is high, inasmuch as income elasticities of demand by commodity groups differ appreciably.[62] In general, change in the composition of aggregate demand barring effects of changes in age composition, will be dominated as now by the rate of growth of average income, which will be at least as high in a stationary as in a growing population. Of course, should cessation of population growth modify inequality in personal income distribution, it could slightly modify aggregate consumption if demonstration effects were slightly reduced as a result.[63] Presumably this effect, should it materialize, might be swamped by other effects.

As I have noted elsewhere,

> the rates of growth of demand for specific products are not closely linked to the rate of population growth. For example, between 1955 and 1965, when employment levels were similar, Gross National Product increased about $3\frac{1}{2}$ percent per year; output per member of the civilian labor force, just over 2 percent; and membership in the civilian labor force, just over $1\frac{3}{8}$ percent compared with a rate of population growth of about $1\frac{5}{8}$ percent. Accordingly, supposing income elasticity of demand for most specific products to lie between just below $\frac{1}{2}$ and just over 2, the rate of growth of aggregate demand for specific products might have been expected to fall mainly within a range of 2 to $5\frac{1}{2}$ percent. The actual range was much wider, even as in 1948–65 when population was growing about $1\frac{3}{4}$ percent per year, and Gross National Product per capita, about 2 percent per year. Then the average annual rate of growth of output (which approximated demand) of selected products and services ranged from over 25 percent to -15 percent and even less. Meanwhile, the demand for services of all sorts rose enough to supply most of the increase in employment recorded in 1948–65. The width of this range of rates is the result mainly of changes in tastes and technology rather than of changes in income and population. Technological changes introduce new products and displace old ones. Tastes adjust to technology, and change for other reasons as well. Moreover, in an age of discretionary time and income, most people have some time and income which they can dispose of in any way that suits them. Under these conditions tastes are volatile and hence highly responsive to newly created opportunities to spend.[64]

Of course, when products are grouped into larger categories, industry sales are more highly correlated with population growth, particularly when the products in question are not luxuries and are oriented to individual rather than industrial consumers.[65]

In general, with population stationary, expenditure upon goods and services characterized by less than unitary income elasticity of demand will decline in *relative* importance, particularly as elasticity moves close to zero with increase in consumption entirely dependent on increase in average income. Demand for goods initially characterized by unitary elasticity of demand will eventually be characterized by declining and finally by zero elasticity. Even goods initially characterized by elasticity in excess of unity will eventually be characterized by unitary elasticity and then by infra-unitary elasticity moving toward zero elasticity. In the long run, therefore, given a stationary population, a state of glut or satiety can approach unless enough new goods and services not wholly substitutable for those already in existence come into being.[66] Such an outcome is likely, however, only in advanced economies enjoying peace. Under these circumstances replacement demand becomes increasingly ascendant. At present, however, these circumstances are not present. Currently of nine categories of goods, Hassan and Johnson found four (food, gasoline and oil, household operation, and other services) with income elasticities less than unity; durable goods with an income elasticity of demand of 2.4343, and housing with one of 0.4586; and three (clothing and shoes, other nondurable goods, and transportation) with elasticities lying between 1.0436 and 1.279.[67]

Inasmuch as some forms of demand and expenditure are dominated by autonomous individuals and others by expenditure units (i.e., families or households), consumption is affected somewhat by change in the ratio of households or spending units to the population. This ratio has increased slightly in recent years, along with population aging and decline in family and household size, even since the 1950s. Moreover, it is expected to decline in the decade ahead.[68] As will be shown, however, it is age of the consumer rather than his family status that affects the consumption of some goods and services, income being given.

As a result of the impact of aging upon individual consumption, as a consequence both of aging as such and of the movement of the individual through his life cycle, population aging affects consumption and demand directly as well as indirectly through such side effects as decrease in mobility.[69] Population aging should, therefore, slow down increase in the instability of consumption and demand associated with the growth of average spending power, together with decrease in the stabilizing influence of the home on consumption.[70] The impact of population aging will depend, however, upon increase in that fraction of individual and family incomes which may be used for "discretionary expenditures," that is, upon expenditures that need not be made at a given time, "are usually not governed by habit," and "are usually not made on the spur of the moment, but rather after considerable deliberation and discussion among family members."[71] The entry of women 45–54 into the labor force must have contributed appreciably to the relative number of families with "discretionary income."[72] Given decline in level of aspiration as families age,[73] however, discretionary expenditure may decline in importance, in part because lifetime income falls and the proportion of lifetime income spent on current consumption rises.[74]

While the advent of a stationary population could increase the wage level and the fraction of the national income going to the human factor as distinguished from that going to owners of scarce natural resources and capital equipment,[75] thus tending to increase the propensity to consume, we shall neglect implications of these possibilities. According to several studies, prospective changes in the rate of population growth will, as remarked earlier, produce only limited effects in the short run. Thus, according to Denton and Spencer, "Aggregate consumption is not affected directly by variations in average household size or in the age distribution of the population. . . . Of course, this does not imply an absence of direct household and age effects on particular *categories* of consumption, but only on the aggregate."[76]

Eilenstine and Cunningham conclude that "the arrival of a stationary population would apparently not mean dramatic shifts in the economy and it certainly would not mean that there would be a dramatic shift away from goods requiring relatively large inputs."[77] The average propensity to consume for a growing population based on 1960 data was only negligibly larger than that for a stationary population.[78] According to their estimates, age and size variables can work "to offset each other's impacts on consumption patterns." The authors' basic conclusion is that "the consumption patterns of a stationary population are sufficiently like those associated with a growing population, so that there is no real reason to fear economic disorder from this source with the cessation of population growth." Their findings "allay the major concerns expressed by Hansen, Billing, Robbins, and others," but, as the authors remark, do not touch upon the fact that "a population with a given total stationary population will contain a larger number of spending units," or upon employment impacts, or upon consequences of oscillation of a population about a stationary equilibrium.[79]

New commodities and services may play an increasingly important role in a stationary population. When new goods are introduced and their use spreads from initial users to nonusers in a position to afford them, the curve describing the growth of the number of users tends to be logistic in shape unless the goods in question bear considerable resemblance to the goods being displaced.[80] For example, the pattern by which television spread differed markedly from that of its predecessor, radio. Of course, given satiation, demand is dominated by replacement unless the services provided by a given type of good begin to be provided by another.[81]

Should the productivity potential of a stationary population be fully realized and average income be relatively higher as a result, aggregate expenditure could prove less stable even though comparatively favorable to trying out new products. For, in a society with discretionary time and discretionary as well as high income, as Reddaway points out and others have since observed, demand for particular products often proves volatile and somewhat transitory and in need of replacement by other sources of demand,[82] especially if income proves "permanent." Eichner and Kregel may be said to have placed this volatility problem in a Keynesian setting when they reformulated Keynesian theory by dividing expenditures upon goods and services into those which are nondiscretionary—"required to keep economic units functioning at a given level of output"—and those which are discretionary—that is, not being closely linked to discretionary income received, are subject to falling below "the level of discretionary income—at least in an *ex ante,* anticipatory sense." As in the Keynesian system, "an ex post *equality between discretionary expenditures (investment) and discretionary income (savings)*" is the *"sole condition for aggregate equilibrium."*[83] Discretionary expenditure thus becomes the "primary factor determining the level of economic activity,"[84] and the type of expenditure to be increased when an *ex ante* imbalance develops between discretionary expenditures and discretionary income. Abstracting from the investment-goods component of discretionary expenditure, however, entrepreneurs may be counted upon to exploit the new empty "wants space"[85] of consumers with uncommitted income by developing new commodities or new combinations of characteristics that give rise to utility, for the lead time is short, as a rule.[86]

While demand for particular commodities may prove volatile, demand for what Lancaster calls the characteristics of particular goods[87] is likely to be stable. For, as has been noted, consumption is dominated by habit, especially in a population that has become stationary, with a relatively large number of persons over 64 and a relatively small number under (say) 35, and adjusted to the impact of aging on the capacity of now relatively old persons to derive utility from particular forms of activity (e.g., forms of recreation).[88] According to Houthakker and Taylor, prices play only a modest role. Moreover, "if income is high enough it is possible for nearly all commodities to become subject to habit formation." "The predominance of habit formation may reflect the high level of income in the United States."[89] "Having decided on a specific family size," say Lionel and David Demery,[90] "the household commits itself to consumption outlays that cannot be redistributed." Habit is reenforced by difficulties in the way of changing consumption patterns.

As noted earlier, entrepreneurial adjustment to changes in consumption patterns associated with aging is analogous to adjustments made in the past to changes originating through technological and related developments. Hence significant problems are not to be expected. There may, of course, be less stress on standardization and more on differentiation and purposeful obsolescence, though such stress may prove objectionable to older elements in the population. Moreover, with a slowing down of the growth of markets to rates often determined by income growth, the propensity to limit competition may be strengthened.

Conclusion

Our stress in this chapter has been upon the economic consequences of cessation of population growth. We have inferred that since adjustment to the advent of a stationary population should not prove difficult, given a *flexible* economy, the net advantages realizable should prove considerable. In contrast W. B. Reddaway describes as "relatively unimportant" the "strictly economic factors" associated with "the prospect of zero population growth" in the United Kingdom. Instead he points to less immediately economic advantages. "On the social and environmental side, however, the advantages from not increasing the number of people in this crowded island seem to me very real."[91] His essay brings out by implication that the nature and degree of net advantage associated with zero population growth depends upon a country's current situation.

X. Cessation of Population Growth: Further Implications

> *Imagination is brought under constraint only when men turn it to practical affairs, in which it is only useful to imagine what is deemed possible.*
>
> G. L. S. Shackle, *Epistemics & Economics*, preface

In this chapter we try to put in terms of conclusions our earlier discussion of the impact of cessation of population growth upon employment, intergenerational relations, and change in the distribution of political power by broad age categories and age-connected concerns. Our treatment continues that in the preceding chapter and builds upon discussion in earlier chapters. In addition, two corollary issues or problems are dealt with. Attention is drawn to regional population decline, a phenomenon of growing as well as nongrowing populations. Attention is drawn also to the fact that a country's capacity for drawing economic advantage from cessation of population growth is conditioned and limited by its international relations.

F. Unemployment

Inasmuch as per capita income in a population is conditioned by the size of the fraction of this population that is gainfully employed, the behavior of employment is important. Of particular concern here is the direct and indirect incidence of unemployment on older persons and upon the flow of funds to retired persons.

Comparison of a growing with a stationary population suggests that the latter will be less prone to unemployment. Let us postulate three stable populations, with a life expectancy of 75 years and fertility patterns yielding growth rate of −1, 0, and +1 percent, respectively.[1] Then the working-age population (i.e., 15–64 years old) will decrease, remain stationary, or increase as follows:

Net rate of total population change (percent)	−1	0	+1
Addition per 1,000 labor-force members	16.2	20.9	26.4
Departure per 1,000 labor-force members	26.2	20.9	16.4
Net change per 1,000 labor-force members	−10.0	0	+10.0

After an economy has become adjusted to a zero rate of population growth, maintaining a given level of employment entails fewer additional adjustments than when it is growing or declining. As a result, the level of material well-being will be high and remain so, particularly if the ratio of gainfully employed to the total as well as to the retired population is maintained at a high level.

When a population is stationary, the labor force is likely to remain steadily employed though not necessarily at as high a level as that at which members of the labor force would settle if not prevented from doing so by man-made barriers. For with the labor force constant and those withdrawing or being removed from the labor force offset by new and mostly relatively young entries, adjustment to oscillation in the number of would-be entries will be minimal, particularly after increase in participation rates for both males and females has virtually ended. Cessation of population growth should also weaken tendencies to economic fluctuation, though the volitional character of investment can always generate some fluctuation.[2] Under the circumstances described, the major need confronting the economy would be that of keeping the economy flexible and thereby facilitating the movement of labor-force members from industries characterized by decline in manpower requirements to those characterized by expansion in manpower needs. When, however, a population is growing steadily, unemployment will develop unless the derived demand for labor continues to rise in keeping with the increase in the flow of persons into the labor force—a rise that is likely to issue in part from increase in actual or prospective increase in discretionary expenditure consequent upon population growth.[3]

When the number of employment-seekers grows at a higher than usual rate, the relative number of persons reported unemployed tends to increase because the derived demand for labor is unlikely to grow rapidly enough at first to absorb all job-seekers. While increase in the rate of growth of labor-force membership may reflect increase in labor-force participation rates (e.g., on the part of women), it will usually echo an upsurge of natality 16–18 or more years earlier. Such upsurge in persons under (say) 20 is likely to add persons under 20 to the labor force faster than derived demand is adequate to absorb them, unless demand is expanding unusually. Not only is unemployment typically much higher among persons under 20; it has been higher since the 1950s, in some measure owing to the past upsurge in natality, though other causal conditions may also be present. Of course, movements in natality reflective of past fluctuations tend to dampen out as time passes.

Some oscillation in natural increase is to be expected whether fertility is at the long-run replacement level or above or below it. For volition enters into fertility as well as into investment. Moreover, various short-period economic cycles may become embedded in economies even in the absence of long-period cycles (e.g., the now apparently defunct 18–20-year "Kuznets Cycle," or the 50-year "Kondratieff Cycle"), and, through their impact upon current employment, income, and expectations, produce variation in fertility that may later contribute to variation in economic activity.[4] Even the cyclical behavior of investment in population-oriented capital such as housing may be much affected by nondemographic variables (e.g., labor costs, interest rates, rental price).[5]

Unemployment, as indicated in chapter VI, has many sources, among them constraints on mobility and substitution, a capacity of greater importance in a stationary than in a growing population,[6] and on the substitutability of labor for capital and resources or of one kind of labor for another.[7] There are also sources that are macroeconomic or cyclical in character or are associated with man-made inflexibility, or originate in individual deficiency,[8] or are sequels to alternatives to self-support. The comparative incidence of these "causes" will change somewhat if population growth ceases, age composition becomes stable, and the degree of mobility essential to interoccupational and interindustrial balance increases. Tendencies toward stability will be strengthened by the fact that with the labor force constant and entries just matching withdrawals, "labor" will be the increasingly scarce "factor" insofar as capital-formation, together with natural-resource–augmenting technical progress, more than offsets labor-augmenting technical progress, a process sometimes partially counterbalanced by increase in the preference of leisure to employment and of household activity to the market.[9]

Unemployment could remain relatively high even if cyclical and related macroeconomic unemployment should become negligible, given a stationary population. We may recall Feldstein's conclusion "that macroeconomic policy is unlikely to lower the permanent rate of unemployment much below 4.5 percent," whereas "a series of specific policies could reduce the unemployment rate for those seeking permanent full-time employment to a level significantly below three percent and perhaps closer to two percent."[10] It is well established that unemployment originates in indisposition to work steadily after entry into the labor force, together with public-welfare measures that conduce to unemployment by supporting these unemployed persons.[11] Of great and increasing importance also, as noted in chapter VI, is restriction of the size of labor markets by overpricing labor and products, mainly as a result of trade-union pressure and minimum wage legislation, especially unfavorable to teen-ager and nonwhite employment, which, along with other employment, may also be complementary to older workers and a condition of their employment.[12] Sometimes, of course, economic expansion coincident with the introduction of a minimum or higher wage may counterbalance what would otherwise have been the result.[13]

While general unemployment affects the economic status of the aged adversely by reducing their support and making it more difficult for them to remain at work, it is causes of actual unemployment of specific older workers that are most subject to direct correction. These causes consist in governmental and trade-union fixation of wages at excessively high levels, and the physical demands of particular employments, demands that are excessive, given the health of older job-seekers and the conditions that characterize the job. While the first of these causes may be eliminated by removing artificial props to wage rates acceptable to older as well as younger workers, correction of the second entails both a focusing of medical attention upon seeming medical barriers to employability and an engineering approach to the task of reducing when possible the physical demands made upon workers by specific modes of employment. A life-cycle human-capital conservation approach may supplement these last two steps, since the overriding objective is conservation of human capital, which tends to peak around age 40 when "the effects of 'depreciation' overwhelm gains through experience."[14]

Employability is conditioned by the quality of a population, a product of both genetic and cultural selection. Cessation of a population's growth will result in a decline in its quality if there are increases in the relative contributions to population growth made by the genetically inferior and / or by the culturally deprived. Should members of these two categories be less sensitive under prevailing conditions to stimuli conducing to family limitation, differential fertility could change enough to affect employability.

The main burden of the argument presented in this section is that fixation of a worker's reservation, or legal, or contractual wage above a minimum level that (given the overhead cost of employing him) makes his employment tolerable or profitable to an employer, will contribute to unemployment directly and / or indirectly. Even if wages are adjusted upward compatibly with increase in productivity in highly productive bellwether industries, corresponding upward adjustment of wages in less productive industries is compatible with maintenance of employment in these industries only if aggregate monetary demand is augmented through inflationary measures.[15]

G. Intergenerational Transfer

While every population is divisible into dependents and nondependents whence flow the human services that operate the economy and generate support of the dependents, problems associated with dependency vary with a population's rate of growth. Transfer of support from nondependent to dependent generations in particular presents financial and fiscal problems in a modern as compared with a simple agricultural economy. In the latter situation children could be useful early, the usefulness of older dependents could be protracted, and support of dependents could be transferred largely within a familial setting. In a modern society, by contrast, transfer of support is subject to anonymity along with fiscal, monetary, and political uncertainty.

Table X.1 serves to illustrate how the problem varies with rate of population growth in a stable male population. In columns 2–4 we present age structures for male populations, based on a life expectancy at birth of 73.9 years combined with fertility rates producing rates of population growth of 1, zero, and −1 percent per year. In column 5 we present the

Table X.1. Age Structure and Dependency

Age Group	+1	0	−1	+1
0–14	26.60	19.99	14.26	31.64
15–54	53.22	52.26	49.29	55.20
55–64	9.30	11.81	14.21	7.29
65 & over	10.89	15.95	22.23	5.87
Total	100.00	100.00	100.00	100.00

Source: Coale and Demeny, Regional Model Life Tables, pp. 148, 168.

age structure of a male population based on a life expectancy of 49.56 years together with fertility yielding a growth rate of 1 percent per year. If we define 0–14 and over-64 as ages of dependency, 15–54 as age of nondependency, and 55–64 as intermediate between dependency and nondependency, several conditions result. First, variation in the relative number of dependents is much affected by the size of the fraction of those in the 55–64 category who elect to become dependents. Second, the age structure of dependents varies, with the older replacing the younger as fertility moves down and life expectancy increases. Third, the ratio of old dependents to young dependents rises as fertility falls and life expectancy increases—e.g., from 0.185 in column 5 to 1.56 in column 4. Fourth, as a result the capacity of a population to support dependents rests markedly upon the degree to which members of the age category 55–64 remain in the nondependent category.

Transfer of support from nondependents to older dependents can be accomplished either through financial mechanisms such as individual annuities or collective pension systems or through national pay-as-you-go arrangements similar to the Social Security System. Ultimately, of course, even annuity and pension systems are pay-as-you-go in character, since the functioning of such a system is based upon continuing activity over time on the part of the relevant nondependent population that operates the economy's facilities which, along with the labor force, produce the pecuniary claims that after a time lag are translated into cash that liquidates these claims. Each arrangement is subject to uncertainty. A straight or near-straight pay-as-you-go system is vulnerable to continuing growth in the ratio of dependents to employed nondependents as well as to the withdrawal of nondependents from the system, as when a city's young population emigrates and shrinks the flow of cash into that city's essentially pay-as-you-go pension fund. The purchasing power of an annuity or pension, even if "variable," is subject to erosion as a result of inflation and its impact upon the purchasing power of money and its sometimes adverse effect upon the value of securities.[16]

Given a stable stationary or declining population, the security of the aged would be very much greater were all of those aged 55–64 to remain in the labor force along with those 15–54, instead of withdrawing into dependence (see Table X.1). Then the ratio of those in the labor force to aged in a dependency category would be about 4 to 1 instead of about 1.9 to 1 (see column 3). Moreover, given column 4 conditions, the ratio would be about 2.9 to 1 instead of about 1.4 to 1. The impact of these ratios is further reduced, of course, given unemployment, inasmuch as unemployed persons do not contribute to the pay-as-you-go flow of funds or to the sources of pension funds.

What has been said may be put in general terms. Let r denote the ratio of employed persons to dependents over 54 years old; y, the average income of an employed person; t, the tax on y for the support of dependents receiving the proceeds of this tax; and i, the average income received by dependents. Then

$$i = ryt; \quad \text{and} \quad i / y = rt$$

So long as r and t remain unchanged and y increases both sufficiently to offset inflation and in an amount that reflects increase in real output per employed person, the real value of i will not be reduced by inflation and will increase with y. The value of r is determined by a population's age composition and labor-force participation on the part of those over 54 years of age.

Given absence of inflation, the eventual return on yt will grow at the rate of increase in y, a rate almost certainly below the rate of interest and the consequent growth of the return on funds invested in an annuity. Given inflation, however, the rate of growth of y in real value may or may not exceed the real return on a corresponding investment in an annuity.[17] Expected inadequacy of i might be supplemented with a private annuity, purchased in an individual's late forties when family-formation, household, and other nondiscretionary expenditures have declined and opportunity for saving has increased.[18]

Provision for the flow of funds to persons in retirement may have to be based in large measure on a pay-as-you-go system. Dependence for maintenance of the income of retired persons cannot suitably be made a charge upon the general revenue system of a country, since the results would be arbitrary and ungoverned by rules of equity; nor can such maintenance always be made wholly dependent upon the financial mechanisms underlying pensions, annuities, and similar contracts. There may not be enough satisfactory outlets for the investment of funds then flowing into the hands of providers of inflation-immune pension and annuity contracts. Net national wealth is not increasing more than 2.5 percent per year, in part because postretirement dependence upon Social Security and company pensions discourages saving and induces early retirement, thus reducing income growth and capital formation as well as the ratio of workers to retired persons.[19] Moreover, should population growth eventually become negative as a result of the current descent of fertility below the replacement level, the ratio of dissavers to savers would increase, and the rate of growth of wealth per capita and in the aggregate could decline.

As of December 31, 1973, when total U.S. assets approximated $9,922 billion, insurance and pension reserves amounted to $458 billion, while corporate equities and bonds, government obligations, mortgages, and other credit instruments totaled $2,975 billion. A pay-as-you-go system such as that described in the preceding paragraph makes little demand upon the slowly growing supply of suitable investments.[20] At present, of course, gross capital requirements of the next five or so years are estimated at 12 percent of projected GNP, compared with the 10.4 percent realized in the preceding decade.[21]

Underlying the arrangement described is intergenerational confidence analogous to intergenerational confidence in an early nineteenth century agricultural economy, perhaps supplemented by the political power of those whose interests are aligned with actual and prospective retired persons.

H. Political Orientation

The distribution of political power, together with governmental policy, reflects a country's age composition, particularly when as many functions have been transferred to the central government as in the United States. When fertility is high, a population is growing, and the relative number of older persons is small, the ratio of younger to older persons is favorable to the economic welfare of the latter, even though their political power is quite limited. As a population ages, however, the economic welfare of a country's older population may become quite sensitive to governmental policy, particularly if, as in the United States, the central government has absorbed functions formerly associated with the private sector and local government. Of overwhelming concern to older persons, of course, is the impact of governmental policy upon the level and the security of the incomes, emoluments, and benefits enjoyed by older persons, especially those who are retired.

Political concerns, like most if not all other concerns, are conditioned by the stage of the life cycle in which an individual finds himself, since political concerns reflect his remaining life expectancy and the constraints imposed by it on his opportunities and ability to realize them, together with particular changes in his vision of the conspectus of economic advantages and disadvantages lying ahead. Because the typical individual is sufficiently future-oriented to anticipate the impact of his aging, and his sensitivity to age-associated policies develops even before he is actually subject to their incidence, his political life cycle will begin to run ahead of his physical life cycle at some point. We shall assume this point in a person's political life cycle to lie in his mid-forties, at which time his children are or soon will be self-sufficient, and he can begin to think seriously of concerns that may or are likely to become real in or after his fifties (e.g., decline in ability to recover from great economic loss). Earlier he will not be free or nearly so of the costs of his dependents and in a good position to accumulate capital, a matter to which financial institutions continually direct an individual's attention.

Aging-oriented concern assumes a number of forms: (a) insurance against the erosion of the means of support of retired persons through inflation; (b) support of measures that augment retained income of retired persons through tax exemption and public defrayal of a portion of the costs of misfortune (e.g., medical expenses); and (c) greater protection of older persons against miscellaneous physical and economic sources of injury (e.g., crime, fraud). With decrease in the ratio of gainfully employed to older dependents and the threat of macroeconomic dissaving, older and middle-aged persons may show increasing concern to prolong membership in the labor force until (say) 70.

As was noted earlier, the population aged 45 and over will probably eventually exceed that aged 18 to 44 years. This is not likely, however, before early in the next century.[22] However, since the propensity to organize and vote is likely to be somewhat stronger among those over 44 than among many of those 18–44, the voting power of those over 44 may become ascendant even before 2000.

I. Population Decline

Decline in the size of the nation's population could set in after the first quarter of the next century should fertility settle around 1.7 or lower and immigration remain low; in fact it could decline about one-tenth between 2020 and 2050. A *persisting* national population decline has not characterized modern countries; for when natural increase has approached zero, countries have tended to encourage marriage and natality and to foster immigration. Many local areas, however, have experienced decline in population, usually as a result of selective net outmigration resulting in changes in age structure often adequate, in conjunction with local attitudes toward fertility, to eventuate in natural decrease. Between 1960 and 1970, according to the 1970 U.S. census, 1,369 of this nation's 3,141 counties experienced decrease in population along with 3 of the nation's 69 SMSAs.[23] Parallel localized population declines have been experienced in low-fertility European countries.

One cannot generalize much from localized population declines other than that the effect of persistent decline is cumulative in character. Because outmigration has only a localized impact and is somewhat offset elsewhere by inmigration, it is insufficient to affect a nation's fertility greatly. Moreover, decline in population at the national level in a modern society tends to proceed too slowly to set a cumulative process in motion in a relatively short period of time. Thus local decline needs to be treated as quite distinct from hypothetical national decline.

Localized population decline, actual and prospective, can intensify greatly public and other financial problems confronting local communities. Both the public and the private infrastructure, together with relevant commitments, of local communities, especially larger cities, are essentially long-term in character, whereas outmigration of capital and population is accomplishable within relatively short time intervals. Such communities, in short, unlike national communities, are open in character, subject to contraction as well as expansion—to contractile forces no longer offset as in the past by aggregate population growth. The planning time horizon of local communities is shorter, therefore, than that of a closed national economy. Accordingly, the temporal framework of urban planning will have to be more closely adjusted to the potential vulnerability of cities to population loss.

While cessation of population growth can accentuate the adverse impact of population-dispersing forces, it should contribute on balance to improvement in the longer-run distribution of the population of the United States and of other countries. For with need to accommodate natural growth out of the way, a clearer total view can be formed of the distribution of population in space, and how to optimize this distribution by taking into account both natural resource constraints and constraints originating in the economic structure of regions and their urban centers. Given such an overview, together with reduction in plant and related unit size essential to realizing economies of both scale and flexibility, it becomes possible greatly to improve the distribution of population in space. For continuing growth in numbers is no longer present to disrupt optimization processes.

J. International Constraints

Prior to the nineteenth century a state, by regulating the growth of its population, could guard itself against adverse effects associated with undue pressure of numbers upon natural resources, the type of pressure to which Malthus and Ricardo pointed. For theirs was a simple economy in which the overriding roles were played by land and labor.[24] Trade did not begin to play a critical role until in the nineteenth century when some countries, initially England, began to become dependent upon foreign sources for critical natural products—and others, in the tradition of Malthus,[25] sought to avoid undue dependence on foreign sources.[26] Moreover, with the continuing growth of population and increase in the variety of raw materials utilized in manufacture, most if not all states ceased to be totally self-sufficient and instead became dependent in part on various foreign sources for raw produce and materials. Each such state found it necessary to earn enough foreign exchange through exportation of goods and services to pay for these critical imports.

While these emerging relationships augmented the population-carrying capacity of many countries, they also modified both the limits to which population growth in these countries might be subject and the character of the set of conditions[27] governing average output there. In particular, net realized and realizable output per head became subject to the course of various terms of trade, and to changes in the internal cost of producing exports. Moreover, superior technologies, adapted both to economizing scarce resources and to producing novel products, and with power to destroy initial original differential advantages, not only were developed but were gradually diffused internationally. Under such paradigmatic circumstances, natural resources and biospheric elements that remain little subject to being replaced by substitutes are likely to rise in relative price as aggregate world demand increases, to the disadvantage of countries lacking these elements.[28]

Given these conditions, two current trends diminish the advantages which advanced countries may derive from cessation of population growth. First, it has been estimated that population will continue to grow in the underdeveloped world and that the crude rate of growth will still be around 2 percent at the close of the century, whereas the rate for the developed world will approximate 0.8 percent if that, given that current fertility is at or below the replacement level.[29] As a result, by 2000 the underdeveloped world may number 5 billion or more, compared with 1.45 billion in the developed world, raising the share of population of the former to about 77 percent from about 68 percent in 1965. Should total GNP increase about 6 percent per year in the underdeveloped world, its amount will be over four times as high in 2000 as in 1975.[30]

Second, such growth of population and output per head will contribute greatly to increase in the consumption of natural resources (e.g., oil, coal), the total reserves of which are fixed in quantity though not always known with accuracy. Demand for these resources usually derives from the use of services embodying these resources, though it may issue as well from quite immediate use of some resources. Depletion of these resources may proceed directly as in the form of reduction of oil reserves, or indirectly as in the degradation of arable land, the amount of which per capita shrinks with population growth.[31] As a result, the relative value of the services derivable from natural resources, together with their own value, will rise, and may put countries endowed with these resources in comparatively favorable positions. Illustrative are countries well endowed with petroleum reserves, or countries still net food exporters (e.g., U.S., Canada, Australia, New Zealand, Argentina, Thailand).

All advanced countries incompletely endowed with the diverse natural resources entering into their gross national production must import some raw materials or products embodying relatively large amounts of these materials. Most advanced countries, lacking exportable raw materials or agricultural produce, must acquire foreign exchange through the exportation of services and fabricated products. Their trading positions tend to be weakened, however, when their favorable methods of production become diffused to other countries, particularly to those with low labor costs. Consider the U.S., for example. It innovates a new product and begins its exportation, sometimes to follow up this action by introducing the product's manufacture into certain foreign countries, perhaps to end up by exporting thence to the United States some of the output originally produced at home. With growth of population, especially in the less developed world, and the international diffusion of new techniques, competition in the production and sale of fabricated products, especially those which are labor-oriented, will increase, thus elevating the relative value of natural resources and foodstuffs, the supply of which is greatly influenced by the available stock of arable land and critical inputs (e.g., oil) complementary to land.[32]

Hitherto the United States has had two means of guarding advantages associated with slow population growth. Its trading position in manufacturing has been "based heavily on a comparative advantage in the generation of innovations,"[33] a base that could become less strong should the factors conducing to innovation become weaker.[34] It is hardly to be expected that multinational enterprise, the main diffuser of competitive technology abroad, will contribute greatly to the security of its country of origin.[35] In contrast with the sometimes transitory character of sources of foreign exchange based upon innovation is that based upon agriculture, source of a set of products for which substitutes are not to be had, inasmuch as the United States has few competitors (e.g., Canada, Australia, New Zealand, Argentina).

In sum, the more dependent a state with a stationary population is upon the exchange of fabricated goods for critical raw materials, the more limited will be the advantages it can draw from cessation of population growth. For it will encounter greater competition in the export area than in the import area. When, however, such a state can export produce sufficient to cover most of its imports, the advantages that it derives from cessation of population growth are quite secure. Given freedom of trade, of course, there may be heavy pressure upon domestic industry with its often inflated wages.

It is to be noted, furthermore, that a country whose population is stationary or declining, even if capable of coping with external commercial pressure, may encounter direct population pressure from adjacent high-fertility resource-short countries. Population grew 2.5–4.3 percent per year in 1970–1974 in countries wherein live about half the world's population. Illustrative is the pressure of the Mexican population, now growing about 3.5 percent per year, against the southwestern border of the United States. The number of Mexican aliens illegally in the United States is estimated at 6–8 million and growing, given the annual addition of 800,000 young people to Mexico's unemployment-ridden labor force, together with connivance by would-be American employers of low-wage aliens and a weak, ill-conceived American immigration policy. Under the circumstances a considerable fraction of the potential longer-run benefits of cessation of America's natural population growth is destined to be dissipated. Most European countries with near-stationary populations, together with Australia and New Zealand, are free of pressure such as has been described, since they do not abut territorially upon countries comparable to Mexico. Even Japan and the Soviet Union are more favorably situated.

K. Residual Inequality

While some conditions described in chapter VII should make for decrease in the inequality with which income is distributed among those aged (say) 20–60, population aging will increase the relative number of persons in and over their sixties, a group whose average real income is relatively low and subject to continuous erosion through inflation. Whereas about

10 percent of the population were 65 or over in 1975, this fraction will have risen to about 16 percent by 2050 should fertility settle at replacement and net immigration continue at 400,000 per year, or slightly above 16 percent should net immigration approximate zero. However, should fertility settle at 1.7, with net immigration continuing at 400,000 annually, the fraction 65 years and older will approximate 21 percent.[36]

Withdrawal of an older individual from the labor force usually results in a lowering of the income which he receives.[37] Moreover, as a rule, the real incomes of retired persons tend to vary inversely with age. This is in part the outcome of the double impact of underparticipation in the growth of output per worker and of inflation. Suppose, for example, that a person enjoying a monetary income x corresponding to average worker income retires on a fixed monetary income $0.8x$. Suppose next that prices rise 5 percent per year; then at the end of a decade the purchasing power of this monetary income would approximate in real terms only about 0.62 of that of the original $0.8x$. Even if the purchasing power of the original $0.8x$ income had remained unchanged, the income of the retiree relative to that of those employed would have declined if he did not share in the fruits of the forces increasing average real income of those employed—about 26 percent if this average grew 3 percent per year. Should both inflation and nonparticipation in the increase in output per worker contribute to the reduction of the *relative* income status of the retiree, diminishing it 8 percent per year, then at the end of ten years the retiree's real income would approximate only about 0.37 of real income per worker instead of 0.8 as originally.

It may be noted that the impact of adverse influences upon the real incomes of persons in and beyond the sixties will reduce the degree to which actual consumption patterns are affected by population aging. The effects of reduction in real incomes of retirees may therefore outweigh effects associated with their aging as such.

As has been indicated earlier, decline in the absolute and relative position of the incomes of the aged can be averted only through a retirement system that corrects for inflation and augments the average retirement income at a rate roughly similar to that at which average wage and salary incomes rise. Such a policy can continue to be carried out, however, only if the ratio of persons in retirement to the active work force is kept low enough to make the money cost of such policy tolerable.

In his search for an optimum population growth rate, Samuelson suggests the existence of a hypothetical optimum rate adequate to displace capital formation and sustain an appropriate ratio of supporters of retired persons to the number of retired.[38] Given such a rate, of course, its maintenance depends upon the social mechanisms in operation—mechanisms whose presence may be dependent upon state intervention.

Conclusion

While the advent of a stationary population may give rise to new problems or make more difficult coping with some already existent problems, it could also bring advantages and capacity to deal effectively with newly emerging problems. Among the advantages associated with a stationary population three stand out: its potentially favorable age structure, given avoidance of early retirement; the potential stability of the ratio of entrants into the labor force to those withdrawing from it; and opportunity to form capital at a relatively high rate per capita. Moreover, realization of these three advantages should not prove difficult. It is essential only that the economy be flexible, free of dominance by labor and other monopolies, together with antieconomic bureaucratic and other restraints; that the assumption of entrepreneurial roles be unimpeded;[39] and that the flow of economic information remain adequate to give guidance to entrepreneurs.

Should the economy not remain flexible and should premature withdrawal from the labor force reduce the productive power of the population relative to its preference for goods and services, state intervention would be likely to win support. Such intervention might not, however, prove equal to the task of restoring flexibility and an adequate flow of relevant information. Coping with the problems of a stationary population may thus be said to depend ultimately upon the adaptability of an economy's mechanisms of adjustment to the maintenance of adequate flexibility, together with the flow of information respecting wants, methods of production and price behavior.

Some economists, as was noted earlier, are less optimistic respecting the impact of stationarity of population under modern conditions, given limits to extension of settlement and the development of appropriate capital-using labor-saving technology and hence to investment and the level of activity. Given these limitations and the likelihood that under zero population growth there will be increase in the tendency to shift preferences from goods to leisure, "it is difficult to believe that sufficient net investment will be generated to propel a modern capitalist system with its inherent property and class relations." So writes Hieser, who concludes that "a radical restructuring of the whole economic system" will be called for, together with "some form of socialism."[40] What action is taken in a country will be conditioned, of course, by the degree to which the economy is already subject to state regulation.

Other economists take a brighter view of zero population growth. For example, Reddaway expects the advantages to outweigh the disadvantages even in a progressive modern economy, such as England or the United Kingdom. "The strictly economic factors seem to me to be relatively unimportant, producing a change in the problems with which administrators will have to grapple, rather than any great effect on gross product per head: sometimes the problems will be eased (e.g., pensions), sometimes made more difficult, but the effects will seldom be large. On the social and environmental side, however, the advantages from not increasing the number of people in this crowded island seem to me very real."[41]

Epilogue

Projection making is an art rather than a science.
A. R. Hall, *Economic Record,* March, 1976, p. 51

Should a virtually stationary or declining population not evolve, the cause
will lie not in improvement in life expectancy but in further change in total
fertility, which declined from slightly over 3 in the early 1960s to about
1.8 in 1976. Allowance for a slight increase in projected life expectancy at
birth does not significantly affect projected populations.[1] Fertility, now
below replacement, could rise above replacement should the average number of lifetime births *expected* by married women aged 18–24 be realized,[2]
a possibility for which June Sklar and Beth Berkov still find some support
in California fertility behavior.[3] Finally, Wachter concludes, in keeping
with Richard Easterlin's model, that since fertility behavior is cyclical, an
upswing in the rate of growth of real wages could stimulate fertility.[4]

The advent of an approximately stationary population in the United
States and various other western countries will bring new problems in its
wake, both problems associated with the absence of population growth and
problems associated with population aging and its probably adverse impact
upon the income situation of the greatly increased number of aged. Slowing down of population growth will also bring in its wake an easing of
some old problems, together with change in the conspectus of options
available. The experience will be novel in that earlier manifestations of
actual or incipient population stationarity were transitory, imposed by adverse circumstances far more than by human volition, which lies at the
heart of prospective stationarity. Not only may the current orientation of
volition persist; it may also carry fertility below the replacement level and
keep it there for a time, thus accentuating problems associated with cessation of population growth.

Given a stationary population, the economy should be less volatile than
at present or in the past. Not only will fluctuations in the annual number
of births and hence later on in the number of entrants into the labor force
be quite small; capital production and consumption, both of which are
subject to considerable variation, should also be somewhat less volatile.
Moreover, habit will dominate consumption in greater measure when a
population is older than at present or in the past. Of course, volatility may
be contributed to by increase in average income and by the need to shift
demand to additional products, given low elasticity of demand for cur-

rently consumed products, but this volatility will not equal that associated with past irregularity in natality and the demand for capital.

Cessation of population growth will give rise to outlets for productive capacity exploitable by private enterprise, private collectivities (e.g., foundations), and agencies of the state, together with a growing demand for leisure; it should even direct attention to economic opportunities and niches currently underexploited. Moreover, given currently inadequate modes of producing support and care for retired and disabled persons in modern societies, a heavy demand for inputs will accompany transformation of the state into what Weldon calls "the household writ large"—into a set of arrangements suited to reduce or remove intergenerational inequality in needs and ability to satisfy them, as well as otherwise repair the currently inadequate communal provisions and practices introduced in place of even more inadequate household and complementary institutions.[5] More generally, there is scope for reordering institutions until the composition of demand is such as matches the potential composition of supply, compatible with full and optimal use of capacity.

Solution of economic problems associated with the advent of a stationary population lies in an empirical approach, assisted by what Harry Johnson calls the "use of trained common sense, supported by but not subordinated to mastery of the tools of the economist's trade." Then problems associated with population trends can be defined by economists, "as they really are," and economists can "set about solving them, and if necessary along the way revolutionize traditional ways of economic thinking about the economic system."[6] However, even given a satisfactory economic approach to economic problems associated with the advent of a stationary population, there would remain many essentially noneconomic problems whose solution would call for the approaches of other sciences (e.g., anthropology, political science, psychology, sociology).

Notes

I. Stationary Population; Stationary Economy

1. J. Fourastié, "De la vie traditionelle à la vie tertiaire," *Population*, XIV, 1959, pp. 417–32. On clues to changes during the Neolithic Revolution see G. B. Kolata, "!Kung Hunter-Gatherers: Feminism, Diet, and Birth Control," *Science*, CLXXXV, Sept. 13, 1974, pp. 932–34; William Petersen, "A Demographer's View of Prehistoric Demography," *Current Anthropology*, XVI, June, 1975, pp. 227–46.

2. Much more detailed illustrations are to be had from A. J. Coale and Paul Demeny, *Regional Model Life Tables and Stable Populations* (Princeton: Princeton University Press, 1966) and United Nations, *The Concept of a Stable Population. Application to the Study of Populations of Countries with Incomplete Demographic Statistics*, Population Study 39, New York, 1968. See also David D. McFarland, "On The Theory of Stable Populations," *Demography*, V, Aug., 1969, pp. 301–22; Nathan Keyfitz, "Age Distribution and the Stable Equivalent," ibid., pp. 261–70; T. J. Espenshade and C. Y. Chan, "Compensating Changes in Fertility and Mortality," ibid., XIII, Aug., 1976, pp. 357–68.

3. N. B. Ryder, "Notes on Stationary Populations," *Population Index*, XII, Jan., 1975, pp. 3–27, esp. pp. 12–13.

4. On the regulation of numbers see A. M. Carr-Saunders, *The Population Problem* (Oxford: Clarendon Press, 1922), chaps. 9–11; W. H. R. Rivers, ed., *Essays on the Depopulation of Melanesia* (Cambridge: University Press, 1927); and A. B. Wolfe's criticism of Carr-Saunders' argument in "Superest Ager," *Quarterly Journal of Economics*, XL, 1925, pp. 172–75. See also R. R. Kuczynski, "British Demographer's Opinions of Fertility," in L. Hogben, ed., *Political Arithmetic* (New York: Macmillan, 1938), chap. 7; A. J. Coale, "The History of the Human Population," *Scientific American*, CCXXXI, Sept., 1974, pp. 40–51; Petersen, "Prehistoric Demography"; E. P. Hutchinson, *The Population Debate* (Boston: Houghton Mifflin, Co., 1967), chap. 2.

5. R. R. Kuczynski reports rates of 3.0 or more in French Canada and parts of Eastern Europe early in the present century. *The Balance of Births and Deaths* (Washington, D.C.: Brookings Institution, 1931), chaps. 2–3, and pp. 61–64; *Birth Registration and Birth Statistics in Canada* (Washington, D.C.: Brookings Institution, 1930), chap. 10; *The Measurement of Population Growth* (New York: Oxford University Press, 1936), pp. 126–27. See also on current rates *Population Bulletin of the United Nations*, No. 7, 1963, chap. 9; W. Brass et al., *The Demography of Tropical Africa* (Princeton: Princeton University Press, 1968), pp. 151–67; Coale, "The History"; United Nations, *Demographic Yearbook, 1975* (New York: United Nations, 1976).

6. See J. Hajnal, "European Marriage Patterns in Perspective," in D. V. Glass and D. E. C. Eversley, eds., *Population in History* (Chicago: Aldine, 1965), chap. 6.

7. Ibid., p. 130.

8. Gy. Ascadi and J. Nemeekeri, *History of Human Life Span and Mortality* (Budapest: Akademiai Kiado, 1970); L. I. Dublin, A. J. Lotka, and M. Spiegelman, *Length of Life*, 2nd ed., (New York: Ronald Press, 1949), chap. 2. On Roman and Medieval mortality see also A. E. R. Boak, *Manpower Shortage and the Fall of the Roman Empire* (Ann Arbor: University of Michigan Press, 1955), pp. 9–17 and references, pp. 131–35. See also Deevey, "Human Population," cited in note 10 below.

9. Dublin et al., *Length of Life*, p. 43. See also Glass and Eversley, *Population in History*, passim; T. H. Hollingsworth, *Historical Demography* (Ithaca: Cornell University Press, 1969), passim; D. V. Glass and Roger Revelle, eds., *Population and Social Change* (London: Arnold, 1972), passim; J. D. Chambers, *Population,*

Economy, and Society in Pre-Industrial England (London: Oxford University Press, 1972). See note 17 below.

10. E.g., see Kingsley Davis's essay and Harrison Brown's introduction in Brown and Edward Hutchings, Jr., *Are Our Descendants Doomed?* (New York: Viking, 1972); also E. S. Deevey, Jr., "The Human Population," *Scientific American,* CCIII, Sept., 1960, pp. 195–205, and Henry Hodges, *Technology in the Ancient World* (Knopf: New York, 1970), chaps. 2–3.

11. On the slowness with which yields increased see Lester Brown, *Increasing World Food Output* (Washington, D.C.: U.S.D.A., 1965), pp. 78, 81, chaps. 3, 8, appendix; Colin Clark, *The Conditions of Economic Progress,* 3rd ed. (London: Macmillan, 1957), chap. 5 and pp. 655–58, 679; Colin Clark and M. R. Haswell, *The Economics of Subsistence Agriculture* (London: Macmillan, 1964, 1967), chaps. 5–6. On upsurges of numbers and their adjustment to the flow of subsistence see K. W. Taylor, "Some Aspects of Population History," *Canadian Journal of Economics and Political Science,* XVI, 1950, pp. 301–13. See also on Europe *Cambridge Economic History of Europe* (Cambridge: University Press, 1941ff.), I, chap. I— II, pp. 160, 167–68, 304—IV, pp. 1–95, esp. 30–32, also 158–59; Colin Clark, *Population Growth and Land Use* (New York: St. Martin's Press, 1967), chaps. 3–4, esp. pp. 69–81; J. C. Russell, *British Medieval Population* (Albuquerque: University of New Mexico Press, 1948), pp. 232, 312–14, and *Medieval Regions and Their Cities* (Bloomington: University of Indiana Press, 1972), pp. 236–37. On Asia see Ryoichi Ishii, *Population Pressure and Economic Life in Japan* (London: P. S. King, 1937), chaps. 1–2; Irene Taeuber, *The Population of Japan* (Princeton: Princeton University Press, 1958), chaps. 1–2; John Durand, "Population Statistics of China, A.D., 2–1953," *Population Studies,* XIII, 1960, pp. 209–56; Ping-ti Ho, *Studies on the Population of China, 1368–1953* (Cambridge: Harvard University Press, 1959). See also United Nations, *The Determinants and Consequences of Population Trends,* I (New York: United Nations, 1973), chap. 2; Douglass C. North and Robert Paul Thomas, "The First Economic Revolution," *Economic History Review,* XXX, May, 1977, pp. 229–41.

12. See Hall's essay in E. E. Rich and C. H. Wilson, eds., *The Cambridge Economic History of Europe* (Cambridge: University Press, 1967), IV, pp. 142–43; see also ibid., chap. 5; also E. A. Wrigley, *Population and History* (New York: McGraw-Hill, 1969). During the Napoleonic wars a 13 percent increase in England's wheat acreage above the 1771 level reduced the average yield per acre by about 8 percent and the marginal yield to 8 bushels. Colin Clark, *The Conditions of Economic Progress,* 2nd ed. (London: Macmillan, 1951), pp. 225–27. This decline may, however, have been due largely to unfavorable weather. J. D. Chambers and G. E. Mingay, *The Agricultural Revolution, 1750–1880* (London: Botsford, 1966), pp. 114–17. See also Gustaf Utterström, "Climatic Fluctuations and Population Problems in Early Modern History," *Scandinavian Economic History Review,* III, 1955, pp. 3–47. On the removal of excess population by plague see A. R. Bridbury, "The Black Death," *Economic History Review,* XXVI, 1973, pp. 557–92.

13. Chambers and Mingay, *The Agricultural Revolution,* pp. 6–11, 15, 199–210, and chaps. 1–4, 7. See also John D. Post, "Famine, Mortality, and Epidemic Disease in the Process of Modernization," *Economic History Review,* XXIX, Feb., 1976, pp. 14–37. In the eighteenth century in England, however, the growth of population centers often was checked by a shortage of fuel due to deforestation and lack of transport to bring in coal. See Phyllis Deane, *The First Industrial Revolution* (Cambridge: University Press, 1965), p. 76.

14. On war losses see B. Urlanis, *Wars and Population,* trans. by Leo Lempert (Moscow: Progress Publishers, 1971). On plague see Post, "Famine, Mortality, and Epidemic Disease"; Russell, *British Medieval Population;* and references in note 16 below.

15. Lynn White, "Technology and Economics in the Middle Ages," *Speculum,* XV, 1940, pp. 141–55, and *Medieval Technology and Social Change* (Oxford: Clarendon Press, 1962).

16. For estimates of population growth before 1750 see M. K. Bennett, *The World's Food* (New York: Harper, 1954), p. 9. See also Clark, *Population Growth*, chap. 3; Simon Kuznets, *Modern Economic Growth. Rate, Structure, Spread* (New Haven: Yale University Press, 1967), chap. 2. On the Black Death and its aftermath see Hollingsworth, *Historical Demography*, pp. 355–88; Clark, *Population Growth*, pp. 82–98; K. Helleiner's chap. 1, in Rich and Wilson, eds., *Cambridge Economic History of Europe*, IV. See also references in next note.

17. See United Nations, *Determinants*, chap. 15, and *The World Population Situation in 1970* (New York: United Nations, 1971), chap. 1; Milos Macura, "The Long Range Outlook," in R. N. Farmer, J. D. Long, and G. J. Stolnitz, eds., *World Population—The View Ahead* (Bloomington: Indiana University Bureau of Business Research, 1968), p. 27. See also United Nations, *Determinants*, 2nd ed., I, 1973, chap. 1; John D. Durand, "The Modern Expansion of World Population," *Proceedings of the American Philosophical Society*, CXI, June, 1967, pp. 136–59; Thomas McKeown, *The Modern Rise of Population*, London, Edward Arnold, 1976.

18. Dublin et al., *Length of Life*, chaps. 2, 4, appendix; *Population Bulletin of the United Nations*, no. 6, 1962, p. 17; Nathan Keyfitz and Wilhelm Flieger, *World Population* (Chicago: University of Chicago Press, 1968); United Nations, *Demographic Yearbook, 1975*.

19. See U.S. Bureau of the Census, *The Two-Child Family and Population Growth: An International View* (Washington, D.C.: 1971); also Tomas Frejka, *The Future of Population Growth: Alternative Paths to Equilibrium* (New York: Wiley & Sons, 1973); Nathan Keyfitz, "On the Momentum of Population Growth," *Demography*, VIII, Feb., 1971, pp. 71–80. According to Gary Littman and Nathan Keyfitz the world's population is growing less rapidly than expected a few years ago; it is expected to number 8.4 billions in 2075 instead of 9.5 or more billion as estimated by the United Nations. Of these only 17.7 percent will be in the developed world. See *The Next Hundred Years*, Working Paper Number 101, Center for Population Studies, Harvard University (Cambridge, Mass., 1977), Preface, pp. 11, 13.

20. For an extreme view see H. von Foerster, P. M. Mora, and L. W. Amiot, "Doomsday: 13 November, A.D. 2026," *Science*, CXXXII, Nov. 4, 1960, pp. 1291–95. They fit empirical curves to population growth over the past 2,000 years.

21. See Tomas Frejka, *Future of Population Growth*, and "The Prospects for a Stationary World Population," *Scientific American*, CCXXIX, April, 1973, pp. 15–23; also his letter of reply to von Foerster's comment based on the article cited in the preceding note. Ibid., July, 1973, p. 8. See also Frejka, "Reflections on the Demographic Conditions Needed to Establish a U.S. Stationary Population Growth," *Population Studies*, XXII, 1968, pp. 379–97. For an optimistic view, see Dudley Kirk's essay in Roger Revelle, ed., *Rapid Population Growth* (Baltimore: The Johns Hopkins Press, 1971), pp. 123–47; also Littman and Keyfitz, *The Next Hundred Years*.

22. See R. Blandy, "The Welfare Analysis of Fertility Reduction," *Economic Journal*, LXXXIV, March, 1974, pp. 109–29; N. E. Terleckyj, ed., *Household Production and Consumption* (New York: Columbia University Press, 1975), Part I; Marc Nerlove, "Household and Economy: Towards a New Theory of Population and Economic Growth" (together with discussion by Zvi Griliches), *Journal of Political Economy*, LXXXII, No. 2, Part II, March / April, 1974, pp. 200–22. See also T. W. Schultz, "The High Value of Human Time: Population Equilibrium," ibid., pp. 2–10, and Schultz, ed., *Economics of the Family: Marriage, Children and Human Capital* (Chicago: University of Chicago Press, 1975). Cf. A. J. Coale, ed., *Economic Factors in Population Growth* (New York: John Wiley & Sons, 1976), Parts I–IV; Boone Turchi, *The Demand for Children: The Economics of Fertility* (Cambridge, Mass.: Ballinger, 1975).

23. Compare K. E. Boulding, "Toward A General Theory of Growth," *Canadian Journal of Economics and Political Science*, XIII, Aug., 1953, pp. 26–40. On growth and form in the biological world see D'Arcy W. Thompson, *On Growth and Form* (Cambridge: University Press, 1917, 1942, 1961).

24. See Lionel Robbins, "On A Certain Ambiguity in the Conception of Stationary Equilibrium," *Economic Journal,* June, 1930, pp. 194–79; J. A. Schumpeter, *History of Economic Analysis* (New York: Oxford University Press, 1954), pp. 55–56, 243, 250, 252, and his *Theory of Economic Development* [1911] (Cambridge: Harvard University Press, 1934); J. D. Pitchford, *The Economics of Population* (Canberra: Australian National University, 1974), chaps. 3–4, esp. pp. 28–31, 35–38, 68–70, and *Population in Economic Growth* (Amsterdam: North Holland, 1924), chaps. 3–4.

25. F. R. Kolb, "The Stationary State of Ricardo and Malthus: Neither Pessimistic nor Prophetic," *Intermountain Economic Review,* III, Spring, 1972, pp. 17–30. See also A. C. Pigou, "The Classical Stationary State," *Economic Journal,* LIII, Dec., 1943, pp. 343–51.

26. *An Inquiry Into the Nature and Causes of the Wealth of Nations,* Modern Library (New York: Random House, 1937), pp. 94–95.

27. Ibid., p. 95. See also Sam Hollander, *The Economics of Adam Smith* (Toronto: University of Toronto Press, 1973), pp. 182–86.

28. As Harvey Leibenstein points out, one need not imply that every wage is at the subsistence level. *A Theory of Economic-Demographic Development* (Princeton: Princeton University Press, 1954), pp. 12–14.

29. David Ricardo, *On the Principles of Political Economy and Taxation,* E. C. K. Gonner, ed. (London: George Bell, 1903), chaps. 5–6, and note on pp. 105–6, where he denies Malthus's view that this stationary state is characterized by stagnation.

30. Ibid., p. 77.

31. Ibid., pp. 112–13, 280, 384.

32. *Principles of Political Economy,* W. J. Ashley, ed. (New York: Longmans Green, 1921), pp. 750–51. See W. C. Bush's model in his "Population and Mill's Peasant-Proprietor Economy," *History of Political Economy,* V, 1973, pp. 110–20; also Pedro Schwartz, *The New Political Economy of J. S. Mill* (Durham: Duke University Press, 1972), chap. 8, esp. pp. 209–12.

33. R. Dorfman, P. A. Samuelson, and R. M. Solow, *Linear Programming and Economic Analysis* (New York: McGraw-Hill, 1958), p. 281. See also P. A. Samuelson on the "logistic law" (which reflects the operation of a limitative factor), in *Foundations of Economic Analysis* (Cambridge: Harvard University Press, 1947), pp. 291–95.

34. *The Distribution of Wealth* (New York: Macmillan, 1899). Cf. F. Y. Edgeworth, "The Theory of Distribution" in *Papers Relating to Political Economy* (London: Macmillan, 1925), pp. 45–46, 49. "The stationary economy is for uncounted thousands of years, and also in historical times in many places for centuries, an incontrovertible fact." J. A. Schumpeter, *The Theory of Economic Development* (Cambridge: Harvard University Press, 1934), p. 83n. On the Austrian conception of stationarity see G. L. S. Shackle, *Epistemics & Economics* (Cambridge: University Press, 1972), pp. 314–18.

35. *Risk, Uncertainty, and Profit* (Boston: Houghton Mifflin, Co., 1921), pp. 144–50; also Knight "Issues in the Economics of Stationary States," *American Economic Review,* XXVI, Sept., 1936, pp. 393–411; Samuelson, *Foundations,* pp. 311–17.

36. *Principles of Economics,* Ninth (variorum) Edition, with annotations by C. W. Guillebaud (London: Macmillan, 1961), I, pp. 366, 320–21, 322, also 691–92.

37. Ibid., pp. 366–67.

38. Ibid., pp. 368–69.

39. *The Economics of Stationary States* (London: Macmillan, 1935), p. 8. Pigou doubted that a stationary state would emerge, given the prospect of "scientific discoveries" and, hence, "new openings for profitable investment." See his *Keynes's 'General Theory'* (London: Macmillan, 1950), pp. 37–38.

40. *The Economics,* p. 10.

41. Ibid., pp. 16–17. Pigou not only called attention as had Marshall to increasing returns and improvement in the "machinery of thought" associated with increase in

population density so long as the elasticity of supply of food and essential raw materials was adequate, but also noted potential if not actual limits to importation of requisite inputs. He added, however, that increase in England's demand for foreign exports was likely to have too little if any effect upon supply prices to affect England's standard of life adversely. *The Economics of Welfare*, 4th ed. (London: Macmillan, 1931), pp. 115–116, 668–669. Under the influence of M. Tarde, Pigou stressed immaterial capital as had Marshall, a form of capital less subject to constraints than was material capital but augmentative of the importance of environmental conditions, since environments "as well as people, have children." Ibid., p. 113.

42. J. M. Keynes, *The General Theory of Employment, Interest and Money* (New York: Harcourt, Brace and Co., 1936), pp. 145–146. According to Shackle stationariness entails learning nothing and forgetting nothing. *Epistemics & Economics*, pp. 270, 478.

43. Keynes, *General Theory*, p. 293.

44. Ibid., pp. 220–221.

45. Ibid., pp. 307–9, also p. 229. See on earlier response to a falling interest rate J. J. Spengler, "Economic Opinion and The Future of The Interest Rate," *Southern Economic Journal*, III, July, 1936, pp. 7–28.

46. Keynes, *General Theory*, p. 318.

47. Ibid., pp. 146, 164.

48. "Some Economic Consequences of A Declining Population," *Eugenics Review*, XXIX, April, 1937, pp. 13–17, esp. p. 17. See my chapters III, IX. Cf. A. C. Pigou, *Keynes's "General Theory,"* (London: 1950), pp. 37–38.

49. See F. H. Hahn and R. C. O. Matthews, "The Theory of Economic Growth: A Survey," Survey V, in *Surveys of Economic Theory*, prepared for the American Economic Association and The Royal Economic Society (London: Macmillan, 1965); Ronald Britto, "Some Recent Developments in the Theory of Economic Growth: An Interpretation," *Journal of Economic Literature*, XI, Dec., 1973, pp. 1343–66. See also R. O. Hieser, "The Economic Consequences of Zero Population Growth," *Economic Record*, XLIX, June, 1973, pp. 241–62. He indicates that in the end zero population growth makes for a stationary state.

50. *Elementary Economics from the Higher Standpoint* (Cambridge: University Press, 1970), p. 53.

51. *The Stationary Economy* (Chicago: Aldine, 1965), p. 25; also Meade, *The Growing Economy* (Chicago: Aldine, 1968), chap. 17. See also on nonconstant returns to scale, F. H. Hahn and R. C. O. Matthews, "The Theory of Economic Growth: A Survey," pp. 55–58.

52. *The Growing Economy*, p. 103.

53. *On Concepts of Capital and Technical Change* (Cambridge: University Press, 1971), pp. 12–13.

54. Ibid., p. 180. The reference to Robinson is to her *The Accumulation of Capital* (London: Macmillan, 1958), pp. 310–11.

55. E.g., see Julius Wolf, *Die Volkswirtschaft der Gegenwart und Zukunft* (Leipzig: 1912), pp. 236ff. The problem was treated by Simon Kuznets in his *Secular Movements in Production and Prices* (New York: Houghton Mifflin Co., 1930).

56. S. K. Kuipers and A. Nentjes conclude that "only if the rate of land-augmenting technical progress is sufficiently high with respect to the growth rates of capital and effective labour, pollution costs will not be a barrier to economic growth"; see "Pollution in a Neo-Classical World: The Classics Rehabilitated?" *De Economist*, CXXI, No. 1, 1973, pp. 52–67, esp. p. 67. See also M. J. Beckman, "The Limits to Growth in a Neoclassical World," *American Economic Review*, LXV, Sept., 1975, pp. 685–99.

57. R. M. Solow, *Growth Theory: An Exposition* (Oxford: Clarendon Press, 1970), pp. 2–4, also pp. 33–38 on technological progress. See also William Nordhaus and James Tobin who find "little reason to worry about the exhaustion of resources which the market already treats as economic goods," given the elasticity of substitu-

tion of other factors for natural resources, together with resource-augmenting technological change. Their view has wide support and is a part of the representative economist's set of long-run expectations. *Economic Growth* (New York: Columbia University Press, 1972), pp. 14–17, 60–70. This volume consists of "Is Growth Obsolete?" by Nordhaus and Tobin, together with discussion; I shall refer to it as *Economic Growth*.

58. P. A. Samuelson, *The Foundations of Economic Analysis* (Cambridge: Harvard University Press, 1947), Part II. See also Bent Hansen, *A Survey of General Equilibrium Systems* (New York: McGraw-Hill, 1970), chap. 18, also chaps. 15–16; Joan Robinson, *Essays in The Theory of Economic Growth* (London: Macmillan, 1963).

59. E.g., see R. M. Solow, *Growth Theory: An Exposition;* also Hansen, *General Equilibrium Systems,* chap. 16 on J. Von Neumann's model.

60. Hansen, *General Equilibrium Systems,* chap. 18, esp. pp. 220–22. See also Britto, "Theory . . . ," p. 1348, on when equality of rate of interest to rate of growth results in equality of savings and investment. "It is impossible for the rate of growth of output to exceed the rate of population growth for a long time, because the scarcity of labour will sooner or later emerge," writes Michio Morishima, *Equilibrium, Stability, and Growth* (Oxford: Clarendon Press, 1964), p. 82.

61. However see Chilsoon Khang, "Equilibrium Growth in the International Economy: The Case of Unequal Natural Rates of Growth," *International Economic Review,* XII, June, 1971, pp. 239–49. But see Paul A. Samuelson, "The Optimum Growth Rate for Population," ibid., XVI, Oct., 1975, pp. 531–38, and Nicholas Georgescu-Roegen, "Energy and Economic Myths," *Southern Economic Journal,* XLI, Jan., 1975, pp. 374–77, reprinted in *Energy and Economic Myths* (New York, Pergamon Press, 1976). See also Ronald Britto, "Steady-State Paths in an Economy with Endogenous Population Growth," *Western Economic Journal,* VIII, Dec., 1970, pp. 390–96; Patrick Guillaumont, "The Optimum Rate of Population Growth," in Coale, ed., *Economic Factors.*

62. See Hahn and Matthews, "The Theory of Economic Growth: A Survey," pp. 110–13; Keynes, *General Theory,* p. 276; also Shackle, *Epistemics & Economics,* chap. 1, esp. pp. 4–7.

63. See Nicholas Georgescu-Roegen, *The Entropy Law and the Economic Process* (Cambridge: Harvard University Press, 1971), p. 281; W. S. Jevons, *The Coal Question,* 3rd ed., A. W. Flux, ed. (London: Macmillan and Co., 1906), chaps. 1, 7–13, 16–17, pp. 9, 11, 220–22, 230–32, 418–24, 459–60.

64. Jevons, *The Coal Question,* p. 232; Mill, *Principles,* p. 477.

65. L. I. Dublin, ed., *Population Problems in The United States and Canada* (Boston: Houghton Mifflin, 1926), chaps. 6–8; Harold Barnett and Chandler Morse, *Scarcity and Growth* (Baltimore: Johns Hopkins Press, 1963).

66. See *The Limits to Growth* (New York: Universe Books, 1972); *World Dynamics* (Cambridge: Wright-Allen Press, 1971). For critiques see W. D. Nordhaus, "World Dynamics: Measurement without Data," *Economic Journal,* LXXXIII, Dec. 1973, pp. 1135–55; Lincoln Gordon, "Limits to the Growth Debate," *Resources* (Resources for the Future), Summer, 1976, pp. 1–6; review by Warren C. Robinson and Robert McGinnis of *Limits to Growth,* in *Demography,* X, May, 1973, pp. 289–99; also H. S. D. Cole, ed., *Thinking About the Future: A Critique of the Limits to Growth* (London: Chattux and Windus, 1974).

67. Mihajlo Mesarovic and Eduard Pestel, *Mankind at the Turning Point* (New York: E. P. Dutton, 1974).

68. Herman E. Daly, ed., *Toward A Steady State Economy* (San Francisco: W. H. Freeman and Co., 1973), p. 14.

69. Nicholas Georgescu-Roegen, "The Entropy Law and the Economic Problem," ibid., pp. 45–48; also Georgescu-Roegen, "Energy and Energy Myth."

70. *Toward A Steady State Economy,* p. 17.

71. E.g., see William Ophuls, "Leviathan or Oblivion," ibid., pp. 215–30. Cf. the options presented by Mesarovic and Pestel, *Mankind at the Turning Point.*

72. See Mancur Olson, ed., *The No-Growth Society,* issued as Vol. 102, No. 4, of

the *Proceedings* of the American Academy of Arts and Sciences, *Daedalus,* Fall, 1973. See especially Olson's introduction, pp. 1–13, the epilogue, pp. 229–41, and essays by Willard R. Johnson and Roland N. McKean.

73. Nordhaus and Tobin, *Economic Growth.* See also references in note 66 above.

74. See Ronald Britto, "Some Recent Developments in the Theory of Economic Growth: An Interpretation," *Journal of Economic Literature,* XI, Dec., 1973, pp. 135–60.

75. See Paul A. Samuelson, "An Economist's Non-Linear Model of Self-Generated Waves," *Population Studies,* XXX, July, 1976, pp. 199, 243–47 and bibliography.

76. E.g., Samuelson, building on R. A. Easterlin's model, concludes that "a possible rebound in fertility in the 1980's is implicit in the Easterlin hypothesis" respecting the United States. Ibid., summary on p. 199.

II. Attitudes toward Population Growth

1. *Papers Relating to Political Economy* (London: Macmillan, 1925), III, p. 65.

2. See parallel arguments of V. Pareto and Alfred Marshall described in "Pareto on Population" in my *Population Economics* (Durham: Duke University Press, 1972), pp. 71–72.

3. "The Limits of Security and Secrecy," *Time,* June 18, 1973, p. 23.

4. Simon Kuznets puts at 1.6 percent per decade the growth of Europe's population between 1000 and 1750 and at not over 0.2 percent per decade the growth of per capita product between 1000 and 1750. *Economic Growth of Nations* (Cambridge: Harvard University Press, 1971), p. 25n., p. 94 and note.

5. We make use of Kuznets's data in ibid., pp. 10–40.

6. See Johnson, *Predecessors of Adam Smith* (New York: Prentice-Hall, 1937), passim, esp. chaps. 12–13; also his *American Economic Thought in the 17th Century* (London: P. S. King, 1932), chap. 6. See also my *French Predecessors of Malthus* (Durham: Duke University Press, 1942), passim; also Michel Cépède, "Exportation de 'terre' et exportation de travail," *Économie Appliquée,* XXII, 1969, pp. 277–94.

7. Slaves were recognized as constituting human capital and varied in price with variation in their supply or their costs of production. See Colin Clark, *The Conditions of Economic Progress,* 3rd ed. (London: Macmillan, 1957), pp. 671–79. Serf labor in Russia and the Austro-Hungarian Empire was only one-half to one-third as efficient as that of Englishmen. Ibid., p. 536. Management theory was not developed enough to generate a theory of human capital. See C. S George, *The History of Management Theory* (Englewood Cliffs: Prentice-Hall, 1968), chaps. 1–3.

8. For example, see H. Michell, *The Economics of Ancient Greece* (Cambridge: University Press, 1940, 1957); A. H. M. Jones, *Athenian Democracy* (Oxford: Blackwell, 1957).

9. A. E. R. Boak, *Manpower Shortage and The Fall of the Roman Empire in the West* (Ann Arbor: University of Michigan Press, 1955), esp. chaps. 1–2, 5. R. M. Haywood takes exception to Boak's well-presented argument in *The Myth of Rome's Fall* (New York: Thomas Y. Crowell Co., 1958), pp. 118–21, also chap. 13.

10. See Clark, *Conditions,* chaps. 11–12, esp. pp. 572ff., 631–43; also C. Clark and M. Haswell, *The Economics of Subsistence Agriculture* (London: Macmillan, 1964), chaps. 5–6; Kuznets, *Economic Growth,* pp. 66–68.

11. *Principles of Economics,* 8th ed., preface, p. xv; this was first written in 1910. On the former importance of land as an asset see Kuznets, *Economic Growth,* pp. 66–69, 106; Clark, *Conditions,* pp. 572–80; R. W. Goldsmith, "The Growth of Reproducible Wealth of the United States of America from 1805 to 1950," in Simon Kuznets, ed., *Income & Wealth of the United States* (Cambridge: Bowes & Bowes, 1952), pp. 247–328, esp. 278–86, 310.

12. E. C. Olson, "Factors Affecting International Differences in Production," *American Economic Review Supplement,* XXXVIII, May, 1948, pp. 502–22.

13. Clark, *Conditions,* chap. 9; W. S. and E. S. Woytinsky, *World Population and*

Production (New York: Twentieth Century Fund, 1953), chap. 13, esp. pp. 424–25, 435–39, also p. 990; S. Lebergott, *Manpower in Economic Growth* (New York: McGraw-Hill, 1964), pp. 510–11; *Population Bulletin of the United Nations,* No. 7, 1963, pp. 134–40.

14. A considerable volume of nonagricultural activities is carried on in rural areas in less-advanced countries. In advanced countries a considerable number of persons employed outside rural areas reside in the latter. See note 24 below.

15. United Nations, *Growth of the World's Urban and Rural Population, 1920–2000* (New York: United Nations, 1969), pp. 24, 31. See also *Population Bulletin of the United Nations,* No. 7, 1963, pp. 137–40.

16. Helmut Haufe, *Die Bevölkerung Europas* (Berlin: Junker and Dünnheinpt, 1936), pp. 225–26. See also W. S. and E. S. Woytinsky, *World Population and Production,* pp. 111–24.

17. M. K. Bennett, *The World's Food* (New York: Harper, 1954), pp. 27, 29–30. See note 23 and text below for Russell's estimates.

18. Agriculture and the progress of urbanization and trade before and after 1000 are dealt with a number of times in *The Cambridge Economic History of Europe* (Cambridge: University Press, 1941ff.), Vols. I–III.

19. E.g., see *Cambridge Economic History of Europe,* III, esp. chap. 1.

20. W. S. and E. S. Woytinsky, *World Population and Production,* p. 413.

21. E.g., see Boak, *Manpower Shortage.*

22. R. Latouche, *The Birth of Western Economy* (London: Methuen, 1961), pp. 97–142, 235–300.

23. J. C. Russell, *Medieval Regions and Their Cities* (Bloomington: University of Indiana Press, 1972), passim and p. 235, and *British Medieval Population* (Albuquerque: University of New Mexico Press, 1948), pp. 304–7. Towns were more congenial than the countryside to plague. See A. R. Bridbury, "The Black Death," *Economic History Review,* XXVI, 1973, pp. 590–92.

24. See Boak, *Manpower Shortage,* chap. 2; Latouche, *Birth of Western Economy,* pp. 67–72, 83–93, 176–208, 244, 273, 308–10. According to the Census of India for 1951, about one-fifth of the labor force living in rural areas was engaged in nonagricultural activities; at that time 83 percent of the labor force lived in rural areas, though only about 70 percent were engaged in agricultural activities. The corresponding fraction engaged in agricultural activities in China in the 1930s was about 70 percent of her population, Clark reports. Often some of the persons reportedly occupied in nonagricultural activities are partly or mainly engaged in agriculture. See Clark, *Conditions,* pp. 496–97.

25. E.g., see Ester Boserup, *The Conditions of Agricultural Growth* (Chicago: Aldine, 1965).

26. E.g., see Clark and Haswell, *Economics of Subsistence Agriculture,* chap. 5; Lester Brown, *Increasing World Food Output* (Washington, D.C.: U.S.D.A., 1965), esp. chaps. 2–3, 8.

27. Clark and Haswell, *Economics of Subsistence Agriculture,* chaps. 6–7; *Conditions,* pp. 313–25; Adam Smith, *An Inquiry,* Bk. III.

28. Adam Smith, *An Inquiry,* p. 146.

29. On pre-railroad transport see Clark, *Conditions,* pp. 312–25; Clark and Haswell, *Economics of Subsistence Agriculture,* chap. 9; P. Deane, *The First Industrial Revolution* (Cambridge: University Press, 1965), chap. 5; also W. S. and E. S. Woytinsky, *World Commerce and Governments* (New York: Twentieth Century Fund, 1955), chaps. 8, 10. On how cities were supplied early in this century see W. P. Hedden, *How Great Cities Are Fed* (Boston: D. C. Heath, 1929). Compare this with the provisioning of ancient Rome described by Boak, *Manpower Shortage,* pp. 65–75.

30. See Brown, *Increasing World Food Output,* pp. 52–57, 66–67. The importance of these external sources to agriculture has increased greatly with the so-called Green Revolution. See Clifton R. Wharton, Jr., "The Green Revolution: Cornucopia or Pandora's Box?" *Foreign Affairs,* XLVII, 1969, pp. 464–76; Leslie Nulty, *The Green*

Revolution in West Pakistan. Implications of Technological Change (New York: Praeger, 1972); Y. Hayami and Vernon Ruttan, *Agricultural Development: An International Perspective* (Baltimore: Johns Hopkins Press, 1971). Under modern conditions sources of what is critical to agriculture often lie outside agricultural countries (e.g., oil, fertilizer).

31. See Clark, *Conditions,* pp. 572–80; also note 11 above.

32. T. K. Rymes, *On Concepts of Capital and Technical Change* (Cambridge: University Press, 1971).

33. J. Chambers and G. Mingay, *The Agricultural Revolution* (London: Botsford, 1966), pp. 115–16, 126, 148–49, 158.

34. W. S. and E. S. Woytinsky, *World Commerce,* pp. 134–51. See also M. M. Postan and H. J. Habakkuk, eds., *Cambridge Economic History of Europe* (1966), VI, Part I, chaps. 3, 6.

35. See my "Adam Smith on Population," *Population Studies,* XXIV, 1970, pp. 377–88. Pre-Smithian writers advocated the exchange of labor-embodying "wrought goods" for food and raw materials of foreign provenance as a means of augmenting the population and labor force of food-short manufacturing countries. E.g., see S. F. Sen, *The Economics of Sir James Steuart* (Cambridge: Harvard University Press, 1957), pp. 75–76.

36. *Principles of Economics,* Ninth Edition, p. xv; this was first included in the sixth edition (1910) preface. See also A. K. Cairncross, *Home and Foreign Investment, 1870–1913* (Cambridge: University Press, 1953), pp. 48, 77, chap. 9. Around the turn of the century Sir William Crookes was warning of the alleged inelasticity of foreign supplies. See below, chap. 3, note 3.

37. *Principles,* pp. xv–xvi. See also on fixity of land and diminishing returns, pp. 148–49 and Bk. IV, chap. 3.

38. *Freedom and Necessity* (London: Allen & Unwin, 1970), p. 62.

39. *Population: A Study in Malthusianism* (New York: Columbia University Press, 1915), chaps. 10–11.

40. *Bevölkerungspolitik nach dem Kriege* (Tübingen: Mohr, 1916).

41. Jena: Fischer, 1929.

42. *Bevölkerungslehre,* Part II. See also A. O. Hirschman, *National Power and the Structure of Foreign Trade* (Berkeley: University of California Press, 1945), Part I.

43. *The Education of Henry Adams* (New York: Modern Library, 1931), chaps. 33–34. These chapters were written in 1904.

44. *Die Volkswirtschaft der Gegenwart u. Zukunft* (Leipzig: A. Deichert, 1912). See also Simon Kuznets, *Secular Movements in Production and Prices* (Boston: Houghton Mifflin, 1930).

45. See J. M. Keynes, *The Economic Consequences of the Peace* (New York: Harcourt, Brace, & Howe, 1920); A. B. Wolfe, "The Population Problem since the World War," *Journal of Political Economy,* in 3 parts, 1928–29, XXXVI–VII.

46. As noted earlier, Jevon's concern rested almost exclusively on the rising cost of coal.

47. Phyllis Deane and W. A. Cole, *British Economic Growth, 1688–1959* (Cambridge: University Press, 1962) p. 141.

48. Most of the people migrating from Europe settled in countries that were sovereign or became so or nearly so; few settled in lands governed from the metropole. See W. S. and E. S. Woytinsky, *World Population and Production,* pp. 56–77.

49. These figures do not include personnel engaged in the production of munitions; that their number became very large is suggested by the fact that in World Wars I and II the ratio of war expenditure to national product rose to 50 percent and higher. See my "Population and Potential Power," in Marcelle Kooy, ed., *Studies in Economics and Economic History* (Durham: Duke University Press, 1972), esp. pp. 134–38. See also Gerry E. Hendershot, "Population Size, Military Power, and Antinatal Policy," *Demography,* X, Nov., 1973, pp. 517–27.

50. B. H. Liddell Hart, *History of the Second World War* (New York: G. P. Putnam's Sons, 1971), pp. 564, 571. See also Charles Fair, *From the Jaws of*

Victory (New York: Simon and Schuster, 1971), chap. 10; Laurence Martin, *Arms and Strategy* (New York: David McKay Co., 1973).

51. See my *France Faces Depopulation* (Durham: Duke University Press, 1938); also E. M. Earle, ed., *Makers of Modern Strategy* (Princeton: Princeton University Press, 1943), pp. 140–54.

52. Otto Prange, *Deutschland's Volkswirtschaft nach dem Kriege* (Berlin: Putkammer und Muhlbrecht, 1915).

53. Based on S. Lebergott, *Manpower in Economic Growth* (New York: McGraw-Hill, 1964), p. 510, and U. S. Bureau of the Census, *Historical Statistics of the United States* (Washington, D.C.: 1960), pp. 710, 736.

54. Lebergott, *Manpower in Economic Growth,* pp. 510, 512, 517.

55. Council of Economic Advisers, *Annual Report* (Washington, D.C.: 1973), pp. 77, 275.

56. Thomas F. Fleming, Jr., "Manpower Impact of Purchases by State and Local Governments," *Monthly Labor Review,* XCVI, June, 1973, pp. 33–39. In 1973 state and local governments generated 16 percent of total civilian employment; in 1959, about 11.9 percent. See also Irving Stern, "Industry Effects of Government Expenditures: An Input-Output Analysis," *Survey of Current Business,* LV, May, 1975, pp. 9–23.

57. U.S. Bureau of the Census, *Statistical Abstract of the United States, 1972,* p. 225. Military expenditure generates less employment per billion dollars, however, than most forms of expenditure, according to a Public Interest Research Group situated in Lansing, Michigan. Durham *Sun,* June 12, 1974, p. 4A.

58. Kuznets, *Economic Growth,* pp. 78, 86–87.

59. Between 1950 and 1971–1972 the number of women in the labor force increased 79 percent, compared with a 20 percent increase in the male component. The long-term rate of decline in hours worked approximated 3 to 4 percent per decade in the nineteenth century; after World War I it may have risen to 4 to 5 percent per decade. Since the number of workers per capita rose not over 1 percent per year, the total input of manhours per capita declined 2–3 percent per year. Ibid., pp. 60–61.

60. Ibid., p. 304.

61. Ibid., pp. 38–40.

62. Ibid., p. 306, also pp. 92–94.

63. Ibid., p. 307.

64. Ibid., pp. 93, 307–8. See also *Revue d'économie politique,* LXXXIII, No. 1, 1973, pp. 1–204, for series of articles on "Les couts de la croissance." See also William Nordhaus and James Tobin, *Economic Growth,* New York: Columbia University Press, 1972.

65. H. A. Simon, *The New Science of Management Decision* (New York: Harper & Row, 1960), p. 38; also *The Shape of Automation for Men and Management* (New York: Harper & Row, 1965), p. 96, also pp. 44–45.

66. *The Shape of Automation,* p. 34.

67. Ibid., p. 40.

68. E.g., under "new era" conditions motherhood as institutionalized supposedly increases woman's share of the total workload. See Jessie Bernard, *The Future of Motherhood* (New York: Deal, 1974). H. J. Heeren anticipates less alarmist reaction to the current decline in fertility than to its decline in the 1920s and 1930s. "Declining Population Growth and Population Policy," *International Social Sciences Journal,* XXVI (2), 1974, pp. 244–54.

69. See Hope T. Eldridge, *Population Policies: A Survey of Recent Developments,* IUSSP, American University, Washington, D.C., 1954; United Nations, *The Determinants and Consequences of Population Trends,* I (New York, 1973), chaps. 16–17.

70. United Nations, *Recent Trends in Fertility in Industrialized Countries* (New York, 1958), esp. chap. 1.

71. E.g., see Alfred Sauvy, *Zero Growth* (New York: Praeger, 1976); also his

"Les charges économiques et les avantages de la croissance de la population," *Population*, XXVII, Jan.–Feb., 1972, pp. 9–26. Cf. the argument that Britain's population is too large in L. R. Taylor, ed., *The Optimum Population for Britain* (New York: Academic Press, 1970).

72. United Nations, *Determinants*, 2nd ed., pp. 564, 566–67. These estimates and projections were made in 1968 and based on assumptions reasonable at the time. Gary Littman and Nathan Keyfitz, on the contrary, anticipate "that births will decline to the point of bare replacement everywhere by the beginning of the 21st century or earlier." *The Next Hundred Years*, Working Paper Number 101, Center for Population Studies, Harvard University (Cambridge, 1977), preface.

73. Ibid., p. 564; United Nations, *The World Population Situation in 1970* (New York, 1971), p. 4.

74. On prospective agricultural land shortage in the United States see David Pimental et al., "Land Degradation: Effects on Food and Energy Resources," *Science*, CXXIV, Oct. 8, 1976, pp. 149–55.

75. E.g., see John P. Holdren and Paul R. Ehrlich, *Global Ecology* (New York: Macmillan, 1973); Nicholas Georgescu-Roegen, *Energy and Economic Myths* (New York: Pergamon, 1976).

76. R. O. Hieser, "The Economic Consequences of Zero Population Growth," *Economic Record*, XLIX, June, 1973, pp. 241–62.

Should fertility and hence the number of births fluctuate more than in the past, concern at this fluctuation will increase appreciably whether it originates in economic fluctuation or in fluctuation in fertility-affecting tastes. For such fluctuation in births can produce fluctuations in the demand for some forms of human resources and physical assets as well as in the employment opportunities confronting relatively large compared with relatively small cohorts.

III. Emerging Concern over the Prospect of a Stationary Population: General Considerations

1. J. M. Keynes, *The Economic Consequences of the Peace* (1919), Vol. 2 of *The Collected Writings of J. M. Keynes* (London: Macmillan, 1971), pp 8–9.

2. See my "Malthus the Malthusian vs. Malthus the Economists," *Southern Economic Journal*, XXIV, 1957, pp. 1–11.

3. Arguments such as Crookes's and Keynes's were criticized as too narrow by R. B. Forrester in "The Limits of Agricultural Expansion," *Economics*, III, 1923, pp. 209–14. See also J. S. Davis, "The Specter of Dearth of Food: History's Answer to Sir William Crookes," in *Facts and Factors in Economic History* (Cambridge: Harvard University Press, 1932), esp. p. 754. In 1950 the Royal Commission on Population expressed the fear that continuing population growth outside Britain, especially in the East, would endanger "Britain's capacity to obtain supplies overseas." *Papers*, III (London: His Majesty's Stationery Office, 1950), pp. 6, 10–13, 58.

4. Keynes, *The Economic Consequences*, pp. 15–16. Cf. Marshall, *Principles*, preface; A. K. Cairncross, *Home and Foreign Investment 1870–1913*, chap. 9, on the advantages derived from Britain's foreign investment.

5. *The Economic Consequences*, in *Collected Writings*, II, p. xxiii.

6. See ibid., pp. xix, xii of preface to French edition of *The Economic Consequences*.

7. See H. G. Moulton and Leo Pasvolsky, *War Debts and World Prosperity* (New York: McGraw-Hill, 1932). This was the last of a series of careful empirical studies conducted by the Brookings Institute of Economics under Moulton's leadership. The first and the one most relevant in the present context was Moulton and C. E. McGuire, *Germany's Capacity to Pay* (New York: McGraw-Hill, 1923).

8. In his "The Theory of Population," Hugh Dalton traced the possibility of using terms of trade to discover changes in population pressure to D. H. Robertson and A. L. Bowley. See *Economica*, VIII, 1928, pp. 28–50, p. 38n; also Robertson, "Word for the Devil," *Economica*, III, 1923, pp. 203–14.

9. *The Economic Consequences,* p. 6.

10. "Population and Unemployment," *Economic Journal,* XXIII, 1923, pp. 447–75, esp. pp. 459, 473. Beveridge elaborated his argument in "Mr. Keynes' Evidence for Over-Population," *Economica,* IV, 1924, pp. 1–20; and "The Fall of Fertility Among European Races," *Economica,* V, 1925, pp. 10–27. Already before the war note had been taken of decline in the birth rate not only in France but elsewhere. E.g., see Julius Wolf, *Der Geburtenrückgang* (Jena: Fischer, 1912). In the 1920s a number of German works appeared on the decline in natality.

11. See Keynes, "A Reply to Sir William Beveridge," *Economic Journal,* XXXIII, 1923, pp. 475–86, esp. pp. 473, 477–79, for Keynes' comments. Keynes might have recognized the presence of the climacteric afflicting Britain had his inquiry been pointed in that direction. E.g., see E. H. Phelps Brown and S. J. Handfield Jones, "The Climacteric of the 1890's; A Study in the Expanding Economy," *Oxford Economic Papers,* IV, 1952, pp. 266–307. See also W. W. Rostow, "The Terms of Trade in Theory and Practice," *Economic History Review,* III, 1950, pp. 1–20, and "The Historical Analysis of the Terms of Trade," ibid., IV, 1951, pp. 53–76.

12. "A Reply," p. 486. Beveridge replied in "Mr. Keynes' Evidence." See also Mark Perlman, "Some Economic Growth Problems and the Part Population Policy Plays," *Quarterly Journal of Economics,* LXXXIX, May, 1975, pp. 247–56.

13. See Quincy Wright, *A Study of War* (Chicago: University of Chicago Press, 1947), II, chaps. 31–32. See also works cited by A. B. Wolfe in his "Since the World War: A Survey of Literature and Research," *Journal of Political Economy,* XXXVI, 1928, pp. 529–59, 662–85, XXXVII, 1929, pp. 87–120, esp. pp. 537–42; also his "Economic Conditions and the Birth Rate After the War," *Journal of Political Economy,* XXV, 1917, pp. 521–41, esp. pp. 540–41. Harold Cox recommended the creation of a "League of Low Birth Rate Nations," prepared to take action, if necessary, against any race that by its too great fecundity is threatening the peace of the world." *The Problem of Population* (New York: G. P. Putnam's Sons, 1923), p. 98.

14. See L. I. Dublin, ed., *Population Problems* (Boston: Houghton Mifflin, 1926). U.S. population capacity was put at about 175 million. Ibid., chap. 7; also chap. 8 on mineral resources. The United States Department of Agriculture put at 300 million the number of people the United States could support at a prewar German standard of living. O. E. Baker put at 250 million the number that could be supported in accordance with tastes current in 1922 and at 400–500 million the number supportable on a "largely vegetarian and dairy diet, so long as the supply of fertilizers held out." For these and other estimates see A. B. Wolfe, "Is There a Biological Law of Human Population Growth?" *Quarterly Journal of Economics,* XLI, 1927, pp. 570–71. On the world situation see also Wolfe's fact-laden series, "The Population Problem Since the World War," *Journal of Political Economy,* 1928, esp. pp. 543–59 and 662–77 on population capacity. See also G. H. Knibbs, *The Shadow of the World's Future* (London: E. Benn, 1928).

15. See A. B. Wolfe, "The Population Problem," esp. pp. 529–42. Wolfe, himself, however, forecast in 1917 that the decline in the birth rate under way in the Western World before the war would continue after the war. He did not even expect that "the legitimate and total [birth] rates" would "manifest the usual normal post-bellum rebound." See his "Economic Conditions," esp. pp. 538–40. See E. M. East's description of the choice before mankind in *Mankind at the Crossroads* (New York: C. Scribner's Sons, 1926).

16. E.g., see Shiroshi Nasu on Japan's population problem in Quincy Wright, ed., *Population* [Harris Foundation Lectures] (Chicago: University of Chicago Press, 1930), pp. 141–207, esp. 205, 207. Thirty-four years earlier, F. Y. Edgeworth, referring to the state of the Japanese economy as of 1615–1860 when numbers grew very little, wrote: "It would seem that the 'stationary state' which some economists have idealized, was not in Japan, a golden age." See his note on "The Stationary State in Japan," *Economic Journal,* V, 1895, pp. 480–81.

17. E.g., see Lionel Robbins "The Optimum Theory of Population," in *London*

Essays in Economics in Honour of Edwin Cannan (London: Routledge, 1920); Edwin Cannan, *A Review of Economic Theory* (London: P. S. King, 1929), chap. 4; and on the ambiguity of criteria, Dalton, "The Theory," pp. 28–50. See also A. B. Wolfe's essay in Dublin *Population Problems*, and his "The Population Problem," esp. pp. 87–93; A. H. Hansen, *Economic Stabilization in an Unbalanced World* (New York: Harcourt Brace and Co., 1932), chap. 13.

18. See my *France Faces Depopulation* (1938), 2nd ed. (Durham: Duke University Press, 1978), esp. chap. entitled "Postlude"; Gérard Calot, ed., "La population de la France," constituting a special June, 1974 number of *Population*, XXIX, 1974, especially chaps. 1, 3; also Wolfe, "The Population Problem," pp. 678–85.

19. See Robert R. Kuczynski *The Measurement of Population Growth* (New York: Oxford University Press, 1936), and *Fertility and Reproduction* (New York: Falcon Press 1932). Also L. I. Dublin, A. J. Lotka, and M. Spiegelman, *The Length of Life*, 2nd ed. (New York: Ronald Press, 1949), chap. 12.

20. *The Balance of Births and Deaths,* I (New York: McGraw-Hill, 1928).

21. L. I. Dublin and A. J. Lotka, "On the True Rate of Natural Increase," *Journal of the American Statistical Association,* XX, Sept., 1925, pp. 205–39. See also their *Length of Life*, 1st ed. (New York, 1936).

22. Kuczynski, *The Balance,* I, chaps. 3–4. See also his *The Measurement of Population Growth,* chaps. 1, 4, 6.

23. Dublin and Lotka, *Length of Life,* chap. 12, and their "On the True Rate."

24. New York, McGraw-Hill, 1933. See Raymond Pearl's delightful review of the report, "America Today and Maybe Tomorrow," *Quarterly Review of Biology,* VIII, March, 1933, pp. 96–101.

25. *Population Trends,* pp. 4–13, 312–70.

26. Ibid., p. 319.

27. Ibid., pp. 312–14; also my "Population Prediction In Nineteenth Century America," *American Sociological Review,* I, Dec., 1936, pp. 905–21.

28. National Resources Committee, *The Problems of a Changing Population* (Washington, D.C.: U.S. Government Printing Office, 1938), pp. 22–26.

29. National Resources Planning Board, *Estimates of the Population of the United States 1940–2000* (Washington, D.C.: 1943), pp. 3ff.

30. See Joseph S. Davis's review of the forecasts in *The Population Upsurge in the United States* (War-Peace Pamphlet No. 12) (Stanford: Food Research Institute, 1949).

31. Royal Commission on Population, *Reports and Selected Papers of the Statistics Committee,* II (London: 1950), esp. pp. 213–301; Kuczynski, *The Balance of Births and Deaths,* I and II; D. V. Glass, *Population Policies and Movements in Europe* (Oxford: Clarendon Press, 1940), and *The Struggle for Population* (Oxford: Clarendon Press, 1936); Alva Myrdal, *Nation and Family* (New York: Harper & Brothers, 1941); chaps. 2, 5; F. W. Notestein et al., *The Future Population of Europe and the Soviet Union* (Geneva: League of Nations, 1944); P. J. Deneffe, *Die Berechnungen über die künftige deutsche Bevolkerungsentwicklung* (Leipzig: Hans Buske, 1938); August Lösch, *Was ist vom Geburtenrückgang zu halten?* Heidenheim (Wurttemberg), 1932; F. Burgdörfer, *Volk ohne Jugend* (Berlin, 1932, 1933, 1935).

32. Kuczynski, *Fertility and Reproduction,* pp. 41–65, and *Measurement,* p. 207 and note. Dublin and Lotka were the first outside Germany to calculate such a table, according to Kuczynski, *Measurement,* p. 207. Lotka and F. R. Sharpe had developed the concept of stable population by 1911. See *Length of Life,* 2nd ed., p. 237n.

33. *Economic Scares* (London: P. S. King and Son, 1933), p. 88. Cannan's articles appeared in the *Economic Journal* in 1895 and 1901; they are reprinted in *Economic Scares,* pp. 108–35.

34. Ibid., p. 89.

35. See my *France Faces Depopulation;* also Elvi Castelot, "Stationary Population in France," *Economic Journal,* XIV, June, 1904, pp. 249–53.

36. *Economic Scares,* p. 132.
37. Ibid., pp. 134–35. In 1932, however, he noted the fall in natality in Germany and elsewhere in Europe. Ibid., p. 135n.
38. On population studies in Australia see Craufurd D. W. Goodwin's *Economic Enquiry in Australia* (Durham: Duke University Press, 1966), chap. 12.
39. On Pearl's work see, e.g., his *The Biology of Population Growth* (New York: Knopf, 1925); *The Natural History of Population* (New York: Oxford University Press, 1939); *Introduction to Medical Biometry and Statistics* (Philadelphia: Saunders, 1923, 1930), 3rd ed., 1940, esp. chaps. 2, 18. For an excellent critique of the logistic and other empirical theories of population forecasting see Wolfe, "Is There A Biological Law of Human Population Growth?" pp. 567–94, and his "The Population Problem," pp. 677–85; also A. J. Lotka, *Elements of Physical Biology* (Baltimore: Williams & Wilkins, 1925), Part II, esp. chap. 7, and Davis, *The Population Upsurge,* passim.
40. E.g., see Spengler, *France Faces Depopulation;* E. Kahn, *Der internationale Geburtenstreik* (Frankfort-am-Main, 1930).
41. E.g., see Vilfredo Pareto, *Trattato di Sociologia generale* (1916, 1923), translated and edited by Arthur Livingston as *The Mind and Society* (New York: Harcourt, Brace and Co., 1935), chaps. 12–13; P. A. Sorokin, *Social and Cultural Dynamics* (New York: American Book Co., 1937), preface, and *Contemporary Sociological Theories* (New York: Harper, 1928), pp. 720–21, 729ff.
42. *The Decline of the West* (1918), II (New York: Alfred A. Knopf, 1926), pp. 104–7, 504–7. See also Sorokin, *Contemporary Sociological Theories,* pp. 304–7.
43. Gini's theory was presented in more summary form in 1929. See "The Cyclical Rise and Fall of Population," in Wright, ed., *Population,* pp. 1–140. See also Sorokin, *Contemporary Sociological Theories,* chaps. 5, 7.
44. Gini, "Cyclical Rise and Fall," pp. 9, 91.
45. E.g., see Maurice Block, *Statistique de la France comparée avec divers pays de l'Europe,* 2nd ed. (Paris, 1875), chaps. 1–2, 6, pp. 484–85, chaps. 10–11.
46. R. R. Kuczynski, "The World's Future Population," in Wright, ed., *Population,* p. 302. Cf. E. B. Attah, "Racial Aspects of Zero Population Growth," *Science,* LXXX, June 15, 1973, pp. 1143–51.
47. *The Balance of Tomorrow* (New York: G. P. Putnam's Sons, 1945), Part II.
48. Ibid., p. 115.
49. F. W. Notestein, "Population and Power in Postwar Europe," *Foreign Affairs,* XXII, April, 1944, pp. 389–403.
50. Unsigned, "World Population," *Life,* September 3, 1945, pp. 45–51.
51. Royal Commission on Population, *Report* (London: His Majesty's Stationery Office, 1949), pp. 134, 225–26. See also PEP (Political and Economic Planning), *Population Policy In Great Britain* (London: S.W.1, PEP, April, 1948).
52. *Life,* September 3, 1945, p. 45.
53. See Glass, *The Struggle for Population* and *Population Policies.*
54. On this legislation and its subsequent development see Glass, *Population Policies,* chaps. 3–4; Cicely Watson's series of fine articles on France and Belgium in *Population Studies,* V, 1952, pp. 261–86, VI, 1953, pp. 3–38, VII, 1953–1954, pp. 14–45, 263–86, VIII, 1954, pp. 46–73, 152–87. Gérard Calot, ed., "La population de la France," chaps. 11–12; my *France Faces Depopulation,* especially "Postlude."
55. On the Swedish program, Swedish opinion, and related matters, see Alva Myrdal, "A Programme for Family Security in Sweden," *International Labour Review,* XXXIX, June, 1939, pp. 723–63, and idem, *Nation and Family* (New York: Harper & Brothers, 1941). See also Gunnar Myrdal's Godkin Lectures, 1938, published as *Population, A Problem for Democracy* (Cambridge: Harvard University Press, 1940); Arthur Montgomery, "Befolkningskommissionen Och Befolknings-frågan," *Ekonomisk Tidskrift,* XLI, September, 1939, pp. 200–21.
56. Gunnar Myrdal, *Population, A Problem,* chap. 7; Alva Myrdal, *Nation and Family,* esp. chaps. 6–8, 16, 17, 19–21. Gustav Cassel, probably the best-known of Sweden's pre-1940 economists, was not much concerned with population trends,

counting upon economic equilibrating tendencies and noting the advantages of a relatively stationary population. See J. J. Spengler, "Cassel on Population," *History of Political Economy,* I, Spring, 1969, pp. 150–72.

57. See *Report,* presented to Parliament in June, 1949.

58. Ibid., pp. 232- 33.

59. Royal Commission on Population, *Papers,* III, pp. 57, 61.

60. See "The Population Problem," reprinted in his *Economic Essays* (London: Macmillan, 1952, 1972). My references are to the 1972 edition, which includes one additional essay. Harrod described in the preface to the 1972 edition how, as "a great believer in the existence of a variety and inequality of stocks," among whom the British (as were the Japanese) were outstanding, he believed it "expedient, for the sake of mankind, that they should not eventually die out." See 2nd edition, p. xii. Harrod expressed concern at the population trend in his *The Trade Cycle* (Oxford: Clarendon Press, 1936), pp. 219–20, 224–25. Also his "Report of the Royal Commission on Population—A Comment," *Journal of Development Studies,* X, 1973–74, pp. 232–53.

61. *Economic Essays,* 2nd ed., pp. 3–41. Even given a redundant population in the British isles there remained wide open places in the world which redundant British could settle. "Report . . . —A Comment," p. 253.

62. Glass, *Population Policies;* Hope T. Eldridge, *Population Policies: A Survey of Recent Developments* (Washington, D.C.: American University, 1954); United Nations, *Incomes in Postwar Europe: A Study of Policies, Growth, and Distribution* (Geneva: United Nations, 1967), chap. 9.

63. See Kingsley Davis and Judith Blake, "Social Structure and Fertility: An Analytic Framework," *Economic Development and Cultural Change,* IV, 1956, pp. 211–245; Edward Pohlman, *Incentives and Compensations in Birth Planning,* Monograph 11 (Chapel Hill, N.C.: Carolina Population Center, 1971).

64. Hans Staudinger, "Germany's Population Miracle," *Social Research,* V, May, 1938, pp. 125–48, esp. pp. 147–48.

65. For a full account see the "Postlude" to my *France Faces Depopulation,* reprinted by Duke University Press in 1978. See also the files of *Population,* which has given a running account of French population movements and policies since its appearance in 1946.

66. Illustrative of French demographic thought is Alfred Sauvy's *Théorie génerale de la population.* (Paris: Presses Universitaire de France, 1966). Sauvy has played a major role in the formation of French demographic policy.

67. Prange, *Deutschland's Volkswirtschaft nach dem Kriege* (Berlin, 1915); F. Y. Edgeworth, "Some German Writings about the War," in his *Papers Relating to Political Economy* III (London: Macmillan, 1925), pp. 215–28, esp. 222.

68. See W. J. Kelly, "Comment on Hendershot's 'Population Size, Military Power, and Antinatal Policy,'" *Demography,* XI, Aug., 1974, pp. 533–35; also note 49 in chap. II above.

69. E.g., see Oleg Zinam, "Optimum Population Growth Concept and the Zero Population Growth Thesis," *Economia Internazionale,* XXVII, May, 1974, pp. 320–38.

IV. Emerging Concern over the Prospect of a Stationary or Declining Population: Economic Considerations

1. For a simple statement of Keynes's view see his "A Self-Adjusting Economic System?" *The New Republic,* Feb. 20, 1935, pp. 35–37. On the ultimately critical character of population growth see R. O. Hieser, "The Economic Consequences of Zero Population Growth," *Economic Record,* XLIX, June, 1973, pp. 241–62. In his *Keynes' Monetary Thought* (Durham: Duke University Press, 1976), Don Patinkin touches a number of times on Keynes's lack of faith in the efficacy of orthodox flexibility-producing mechanisms.

2. Douglas, *The Theory of Wages* (New York: Macmillan, 1934), pp. 150–55; 438–43, 457; Knight, "Professor Fisher's Interest Theory: A Case in Point," *Journal of Political Economy*, XXXIX, April, 1931, pp. 176–212, esp. 208–10. See also my "Economic Opinion and the Future of the Interest Rate," *Southern Economic Journal*, III, 1936, pp. 7–28, and "Cassel on Population," *History of Political Economy*, I, Spring, 1969, pp. 150–72.

3. Douglas, *The Theory of Wages*, pp. 150–55, 501–2; Pigou, *The Theory of Unemployment* (London: Macmillan, 1933), p. 97. Here Douglas does not refer to unemployment of a seasonal, cyclical, or technological nature. *The Theory of Wages*, p. 502.

4. *The Theory*, Part II, chap. 9, pp. 96–97.

5. *The Theory*, Part II, chap. 10, p. 106, also Part IV, on how monetary factors could modify the assumption of *ceteris paribus*.

6. Ibid., pp. 236–37, also 238–43. See also p. v and pp. 250–51.

7. "Elasticity of Supply as a Determinant of Distribution," in J. H. Hollander, ed., *Economic Essays Contributed in Honor of John Bates Clark* (New York: Macmillan, 1927), pp. 71–118, esp. pp. 95–96; *The Theory of Wages*, pp. 482–83.

8. Douglas, "Elasticity of Supply," p. 116; A. H. Hansen, *Economic Stabilization in an Unbalanced World* (New York: Harcourt, Brace and Co., 1932), pp. 232–33. Earlier Hansen noted some effects of population growth, such as the impact of surplus agricultural population and the destabilizing influence of population growth in general, an influence remarked by European writers on the business cycle. See Hansen, *Business Cycle Theory* (Boston: Ginn and Co., 1977), pp. 4, 74–75, 114–115.

9. Hansen, *Economic Stabilization*, chaps. 13–15, esp. p. 238.

10. Ibid., chaps. 9–10, 21, 24.

11. Clark, *Economics of Planning Public Works* (Washington, D.C.: National Planning Board, 1935), pp. 43, 47, 49, 85–100.

12. Clark, *Strategic Factors in Business Cycles* (New York: National Bureau of Economic Research, 1934), pp. 132, 141–42, 225. While he later admitted the possibility of "an inherent tendency to oversaving or underinvestment," he rejected the proposal that public investment fill the gap, noting that such a policy would prove cumulatively depressive. See his contribution to National Resources Planning Board, *The Structure of the American Economy*, Part II, *Toward Full Use of Resources* (Washington, D.C.: 1940), pp. 20–26, esp. pp. 24–26.

13. *The Theory*, Part V, chap. 8, esp. p. 287. See also Lionel Robbins, "Notes on Some Probable Consequences of the Advent of a Stationary Population in Great Britain," *Economica*, IX, 1929, pp. 71–82. Pigou neglected the impact of population change in his *Industrial Fluctuations* (London: Macmillan, 1927).

14. E.g., see Guy Chapman, *Culture and Survival* (London: Jonathan Cape, 1940), chaps. 8–10; Enid Charles, *The Twilight of Parenthood* (New York: W. W. Norton and Co., 1934), chaps. 5–6, and "The Effects of Present Trends In Fertility and Mortality Upon the Future Population of Great Britain and Upon Its Age Composition," in Lancelot Hogben, ed., *Political Arithmetic* (New York: Macmillan, 1938), chap. 2; also *Population Policy in Great Britain*, a Report by Political and Economic Planning (London: 1948), chap. 2. See also Adolph Landry, "La révolution démographique," in *Economic Essays In Honour of Gustav Cassel* (London: Allen & Unwin, 1933), pp. 357–68.

15. See A. H. Hansen, *A Guide to Keynes* (New York: McGraw-Hill, 1953), chaps. 1, 13; Dudley Dillard, *The Economics of John Maynard Keynes* (New York: Prentice-Hall, 1948), chap. 12; L. R. Klein, *The Keynesian Revolution* (New York: Macmillan, 1947), passim; Paul Lambert, "The Evolution of Keynes's Thought From the Treatise on Money to the 'General Theory'," *Annals of Public and Co-Operative Economy*, 1969, pp. 1–21. See also Vincent Tarascio's formalization of Keynes's theory of growth in "Keynes on the Sources of Economic Growth," *Journal of Economic History*, XXXI, June, 1971, pp. 429–44.

16. Eprime Eshag, *From Marshall to Keynes* (Oxford: Blackwell, 1963), pp.

128–44. In the first Keynes Lecture, E. A. G. Robinson observed that "much of what Keynes first taught our generation has now become so completely absorbed into the orthodoxy of economics that it is forgotten how great was the revolution in our whole method of thought that he pioneered and others have continued to develop." "John Maynard Keynes: Economist, Author, Statesman," *Economic Journal*, LXXXII, June, 1972, p. 542.

17. *A Treatise on Money*, II (New York: Harcourt, Brace and Co., 1930), chap. 30, pp. 188–89. See also 203–4, 377–80 on the "natural-rate" and the "tendency for the market rate" not to adjust quickly to changes in the natural rate; also pp. 183–84 on the stickiness of wages in a "Modern World of organised Trade Unions and a proleterian electorate" that makes them "overwhelmingly strong."

18. Ibid., pp. 377–78.

19. Ibid., p. 378.

20. Ibid., p. 379, and see pp. 377–87.

21. Ibid., p. 384.

22. *General Theory*, chaps. 16–20.

23. "Some Consequences of a Declining Population," *Eugenics Review*, XXIX, April, 1937, pp. 13–17, p. 15.

24. Ibid., p. 15.

25. Ibid.

26. Ibid., p. 16.

27. Ibid.

28. Ibid., pp. 16–17. Keynes did not make use in his *General Theory* of the concept of "natural rate of interest," widely used in the *Treatise*.

29. *General Theory*, pp. 217–18, also 325–26.

30. Ibid., pp. 220–21, 293, 319–20, also 213–14 on labor "as the sole factor of production."

31. Ibid., pp. 213–21, 306–9, also 317–18 on lengthening the trade cycle.

32. Ibid., pp. 161, 164, 220–21, 324–29, 335, 349, 351, 374–81.

33. Ibid., pp. 202, 205, 238, 246, 263–65, 316–18. See also Dillard, *Economics of John Maynard Keynes*, pp. 142–55, 176–77; Hansen, *A Guide to Keynes*, pp. 45–54, 207–14; D. G. Champernowne, "Expectations and the Links Between the Economic Future and the Present," in Robert Lekachman, *Keynes' General Theory. Reports of Three Decades* (New York: St. Martin's Press, 1964), pp. 174–202.

34. J. R. Hicks, "Mr. Keynes' Theory of Employment," *Economic Journal*, XLVI, June, 1936, pp. 252–53. One result of Keynes's *General Theory* was greater emphasis upon the role of long-term expectation as distinguished from short-term expectation as treated in business cycle theory. See for a sample of papers on expectations those listed in American Economic Association, *Readings In Business Cycle Theory* (Philadelphia: Blakiston Co., 1944), pp. 475–76.

35. *Value and Capital*, 2nd ed. (Oxford: Clarendon Press, 1946), p. 302 and note.

36. Dillard, *Economics of John Maynard Keynes*, p. 155. See Hansen, *Full Recovery or Stagnation?* (New York: Norton, 1938), pp. 289, 303–18; also Benjamin H. Higgins, "The Doctrine of Economic Maturity," *American Economic Review*, XXXVI, March, 1946, pp. 133–41, and "The Theory of Increasing Unemployment," *Economic Journal*, LX, June, 1950, pp. 255–74.

37. J. Steindl, *Maturity and Stagnation In American Capitalism* (Oxford: Blackwell, 1952). See also Paul M. Sweezy, "John Maynard Keynes," in Lekachman, *Keynes' General Theory*, pp. 297–314, and Sweezy, *The Theory of Capitalist Development* (New York: Oxford University Press, 1942), chap. 12.

38. J. A. Schumpeter, *Capitalism, Socialism, and Democracy*, 2nd ed. (New York: McGraw-Hill, 1945), chap. 7, pp. 82–83, also chap. 9.

39. Ibid., chaps. 9–11.

40. Ibid., chaps. 11–13.

41. Ibid., chap. 14. See also Schumpeter's *Business Cycles*, II (New York: Mc-Graw-Hill, 1939), pp. 697–700 on "the loosening of the family tie."

42. Ibid., pp. 497–98, 699, 1935–37, I, p. 311; *Capitalism, Socialism*, Part II,

cf. C. O. Hardy's critique, "Schumpeter on Capitalism, Socialism and Democracy," *Journal of Political Economy,* LIII, Dec., 1945, pp. 348–56.

43. "Economic Progress and Declining Population Growth," *American Economic Review,* XXIX, 1939, pp. 1–15, reprinted with slight modification in Gottfried Haberler, ed., *Readings in Business Cycle Theory* (Philadelphia: Blakeston, 1944), pp. 366–84. See also Hansen's and related views in *Report of the Temporary National Economic Committee,* Part IX, *Savings and Investment* (Washington, D.C.: U. S. Government Printing Office, 1940).

44. *Readings,* p. 370. For a more formal statement see Ben H. Higgins, "The Concept of Secular Stagnation," *American Economic Review,* XL, March, 1950, pp. 160–66, and "The Theory of Increasing Underemployment," *Economic Journal,* LX, June, 1950, pp. 255–74.

45. Hansen, *Readings,* p. 376.

46. Ibid., pp. 374–75.

47. Ibid., pp. 378–79.

48. Ibid., pp. 380–81.

49. Ibid., p. 381.

50. Ibid., pp. 383–84.

51. *Fiscal Policy and Business Cycles* (New York: Norton, 1941); also *Economic Policy and Full Employment* (New York: McGraw-Hill, 1947).

52. *Business Cycles and National Income* (New York: Norton, 1951), p. 488.

53. Ibid., pp. 75–76. With investment dependent on population growth, inventions, and the discovery and development of new territory and resources, the essential issue was: "Are the automatic forces making for investment outlets as strong in our world today as in the century preceding World War I?" See *Economic Policy and Full Employment,* p. 298.

54. *Keynes' General Theory.* See also Mark Perlman, "Some Economic Growth Problems and the Part Population Policy Plays," *Quarterly Journal of Economics,* LXXXIX, May, 1975, pp. 247–56.

55. See *Readings in Business Cycle Theory* (1944), pp. 451–57, 460–65, 471–74, 476–85, esp. 484–85. See also Melvin D. Brockie, "Population Growth and the Rate of Investment," *Southern Economic Journal,* XVII, July, 1950, pp. 1–15; H. A. Adler, "Absolute or Relative Decline in Population Growth," *Quarterly Journal of Economics,* LIX, Aug., 1945, pp. 626–34.

56. Chicago, Machinery and Allied Products Institute, 1945. See also Martin V. Jones's essay, "Secular Trends and Idle Resources," *Journal of Business* of the University of Chicago, XVII, No. 4, Part 2, October, 1944, p. 76. Hansen replied to Terborgh's critique in his *Economic Policy and Full Employment* (New York: McGraw-Hill, 1947), Appendix B, pp. 298–306. See also the extensive bibliography in William J. Serow, "The Economics of Stationary and Declining Populations: Some Views from the First Half of the Twentieth Century," in Joseph J. Spengler, ed., *Zero Population Growth: Implications* (Chapel Hill: Carolina Population Center, 1975), chap. 2.

57. E.g., see Joan Robinson, *Essays in the Theory of Employment* (New York: Macmillan, 1937), Part II, esp. pp. 153–61; A. R. Sweezy, "Population Growth and Investment Opportunity," *Quarterly Journal of Economics,* LV, Nov., 1940, pp. 64–79, esp. 77–79.

58. *Economic Essays* (London: Macmillan, 1972), p. 273.

59. Ibid., pp. 274–75.

60. Ibid., p. 276.

61. R. F. Harrod, *The Trade Cycle* (Oxford: Clarendon Press, 1936), pp. 106–8, 219–25. Harrod refers to Keynes's *General Theory* a number of times. See also Harrod's "Modern Population Trends," *Manchester School of Economics and Social Studies,* X, March, 1939, pp. 1–20.

62. *Trade Cycle,* p. 101; W. B. Reddaway, "Special Obstacles to Full Employment In a Wealthy Community," *Economic Journal,* XLVII, June, 1937, pp. 297–307, esp. 298, 304; also Reddaway, *The Economics of A Declining Population* (New York: Macmillan, 1939), pp. 107–8, and 117–19 on the increased sensitivity of

capital outley to variation. Cf. F. Lafitte, "The Economic Effects of a Declining Population," *Eugenics Review,* XXXII, 1940, pp. 121–34.

63. A. Loveday, et al., *The World's Future. The Halley Stewart Lectures, 1937* (London: Allen and Unwin, 1938).

64. Royal Commission on Population (London: His Majesty's Stationery Office, 1949) *Report of the Economics Committee,* p. 13.

65. Ibid., pp. 60–61. The PEP report on *Population Policy in Great Britain* placed stress upon improving the quality of the population and encouraging an average of considerably more than two children." See PEP (Political and Economic Planning), *Population Policy in Great Britain* (London: S. W. I., PEP, April, 1948), Parts 2–5.

66. "Declining Investment Opportunity," in Seymour E. Harris, *The New Economics* (New York, Knopf: 1947), pp. 424–35, esp. pp. 430–31. See also Alan R. Sweezy, "The Natural History of the Stagnation Thesis," in Spengler, *Zero Population Growth: Implications,* pp. 24–43.

67. "Declining Investment Opportunity," pp. 433–34; also Sweezy's and Aaron Owens's, "The Impact of Population Growth on Employment," *American Economic Review,* LXIV (2), May, 1974, pp. 45–50. Cf. J. E. Meade, *Trade and Welfare,* II (London: Oxford University Press, 1955), pp. 93–94, where Meade, assumes that "if the welfare of all generations is to be maximized the community must go on saving and accumulating . . . so long as the marginal product of capital is greater than zero"—that is, until "all consumers' needs" have been "satisfied" and a "product glut" has developed, or until, even though consumers' needs remain unsatisfied and the labor force is susceptible of further increase, fixity of the supply of land with which labor and capital can work sets a limit to further growth and introduces a "capital glut." *Trade and Welfare,* p. 93.

68. Sweezy, "Declining Investment Opportunity," p. 455, reports of the Council of Economic Advisers; also Simon Kuznets, *Capital in the American Economy* (Princeton: Princeton University Press, 1961), chap. 3.

69. Warren L. Smith, *Macroeconomics* (Homewood, Ill.: Irwin, 1970), pp. 192–93. On interest elasticity see W. H. White, "Interest Inelasticity of Investment Demand," *American Economic Review,* XLVI, Sept., 1956, pp. 565–87.

70. Smith, *Macroeconomics,* pp. 452–53. Cf. Evsey Domar, "Expansion and Employment," *American Economic Review,* XXXVII, March, 1947, pp. 34–55; and see also Richard X. Chase, "Keynes and U.S. Keynesianism: A Lack of Historical Perspective and the Decline of the New Economics," *Journal of Economic Issues,* IX, Sept., 1973, pp. 441–70.

71. "Stationary Population—Stagnant Economy," *Social Research,* VI, May, 1939, pp. 141–52.

72. Hans Neisser, "The Economics of a Stationary Population," *Social Research,* XI, Nov., 1944, pp. 470–90, esp. pp. 475–88.

73. Ibid., pp. 484–88.

74. Ibid., p. 483.

75. E.g., see Benjamin Higgins, "Concepts and Criteria of Secular Stagnation," in Higgins et al., *Income, Employment and Public Policy, Essays in Honor of Alvin H. Hansen* (New York: W. W. Norton, 1948), chap. 4, pp. 98–100; Evsey D. Domar, "Investment Losses, and Monopolies," ibid., chap. 2, pp. 39–44; Clarence L. Barber, "Population Growth and the Demand for Capital," *American Economic Review,* XLIII, March, 1953, pp. 133–39; Leon Goldenberg, "Savings in A State with A Stationary Population," *Quarterly Journal of Economics,* LXI, Nov., 1946, pp. 40–65.

76. See Richard M. Goodwin, "Secular and Cyclical Aspects of the Multiplier and the Accelerator," in Higgins et al., *Income, Employment and Public Policy,* chap. 5; Joseph J. Spengler, "Population Movements, Employment, and Income," *Southern Economic Journal,* V, Oct., 1938, pp. 129–57; S. C. Tsiang, "The Effect of Population Growth on the General Level of Employment and Activity," *Economica,* IX (NS), Nov., 1942, pp. 325–32.

77. *Bevölkerungswellen und Wechsellagen* (Jena: Gustav Fischer, 1936), and

"Population Cycles as a Cause of Business Cycles," *Quarterly Journal of Economics,* LI, Aug., 1937, pp. 649–62.

78. *Business Cycles and Economic Growth* (New York: McGraw-Hill, 1958), pp. 288ff., also pp. 227–28, 263, 265. Cf. Jan Tinbergen and J. J. Polak, *The Dynamics of Business Cycles* (Chicago University of Chicago Press, 1950), pp. 24–26, 112, 132–35, 247, 258.

79. E.g., see R. C. O. Matthews, *The Business Cycle* (Chicago: University of Chicago Press, 1959).

80. "The Economics of an Aging Population," *Lloyd's Bank Review,* No. 27, 1953, pp. 25–36.

81. Ibid., pp. 34–36.

82. *The Economics of a Declining Population,* p. 40.

83. Ibid., chaps. 2–3, esp. pp. 60, 68, 89–90.

84. Ibid., chap. 4.

85. Ibid., chap. 5 and appendix B.

86. Ibid., pp. 153–60, 167, 214.

87. Ibid., chap. 8.

88. Ibid., chap. 10. Australian trade would also be adversely affected. Ibid., p. 215. Cf. J. R. Hicks's discussion of the impact of slowing population growth in advanced countries upon underdeveloped countries' terms of trade and access to foreign capital. "Growth and Anti-Growth," *Oxford Economic Papers,* XVIII, Nov., 1966, pp. 257–69.

89. Reddaway, *The Economics,* pp. 220–26.

90. Ibid., p. 226.

91. Ibid., pp. 231–32.

92. Ibid., p. 237.

93. Ibid., pp. 238–45, also Appendix A. These proposals are the reverse of anti-natalist programs. E.g., see B. Berelson, "Beyond Family Planning," *Science,* CLXIII, Feb. 7, 1969, pp. 533–43.

94. Published as a Supplement to *Population Studies,* May, 1970.

95. Ibid., pp. 25–31.

96. "Some Macroeconomics of Population Levelling," in Commission on Population Growth and the American Future, *Economic Aspects of Population Change,* E. R. Morss and Ritchie H. Reed, eds., Vol. II of Commission Research Reports (Washington, D.C.: U.S. Government Printing Office, 1972), pp. 75–84, esp. pp. 81–82.

97. Ibid., pp. 85–89. However, Paul Douglas's 1925 forecast has been borne out, namely, that the family allowance system would spread widely (though not on populationist grounds as such). See his essay in L. I. Dublin, ed., *Population Problems in the United States and Canada* (Boston: Houghton Mifflin, 1926), chap. 18.

98. A. J. Coale, ed., *Demographic and Economic Change in Developed Countries* (Princeton: Princeton University Press, 1960), p. 371. Cf. J. R. Hicks's conclusion cited in note 35 above.

99. The data are taken from *Current Population Reports,* Series P-25, No. 601, October, 1975, Tables 9, 12.

100. Japan Information Service (Consulate General of Japan, New York), XXII, No. 22, Nov. 16, 1976, pp. 1–2.

101. With fertility at the replacement level, school and college enrollment will rise and fall owing to echo effects but not move to a stable level until in the early twenty-first century. E.g., see Bureau of the Census, *Current Population Reports,* "Projections of School and College Enrollment: 1971 to 2000," Series P-25, No. 473, Jan., 1972.

V. Age Composition

1. E.g., United Nations, *The Determinants and Consequences of Population Trends,* 2nd ed., Vol. I, pp. 274–81.

2. A. J. Coale, *The Growth and Structure of Human Populations* (Princeton: Princeton University Press, 1972), p. 206; see also A. W. Lopez, *Some Problems in a Stable Population Theory* (Princeton: Princeton University Press, 1961), passim; United Nations, *The Concept of a Stable Population* (New York: United Nations, 1968), chap. 1, esp. pp. 3–8.

3. What follows in this and the two succeeding paragraphs is based on N. B. Ryder's excellent "Notes on Stationary Populations," *Population Index,* XLI, Jan., 1975, pp. 3–27.

4. United Nations, *The Concept of a Stable Population, Population Studies,* No. 39 (New York, 1968), p. 5; also J. H. Pollard, *Mathematical Models for the Growth of Human Populations* (Cambridge: University Press, 1973).

5. See T. N. E. Greville, ed., *Population Dynamics* (New York: Academic Press, 1972), esp. chap. 1, "Population Waves," by Nathan Keyfitz.

6. Coale, *The Growth,* esp. chaps. 2–3; Ryder, "Notes," pp. 14–17.

7. United Nations, *The Concept,* p. 168, and *The Aging of Populations,* pp. 26–30.

8. Ansley J. Coale, "Increases in Expectation of Life and Population Growth," International Union for the Scientific Study of Population, *International Population Conference* (Vienna, 1959), pp. 36–41; also *The Growth,* pp. 58–60. See also Coale, "Age Composition in the Absence of Mortality and Other Odd Circumstances," *Demography,* X, Nov., 1973, pp. 537–42.

9. United Nations, *The Aging,* pp. 26–27.

10. Ibid., pp. 28–41; also United Nations, *The Concept,* pp. 4–8.

11. See U.S. Bureau of the Census, *Current Population Reports,* Series P-25, No. 448, Aug. 6, 1970, pp. 2–4, 50.

12. *Current Population Reports,* Series P-25, No. 601, Oct., 1975, pp. 31–32, 120, 141–42.

13. These tables are based on Projections W, V, and Y, taken or derived from *Current Population Reports,* P-25, No. 480, April, 1972.

14. For a model comparable to that underlying Projection Y, see A. J. Coale, "Alternative Paths to a Stationary Population," Commission on Population Growth and the American Future, Research Reports, Vol. I, *Demographic and Social Aspects of Population Growth,* pp. 594–95, on the changes required in total fertility between 1970 and 2005 in order to hold the number of births constant.

15. *Current Population Reports,* Series P-25, No. 480, April, 1972, pp. 4–6. See also Coale, "Alternative Paths," pp. 595–96, Tomas Frejka, *The Future of Population Growth* (New York: Wiley, 1973), and "Demographic Paths to a Stationary Population: The U.S. in International Comparison," in Commission on Population Growth and the American Future, *Research Reports,* Vol. I, pp. 627–43, esp. 633–34.

16. *Current Population Reports,* Series P-25, No. 601, Oct., 1975, pp. 2, 36, 121, and ibid., No. 541, Feb., 1975, pp. 3–5. Total fertility approximated 1.76 in 1976. Ibid., Series P-20, No. 308, June, 1972, p. 2.

17. Some attention will be given to dependency costs later on.

18. E.g., see Coale, "Alternative Paths," pp. 591–603; Ryder, "A Demographic Optimum Projection for the United States," in Commission on Population Growth and the American Future, *Research Reports,* Vol. I, pp. 605–22.

19. E.g., see James B. Pick, "Display of Population Age Structure," *Demography,* XI, Nov., 1974, pp. 673–82; also F. T. Denton and B. G. Spencer, "Some Demographic Consequences of Changing Cohort Fertility Patterns: An Investigation Using the Gompertz Function," *Population Studies,* XXVIII, July, 1974, pp. 209–18, and "A Simulation Analysis of the Effects of Population Change on a Neoclassical Economy," *Journal of Political Economy,* LXXXI, No. 2, Part 1, March–April, 1973, pp. 356–76.

20. See Coale, "Alternative Paths," pp. 591–603.

21. Births per year rose from 2,647,000 in 1935–1944 to an average of 3,966,000 in 1945–1964.

22. See Frejka, "Demographic Paths," and *Reference Tables to the Future of Population Growth, Alternative Paths to Equilibrium* (New York: Population

Council, 1972), pp. 97, 164–72; "Reflections on the Demographic Conditions Needed to Establish a U.S. Stationary Population," *Population Studies,* XXII, Nov., 1968, pp. 379–97.

23. Ryder, "Demographic Optimum Projection."

24. On factors affecting variability in natality and births as it bears upon population projection see *Current Population Reports,* P-25, No. 601, "Projections of the Population of the United States: 1975 to 2050," Oct., 1975, pp. 1–7, 21–32.

25. On the purely demographic aspects of birth variability see Ronald Lee, "The Formal Dynamics of Controlled Populations and The Echo, The Boom and The Bust," *Demography,* XI, Nov., 1974, pp. 563–86; also Keyfitz, "Population Waves," in Greville, *Population Dynamics,* pp. 1–37. On past economic effects see Richard Easterlin, *Population, Labor Force, and Long Swings in Economic Growth* (New York: Columbia University Press, 1968). On Paul Samuelson's formalization of Easterlin's model and its implication of a birth upsurge see his "An Economist's Non-Linear Model of Self-Generated Fertility Waves," *Population Studies,* XXX, July, 1976, pp. 243–48.

26. Of the 4,970,000 Mexican immigrants supposedly entering the United States in 1946–1965, about 88 percent entered illegally. Parker Frisbie, "Illegal Migration from Mexico to the United States. A Longitudinal Analysis," *International Migration Review,* IX, Spring, 1975, pp. 3–14, esp. p. 5; W. A. Fogel, "Immigrant Mexicans and the U.S. Labor Force," *Monthly Labor Review,* XCVIII, May, 1975, pp. 44–46; also V. M. Briggs, "Illegal Aliens: The Need for a More Restrictive Border Policy," *Social Science Quarterly,* LVI, Dec., 1975, pp. 477–84, and W. Gordon, "The Case for a Less Restrictive Border Policy," ibid., pp. 485–91. See also Elliott Abrams and F. S. Adams, "Immigration Policy—Who Gets in and Why?" *The Public Interest,* No. 38, Winter, 1975, pp. 3–29, esp. p. 21.

27. On the nature of this effect see Coale, "Alternative Paths," pp. 598–602.

28. See my "Effects Produced in Receiving Countries by Pre-1939 Immigration," in Brinley Thomas, ed., *The Economics of International Migration* (London: Macmillan, 1958), pp. 17–51; also ibid., parts III, VI; also J. G. Williamson, "Migration to the New World: Long Term Influences and Impact," *Explorations in Economic History,* XI, Summer, 1974, pp. 357–89.

29. See *Current Population Reports,* P-25, No. 601, "Projections of the Population of the United States: 1975 to 2050," Oct., 1975, pp. 26–27, 31, 120, 121, 134, 141; also Coale, "Alternative Paths."

30. *Current Population Reports,* Series P-23, No. 43, Feb., 1973, pp. 21–25. See also *Bulletin* of Metropolitan Life Insurance Co., New York, Dec., 1975.

31. E.g., see on the role of environment in the causation of cancer, John Cairnes, "The Cancer Problem," *Scientific American,* CCXXXIII, Nov., 1975, pp. 64–78.

32. Coale, "Increases in Expectation of Life."

33. *Current Population Reports,* P-25, No. 541, Feb., 1975, pp. 4–5; ibid., No. 601, Oct., 1975, pp. 25–26. See also ibid., P-23, No. 59, May, 1976, pp. 25–45.

34. J. S. Davis, *The Population Upsurge in the United States* (Stanford: Stanford University, 1949); also *Current Population Reports,* P-25, No. 601, Oct., 1975, pp. 16–21.

35. *Current Population Reports,* P-20, No. 265, June, 1974, p. 3.

36. *Current Population Reports,* P-25, No. 601, Oct., 1975, pp. 1–7, also ibid., P-23, No. 52 (1975), *Some Recent Changes in American Families,* by Paul C. Glick.

37. *Current Population Reports,* P-25, No. 613, Nov., 1975, and No. 601, Oct., 1975, esp. pp. 135, 138, 141.

38. The above data are from *Current Population Reports,* P-25, No. 601, Oct., 1975.

39. Charles F. Westoff, "The Decline of Unplanned Births in the United States," *Science,* CXCI, Jan. 9, 1976, pp. 38–41; R. H. Weller, "Number and Timing Failures Among Legitimate Births in the United States: 1968, 1969, 1972," *Family Planning Perspectives,* VIII, May–June, 1976, pp. 111–16; Boone Turchi, *The Demand for Children* (Cambridge, Mass.: Ballinger, 1975).

40. See Turchi, *The Demand for Children,* chap. 7. See also Judith Blake, "Can We Believe Recent Data on Birth Expectations in the United States?" *Demography,* XI, Feb., 1974, pp. 25–44, and comments by Larry Bumpass and David L. Kruegel, ibid., XII, Feb., 1975, pp. 155–61; J. Sklar and B. Berkov, "The American Birth Rate: Evidences of a Coming Rise," *Science,* CLXXXIX, Aug. 29, 1975, pp. 693–700; and comment by Harry Rosenberg, ibid., CXCI, Feb. 6, 1976, pp. 424–26. On substitution effects see D. J. O'Hara, "Microeconomic Aspects of Demographic Transition," *Journal of Political Economy,* LXXXIII, Dec., 1975, pp. 1203–16.

41. Glick, *Some Recent Changes in American Families;* Yoram Ben-Porath, "First Generation Effects on Second Generation Fertility," *Demography,* XII, Aug., 1975, pp. 397–406; J. C. Frumenthal, "Birth Trajectory under Changing Fertility Conditions," *Demography,* XII, Aug., 1975, pp. 447–54; N. K. Namboodri's review of Schultz, *Economics of the Family,* ibid., pp. 561–69; David Gutman, "The New Mythologies and Premature Aging in the Youth Culture," *Social Research,* XL, Summer, 1973, pp. 248–68, esp. 265–68.

42. E.g., see Glen G. Cain and Adriana Weininger, "Economic Determinants of Fertility: Results from Cross-Sectional Aggregate Data," *Demography,* X, May, 1973, pp. 205–24. See also P. S. Fisher and W. C. Quinn, "A Cross-Section Analysis of Fertility," *The American Economist,* XIX, Fall, 1975, pp. 64–68; T. W. Schultz, *Economics of the Family: Marriage, Children and Human Capital* (Chicago: University of Chicago Press, 1975); Turchi, *The Demands for Children.* But cf. E. B. Sheldon, ed., *Family Economic Behavior* (Philadelphia: Lippincott, 1973), and G. B. Terry, "Rival Explanations in the Work-Fertility Relationship," *Population Studies,* XXIV, July, 1975, pp. 191–206.

43. E.g., see Charles F. Hohm, "Social Security and Fertility: An International Perspective," *Demography,* XII, Nov., 1975, pp. 620–44; P. A. Neher, "Peasants, Procreation, and Pensions," *American Economic Review,* LXI, June, 1971, pp. 380–89, also ibid., LXII, Dec., 1972, p. 979.

44. Harry Rosenberg, "U.S. Fertility Rates: What Birth Rates Specific for Age and Parity of Women Tell Us," *Proceedings of the American Statistical Association,* Social Statistics Section, 1975, pp. 621–26; also note 40 above.

45. *Current Population Reports,* P-25, No. 601, p. 15. See also Ernest B. Attah, "Racial Aspects of Zero Population Growth," *Science,* CLXXX, June 15, 1973, pp. 1143–51.

46. Cf. *Current Population Reports, Series* P-20, No. 277, Feb., 1975, pp. 26, 28; R. B. Rajonc and G. B. Markus, "Birth Order and Intellectual Development," *Psychological Review,* LXXXII, Jan., 1975, pp. 26–44; D. N. De Tray, "Child Quality and the Demand for Children," *Journal of Political Economy,* March / April supplement, LXXXI, Part 2, March–April, 1973, pp. 70–95; Assaf Raziu and Uri Ben-Zion, "An Intergenerational Model of Population Growth," *American Economic Review,* LXV, Dec., 1975, pp. 923–933.

47. E.g., see *Current Population Reports,* Series P-25, No. 601, Oct., 1975, p. 19.

48. E.g., see table of reproduction rates in *Population Index,* XLII, April, 1976, pp. 362–72.

49. The data in Table V.10 identify only peaks as they appear in the table, not in the complete series, peaks in which may come a few years earlier or later.

50. Cf. George L. Brinkman, "The Effects of Zero Population Growth on the Spatial Distribution of Economic Activity," *American Journal of Agricultural Economics,* LIV, Dec., 1972, pp. 964–71.

VI. Age Structure and Economic Well-Being: Labor-Force/Population Ratio

1. On relevant differences between more and less advanced countries see United Nations, *The Determinants and Consequences of Population Trends,* 2nd ed., 1973, chap. 9, and *Demographic Aspects of Manpower, Population Studies,* No. 33, 1962.

2. E.g., see William Serow, "Slow Population Growth and Relative Size and

Productivity of the Male Labor Force," *Atlantic Economic Journal,* IV (2), Spring, 1976, pp. 61–68.

3. U.S. Bureau of the Census, "Demographic Aspects of Aging and the Older Population in The United States," *Current Population Reports,* P-53, No. 59, May, 1976, pp. 3–10. The 21 percent figure is associated with fertility of 1.7 compared with a 2.1 replacement rate. This report was prepared by J. S. Siegel et al. See also Lenore E. Bixby, *Demographic and Economic Characteristics of the Aged,* Research Report No. 45 / DHEW Publication No. (SSA), 75–11802, Washington, D.C., 1975.

4. *Current Population Reports,* P-53, No. 59, May, 1976, pp. 49–58; Howard N. Fullerton, Jr., and Paul O. Flaim, "New Labor Force Projections to 1990," *Monthly Labor Review,* XCIX, Dec., 1976, pp. 3–13, esp. p. 5. See also Bureau of the Census, "Social and Economic Characteristics of the Older Population, 1974," *Current Population Reports,* Series P-23, No. 57, Nov., 1975, pp. 3, 24–25, 36–37.

5. Howard N. Fullerton, Jr., and James J. Byrne, "Length of Working Life for Men and Women, 1970," *Monthly Labor Review,* XCIX, Feb., 1976, pp. 31–35; U.S. Department of Labor, "The Length of Working Life for Males, 1900–60," *Manpower Report,* No. 8, Washington, D.C., July, 1963; Howard N. Fullerton, Jr., "A Table of Expected Working Life for Men, 1968," *Monthly Labor Review,* XCIV, June, 1971, pp. 49–55, and "A New Type of Working Life Table for Men," ibid., XCV, July, 1972, pp. 20–27. Cordelia Reimers finds that the average age at retirement has been more stable than is commonly assumed. See "Is the Average Age at Retirement Changing?" *Journal of American Statistical Association,* LXXI, Sept., 1976, pp. 552–58. See also references in note 4 above and Ewan Clague et al., *The Aging Worker and the Union* (New York: Praeger, 1971), Parts I, III.

6. G. H. Moore and Janice N. Hedges, "Trends in Labor and Leisure," *Monthly Labor Review,* XCIV, Feb., 1971, pp. 3–11, esp. p. 10. See also Harl E. Ryder, Frank P. Stafford, and Paula E. Stephan, "Labor, Leisure and Training over the Life Cycle," *International Economic Review,* XVII, Oct., 1976, pp. 651–74.

7. C. L. Gilroy, "Investment in Human Capital and Black-White Unemployment," *Monthly Labor Review,* XCVIII, July, 1975, pp. 13–21. See also R. D. Bednarzek, "Involuntary Part-Time Work: A Cyclical Analysis," ibid., Sept., 1975, pp. 12–18; H. H. Winsborough, "Age, Period, Cohort, and Education Effects on Earnings by Race," in K. C. Land and Seymour Spilerman, *Social Indicator Models* (New York: Russell Sage Foundation, 1975, pp. 201–17; Paula E. Stephan, "Human Capital Production: Life Cycle Production with Different Learning Technologies," *Economic Inquiry,* XIV, Dec., 1976, pp. 539–57.

8. On the high value of housewives' time see Reuben Gronau, "The Evaluation of Housewives' Time," in Milton Moss, ed., *The Measurement of Economic and Social Performance* (New York: Columbia University Press, 1973), pp. 163–92. See also references in notes 9 and 14 below.

9. On the increasing significance of "leisure" or "time free of the necessity to earn a living," see Moore and Hedges, "Trends in Labor and Leisure," pp. 3–11. These trends are manifest in trade-union demands for an increasing number of holidays, and are affected by opportunities for household production. E.g., see N. E. Terleckyj, ed., *Household Production and Consumption* (New York: Columbia University Press, 1975).

10. U.S. Bureau of the Census, *Historical Statistics of the United States, Colonial Times to 1957,* Washington, D.C., 1960, pp. 70–71; *Statistical Abstract of the United States,* 1973, p. 219; U.S. Bureau of the Census, "A Statistical Portrait of Women in the U.S.," *Current Population Reports,* P-23, No. 58, April, 1976; Valerie K. Oppenheimer, *The Female Labor Force In The United States* (Berkeley: Institute of International Studies, 1970).

11. On labor force development see Gertrude Bancroft, *The American Labor Force* (New York: Wiley, 1958); C. D. Long, *The Labor Force Under Changing Income and Employment* (Princeton: Princeton University Press, 1958); John D. Durand, *The Labor Force in the United States 1890–1960* (New York: Social Science Research Council, 1948); A. J. Jaffe et al., "Labor Force," *International Ency-*

clopedia of the Social Sciences, VIII, New York, 1968, pp. 469–91; John Durand, *The Labor Force in Economic Development* (Princeton: Princeton University Press, 1976); Oppenheimer, *The Female Labor Force.*

12. D. Pimental et al., "Food Production and the Energy Crisis," *Science,* CLXXXII, Nov. 2, 1973, p. 444.

13. See Stanley Lebergott, *Manpower in Economic Growth: The United States Record Since 1800* (New York: McGraw Hill, 1964).

14. See William D. Nordhaus and James Tobin, *Economic Growth* (New York: Columbia University Press, 1972), pp. 9–12, esp. p. 12; also Gronau, "Housewives' Time," pp. 182–84.

15. A. L. Gitlow, *Labor and Manpower Economics* (Homewood, Ill.: Irwin, 1971), pp. 173–78.

16. U.S. Dept. of Manpower Administration, *Manpower Report of the President,* Washington, D.C., 1975, p. 270. The shorter-hours movement tends both to reduce persistent unemployment, by reducing the total labor supply, and to encourage off-setting moonlighting. Jan Mossen and Martin Bronfenbrenner, "The Shorter Work Week and the Labor Supply," *Southern Economic Journal,* XXXIII, Jan., 1967, pp. 322–31. See also S. R. Finkel and V. J. Tarascio, *Wage and Employment Theory* (New York: Ronald Press, 1971), pp. 119–21. According to R. Shiska and B. Rostker, moonlighting is positively correlated with family size and the relative reward of moonlighting, but negatively correlated with age. "The Economics of Multiple Job Holding," *American Economic Review,* LXVI, June, 1976, pp. 298–308.

17. Moore and Hedges, "Trends in Labor and Leisure," pp. 7–8.

18. Ibid., pp. 4–5. See also J. F. Dewhurst, *America's Needs and Resources* (New York: Twentieth Century Fund, 1955), p. 40, for higher estimates of weekly hours in the 1870s.

19. Janice N. Hedges, "How Many Days Make a Workweek?" *Monthly Labor Review,* XCVIII, April, 1975, pp. 29–36.

20. See *Monthly Labor Review,* XCVIII, Jan., 1975, p. 51.

21. See Fullerton, "A Table of Expected Working Life for Men, 1968," pp. 51–52.

22. Ibid., p. 50.

23. Hedges, "How Many Days Make a Workweek?" "A Look at the 4-Day Work-week," *Monthly Labor Review,* XCVI, Feb., 1973, pp. 3–8. The availability of part-time work has been an important inducement to labor-force participation, especially by women. See "A Statistical Portrait," *Current Population Reports,* P-23, No. 58, pp. 26–31.

24. Moore and Hedges, "Trends in Labor and Leisure," p. 11.

25. *Manpower Report of the President,* pp. 208–9. See also Fullerton and Flaim, "New Labor Force Projections," who indicate that despite increase in labor-force participation rates for women, the work force will grow more slowly because a smaller number of youths will be reaching working age.

26. *Manpower Report of the President, 1975,* p. 31. In late 1974 the number of persons wanting jobs but "not looking" was 5.2 percent as large as the civilian labor force. Ibid. See also D. S. Hammermesh, "A Note on Income and Substitution Effects in Search Unemployment," *Economic Journal,* LXXXVII, June, 1977, pp. 312–14, and *Jobless Pay and the Economy* (Baltimore: The Johns Hopkins Press, 1977).

27. See also Bancroft, *The American Labor Force,* pp. 207–8, and passim; Long, *The Labor Force,* chaps. 5–7. On earlier experience see Lebergott, *Manpower in Economic Growth,* pp. 125–30, 519–52.

28. Fullerton, "A New Type of Working Life Table for Men," pp. 23–25.

29. See Marion Gross Sobol, "A Dynamic Analysis of Labor Force Participation of Married Women of Childbearing Age," *Journal of Human Resources,* Vol. 8, Fall, 1973, pp. 497–505; Hilda Kahne, "Economic Perspectives on the Roles of Women in the American Economy," *Journal of Economic Literature,* XIII, Dec., 1975, pp. 1249–92; Jacob Mincer, "Labor Force Participation of Married Women:

A Study of Labor Supply," in National Bureau of Economic Research, *Aspects of Labor Economics* (Princeton: Princeton University Press, 1962), pp. 63–97, Oppenheimer, *The Female Labor Force.*

30. G. Terry, "Rival Explanations in the Work-Fertility Relationship," *Population Studies,* XXIV, July, 1975, pp. 191–206.

31. U.S. Department of Labor, "Work Life Expectancy and Training Needs of Women," *Manpower Report,* No. 7, Washington, D.C., May, 1967.

32. U.S. Dept. of Labor, Bureau of Labor Statistics, *Handbook of Labor Statistics, 1974,* Table 2, p. 31, reprinted in *Manpower Report of the President,* p. 57.

33. E.g., see D. F. Johnston, "The U.S. Labor Force: Projection to 1990," *Monthly Labor Review,* XCVI, July, 1973, pp. 3–13; Fullerton, "A New Type of Working Life Table for Man," pp. 20–27, and "Sensitivity of Generation Tables of Working Life for Men to Different Projections of Labor Force Participation Rates and Mortality Rates," *Proceedings of the American Statistical Association,* Social Statistics Section, 1972. See Archibald Evans, *Flexibility in Working Life,* Paris: Organization for Economic Co-operation and Development, 1973. See also note 38 below.

34. Marc Rosenblum, "On the Accuracy of Labor Force Projections," *Monthly Labor Review,* XCV, Oct., 1972, pp. 22–29; Fullerton and Flaim, "New Labor Force Projections."

35. E.g., Carolyn Shaw Bell writes in "Age, Sex, Marriage, and Jobs": "If there are structural problems that prevent full employment, they consist of trouble spots in the economy, not in the labor force. They are barriers to the employment of *people,* whether they are black or white, male or female, under 20 or over 50. These are the proper areas for investigation and policy." See *The Public Interest,* No. 31, Winter, 1973, pp. 76–77, esp. p. 87. See also B. G. Spencer, "Determinants of the Labour Force Participation of Married Women: A Micro-Study of Toronto Households," *Canadian Journal of Economics,* VI, May, 1973, pp. 722–38; Jacob Mincer, "Labor Force Participation of Married Women."

36. *Manpower Report of the President,* pp. 250–51.

37. On participation-affecting factors see James A. Sweet, *Women in the Labor Force* (New York: Seminar Press, 1973).

38. D. F. Johnston, "Illustrative Projections in the Labor Force of the United States to 2040," in Commission on Population Growth and The American Future, Research Report II, *Economic Aspects of Population Change* (Washington, D.C.: U.S. Government Printing Office, 1972), pp. 159–88, Table 1.

39. E.g., see Matilda W. Riley, ed., *Aging and Society,* 3 vols. (New York: Russell Sage Foundation, 1972); A. T. Welford and J. E. Birren, *Behavior, Aging and the Nervous System* (Springfield, Ill.: C. C. Thomas, 1965); R. H. Williams et al., eds., *Processes of Aging* (New York: Atherton Press, 1963); L. F. Koyl, *Employing the Older Worker: Matching the Employee to the Job* (Washington, D.C.: National Council on the Aging, Inc., 1974). See also note 46 below.

40. Y. Weiss, "On the Optimal Lifetime Patterns of Labour Supply," *Economic Journal,* LXXXII, Dec., 1972, pp. 1293–1315. Cf. L. Thurow, "The Optimum Life Time Distribution of Consumption and Expenditures," *American Economic Review,* LIX, June, 1969, pp. 324–30. See also A. S. Blinder on sources and effects of distribution patterns and status-oriented wealth and income, *Journal of Political Economy,* LXXXIII, June, 1975, pp. 447–61; Juanita M. Kreps, *Lifetime Allocation of Work and Income* (Durham: Duke University Press, 1971).

41. On some of these problems see A. J. Jaffe et al., *Disabled Workers in the Labor Market* (Totowa, New Jersey: Bedminster Press, 1964); R. W. Conley, *The Economics of Vocational Rehabilitation* (Baltimore: Johns Hopkins Press, 1965); Williams et al., *Processes of Aging,* II, passim.

42. See H. L. Sheppard, ed., *Towards an Industrial Gerontology* (Cambridge: Schenkman Pub. Co., 1970), especially chap. 3 by Solomon Barkin; L. D. Haber, "Age and Capacity Devaluation," *Health and Social Behavior,* Sept., 1970, p. 8. On "humanizing" work and workplaces see S. A. Levitan and W. B. Johnston, *Work is Here to Stay, Alas* (Salt Lake City: Olympus Publishing Co., 1973); also L. E.

Björk, "An Experiment in Work Satisfaction," Scientific American, CCXXXII, March, 1975, pp. 17–23; Koyl, Employing the Older Worker. The entire subject including labor force participation on the part of older persons is dealt with by W. G. Bowen and T. A. Finegan, The Economics of Labor Force Participation (Princeton: Princeton University Press, 1969). See also James H. Schulz, "The Economic Impact of an Aging Population," Gerontologist, XII, Spring, 1973, pp. 111–18, and The Economics of Aging (Belmont, Ca.: Wadsworth, 1976).

43. See G. S. Hamilton and J. D. Roessner, "How Employers Screen Disadvantaged Job Applicants," Monthly Labor Review, XCV, Sept., 1972, pp. 14–21.

44. Michael J. Boskin, "Social Security and Retirement Decisions," Economic Inquiry, XV, Jan., 1977, pp. 1–25; Haber, "Age and Capacity Devaluation"; C. R. Hill, "Education, Health and Family Size as Determinants of Labor Market Activity for the Poor and Nonpoor," Demography, VIII, Aug., 1971, pp. 379–88, esp. 382–83, 387–88. See also Riley, Aging and Society, passim, esp. I, chap. 18, III, chap. 5; Williams et al., Processes of Aging, part 7; also Welford and Birren, Behavior, Aging and the Nervous System; F. T. Denton and B. G. Spencer, "Health-Care Costs when the Population Changes," Canadian Journal of Economics, VII, Feb., 1975, pp. 34–48. According to H. H. Winsborough "Age, Period, Cohort, and Education Effects," pp. 209–10, depreciation of human capital begins to overwhelm gains through experience around age 40.

45. On reasons for not working see Riley, Aging and Society, III, p. 180, and U.S. Bureau of the Census, Current Population Reports, Series P-23, No. 49, 1974, pp. 150–51. Poor health has reduced by 37 percent the annual earnings of the average disabled man who remains in the labor force. See Harold L. Luft, "The Impact of Poor Health on Earnings," The Review of Economics and Statistics, LVII, Feb., 1975, pp. 43–57, esp. 43–52; also Joseph M. Davis, "Impact of Health on Earnings and Labor Market Activity," Monthly Labor Review, XCV, Oct., 1972, pp. 46–49.

46. U.S. Dept. of Health, Education, and Welfare, Current Estimates from the Health Interview Survey, U.S., 1973, Rockville, Md., Oct., 1974, pp. 15–19, and Acute Conditions, DHEW Publication No. (HRA) 75–1525, Series 10, No. 98, Jan., 1975, Tables, A, B, 10, and pp. 1–7. See also Acute Conditions, Series 10, No. 104, March, 1976; Otto Pollak, Social Adjustment in Old Age (New York: Social Science Research Council, 1948); U.S. Dept. of Health, Education, and Welfare, Health. United States, 1975, DHEW Publication No. (HRA) 76–1232, Rockville, Md., 1976.

47. See Williams et al., Processes of Aging, esp. Vol. II, chap. 44, p. 338. See also W. A. Chance, "Long-Term Labor Requirements and Output of the Educational System," Southern Economic Journal, XXXII, April, 1966, pp. 417–28; R. C. Atchley, The Sociology of Retirement (New York: Halsted, 1975); J. M. Dirken, Functional Age of Industrial Workers (Groningen: Wolters-Noordhoff, 1972); G. Marbach, Job Redesign for Older Workers (Paris: OECD, 1968).

48. E.g., see Mincer, "Labor Force Participation of Married Women"; also on the use of time see Gary Becker, "A Theory of the Allocation of Time," The Economic Journal, LXXV, 1965, pp. 493–517.

49. E.g., see John D. Owen, The Price of Leisure (Rotterdam: Rotterdam University Press, 1969); Finkel and Tarascio, Wage and Employment Theory, pp. 118–22, 193–99. About 25 percent of the long-term increase in the demand for leisure is attributable to a decline in market recreation prices; much of the rest is associated with income increase. John D. Owen, "The Demand for Leisure," Journal of Political Economy, LXXIX, Jan.–Feb., 1971, pp. 56–76, esp. 56, 79.

50. In 1974 "discouraged workers" numbered 686,000, of whom 145,000 were over 60 years old. See Julius Shiskin and R. L. Stein, "Problems in Measuring Unemployment," Monthly Labor Review, XCVIII, Aug., 1975, pp. 3–10. See also James J. Byrne, "Occupational Mobility of Workers," ibid., Feb., 1975, pp. 53–59; Finkel and Tarascio, Wage and Employment Theory, pp. 121–22, 193–99; Lowell E. Gallaway, "Age and Labor Mobility Patterns," Southern Economic Journal, XXXVI, Oct., 1969, pp. 171–80, and "Labor Mobility, Resource Allocation, and Structural

Unemployment," *American Economic Review,* LIII, Sept., 1963, pp. 694–716; Glen S. Cain, "The Challenge of Segmented Labor Market Theories to Orthodox Theory," *Journal of Economic Literature,* XIV, Dec., 1976, pp. 1215–55. But cf. H. S. Parnes, *Research on Labor Mobility* (New York: Social Science Research Council), 1954, and references in note 6 in chap. 10.

51. See Lionel Robbins, "On the Elasticity of the Demand for Income in Terms of Effort," *Economica,* X, June, 1930, pp. 123–29; Milton Friedman, *Price Theory. A Provisional Text* (Chicago: Aldine, 1962), p. 204; also John D. Owen, *The Price;* Peter Kranz, "What Do People Do All Day?" *Behavioral Science,* XV, 1970, pp. 286–91; Unsigned, "Time for Recreation Desired More than Money," *Ohio State University Monthly,* April, 1975, p. 9.

52. Finkel and Tarascio, *Wage and Employment Theory,* chap. 5, esp. 122–23, also 111–12, 115–17, 126–29. See also Gitlow, *Labor and Manpower Economics,* Part III.

53. On the unemployment-generating effects of minimum wages see Douglas K. Adie, "Teen-Age Unemployment and Real Federal Minimum Wages," *Journal of Political Economy,* LXXXI, No. 2, Part I, March–April, 1973, p. 441.

54. Ibid., p. 441. A heavy influx of young persons into the labor market 20 or so years after a baby boom may accentuate other sources of teenage unemployment.

55. There is some tendency, however, though not a strong one, for additional members of a family to seek employment when the main breadwinners are unemployed. See J. E. Parker and L. B. Shaw, "Labor Force within Metropolitan Areas," *Southern Economic Journal,* XXXIV, April, 1968, pp. 538. According to P. S. Barth, however, "An increase in the employment rate will not bring about a very noticeable amount of 'hidden unemployment,' nor will a continued decline in the rate alone precipitate a major inflow of workers into the labor force." See his "Unemployment and Labor Force Participation," *Southern Economic Journal,* Vol. 34, Jan., 1968, pp. 375–82, esp. p. 382.

56. See C. C. von Weiszsäcker, *The Political Economy of Stability in Western Countries* (Stockholm: Almqvist & Wiksell, 1972); H. G. Johnson and P. Mieszkowski, "The Effects of Unionization on the Distribution of Income: A General Equilibrium Approach," *Quarterly Journal of Economics,* LXXXIV, 1970, pp. 539–61; also J. J. Spengler, "Power Blocs and the Formation and Content of Economic Decisions," *American Economic Review / Supplement,* XL, May, 1950, pp. 413–30. The economic status of retired workers may reflect their experience as labor-force members, since worker-wealth ownership declines after retirement. See A. F. Shorrocks, "The Age-Wealth Relationships: A Cross-Section and Cohort Analysis," *The Review of Economics and Statistics,* LVII, 1975, pp. 155–63; Alan Fox, "Work Status and Income Change, 1968–72: Retirement History Study Preview," *Social Security Bulletin,* XXXIX, Dec., 1976, pp. 15–28.

57. Suggestive is G. L. Perry's "Changing Labour Markets and Inflation," *Brookings Papers Econ. Activity,* I, No. 3 (1970), pp. 411–41; also William Fellner, "Theoretical Foundations of the Failure of Demand-Management Policies: An Essay," *Journal of Economic Literature,* XIV, March, 1976, pp. 34–53, esp. 45–52.

58. See Martin Feldstein, "The Economics of the New Unemployment," *The Public Interest,* No. 33, 1973, pp. 3–42, esp. pp. 3, 41; also B. U. Ratchford's "Institutionalized Inflation," *South Atlantic Quarterly,* Autumn, 1974, pp. 516–28. See also Gitlow, *Labor and Manpower Economics,* passim; Geoffrey H. Moore, *Recession Related Unemployment,* Reprint No. 29 (Washington, D.C.: American Enterprise Institute, March, 1975); Victor Tabbush, "Underemployment," *Arizona Review,* XXIV, April, 1975, pp. 9–12; also Fellner, "Theoretical Foundations."

59. H. G. Grubel, D. Maki, and S. Sax, "Real and Insurance-Related Unemployment in Canada," *Canadian Journal of Economics,* VIII, May, 1975, pp. 174–91, esp. p. 174, also bibliography. On the role of job search see also C. A. Pissarides, "Risk, Job Search, and Income Distribution," *Journal of Political Economy,* LXXXII, Nov.–Dec., 1974, pp. 1255–67.

60. Feldstein, "The Economics," passim. Were the unemployed required to fill

jobs for which they were physically and mentally qualified or forfeit unemployment compensation, unemployment would be appreciably reduced. E.g., see R. S. Livingstone, "Unemployment—A Story the Figures Don't Tell," *U.S. News & World Report,* Nov. 18, 1974, pp. 43–45. Such policy is all the more pertinent in view of the fact that arbitrariness and noncompetition have much to do with the wage structure and excessive wage rates. E.g., see Michael Fortes, "Job Evaluation and Income Policy," *Lloyds Bank Review,* No. 114, Oct., 1974, pp. 38–48.

61. Bell, "Age, Sex, Marriage, and Jobs," pp. 84–86.

62. James S. Coleman, *Youth: Transition to Adulthood* (Chicago: U. of Chicago Press, 1974).

63. Alan Fechter, *Public Employment Programs,* Evaluative Study No. 20 (Washington, D.C.: American Enterprise Program, May, 1975), esp. pp. 34–35.

64. Martin Feldstein, "Social Security, Induced Retirement, and Aggregate Capital Accumulation," *Journal of Political Economy,* LXXXII, Sept.–Oct., 1974, pp. 905–26. This argument is more fully developed by Alicia Munnell, *The Effect of Social Security on Personal Saving* (Cambridge: Ballinger, 1974). See also Munnell, "Private Pensions and Saving: New Evidence," *Journal of Political Economy,* LXXXIV, Oct., 1976, pp. 1013–32.

65. See Charles Upton's review of Munnell's 1974 study in *Journal of Political Economy,* LXXXIII, Oct., 1975, pp. 1090–92.

66. John Rawls, *A Theory of Justice* (Cambridge: Harvard University Press, 1971), pp. 284–93, esp. p. 293.

67. Today, writes Carolyn Shaw Bell, it is essential that "we stop having families as the focus of our concerns" and instead make the individual within and outside the family the central focus for purposes of policy. "Let's Get Rid of Families," *Newsweek,* LXXXIX, May 9, 1977, p. 19.

68. As a rule only federal retirement benefits are compensated for inflationary price increases. See *The Effect of Inflation on Federal Expenditures,* Background Paper No. 9, June 18, 1976, Congressional Budget Office, Washington, D.C., esp. pp. 23–41.

69. Edgar K. Browning,, "Social Insurance and Intergenerational Transfers," *Journal of Law and Economics,* XVI, Oct., 1973, pp. 215–37. Browning compares his proposal with proposals put forward by James Buchanan and Milton Friedman.

70. On the impact of a city's demographic and economic contraction upon its ability to meet pension claims see *New York City's Financial Crisis,* a study prepared for the Joint Committee, Congress of the United States, Washington, D.C., 1975, esp. pp. 11–18; also Tom Stevenson, "In Hock to Pensions," *New Republic,* CLXXV, Aug. 7, 1976, pp. 23–25; Thomas P. Bleakney, "Problems and Issues in Public Employee Retirement Systems," *Journal of Risk and Insurance,* XL, March, 1973, pp. 39–46.

71. Paul Samuelson, *The Collected Scientific Papers of Paul A. Samuelson,* ed. by J. E. Stiglitz (Cambridge: M.I.T. Press, 1966), I, p. 473. Elsewhere Samuelson shows how social security systems such as the American are suboptimum, yet made optimal by myopia. See "Optimum Social Security in a Life-Cycle Growth Model," *International Economic Review,* XVI, Oct., 1975, pp. 539–544; also his "The Optimum Growth Rate for Population," ibid., pp. 531–38.

72. J. A. Pechman, H. J. Aaron, and H. K. Taussig, *Social Security Perspectives for Reform* (Washington, D.C.: Brookings Institution, 1968), p. 72.

73. Henry Aaron, "The Social Insurance Paradox," *Canadian Journal of Economics and Political Science,* XXXII, August, 1966, pp. 371–74.

74. I am indebted to Dr. Angelica Michail of Metropolitan Life for the basic data relating to FPPA contracts.

75. T. D. Hogan, "The Implications of Population Stationarity for the Social Security System," *Social Science Quarterly,* LV, June, 1974, pp. 151–58.

76. On the cost of children see Boone Turchi, The Demand for Children (Cambridge: Ballinger, 1975); Thomas J. Espenshade, "The Value and Cost of Children," *Population Bulletin,* XXXII(1), April, 1977.

77. Let W / Y denote the ratio of national wealth of all sorts to national income. If this ratio stands around 5 and life expectancy approximates 72 years, $100 / 72 =$ 1.4 percent of a stationary population will die annually and occasion on an average the transfer of 1.4 percent of the national wealth to those still living, an amount approximating 7 percent of Y if $W / Y = 5$. Of course, since only the major fraction of those assets is owned by older persons, the actual percentage falls short of 7.

78. What I have called floating rents are the rents imputable to national property for which the state receives little compensation (e.g., airways, channels) and to uncompensated state and eleemosynary investment in human capital (e.g., education), science, and technological progress. These floating rents pass largely into the hands of labor and enterprise, making wages and profits higher than they would otherwise be.

79. On pensions see Institute of Life Insurance, *Pension Facts 1975* (New York: 1976); also N. B. Ture, *The Future of Private Pensions* (Washington, D.C.: American Enterprise Institute, 1976).

80. *Report* of the Advisory Council on Social Security to the Secretary of Health, Education and Welfare, March 6, 1975, Washington, D.C., pp. 119–22. See also Robert S. Kaplan, *Financial Crisis in the Social Security System* (Washington, D.C.: American Enterprise Institute, 1976); *Report* of the Panel on Social Security Financing to the Committee on Finance, United States Senate, Pursuant to S. Res. 350, 93rd Congress, Feb., 1975; A. Haworth Robertson, "OASDI: Fiscal Basis and Long-Range Cost Projections," *Social Security Bulletin*, XL, Jan., 1977, pp. 20–27, 48; Yung-Ping Chen and Kwang-win Chu, "Tax-Benefit Ratios and Rates of Return under OASI: 1974 Retirees and Entrants," *Journal of Risk and Insurance*, XLI, June, 1974, pp. 189–206. See also Alicia Munnell, *The Future of Social Security* (Washington, D.C.: Brookings Institution, 1976); George E. Rejda and Richard J. Sheply, "The Impact of Zero Population Growth on OASDHI Program," *Journal of Risk and Insurance*, XL, Sept., 1973, pp. 313–25; Boone Turchi, "Stationary Populations: Pensions and the Social Security System," in Spengler, ed., *Zero Population Growth: Implications*, pp. 75–94; James H. Schulz, "The Economic Impact of an Aging Population," *Gerontologist*, XIII, Spring, 1973, pp. 111–18, and Schulz et al., *Providing Adequate Retirement Income: Pension Reform in The United States and Abroad* (Hanover, N.H.: University Press of New England, 1974).

81. On retirement see Lenore E. Bixby, "Retirement Patterns in the United States: Research and Policy Interaction," *Social Security Bulletin*, XXXIX, Aug., 1976, pp. 3–19; also Bixby et al., *Demographic and Economic Characteristics of the Aged*, esp. chaps. 3–4.

82. Serow, "Slow Population Growth"; also M. J. Brennan, P. Taft, and M. B. Schupack, *The Economics of Age* (New York: Norton, 1967).

VII. Age Structure and Economic Well-Being: Vertical and Horizontal Mobility

1. A. J. Coale and Paul Demeny, *Regional Model Life Tables and Stable Populations* (Princeton: Princeton University Press, 1966), p. 25.

2. See N. B. Ryder, "Notes on Stationary Populations," *Population Index*, XII, Jan., 1975, pp. 22–23; United Nations, *The Aging of Populations and Its Economic and Its Economic and Social Implications* (New York: United Nations, 1955), p. 56.

3. The number in the c category varies with the state of the labor market and *ceteris paribus* with age of worker insofar as propensity to change employment weakens with age of worker. The "quit" rate varies inversely with the "lay-off" rate and with the "job vacancy" rate. E.g., see U.S. Dept. of Labor, *Manpower Report of the President*, March, 1973, p. 16; also on the dual character of labor markets and quit rates, N. Bosanquet and P. B. Doerringer, "Is There a Dual Labour Market in Great Britain?" *Economic Journal*, LXXXIII, June, 1973, pp. 421–34, esp. 424–25; Glen G. Cain, "The Challenge of Segmented Labor Market Theories to Orthodox

Theory: A Survey," *Journal of Economic Literature,* XIV, Dec., 1976, pp. 1215–57.

4. Presumably *b* and *c* may be inversely related. For when employment rises and *b* declines, *c* may increase, since as a result of improvement in employment prospects the propensity to consider change in employment tends to increase.

5. Between 1970 and 1990 the percentage has been and is expected to be in the neighborhood of 60–61. See U.S. Bureau of the Census, *Statistical Abstract of the United States: 1974* (Washington, D.C.: 1974), Table 543, p. 337.

6. See my "Prospective Population Changes and Price Level Tendencies," *Southern Economic Journal,* XXXVIII, April, 1972, pp. 459–67. On labor reserve see C. G. Gellner, "Enlarging the Concept of a Labor Reserve," *Monthly Labor Review,* XCVIII, April, 1975, pp. 20–28. He estimated that in 1973 there were about 4.5 million persons outside the labor force who wanted a job "now," a number equal to about 5 percent of those in the labor force. Ibid., pp. 20–21. There were also nearly two million who had held jobs within the previous 12 months but were not currently seeking employment. Ibid., pp. 23–24. There were still others. Indeed, the 88.7 million in the labor force in 1973 represented over 100 million who were "active participants at some time or other." Ibid., p. 27.

7. Based on Coale and Demeny, *Regional Model Life Tables,* p. 168.

8. See his "Individual Mobility in a Stationary Population," *Population Studies,* XXVII, July, 1973, pp. 335–52. See also Louis Henry, "Pyramides, statuts et carrières," 2 parts, *Population,* XXVI, 1971, pp. 463–86, XXVII, 1972, pp. 599–636.

9. "Individual Mobility," pp. 335–36.

10. Ibid., p. 338 and Table 2.

11. Ibid., pp. 339–40, 346–47.

12. Ibid., p. 341.

13. Ibid., p. 346. While this favorable situation may encourage fertility on the part of the small cohort, the labor supply would not be much affected for 18–20 years.

14. E.g., see Milton Friedman, *Capitalism and Freedom* (Chicago: University of Chicago Press, 1962), chap. 9. See also Stephen P. Dresch, "Demography, Technology, and Higher Education: Toward a Formal Model of Educational Adaptation," *Journal of Political Economy,* LXXXIII, June, 1975, pp. 535–70. See also Harvey L. Browning, "Speculation on Labor Mobility in a Stationary Population," in Spengler, ed., *Zero Population Growth,* pp. 56–74.

15. For example, the ratio of peak to beginning salaries of academic economists according to one study ranged between around 1.6 and around 1.9. See George E. Johnson and Frank P. Stafford, "Lifetime Earnings in a Professional Labor Market: Academic Economists," *Journal of Political Economy,* LXXXII, May–June, 1974, pp. 549–69, esp. pp. 558, 568, also pp. 550–56 on the effect of professional experience on salary profiles. On some conditions affecting earnings profiles see also Y. Weiss, "On the Optimal Lifetime Pattern of Labour Supply," *Economic Journal,* LXXXII, Dec., 1972, pp. 1293–1315. On the impact of "ability" on age-earnings profiles see Paul T. Taubman and Terrence Wales, "The Inadequacy of Cross-Section Age-Earnings Profiles When Ability is Not Held Constant," *Annals of Economic and Social Measurement,* I, No. 3, July, 1972, pp. 363–68. See also idem, *Higher Education and Earnings* (New York: McGraw-Hill, 1974).

16. The term "nearly" is used because the capacity of some members of the labor force to benefit from exosomatic improvements is limited, with the result that their relative position declines. E.g., see Raymond Boudon, *Education, Opportunity, and Social Inequality* (New York: Wiley, 1974); also Paul Taubman and Terrence Wales, "Mental Ability and Higher Educational Attainment in the Twentieth Century," National Bureau of Economic Research Occasional Paper, No. 118, New York, 1972.

17. See C. A. Pissarides, "Risk, Job Search, and Income Distribution," *Journal of Political Economy,* LXXXII, Nov.–Dec., 1974, pp. 1255–67. See also D. O. Parsons, "Quit Rates Over Time: A Search and Information Approach," *American Economic Review,* LXIII, June, 1973, pp. 390–401; also J. M. Barron, "Search in the Labor Market and the Duration of Unemployment: Some Empirical Evidence," *American Economic Review,* LXV, Dec., 1975, pp. 934–42.

18. See Harvey C. Lehman, *Age and Achievement* (Princeton: Princeton University Press, 1953); also Frank Clemente and Jon Hendricks, "A Further Look at the Relationship Between Age and Productivity," *The Gerontologist*, XIII, Spring, 1973, pp. 106–10 and bibliography.

19. "The Impact of Population Growth on Employment," *The American Economic Review*, LXIV(2), May, 1974, pp. 44–50, esp. p. 49; also A. J. Owens, "Will Zero-Population Growth Hamper Scientific Creativity?" *Physics Today*, Vol. 26, Oct., 1973, pp. 9–13.

20. Sweezy and Owens, "Impact of Population Growth," p. 49. See also Lehman, *Age and Achievement*.

21. "The Impact of Population Growth on Economic Welfare—Nontraditional Elements," in Roger Revelle et al., eds., *Rapid Population Growth*, published for the National Academy of Sciences (Baltimore: The Johns Hopkins Press, 1971), p. 188.

22. Ibid., p. 189.

23. Ibid., p. 195. On qualifications respecting this "effect" see Leibenstein's introduction to "Population: A Symposium," *Quarterly Journal of Economics*, LXXXIX, May, 1975, esp. pp. 230–32.

24. For a somewhat pessimistic view of the impact of population aging see Alfred Sauvy, *General Theory of Population*, trans. by Christophe Compos (New York: Basic Books, 1969), pp. 303–19.

25. *Statistical Bulletin* of Metropolitan Life Insurance Co., LVI, Sept., 1975, pp. 8–9. See also S. H. Preston, "Effect of Mortality Change on Stable Population Parameters," *Demography*, XI, Feb. 1974, pp. 119–36.

26. Based on Tables 8 and 11 in *Current Population Reports*, Series P-25, No. 601, Oct., 1975. See also F. R. Eisele, ed., *Political Consequences of Aging*, Annals of the American Academy of Political and Social Science, Vol. 415, Sept., 1974.

27. See book review, *Journal of Economic Literature*, XV, June, 1977, p. 544.

VIII. Population Growth and Output Growth

1. Joseph A. Schumpeter, *Business Cycles*, I (New York: McGraw-Hill, 1939), p. 74; also Jan Tinbergen and J. J. Polak, *The Dynamics of Business Cycles* (University of Chicago Press, 1949), chaps. 9, 15.

2. D. W. Jorgenson and Z. Griliches, "The Explanation of Productivity Change," *Review of Economic Studies*, XXXIV, July, 1967, pp. 249–82, esp. 249–50; Mark Z. Fabrycy, "Determinants of Total Factor Productivity," *Western Economic Journal*, IX, Dec., 1971, pp. 408–18.

3. E.g., see J. Tinbergen, "Zur Theorie der langfristigen Wirtschaftsentwicklung," *Weltwirtschaftliches Archiv*, LV, May, 1942, pp. 511–49.

4. Illustrative of measurement problems is the Jorgenson-Griliches paper, "Explanation of Productivity Change," reprinted in *Survey of Current Business*, XLIX, Part II, May, 1969, together with E. F. Denison's critique, "Some Major Issues in Productivity Analysis: An Examination of Estimates by Jorgensen and Griliches," ibid., pp. 1–27. See also C. Kennedy and A. P. Thirlwall, "Technical Progress: A Survey," *Economic Journal*, LXXXII, March, 1972, pp. 11–72; Allen C. Kelley, "The Role of Population in Models of Economic Growth," *American Economic Review*, LXIV, No. 2, May, 1974, pp. 39–44.

5. See Friedman's discussion of Simon Kuznets, "Population Change and Aggregate Output" in the symposium volume, *Demographic and Economic Change in Developed Countries* (National Bureau of Economic Research), edited by Ansley J. Coale (Princeton: Princeton University Press, 1960), pp. 345–46.

6. Ibid., pp. 346–49. Richard Quandt also notes the importance of external economies in his comment on Kuznets's paper. Ibid., pp. 342–43.

7. Simon Kuznets, *Population, Capital, and Growth* (New York: Norton, 1973), p. 91. Cf. Donald B. Keesing, "Small Population As A Political Handicap to National Development," *Political Science Quarterly*, LXXXIV, March, 1969, pp. 50–60.

8. Cf. Schumpeter, *Business Cycles*, II, p. 699. See also A. J. Coale and E. M.

Hoover, *Population Growth and Economic Development in Low-Income Countries* (Princeton: Princeton University Press, 1958).

9. E. F. Denison, *Why Growth Rates Differ* (Washington, D.C.: Brookings Institution, 1967), pp. 9–11; also Denison, "Classification of Sources of Growth," *Review of Income and Wealth*, Series 18, March, 1972, pp. 1–25; A. C. Kelley, "Demographic Changes and American Economic Development, Past, Present and Future," in Commission on Population Growth and the American Future, Research Reports, Vol. II, *Economic Aspects of Population Change* (Washington, D.C.: U.S. Govt. Printing Office, 1972), pp. 9–48; Kuznets, "Population Change and Aggregate Output," in Coale, ed., *Demographic and Economic Change*, pp. 328–36. On past population growth and scale economies in the United States see also Allen C. Kelley, "Scale Economies, Inventive Activity, and The Economics of American Population Growth," *Explorations In Economic History*, X, Fall, 1972, pp. 35–52.

10. Denison, *Why*, p. 9. See also Donald B. Keesing, "The Impact of Research and Development on United States Trade," *Journal of Political Economy*, LXXV, Feb., 1967, pp. 38–48; F. M. Fisher and Peter Temin, "Returns to Scale in Research and Development: What Does the Schumpeterian Hypothesis Imply?" *Journal of Political Economy*, LXXXI, Jan.–Feb., 1973, pp. 56–70.

11. Kuznets, "Population Change," pp. 328–30.

12. "Demographic Changes," pp. 13–14.

13. Ibid., p. 20, also pp. 18–19.

14. Denison, *Why*, p. 9.

15. Ibid., p. 9.

16. Cf. Kuznets, "Population Change," pp. 326–28, 337.

17. Denison, *Why*, p. 9.

18. "Demographic Changes," pp. 13–14, also 15–20.

19. Denison, *Why*, p. 10; Kuznets, "Population Change," p. 326.

20. Lowell E. Gallaway, *Manpower Economics* (Homewood, Ill.: Irwin, 1971), pp. 17–25. See also chapters VI–VII above.

21. Ibid., p. 27.

22. Ibid., p. 29.

23. W. G. Bowen and T. A. Finegan, *The Economics of Labor Force Participation* (Princeton: Princeton University Press, 1969), pp. 227–31.

24. *Manpower Report of the President*, 1975, p. 309.

25. Ibid., p. 271. See also Robert Shishko and Bernard Rostker, "The Economics of Multiple Job Holding," *American Economic Review*, LXVI, June, 1976, pp. 298–308, also bibliography.

26. J. S. Mill, *Principles of Political Economy* (1848) (London: Longmans Green, 1921), Bk. IV, chap. 6.

27. A. A. Young, "Increasing Returns and Economic Progress," *Economic Journal*, XXXVIII, Dec., 1928, pp. 527–42, esp. p. 534.

28. Ibid., pp. 534, 536.

29. Colin Clark, *Population Growth and Land Use* (New York: St. Martin's Press 1967), p. 261.

30. Ibid., pp. 260–61, 266. Clark cites P. J. Verdoorn, "Fattori che regolano lo sviluppo della produttività del lavoro," *L'industria*, 1949.

31. Clark, *Population Growth*, p. 264.

32. F. H. Hahn and R. C. O. Matthews, "Theory of Economic Growth: A Survey," in *Surveys of Economic Theory*, II, prepared for the American Economic Association and The Royal Economic Society (London: Macmillan, 1965), pp. 55–58.

33. See R. E. Rowthorn, "What Remains of Kaldor's Law?" *Economic Journal*, LXXXV, March, 1975, pp. 10–19, esp. 10. Kaldor's law was put forward in *Causes of the Slow Rate of Growth of the United Kingdom; An Inaugural Lecture* (Cambridge: University Press, 1966). See also J. Cornwall, "Diffusion, Convergence, and Kaldor's Laws," *Economic Journal*, LXXXVI, June, 1976, pp. 307–14.

34. Rowthorn, "What Remains?" pp. 18–19.

35. See N. Kaldor, "Economic Growth and the Verdoorn Law: A Comment on

Mr. Rawthorn's Article," *Economic Journal,* LXXXV, Dec., 1975, pp. 891–96, and R. E. Rowthorn, "A Reply to Lord Kaldor's Comment," ibid., pp. 897–901. See also Paul Samuelson, "Scale Economies and Non-Labor Returns at the Optimum Population," *Eastern Economic Journal,* I, April, 1974, pp. 125–27; Robert E. Cole, "Optimal Population and Returns to Scale," *Demography,* IX, May, 1972, pp. 241–48.

36. *Why Growth Rates Differ,* and *Accounting for United States Economic Growth* (Washington, D.C.: Brookings Institution, 1974).

37. *Why,* chaps. 17–18. For a somewhat different interpretation see R. C. O. Matthews, "Why Growth Rates Differ," *Economic Journal,* LXXXIX, June, 1969, pp. 261–68.

38. *Accounting,* pp. 71–72.

39. Denison, *Why,* chap. 17, pp. 232–33.

40. Ibid., p. 255. On scale economies in developing countries see H. B. Chenery and L. Taylor, "Development Patterns: Among Countries and Over Time," *Review of Economics and Statistics,* L, Nov., 1968, pp. 391–416.

41. *Accounting,* p. 75. See also chap. 6 and pp. 314–17.

42. Clark, *Population Growth,* p. 260.

43. E. F. Denison, "The Shift to Services and the Rate of Productivity Change," *Survey of Current Business,* October, 1972, pp. 20–35, esp. p. 29. Clopper Almon and his associates anticipate a greater slowdown, in part because of a shift of employment into less productive sectors and in part because of a decline in the growth rate in individual sectors. *1985: Interindustry Forecasts of the American Economy* (Lexington, Mass.: D. C. Heath, 1974), chaps. 1, 9.

44. See Jorgenson and Griliches, "The Explanation of Productivity Change," reprinted with corrections in *Survey of Current Business,* XLIX, May, 1969, Part II, pp. 29–64, esp. 53–58. Denison's reply, "Some Major Issues in Productivity Analysis: An Examination of Estimates by Jorgenson and Griliches," ibid., pp. 1–27. See also Kennedy and Thirlwall, "Technical Progress," pp. 26–27; J. E. La Tourette, who reports "the experience of decreasing returns to scale in total manufacturing during the period 1926–72," in Canada, in "Economies of Scale and Capital Utilization in Canadian Manufacturing, 1926–72," *Canadian Journal of Economics,* VIII, Aug., 1975, pp. 448–55.

45. D. W. Jorgenson and L. R. Christensen, "U.S. Real Product and Real Factor Input, 1929–1967," *Review of Income and Wealth,* Series 16, March, 1970, pp. 19–50, esp. p. 47.

46. *Accounting,* p. 114.

47. See Usher's review of Denison's *Accounting,* in *Canadian Journal of Economics,* VIII, Aug., 1975, pp. 476–80.

48. C. R. Hulten, "Technical Change and the Reproducibility of Capital," *American Economic Review,* LXV, Dec., 1975, pp. 956–65.

49. F. M. Westfield, "Technical Progress and Returns to Scale," *Review of Economics and Statistics,* XLVIII, Nov., 1966, pp. 432–41, esp. p. 440.

50. See Kuznets, "Population Change," pp. 330–34, together with comments of Quandt and Friedman, pp. 344–45, 348, and Kelley, "Demographic Changes," p. 14, also 20–28. Cf. also Schumpeter who states that "provision for an indefinite family future is of central importance in the scheme of bourgeois motivation, and much driving power may be eliminated by childlessness" (*Business Cycles,* II, p. 1036) and M. J. Farrell ("The New Theories of the Consumption Function," *Economic Journal,* LXIX, Dec., 1959, sec. ix), who suggests that although parents tend to be generous to children while alive, they are not inclined to save for posterity.

51. Farrell, "New Theories," sec. vi; F. Modigliani and R. Brumberg, *Utility Analysis and Aggregate Consumption Functions: An Attempt at Integration* (New York: Photocopy, 1953); also John Cornwall, *Growth and Stability in a Mature Economy* (New York: John Wiley & Sons, 1972), chap. 5 on family-related expenditure; J. J. Spengler, *Declining Population Growth Revisited* (Chapel Hill, N.C.: Carolina Population Center, 1971).

52. Clark, *Population Growth,* pp. 267, 268. Cf. Schumpeter, *Business Cycles,* pp. 699, 1035–36.

53. f. Robert A. Gordon, "Population Growth, Housing, and the Capital Coefficient," *American Economic Review,* XLVI, June, 1956, pp. 307–22.

54. John W. Kendrick, *Productivity Trends in the United States* (Princeton: Princeton University Press, 1961), pp. 99–102.

55. Simon Kuznets, *Capital in the American Economy* (Princeton: Princeton University Press 1961), pp. 332–33, also on the relation of capital to output, ibid., pp. 78–90; *Economic Growth of Nations* (Cambridge: Harvard University Press, 1971), pp. 61–73, and *Modern Economic Growth* (New Haven: Yale, University Press, 1967), pp. 76–77, 252–62, 421.

56. W. M. Corden, "The Economic Limits to Population Increase," *Economic Record,* XXXI, Nov., 1955, pp. 242–60, esp. 259–60.

57. G. A. Akerlof and J. E. Stiglitz, "Capital, Wages and Structural Unemployment," *Economic Journal,* LXXIX, June, 1969, pp. 269–81.

58. See Kuznets, *Capital;* Raymond Goldsmith and Christopher Saunders, eds., *The Measurement of National Wealth,* Vol. 8 in Income and Wealth Series (Chicago: Quadrangle Books, 1959), pp. 1–34, esp. 31–32. See also Goldsmith, "A Synthetic Estimate of the National Wealth of Japan, 1885–1973," *Review of Income and Wealth,* Series 21, June, 1975, pp. 125–51; Spengler, *Declining Population Growth Revisited.*

59. T. W. Schultz, *Human Resources* (National Bureau of Economic Research) (New York: Columbia University Press, 1972), p. 59. See also Kuznets, *Economic Growth of Nations,* 76–77, 88–92.

60. J. Morth, "Human Capital: Deterioration and Net Investment," *Review of Income and Wealth,* Series 19, Sept., 1973, pp. 279–302.

61. On widening and deepening investment in education see Marcelo Selowsky, "On the Measurement of Education's Contribution to Growth," *Quarterly Journal of Economics,* LXXXIII, Aug., 1969, pp. 449–63.

62. On these and related issues see references in the note following. See also Robert Solow, "The Economics of Resources or the Resources of Economics," *American Economic Review,* LXIV, May, 1974, pp. 1–14.

63. Aspects of the comparative impact of population growth and average-income growth upon fixed and depletable assets are treated in Commission on Population Growth and the American Future, Research Reports, Vol. 3, *Population, Resources, and the Environment,* edited by R. G. Ridker (Washington, D.C.: U.S. Government Printing Office, 1972). See also ibid., Vol. 2; National Academy of Sciences and National Research Council, *Resources and Man* (San Francisco: Freeman, 1969); Sterling Brubaker, *To Live on Earth* (Baltimore: The Johns Hopkins University Press, 1972); H. T. Odum, *Environment, Power, and Society* (New York: Wiley, 1971); Ralph E. Lapp, *The Logarithmic Century* (Englewood Cliffs: Prentice Hall, 1973), esp. chaps. 3–5, 9; Nicholas Georgescu-Roegen, *Energy and Economic Myths* (New York: Pergamon, 1976), Part I; idem, *The Entropy Law and the Economic Process* (Cambridge: Harvard University Press, 1971).

64. Technical progress can extend the range of direct and indirect technical substitutes for given scarce resources as well as reduce input of depletable resources per unit of output. However, technical progress itself may prove subject to limitations even as Julius Wolf anticipated. See *Die Volkswirtschaft der Gegenwart u. Zukunft* (Leipzig: A. Deichert, 1912), pp. 236–37; Simon S. Kuznets, *Secular Movements in Production and Prices* (Boston: Houghton Mifflin, 1930), chap. 1, esp. pp. 11–41. Moreover, when technologies require specialized materials, these materials, if in short supply, can constrain these technologies. E.g., see A. L. Hammond, "Lithium: Will Short Supply Constrain Energy Technologies?" *Science,* CXVI, March 12, 1976, pp. 1037–38. See also N. Georgescu-Roegen, "Dynamic Equilibrium and Economic Growth," *Economie Appliquée,* XXVII(4), 1974, p. 542.

65. E.g., see T. W. Schultz, ed., *Marriage, Children and Human Capital* (Chicago: University of Chicago Press, 1975), and critiques by Mark Perlman, F. D. Bean,

and N. K. Namboodri, *Demography*, XII, August, 1975, pp. 549–69; Gary Becker and H. Gregg Lewis, "On the Interaction between the Quantity and the Quality of Children," *Journal of Political Economy*, LXXXI(2), March–April, 1973, pp. S279–S288.

66. National Bureau of Economic Research, *54th Annual Report*, Sept., 1974, pp. 81–85.

67. Union membership may run counter to work-choice options. R. E. B. Lucas, "The Distribution of Job Characteristics," *Review of Economics and Statistics*, LVI, Nov., 1974, pp. 538–39.

68. Paul Taubman and Terrence Wales, "The Inadequacy of Cross-section Age-Earning Profiles When Ability Is Not Held Constant," *Annals of Economic and Social Measurement*, I, July, 1972, pp. 363–68, esp. 366–68. Cf. R. Boudon, *Education, Opportunity, and Social Inequality* (New York: Wiley, 1974); also Finis Welch, "Human Capital Theory: Education, Discrimination, and Life Cycles," *American Economic Review*, LXV, May, 1975, pp. 63–73.

69. L. C. Solomon, "Definition of College Quality and Its Impact on Earnings," *Explorations in Economic Research*, Occasional Paper, National Bureau of Economic Research, Vol. 2, Fall, 1975, pp. 537–87, esp. p. 583; also Paul Wachlit, "The Effect of School Quality on Achievement, Attainment Levels, and Lifetime Earnings," ibid., pp. 502–36.

70. M. J. Beckman, "The Limits to Growth in a Neoclassical World," *American Economic Review*, LXV, Sept., 1975, pp. 695–99, esp. p. 699.

71. See Harold Lydall's review in *Economic Journal*, LXXXV, March, 1975, pp. 186–87.

72. R. L. Gordon, "Conservation and the Theory of Exhaustible Resources," *Canadian Journal of Economics*, XXXII, Aug., 1966, pp. 319–326; also A. C. Fisher and J. V. Krutilla, "Conservation, Environment, and the Rate of Discount," *Quarterly Journal of Economics*, LXXXIX, Aug., 1975, pp. 358–70.

73. N. Georgescu-Roegen, "Energy and Economic Myths," *Southern Economic Journal*, XLI, Jan., 1975, pp. 374–76; but cf. M. C. Weinstein and R. L. Zeckhauser, "Optimal Consumption of Depletable Resources," *Quarterly Journal of Economics*, LXXXIX, Aug., 1975, pp. 371–92.

74. According to some estimates net investment in human capital sometimes roughly approximates net investment in other assets. See Morth, "Human Capital," p. 297.

75. E.g., see Kennedy and Thirlwall, "Technical Progress"; I. B. Kravis, "A Survey of International Comparisons of Productivity," *Economic Journal*, LXXVI, March, 1976, pp. 1–44; Edwin Mansfield, *The Economics of Technical Change* (New York: Norton, 1968), and "Contribution of R & D to Growth in the United States," *Science*, CLXXV, Feb. 4, 1972, pp. 477–86; Denison, *Accounting* and *Why;* Jorgensen and Griliches, "The Explanation of Productivity Change."

76. M. Z. Fabrycy, "Determinants of Total Factor Productivity." See also E. F. Denison and W. K. Chung, *How Japan's Economy Grew So Fast* (Washington, D.C.: Brookings Institution, 1976). The authors point to the contribution of both indigenous and borrowed technology, together with economies of scale, and increase in capital and labor made possible in part by the movement of labor from agriculture to industry.

77. *Accounting*, chap. 9, esp. pp. 127–28, also pp. 340–47.

78. Mansfield, "Contribution," p. 477, and *The Economics;* R. Solow, "Technical Change and the Aggregate Production Function," *Review of Economics and Statistics*, XXXIX, Aug., 1957, pp. 312–20.

79. Mansfield, *The Economics*, pp. 4–5, 40–42; also "Contribution."

80. I. B. Kravis ("A Survey," p. 41) concludes from his international and his interindustry comparisons that "only the total size of the market emerges from the studies with any degree of consistency as being associated with industry-to-industry differences in relative productivity, and there the line of causation probably runs both ways."

81. Georgescu-Roegen, "Energy and Economic Myths," p. 367.

82. Ibid., p. 368. See also R. E. Miles, *Awakening from the American Dream* (New York: Universe Books, 1976).

83. *Accounting*, p. 127. See also C. Daugherty and Marcelo Selowski, "Measuring the Effects of Misallocation of Labor," *Review of Economics and Statistics*, LV, 1972, pp. 38–46.

84. B. S. Schiller, "Job Search Media: Utilization and Effectiveness," *Quarterly Review of Economics and Business*, XV, Winter, 1975, pp. 55–64. On the effect of education, income level, and so on, on job search and employment see Stanley P. Stephenson, Jr., "The Economics of Youth Job Search Behavior," *Review of Economics and Statistics*, LVIII, Feb., 1976, pp. 104–11.

85. On anticipations see M. I. Kamien and N. L. Schwartz, "Some Economic Consequences of Anticipating Technical Advance," *Western Economic Journal*, X, June, 1973, pp. 123–38.

86. For illustrations of the impact of power blocs see V. L. Bassie, "The Positive Relationship Between Unemployment and Price Changes," *Quarterly Review of Economics and Business*, XV, Autumn, 1975, pp. 7–16.

87. E.g., see H. Grubel, Dennis Maki, and Shelly Sax, "Real and Induced Unemployment in Canada," *Canadian Journal of Economics*, VIII, May, 1975, pp. 151–73; Martin Feldstein, "The Economics of the New Unemployment," *The Public Interest*, No. 33, Fall, 1973, pp. 3–42, esp. pp. 23–25, 29–36, 42; Gene Chapin, "Unemployment Insurance, Job Search, and the Demand for Leisure," *Western Economic Journal*, IX, March, 1973, pp. 102–7.

88. Michael C. Lovell, "The Minimum Wage, Teenage Unemployment, and the Business Cycle," *Western Economic Journal*, X, Dec., 1972, pp. 414–27; Feldstein, "The Economics," pp. 14–17; J. H. McCulloch, "The Effect of a Minimum Wage Law in the Labour-Intensive Sector," *Canadian Journal of Economics*, VII, May, 1974, pp. 316–18; Gallaway, *Manpower Economics*, chaps. 7–8; H. G. Johnson, "Minimum Wage Laws: A General Equilibrium Analysis," *Canadian Journal of Economics*, II, 1969, pp. 599–604; H. G. Johnson and Peter Mieszkowski, "The Effects of Unionization on the Distribution of Income: A General Equilibrium Approach," *Quarterly Journal of Economics*, LXXXIV, Nov., 1970, pp. 539–61.

89. E. F. Denison, *The Sources of Economic Growth in the United States and the Alternatives Before Us* (Committee for Economic Development, Supplementary Paper No. 13), New York, 1962, pp. 204–6.

90. *Manpower Economics*, chaps. 3–4, pp. 42, 54. On "stayers" see also Larry Shroeder, "An Information-Theoretic Analysis of Occupational Mobility Paths," *Quarterly Review of Economics and Business*, XV, Winter, 1975, pp. 20–21.

91. Gallaway, *Manpower Economics*, chap. 5, p. 70.

92. T. W. Schultz, "The Value of the Ability to Deal with Disequilibria," *Economic Literature*, XIII, Sept., 1975, pp. 827–46. See also J. G. Scoville, "Education and Training Requirements for Occupations," *Review of Economics and Statistics*, XLVIII, 1966, pp. 387–94.

93. C. R. S. Dougherty, "Substitution and the Structure of the Labor Force," *Economic Journal*, LXXXII, March, 1972, pp. 170–82.

94. "Population Change," pp. 326–30, 334, 336–37.

95. Denison, *Why*, p. 186. As we indicate below, however, even very large countries may be seriously constrained by heavy dependence upon foreign sources for raw materials.

96. E. A. G. Robinson, ed., *Economic Consequences of the Size of Nations* (London: Macmillan, 1960), p. xviii. On factors influencing size of state and governmental costs see Allen C. Kelley, "Demographic Change and the Size of the Governmental Sector," *Southern Economic Journal*, XLIII, Oct., 1976, pp. 1058–65 and bibliography. See also section 3 below.

97. *Why*, pp. 230, 231, 234.

98. F. L. Pryor, "Size of Establishment in Manufacturing," *Economic Journal*, XXXII, June, 1972, pp. 547–66. On internal limits to firm size see P. H. Rubin, "The

Expansion of Firms," *Journal of Political Economy*, LXXXI, Aug., 1973, pp. 936–49.

99. Kuznets, "Population Change," in Coale, *Demographic and Economic Change*, pp. 336–37, and Friedman's comment, ibid., p. 349; also Harvey Leibenstein, "The Impact of Population Growth on Economic Welfare—Nontraditional Elements," in Roger Revelle, ed., *Rapid Population Growth* (Baltimore; Johns Hopkins Press, 1971), pp. 175–198.

100. "Population Change," pp. 328–30. E. M. Hoover points out, however, that many obstacles stand in the way of developing talent when it is born. See his "Basic Approaches to the Study of Demographic Aspects of Economic Development: Economic Demographic Models," *Population Index*, XXXVII, April–June, 1971, pp. 66–75.

101. Kelley, "Demographic Changes," p. 14; also J. D. Pitchford, *Population In Economic Growth* (Amsterdam: North Holland, 1924), pp. 54–70.

102. For a number of models based upon population as an endogenous factor see Jürg Niehans, "Economic Growth with Two Endogenous Factors," *Quarterly Journal of Economics*, LXXVII, Aug., 1963, pp. 349–71. See also Hahn and Matthews, "Theory of Economic Growth," pp. 23–26.

103. Illustrative is Ronald Lee's "The Formal Dynamics of Controlled Populations and The Echo, The Boom and The Bust," *Demography*, XI, Nov., 1974, pp. 463–86. On postwar fertility patterns see Arthur A. Campbell, "Beyond the Demographic Transition," ibid., pp. 549–62.

104. See Simon Kuznets, *Postwar Economic Growth* (Cambridge: Harvard University Press, 1964), chap. 1.

105. Wassily Leontief, "Structure of the World Economy," *American Economic Review*, LXIV, Dec., 1974, p. 823; see also M. Mesarovic and E. Pestel, *Mankind at the Turning Point* (New York: E. P. Dutton, 1974), p. 20.

106. E.g., see Raymond Vernon, *Sovereignty at Bay* (New York: Basic Books, 1971).

107. E.g., see S. D. Kramer, "State Power and the Structure of International Trade," *World Politics*, XXVIII, April, 1976, pp. 317–47; also Edward Friedland, "Oil and The Decline of Western Power," *Political Science Quarterly*, XC, Fall, 1975, pp. 432–50. See also D. B. Keesing, "Small Population as a Political Handicap to National Development," *Political Science Quarterly*, LXXXIV, March, 1969, pp. 50–60.

108. G. J. Stigler, *The Organization of Industry* (Homewood, Ill.: Irwin, 1968), chap. 7, esp. pp. 88–89.

109. D. B. Keesing, "Population and Industrial Development: Some Evidence From Trade Patterns," *American Economic Review*, LVIII, June, 1968, pp. 448–55, esp. p. 455; Robinson, *Economic Consequences*, p. xviii.

110. E.g., on Norway see Z. Griliches and V. Ringstad, *Economies of Scale and the Form of the Production Function* (Amsterdam: North-Holland Publishing Co., 1971), esp. p. 160.

111. Charles I. Taylor and M. C. Hudson, *World Handbook of Political and Social Indicators*, 2nd ed. (New Haven: Yale University Press, 1972), pp. 372–77. See also D. B. Keesing and D. R. Sherk, "Population Density in Patterns of Trade and Development," *American Economic Review*, LXI, Dec., 1971, pp. 956–61.

112. On the role of resources see Pitchford, *Population in Economic Growth*, chap. 8. On U.S. dependence on foreign sources, see Vivian E. Spencer, *Raw Materials in the United States Economy: 1900–1969*, U.S. Bureau of Mines, Working Paper 35, (Washington, D.C.: U.S. Government Printing Office, 1972); E. Conecion, ed., *The Mineral Position of the United States, 1975–2000* (Madison: University of Wisconsin Press, 1972); Ralph W. Marsden, ed., *Politics, Minerals, and Survival* (Madison: University of Wisconsin Press, 1974).

113. These data are based on the World Bank Atlas, 1975. The economic behavior of some small countries is described in Robinson, *Economic Consequences*.

114. See H. B. Chenery, "Patterns of Industrial Growth," *American Economic Review*, L, Sept., 1960, pp. 624–54; D. B. Keesing, "Outward-Looking Policies and

Economic Development," *Economic Journal,* LXXVII, June, 1967, pp. 304–26; Martin Bronfenbrenner, "Predatory Poverty on the Offensive, The UNCTAD Record," *Economic Development and Cultural Change,* XXIV, June, 1976, pp. 825–32.

115. Cf. Irving Hoch's interesting paper on consequences of city growth. "City Size Effects, Trends, and Policies," *Science,* CXCIII, Sept. 3, 1976, pp. 856–63.

116. Elmer Plischke, *Microstates in World Affairs* (Washington, D.C.: American Enterprise Institute, 1977), pp. 2, 17–20.

117. Ibid., pp. 22–23, also Appendix A.

118. Donald B. Keesing, "National Diversity and World Progress," *World Development,* III, April, 1975, pp. 191–99, esp. 199.

IX. Cessation of Population Growth: Implications, Problem Areas

1. G. J. Stigler, *The Organizations of Industry* (Homewood, Ill.: Irwin, 1968), p. 229.

2. Israel M. Kirzner, *Competition and Entrepreneurship* (Chicago: University of Chicago Press, 1973), chap. 2, p. 39, also pp. 79–84.

3. Ibid., pp. 69, 221.

4. Ibid., p. 45.

5. Ibid., p. 68.

6. Ibid., p. 83.

7. Tamara K. Hareven, "The Last Stage: Historical Adulthood and Old Age," *Daedalus,* CV, Fall, 1976, pp. 13–28, esp. 19–21.

8. On the hardness of old age see Simone de Beauvoir, *The Coming of Age,* trans. Patrick O'Brien (New York: Putnam, 1972). See also N. B. Ture, *The Future of Private Pension Plans* (Washington, D.C.: American Enterprise Institute, 1976), chap. 2; Lenore Bixby et al., *Demographic and Economic Characteristics of the Aged.*

9. As Arrow points out, "uncertainty can tend to destroy markets" and the "absence of some markets for future goods may cause others to fail." Therefore, for example, "the demand for future capital goods will depend on expectations about the product at some still more removed time." K. J. Arrow, "Limited Knowledge and Economic Analysis," *American Economic Review,* LXIV, March, 1974, pp. 1–10, esp. p. 9. W. Beckerman writes: "Growth, at least over a very wide range, depends on expectations and is therefore limited by what people expect it to be." See his "The Determinants of Economic Growth," in P. D. Henderson, ed., *Economic Growth in Britain* (London: Weidenfeld Nicholson, 1966), pp. 69, 73.

10. E.g., see James S. Duesenberry, *Business Cycles and Economic Growth* (New York: McGraw Hill, 1958), pp. 227–28, 263, 265, 288; also Harold W. Watts, "Long-run Income Expectations and Consumer Saving," in T. F. Dernburg, R. N. Rosett, and H. W. Watts, *Studies in Household Economic Behavior* (New Haven: Yale University Press, 1958), pp. 101–44. However, see E. H. Phelps Brown (with Margaret H. Brown), *A Century of Pay* (New York: St. Martins Press, 1968), pp. 323–24. They found that although population growth supposedly made for expanding markets, and adaptability of the labor force, there was little correlation in West European countries between rate of increase of productivity and real wages and that of population.

11. See S. A. Ozga, *Expectations in Economic Theory* (London: Weidenfeld and Nicholson, 1965); also G. L. S. Shackle, *Epistemics & Economics* (Cambridge: University Press, 1972), pp. 134, 218, 223–24, 233, 447–48, also chap. 34.

12. Keynes, *General Theory,* p. 294. See Shackle's comments on Keynes's chapter 12, *Epistemics,* pp. 222–26.

13. Keynes questioned the helpfulness of mathematical models relating to the future on the ground of "the complexities and interdependencies of the real world." *General Theory,* chap. 2, p. 298. Cf. Michael D. McCarthy, *The Wharton Quarterly*

Econometric Forecasting Model Mark III (Philadelphia: Wharton School, University of Pennsylvania, 1972). This work illustrates difficulties attendant upon short-term forecasting, a mode of forecasting subject to some improvement through judgmental intervention, a form of intervention of greater importance in long-run planning.

14. However, See Franco Modigliani and E. Gruneberg, "The Predictability of Social Events," *Journal of Political Economy,* LXII, Dec., 1954, pp. 465–78; also Ian H. Wilson, "Socio-Political Forecasting: A New Dimension to Strategic Planning," *Michigan Business Review,* July, 1974, pp. 15–25, and J. R. Stodden, "Inflation—Temporary or Ongoing Is The Question for the 1970's," *Business Review,* Federal Reserve Bank of Dallas, June, 1975, pp. 1–6. See also J. M. Burgers, "Causality and Anticipation," *Science,* CLXXXIX, July 18, 1975, pp. 194–98; V. F. Weisskopf, "The Frontiers and Limits of Science," *Bulletin of the American Academy of Arts and Sciences,* XXVIII, March, 1975, pp. 15–26.

15. See John Cornwall, *Growth and Stability in a Mature Economy* (New York: Wiley, 1972).

16. W. Nordhaus and J. Tobin, *Economic Growth* (New York: Columbia University Press, 1972), pp. 14–18, 60–70. See also Glenn Hueckle, "A Historical Approach to Future Economic Growth," *Science,* CLXXXVII, March 14, 1975, pp. 925–31.

17. H. Daly, ed., *Toward a Steady State Economy* (San Francisco: Freeman, 1973); N. Georgescu-Roegen, "Energy and Economic Myths," *Southern Economic Journal,* XLI, Jan. 1975, pp. 374–77.

18. E.g., see J. B. Wiesner, "Has the U.S. Lost its Initiative in Technological Innovation?" *Technology Review,* LXXVIII, July–Aug., 1976, pp. 55–60.

19. *General Theory,* p. 161. "Pure" expectations need to be distinguished, at least in part, from views of the future conditioned by age, time horizon, resiliency of the economy and structure of the labor force, life style, proneness to experimentation and risk assumption, and so on. See also Don Patinkin, "Keynes' Monetary Thought," *History of Political Economy,* VIII, Spring, 1976, pp. 98, 118, 136–37, 141–42. On the impact of futures markets see C. J. Bliss, "Prices, Markets and Planning," *Economic Journal,* LXXXII, March, 1972, pp. 97–99. On expectation as "search" see Shackle, *Epistemics,* pp. 365–69.

20. See R. C. O. Matthews, *The Business Cycle* (Chicago: University of Chicago Press, 1959), pp. 60–62, 275; G. Haberler, *Prosperity and Depression* (Take Success: United Nations, 1946) chap. 6, pp. 180–83, 252–53. J. M. Culbertson points to the need to distinguish between "expectations . . . explained in terms of feedbacks" and expectations "given externally in a *ceteris paribus* world of comparative statics." *Macroeconomic Theory and Stabilization Policy* (New York: McGraw-Hill, 1968), p. 42.

21. J. A. Kregel, "The Modelling Methodology in the Face of Uncertainty: The Modelling Methods of Keynes and the Post-Keynesians," *Economic Journal,* LXXXVI, June, 1976, pp. 209–25, esp. 209–12, 213, 218–25; R. X. Chase, "Keynes and U.S. Keynesianism: A Lack of Historical Perspective and the Decline of the New Economics," *Journal of Economic Issues,* IX, Sept., 1975, pp. 446–48; E. Roy Weintraub, "'Uncertainty' and the Keynesian Revolution," *History of Political Economy,* VII, 1975, no. 4, pp. 530–48, esp. pp. 530–35. See also Shackle, *Epistemics,* chap. 34, p. 400.

22. *General Theory,* pp. 307–8, also 220–21, 318.

23. "Some Economic Consequences of a Declining Population," *Eugenics Review,* XXIX, April, 1937, pp. 13–14; also Vincent Tarascio's model based on this essay, "Keynes on the Sources of Economic Growth," *Journal of Economic Growth* XXXI, June, 1971, pp. 429–44, and Keynes' "The General Theory of Employment," *Quarterly Journal of Economics,* LI, Feb., 1937, pp. 209–23.

24. A. C. Pigou, *Keynes's 'General Theory'* (London: Macmillan, 1950), pp. 37–38 and note.

25. *Trade and Welfare,* II (London: Oxford University Press, 1955), p. 94. Savings should "continue until the state of glut is reached." *Ibid.,* p. 95.

26. Roy Radner, "Satisficing," *Journal of Mathematical Economics*, II, June–Sept., 1975, pp. 253–62, esp. p. 253. "It is probably not good positive theory to take very seriously an assumption that anyone behaves according to a sequential strategy that maximizes an expected lifetime (or infinite) horizon utility, nor is it good advice to a manager to recommend adoption of the solution of an optimization problem that there is no prospect of solving in the next hundred years." Ibid., p. 253. See also R. M. Goodwin, *Elementary Economics*, pp. 184–90, on an "optimal sequence of decisions directly affecting population" and complications associated therewith. "A world which looks to tomorrow is a world bent upon exploiting uncertainty, un-knowledge," writes Shackle in *Epistemics*, p. 164, also p. 165.

27. Radner, "Satisficing," p. 254; also S. J. Turnowski, "Empirical Evidence on the Formation of Price Expectations," *Journal of the American Statistical Association*, LXV, Dec., 1976, pp. 1441–54, and C. L. Hedrick, "Expectations and the Labor Supply," *American Economic Review*, LXIII, Dec., 1973, pp. 968–74, esp. 973.

28. L. M. Lachmann, "From Mises to Shackle: An Essay on Austrian Economics and the Kaleidic Society," *Journal of Economic Literature*, XIV, March, 1976, pp. 54–62, esp. p. 59.

29. A. D. Knox, "The Acceleration Principle and the Theory of Investment: A Survey," *Economica*, XIX, Aug., 1952, pp. 269–97.

30. "Anticipation of technical advance tends to delay scrapping of old equipment and retard installation of new, with current output and price higher than if technology is stagnant. Selection among currently competing technologies is also affected by the course future technical advance is expected to follow." See M. I. Kamien and N. L. Schwartz, "Some Economic Consequences of Anticipating Technical Advance," *Western Economic Journal*, X, June, 1972, pp. 123–38, esp. p. 137. As Nathan Rosenberg notes, however, "the very rapidity of the overall pace of technological improvement may make a postponed decision privately (and perhaps even socially) optimal." See "On Technological Expectations," *Economic Journal*, LXXXVI, Sept., 1976, pp. 523–35, esp. p. 535.

31. This argument is parallel to J. Bain's observation that large-scale capital requirements block entry and hence guard early comers against competition by later comers. See *Barriers to New Competition* (Cambridge: Harvard University Press, 1956), chaps. 3, 5.

32. E.g., see George Katona, *Psychological Economics* (New York: Elsevier, 1975), chaps. 9–11. See, however, Watts, "Long-run Income Expectations," pp. 103–8, on the role of long-run income expectations in spending and saving.

33. In the absence of genetic counseling "in a few generations, the ethic which guides medical practice will have seriously damaged the heritage of countless previous generations. Having thwarted the historical process of natural selection against such disadvantageous genes, civilization must provide an acceptable substitute." Philip Handler, ed., *Biology and the Future of Man* (New York: Oxford University Press, 1970), p. 911.

34. E.g., see G. B. Terry, "Rival Explanations in the Work-Fertility Relationship," *Population Studies*, XXIX, July, 1975, pp. 191–206; T. J. Espenshade, "The Price of Children and Socio-Economic Theories of Fertility: A Survey of Alternative Methods of Estimating the Parental Cost of Raising Children," ibid., XXVI, July, 1972, pp. 207–22; N. K. Namboodri, "Some Observations on the Economic Framework for Fertility Analysis," ibid., pp. 185–206. See also M. G. Groat, R. L. Workman, and A. G. Neal, "Labor Force Participation and Family Formation: A Study of Working Mothers," *Demography*, XIII, Feb., 1976, pp. 115ff. They found "lower fertility, longer first birth intervals, and earlier use of birth control were associated with the longest work durations, the highest status jobs, and work before the birth of the first child."

35. R. Blandy, "The Welfare Analysis of Fertility Reduction," *Economic Journal*, LXXXIV, March, 1974, pp. 109–29, esp. p. 110. Cf. A. R. Sweezy, "The Economic

Explanation of Fertility Changes in the United States," *Population Studies*, XXV, pp. 255–68; also Erland Hofstee, "Birth Variation in Populations Which Practice Family Planning," ibid., pp. 315–26; also U.S. Bureau of the Census, *Current Population Reports*, Series P-20, no. 308, "Fertility of American Women: June, 1976," June 1977, pp. 1–7.

36. On controversy respecting the degree to which economic factors determine fertility see Harvey Leibenstein, "An Interpretation of the Economic Theory of Fertility: Promising Paths or Blind Alley," *Journal of Economic Literature*, XII, June, 1974, pp. 457–79, M. C. Keeley's critique and Leibenstein's reply, ibid., XIII, June, 1975, pp. 461–72, and bibliography.

37. A. S. Eichner and J. A. Kregel, "An Essay on Post-Keynesian Theory: A New Paradigm in Economics," *Journal of Economic Literature*, XIII, Dec., 1975, pp. 1293–1314, esp. 1294; authors' italics.

38. E.g., see A. D. Knox, "The Acceleration Principle and the Theory of Investment: A Survey," *Economics*, XIX, Aug., 1952, pp. 269–97; also J. J. Spengler, "Population Movements, Employment, and Income," *Southern Economic Journal*, V, Oct., 1938, pp. 129–57, sections vii–x; J. Tinbergen, "Statistical Evidence on the Acceleration Principle," *Economica*, V, May, 1938, pp. 164–76.

39. On this concern, effectively expressed by A. H. Hansen in a number of studies, see Maurice W. Lee, *Macroeconomics: Fluctuations, Growth, Stability* (Homewood, Ill.: Irwin, 1967, pp. 116–26; A. L. Levine, "Economic Science and Population Theory," *Population Studies*, XIX, Nov., 1965, pp. 139–54. Among the most critical early replies to Hansen were George Terborgh's *The Bogey of Economic Maturity* (Chicago: Machinery and Allied Products Institute, 1945), and Marvin V. Jones's *Secular Trends and Idle Resources*, which appeared as Part 2 of the Vol. 17, Oct., 1944 number of the *Journal of Business of the University of Chicago*. See also Clarence L. Barber's critique, "Population Growth and the Demand for Capital," *American Economic Review*, XLIII, March, 1943, pp. 133–39, and John Cornwall's assessment of "Vulgar" stagnation theory, in *Growth and Stability in a Mature Economy* (New York: Wiley, 1972). See also H. L. Reed, "Economists on Industrial Stagnation," *Journal of Political Economy*, XLVIII, 1940, pp. 244–50.

40. In 1930 gross national product in real terms fell below the 1929 level, not to return thereto until 1937. The U.S. population increased about 7.2 percent in the 1930s compared with per decade rates of about 15.5 percent in 1910–1930, and higher rates earlier. Whereas the annual number of immigrants averaged 1,035,000 in 1910–1914, it fell to 280,000 in prosperous 1929, in the main because of restrictions on immigration, and to 23,000 in depressed 1933, rising to only 63,000 by 1938. See U.S. Bureau of the Census, *Historical Statistics of the United States*, Bicentennial Edition, Washington, D.C., 1975. Official immigration data are incomplete in that they do not include the allegedly large annual inflow of illegal immigrants.

41. Alfred Sauvy and Joseph Stassart refer to "capital widening" as "demographic investment" and "capital deepening" as "economic investment." Alfred Sauvy, *General Theory of Population*, trans. by Christophe Campos (New York: Basic Books, 1969), p. 180; Joseph Stassart, *Les avantages et les inconvienients économiques d'une population stationnaire* (The Hague: Nijhoff, 1965), passim. Recently W. B. Reddaway estimated that a complete disappearance of the market for capital associated with population growth in the United Kingdom would not seriously reduce the demand for capital. Moreover, this reduction could easily be offset. "The Economic Consequences of Zero Population Growth," *Lloyd's Bank Review*, No. 124, April, 1977, pp. 14–30, esp. 20–22.

42. S. Kuznets, *Capital in the American Economy* (Princeton: Princeton University Press, 1961), chap. 7, esp. pp. 333, 340–41, 349, 425; also his *Population, Capital, and Growth* (New York: W. W. Norton, 1973), and Brinley Thomas, *Migration and Economic Growth* (Cambridge: Cambridge University Press, 1954). Real net national wealth per capita increased 1.3 percent per year in 1925–1975, with the rate ranging from 0.2 percent in 1929–1948 to 2.6 in 1925–1929; it grew

about 1.4 percent between 1775 and 1975. See J. W. Kendrick, "Measuring America's Wealth," *Morgan Guaranty Survey,* May, 1976, pp. 5–13, esp. pp. 6–7.

43. Given a wealth–income ratio *W / Y* of 3.5 or 4.0 to 1, maintaining a constant wealth/population ratio would absorb inputs approximating 3.5 or 4.0 percent of the national income in addition to investment in "human capital" not otherwise covered. In the 1960s the ratio of tangible reproducible assets—then 77 percent of all tangible assets compared with 82 percent in 1952—to national income approximated 3 to 1, and that of all tangible assets to national income approximated 4 to 1. On tangible assets, reproducible and not reproducible, see U.S. Bureau of the Census, *Historical Statistics of the United States, Colonial Times to 1970, Bicentennial Edition,* Part I, (Washington, D.C.: 1975), p. 252. In 1965 the value of educational capital approximated 0.53 of that of net reproducible capital. Nordhaus and Tobin, *Economic Growth,* p. 30.

44. The age composition of the population was changing in 1952–1968; the median age fell from 29.9 in 1950 to 26.8 in 1970.

45. In 1952 structures constituted 62.6 percent of total reproducible assets; in 1968, 60.8 percent. The corresponding percentages for producer durables are 15.8 and 16.9; for consumer durables, 9.2 and 11.7. Computed from *Historical Statistics,* I, p. 252.

46. Kuznets, *Capital,* pp. 92–96, 393–96. Increase in the relative number of old persons may slow deferrable replacement inasmuch as an individual's demand for a good tends to be conditioned by the ratio of his life expectancy to the average life of the product under consideration.

47. The replacement rate is much lower for residential and business structures than for durables, public and private. For data see tables in *Survey of Current Business,* XLVII, Dec., 1967, pp. 46–47; J. C. Musgrave, "New Estimates of Residential Capital in the United States, 1925–73," ibid., LIV, Oct., 1974, pp. 32–38. With capital consumption around 15 percent of Gross National Product and total reproductive resources amounting to about 2.75 times Gross National Product, only 5–6 percent of reproductive assets would be replaced annually.

48. *Annual Report of the Council of Economic Advisers* (Washington, D.C., 1974), p. 265.

49. Ibid., pp. 324, 330.

50. Per capita disposable income in 1958 dollars increased from $1,236 in 1929 to $2,890 in 1973, or 134 percent. Had the ratio of disposable to national income remained as in 1929, per capita disposable income would have increased about 154 percent. Ibid., pp. 268–69.

51. Writing of the past in 1960, Kuznets suggested as "a reasonable impression" that "the limitation on savings available for financing capital formation held down capital formation levels and may have accounted for the decline in the *net* capital formation proportion." *Capital,* p. 399.

52. Kuznets, *Capital,* p. 95. "Gross capital formation accounted for about one-fifth of gross national product" between 1869 and 1955. Ibid., p. 396.

53. Ibid., p. 268.

54. U.S. Bureau of the Census, *Historical Statistics,* Part 1, p. 229.

55. Council, *Annual Report,* 1974, pp. 249, 264–65.

56. Robert Dorfman, summarizing E. S. Phelps's central theme, notes the importance of increase in equipment per worker, a sequel to technological progress and growing source of demand for capital. See Phelps, "Some Macroeconomics of Population Leveling," in Commission on Population Growth and the American Future, *Research Reports* (Washington, D.C., Government Printing Office, 1972), II, pp. 71–84; also Dorfman's comments, ibid., pp. 85–89. "The only major source of new investment opportunity lies in technical progress. However, if technical progress is *neutral,* as is so often supposed, all investment induced by technical change could be financed from amortization funds. *Net* investment would still trend to zero as would net profits." So writes R. O. Hieser, "The Economic Consequences of Zero Population Growth," *The Economic Record,* XLIX, June, 1973,

pp. 241–62. See also E. S. Phelps, "Population Increase," *Canadian Journal of Economics,* I, Aug., 1968, pp. 497–518; Roy Harrod, "Les relations entre l'investissement et la population," *Revue économique,* VI, May, 1955, pp. 356–67.

57. As of June 30, 1975 securities listed on American exchanges were valued at $795.5 billions. *Annual Report of Security and Exchange Commission* for year ending June 30, 1975, p. 196. As of December 31, 1973, U.S. assets were estimated at $9,922 billions, of which 458 billion were in insurance and pension reserves, 2,186 billion were in corporate equities and bonds, government obligations, and mortgages, and 789 billion were in other credit instruments. Kendrick, "Measuring," p. 9.

58. Kendrick, "Measuring," p. 13. See also Henry C. Wallich, "Is There a Capital Shortage?" *Challenge,* XVIII, Sept.–Oct., 1975, pp. 30–43.

59. Wallich, "Is There?" p. 31. Cf. also L. R. Christensen and D. W. Jorgenson, "U.S. Income, Saving, and Wealth, 1929–1969," *Review of Income and Wealth,* Series 19, No. 4, Dec., 1973.

60. "Little is known about consumer behavior," writes Robert Ferber in "Consumer Economics, A Survey," *Journal of Economic Literature,* XI, Dec., 1973, pp. 1303–42, esp. p. 1332. See also Marc Nerlove's excellent review of the work of K. J. Lancaster and D. S. Ironmonger in *Journal of Political Economy,* LXXXIII, Oct., 1975, pp. 1084–89.

61. Cornwall, *Growth,* pp. 19, 78–79, also pp. 261–63, on offsets to savings.

62. E.g., see Zuhair A. Hassan and S. R. Johnson, "Consumer Demand Parameters for the U.S.: A Comparison of Linear Expenditures, Rotterdam and Double-Log Estimates," *Quarterly Review of Economics and Business,* XVI, Spring, 1976, pp. 77–92; also D. Eilenstine and J. P. Cunningham, "Projected Consumption Patterns for a Stationary Population," *Population Studies,* XXVI, July, 1972, pp. 228–30, on the response of particular categories of consumer expense to age and size changes. See also F. T. Denton and B. G. Spencer, "Household and Population Effects on Aggregate Consumption," *Review of Economics and Statistics* 58, Feb., 1976, pp. 86–95; and Robert W. Resek and Frederick Siegel, "Consumption Demand and Population Growth Rates," *Eastern Economic Journal,* I, Oct., 1974, pp. 282–90.

63. A. S. Blinder, "Distribution Effects and the Aggregate Consumption Function," *Journal of Political Economy,* LXXXIII, June, 1975, pp. 447–76, esp. p. 472. Average income moves down with age beyond the late fifties. See Michael K. Taussig, *Alternative Measures of the Distribution of Economic Welfare* (Princeton: Industrial Relations Section, Princeton University, 1973), p. 13 and chap. 5. See also Bixby et al., *Demographic and Economic Characteristics of the Aged.*

64. Joseph J. Spengler, *Declining Population Growth Revisited* (Chapel Hill: Carolina Population Center [Monograph 14], 1971), p. 12. The data are taken mainly from Francis L. Horst, "Patterns of Output Growth," *Survey of Current Business,* XLVI, Nov., 1966, pp. 18–25.

65. J. A. Howard and D. R. Lehman, "The Effect of Different Populations on Selected Industries in the Year 2000," in Commission on Population Growth and the American Future, Research Report II, *Economic Aspects of Population Change,* Washington, D.C., 1972, pp. 141–58, esp. 147–49. See also David Jones, "Projections of Housing Demand to the Year 2000, Using Two Population Projections," ibid., pp. 301–32; T. C. Marcin, "The Effect of Declining Population Growth on Housing Demand," *Challenge,* 19, Nov.–Dec., 1976, pp. 30–33.

66. See Spengler, *Declining Population Growth,* pp. 13–19. Cf. Meade, *Trade and Welfare,* II, p. 94, on "product glut" and "capital glut." On the impact of low elasticity of demand for agricultural products see William J. Serow, "The Implications of Zero Growth for Agricultural Commodity Demand," *American Journal of Agricultural Economics,* LIV, Dec., 1972, pp. 955–63, and "The Effects of Zero Population Growth on the Spatial Distribution of Economic Activity," ibid., pp. 964–71.

67. Hassan and Johnson, "Consumer Demand," pp. 84–85, also pp. 86–89 on somewhat comparable estimates. See also on the impact of nongrowth of population

Eilenstine and Cunningham, "Projected Consumption," p. 228; also F. T. Denton and Byron G. Spencer, "Health Care Costs When the Population Changes," *Canadian Journal of Economics,* VIII, Feb., 1975, pp. 34–48.

68. U.S. Bureau of the Census, "Households and Families by Type," *Current Population Report,* Series P-20, No. 296, Sept., 1976, p. 4; E. C. Bratt et al., "Construction in an Expanding Economy: 1960–2000," reprinted from *Construction Review,* Sept., 1961, p. 3. See also R. G. Ridker, "The Economy, Resource Requirements, and Pollution Levels," in Commission on Population Growth and the American Future, Research Report III, *Population, Resources, and The Environment* (Washington, D.C.: U.S. Government Printing Office, 1972), chap. 2, p. 41; and Jacob S. Siegel, "Development and Accuracy of Projections of Population Households in the United States," *Demography,* IX, Feb., 1972, pp. 51–68. On the economic role of the family see Eleanor B. Sheldon, ed., *Family Economic Behavior* (Philadelphia: J. B. Lippincott, 1973).

69. E.g., see Robert Ferber, "Research on Household Behavior," *American Economic Review,* LII, March, 1962, pp. 19–63; Larry H. Long and Celia G. Boertlein, "The Geographical Mobility of Americans: An International Comparison," *Current Population Reports: Special Studies Series,* Series P-23, No. 4 (Washington, D.C.: Bureau of the Census, 1976), pp. 7–30.

70. See W. H. Lough, *High-Level Consumption* (New York: McGraw-Hill, 1935), pp. 108, 166, 171–72, 179. Young persons, unlike old persons, can look forward to increasing income and accommodate their saving and spending to these income expectations. See Watts, "Long-run Income Expectations," pp. 109–10. They are less habit-ridden, more receptive to new "wants."

71. Katona, *Psychological Economics,* chap. 1, esp. pp. 22–23, 26–28, 29, also pp. 180–82, 186, 254–55, 396 on age and income expectations. See also A. H. Johnson, G. E. Jones, and D. B. Lucas, *The American Market of the Future* (New York: New York University, 1966).

72. Katona, *Psychological Economics,* pp. 290–393. In 1974 wives' earnings accounted for 26.5 percent of median family income: U.S. Bureau of the Census, "A Statistical Portrait of Women in the U.S.," *Current Population Reports,* Series P-23, No. 58, April, 1976, p. 52.

73. See G. Schmöelders and B. Biervert, "Level of Aspiration and Consumption Standard: Some General Findings," in B. Strumpel, J. N. Morgan, and E. Zahn, eds., *Human Behavior in Economic Affairs* (Washington: Jossey-Bass, Inc., 1972), pp. 213–28, esp. pp. 219–21.

74. D. M. Heien, "Demographic Effects and the Multiperiod Consumption Function," *Journal of Political Economy,* LXXX, Jan.–Feb., 1972, pp. 125–39, esp. 134–37; Sidney Goldstein, *Study of Consumer Expenditures, Incomes, and Savings* (Philadelphia: University of Pennsylvania, 1960), chap. 18. Median family income with head 65 years and over was 41 percent below the national average and 54 percent below that of families with head 45–54 years old. *Current Population Reports,* Series P-60, Consumer Income, No. 103, Sept., 1976, p. 19.

75. For discussions of the issue see Martin Bronfenbrenner, *Income Distribution Theory* (Chicago: Aldine, 1971), esp. chap. 16; C. E. Ferguson, *The Neoclassical Theory of Production and Distribution* (Cambridge: University Press, 1969). I have passed over the neo-Cambridge revolt because it does not deal directly with the orthodox labor-capital problem.

76. Denton and Spencer, "Household and Population Effects," pp. 86–95, esp. p. 93.

77. Eilenstine and Cunningham, "Projected Consumption," pp. 223–31, esp. p. 228.

78. Ibid., p. 227.

79. Ibid., pp. 227–28, 230–31.

80. See Torsten Hägerstrand, "Quantitative Techniques For Analysis of the Spread of Information and Technology," in C. A. Anderson and Mary Jean Bowman, eds., *Education and Economic Development* (Chicago: Aldine, 1965), chap. 12; D. S. Ironmonger, *New Commodities and Consumer Behaviour* (Cambridge:

University Press, 1972); A. Brown and A. Deaton, "Models of Consumer Behavior: A Survey," *Economic Journal,* LXXXII, Dec., 1972, pp. 1145–136, esp. 1226–27.

81. Cf. Brown and Deaton, "Models," pp. 1222–24. New products move through a life cycle, with price elasticity of demand initially high and sales volume increasing until little room for expansion remains and aggregate sales rise slowly in the absence of emerging substitutes. See L. T. Wells, ed., *The Product Life Cycle and International Trade* (Boston: Harvard Graduate School of Business Administration, 1972).

82. See W. B. Reddaway, *The Economics of a Declining Population* (London: Allen & Unwin, 1939) and "Special Obstacles to Full Employment in a Wealthy Economy," *Economic Journal,* XCVII, June, 1937, pp. 297–307. See also Lewis Schiffer, *Consumer Discretionary Behavior* (Amsterdam: North Holland Publishing Co., 1964); Staffan Burenstam Linder, *The Harried Leisure Class* (New York: Columbia, 1970).

83. A. S. Eichner and J. A. Kregel, "An Essay on Post-Keynesian Theory: A New Paradigm in Economics," *Journal of Economic Literature,* XIII, Dec., 1975, pp. 1293–1314, esp. pp. 1300–1301.

84. Ibid., p. 1301.

85. Cf. Brown and Deaton, "Models," p. 1227.

86. E.g., see Kelvin J. Lancaster, *Consumer Demand: A New Approach* (New York: Columbia University Press, 1971). Illustrative of frequent reports on new products is unsigned, "The Great Rush for New Products," *Time,* Oct. 24, 1969, pp. 92–93; also unsigned, "A Wave of New Products for Work, Play, Travel," *U.S. News & World Report,* LXXXI, Nov. 29, 1976, pp. 73–75.

87. Lancaster, *Consumer Demand.*

88. On the impact of changes in age composition on outdoor recreation see Charles J. Cicchetti, "Outdoor Recreation and Congestion," in R. G. Ridker, ed., *Population, Resources, and The Environment,* chap. 6, esp. pp. 163–67, 172.

89. H. S. Houthakker and L. D. Taylor, *Consumer Demand in the United States: Analysis and Projections* (Cambridge: Harvard University Press, 1970), pp. 304–5. See also Brown and Deaton, "Models," pp. 1223–24; Heien, "Demographic Effects," pp. 131–33.

90. "Demographic Change and Aggregate Consumption UK: 1950–1973," in Hamish Edwards, ed., *Population, Factor Movements and Economic Development* (Cardiff: University of Wales Press, 1976), p. 157.

91. "The Economic Consequences," p. 29.

X. Cessation of Population Growth: Further Implications

1. See Ryder, "Notes on Stationary Populations," *Population Index,* XII, Jan., 1975, pp. 22–23.

2. J. Tinbergen, "Statistical Evidence on the Accelerator Principle," *Economica,* V, May, 1938, pp. 164–76. Hicks suggests that differences in the life-span of different types of capital goods will swamp the impact of any one type of capital good. J. R. Hicks, *A Contribution to the Theory of the Trade Cycle* (Oxford: Oxford University Press, 1950), pp. 51–52.

3. E.g., see A. Eichner and J. Kregel, "An Essay on Post-Keynesian Theory," *Journal of Economic Literature,* XIII, Dec., 1975, pp. 1300–3; also Alan Sweezy and Aaron Owens, "The Impact of Employment Growth on Employment," *American Economic Review, Papers and Proceedings,* LXIV(2), May, 1974, pp. 44–50. On the inadequacy of the employment rate as a measure of welfare see Stewart Schwab and John J. Seater, "The Unemployment Rate: Time to Give it a Rest," *Business Review* of the Federal Reserve Bank of Philadelphia, May–June, 1977, pp. 11–18.

4. On these cycles see R. C. O. Matthews, *The Business Cycle;* N. J. Mass,

"Modeling Cycles in the National Economy," *Technology Review,* LXXIX, March–April, 1976, pp. 43–52; R. A. Easterlin, *Population, Labor Force, and Long Swings* (New York: Columbia University Press, 1968). The U.S. birth rate rose from 18.4 in 1936 to 25.1 in 1953–1957; the total fertility rate fell from 3.6 in 1960 to 1.76 in 1976. Lifetime births expected per wife 18–24 years old may or may not be realized, since such expectations change as conditions of life change. *Current Population Reports,* Series P-20, No. 308, June, 1977, pp. 1–7.

5. Neil A. Stevens, "Housing: A Cyclical Industry on the Upswing," *Review* of Federal Reserve Bank of St. Louis, LVIII, Aug., 1976, pp. 15–20. See also A. Thomas King, "The Demand for Housing: Integrating the Roles of Journey to Work, Neighborhood Quality, and Prices," together with comments by Gregory Ingram, in Nestor E. Terlickyj, ed., *Household Production and Consumption* (NBER) (New York: Columbia University Press, 1975), pp. 451–87. See also George Katona and Burkhard Strumpel, "Consumer Investment versus Business Investment," *Challenge,* XVIII, Jan.–Feb., 1976, pp. 12–16; T. C. Marcin, "The Effect of Declining Population on Housing Demand," *Challenge,* XIX, Nov.–Dec., 1976, pp. 30–33; David Jones, "Projections of Housing Demand to the Year 2000, Using Two Projections," Commission on Population Growth and the American Future, Research Report II, *Economic Aspects of Population Change,* Washington, D.C.: U.S. Government Printing Office, 1972.

6. Substitution is constrained by emphasis on "firm-specific" skills, the use of which may not be transferable. See Donald Davidson and B. C. Eaton, "Firm-Specific Human Capital: A Shared Investment or Optimal Entrapment," *Canadian Journal of Economics,* IX, Aug., 1976, pp. 462–72. Mobility is high in the American labor force; 32 percent of all persons working in 1970 had transferred from their occupations in 1965. See Dixie Sommers and Alan Eck, "Occupational Mobility in the American Labor Force," *Monthly Labor Review,* C, Jan., 1977, pp. 3–19. On residential and job mobility see L. H. Long, "New Estimates of Migration Expectancy in the United States," *Journal of American Statistical Association,* LXVIII, March, 1973, pp. 37–43 and bibliography.

7. C. R. S. Dougherty has found the elasticity of substitution between different kinds of labor to be "invariably high" and that between labor and capital to be positive. See "Substitution and the Structure of the Labor Force," *Economic Journal,* LXXXII, March, 1972, pp. 172–73. See also D. B. Humphrey and J. R. Moroney, "Substitution Among Capital, Labor, and Natural Resource Products in American Manufacturing," *Journal of Political Economy,* LXXXIII, Feb., 1975, pp. 57–82.

8. On frictional and structural unemployment, together with age and sex as factors in employment, see R. A. Gordon, "Some Macroeconomic Aspects of Manpower Policy," in Lloyd Ulman, ed., *Manpower Problems in the Policy Mix* (Baltimore: The Johns Hopkins Press, 1973), chap. 1. See also Eli Ginzberg, ed., *Jobs for Americans* (Englewood Cliffs, N.J.: Prentice-Hall, 1976).

9. In 1965, Nordhaus and Tobin estimate, nonmarket activity accounted for a volume of output worth nearly half as much as Gross National Product in that year. *Economic Growth* (New York: Columbia University Press, 1972), p. 55. Under the impact of rising prices, imports, income taxes, together with improvements in small-scale technology, this fraction will rise, thus intensifying withdrawal from the labor force in areas favorable to domestic activities.

10. Martin Feldstein, "The Economics of the New Unemployment," *The Public Interest,* No. 33, Fall, 1973, pp. 3–42, esp. p. 41. See also William Fellner, "Theoretical Foundations of the Failure of Demand-Management Policies: An Essay," *Journal of Economic Literature,* XIV, March, 1976, pp. 34–53, esp. 45–52.

11. Feldstein, "The Economics," pp. 12–15, 29–35. See also Elizabeth Durbin's account of AFDC families in New York City in Cynthia B. Lloyd, ed., *Sex Discrimination and the Division of Labor* (New York: Columbia University Press, 1975); N. Swan, P. McRae, and C. Steinberg, *Income Maintenance Programs: Their Effect on Labour Supply and Aggregate Demand in the Maritimes* (Ottawa: Eco-

nomic Council of Canada, 1976); Martin Feldstein, "Temporary Layoffs in the Theory of Unemployment," *Journal of Political Economy,* LXXXIV, Oct., 1976, pp. 937–58; M. D. Ornstein, *Entry into the American Labor Force* (New York: Academic Press, 1976); W. F. Barnes and Ethel B. Jones, "Woman's Increasing Unemployment: A Cyclical Interpretation," *Quarterly Review of Economics and Business,* XV, Summer, 1975, pp. 61–70; Samuel A. Rea, Jr., "Unemployment Insurance and Labour Supply; A Simulation of the 1971 Unemployment Insurance Act," *Canadian Journal of Economics,* X, May, 1977, pp. 263–78, esp. 278.

12. Feldstein, "The Economics," pp. 14–21; Dean A. Worcester, *Beyond Welfare and Full Employment: The Economics of Optimal Employment without Inflation* (Lexington, Mass.: D. C. Heath, 1972); Jacob Mincer, "Unemployment Effects of Minimum Wages," *Journal of Political Economy,* LXXXIV, No. 4, Part 2, Aug., 1976, pp. S87–S104, esp. S87, S100, and S103; also on factors affecting employment of women, Lloyd, *Sex Discrimination;* Hilda Kahne and A. I. Kohen, "Economic Perspectives on the Roles of Women in the American Economy," *Journal of Economic Literature,* XIII, Dec., 1975, pp. 1249–92. Excessive reservation wages also prevent employment. See S. P. Stephenson, Jr., "The Economics of Youth Job Search Behavior," *Review of Economics and Statistics,* LVIII, Feb., 1976, pp. 104–11. Inflation, often resorted to as a means to reduce unemployment whatever its initial cause, may in turn give rise to unemployment. See Milton Friedman, "Nobel Lecture: Inflation and Unemployment," *Journal of Political Economy,* LXXXV, June, 1974, pp. 451–72.

13. E.g., see P. G. Cotteritt and W. J. Wadycki, "Teenagers and the Minimum Wage in Retail Trade," *Journal of Human Resources,* XI, Winter, 1976, pp. 69–85.

14. H. H. Winsborough, "Age Period, Cohort, and Education Effects on Earnings by Race," in K. C. Land and Seymour Spilerman, eds., *Social Indicator Models* (New York: Russell Sage Foundation, 1975), pp. 209–10.

15. See Juanita M. Kreps and J. J. Spengler, "Equity and Social Credit for the Retired," in Kreps, ed., *Employment, Income, and Retirement Problems of the Aged* (Durham: Duke University Press, 1963), pp. 198–229. Underlying interindustry differences in the ratio of the earnings structures of particular industries to their per worker productivity structure is the fact that late-comer industries always have to pay more to attract workers from established industries. See Mark A. Lutz, "The Evolution of the Industrial Earnings Structure: The 'Geological Theory,' " *Canadian Journal of Economics,* IX, Aug., 1976, pp. 473–91. See also W. J. Baumol, "Macroeconomics of Unbalanced Growth: The Anatomy of Urban Crisis," *American Economic Review,* LXVII, June, 1967, pp. 415–26.

16. E.g., see A. Deutsch, "Inflation and Guaranteed Pension Plans," *Canadian Journal of Economics,* VIII, Aug., 1975, pp. 447–48; James E. Pesando, "Inflation and Guaranteed Formula Pension Plans," ibid., IX, Aug., 1976, pp. 529–31.

17. Cf. J. O. Blackburn, "The Social Insurance Paradox: A Comment," *Canadian Journal of Economics and Political Science,* XXXIII, Aug., 1967, pp. 445–46.

18. E.g., see Juanita Kreps, *Lifetime Allocation of Work and Income* (Durham: Duke University Press, 1971), esp. Part III.

19. See Martin Feldstein, "Social Security, Induced Retirement, and Aggregate Capital Accumulation," *Journal of Political Economy,* LXXXII, Sept.–Oct., 1974, pp. 905–26; Alicia H. Munnell, "Private Pensions and Saving: New Evidence," ibid., LXXXIV, Oct., 1976, pp. 1013–32, and *The Effect of Social Security on Personal Savings* (Cambridge, Mass.: Ballinger, 1974), and *The Future of Social Security* (Washington, D.C.: Brookings Institution, 1976).

20. On wealth data see John W. Kendrick, "Measuring America's Wealth," *Morgan Guaranty Survey,* May, 1976, pp. 507–13, esp. pp. 6, 9.

21. Ibid., p. 13.

22. If fertility remains at the replacement level, 2.1, the above fraction over 45 will not exceed 0.5 until in the second decade of the next century. But should fertility soon settle around 1.7, this fraction will exceed one-half in the first decade of the next century. Estimates based on U.S. Bureau of the Census, *Current Popu-*

lation Reports, Series P-25, No. 601, Washington, D.C., 1975. See also ibid., Series P-20, No. 308, 1977.

23. On local depopulation see C. L. Beale, "Natural Decrease of Population: The Current and Prospective Status of an Emergent American Phenomenon," *Demography,* VI, May, 1969, pp. 91–100; H. C. Chang, "Natural Population Decrease in Iowa Counties," ibid., XI, Nov., 1974, pp. 657–72; W. C. Baer, "On The Death of Cities," *Public Interest,* No. 45, Fall, 1976, pp. 3–19.

24. Cf. Oswald St. Clair, *A Key to Ricardo* (London: Routledge & Kegan Paul, 1957), chap. 1. In the eighteenth century, however, the barrier to the growth of many population and industrial centers was not food but fuel, since wood had been exhausted and coal could not be made generally available before canals were developed. See Phyllis Deane, *The First Industrial Revolution* (Cambridge: University Press, 1965), pp. 75–76.

25. E.g., England, already in 1800 a net importer of corn "except in years of abundant harvest," by 1840 "was feeding between 10 and 15 per cent of its population on foreign wheat." Deane, *The First Industrial Revolution,* p. 189.

26. A. O. Hirschman, *National Power and the Structure of International Trade* (Berkeley: University of California Press, 1945). For example, in his *Agrar-und Industriestaat* (Jena: Fischer, 1902), Adolf Wagner warned (as had T. R. Malthus over eight decades earlier) against the consequences of continuing population growth and the ascendancy of manufacturing over agriculture to a degree making Germany dependent on foreign sources for a significant fraction of its foodstuffs and critical materials and hence subject to foreign powers (e.g., the United States, "that country and people, of the crassest national economic egotism, . . . capable of anything") in times of peace as well as war. Lujo Brentano, in *Die Schrecken des überwiegenden Industriestaats* (Berlin, 1901) expressed greater optimism, pointing to increasing return in manufacturing, the supposedly many sources of food supply (rye having been imported since 1852), the belief that a European war could not last more than a year, and the military and fiscal dependence of a state upon manufacture. See F. W. Taussig, *Selected Readings in International Trade and Tariff Problems* (Boston: Ginn and Co., 1921), pp. 343–70, 392–416; also Gottfried von Haberler, *The Theory of International Trade with Its Application to Commercial Policy,* trans. A. Stonier and F. Benham (New York: Macmillan, 1936), pp. 243, 285–90.

27. E.g., see W. M. Corden, "The Economic Limits to Population Increase," *Economic Record,* XXXI, 1955, pp. 242–60.

28. On the exploitative aspects of cartellization of these resources and elements see Sanford Rose, "Third World 'Commodity Power' is a Costly Illusion," *Fortune,* XCIV, Nov., 1976, pp. 147–54, 158–60.

29. United Nations, *The Determinants and Consequences of Population Trends,* I, 1973, p. 564. Net reproduction is near or below the replacement level in much of the developed world. See *Population Index,* XLII, April, 1976, pp. 360–72; also Simon Kuznets, "Fertility Differentials Between Less Developed and Developed Regions: Components and Implications," *American Philosophical Society,* CXIX, Oct. 15, 1975, pp. 363–96. It remains possible, however, that fertility will decline enough in some countries to bring the rate of growth in the underdeveloped world below the levels reported in the text above. Gary Littman and Nathan Keyfitz estimate the world's population in 2075 at 8.44 billion of which 6.94 billion, or 82.2 percent, will live in undeveloped countries. *The Next Hundred Years,* Working Paper Number 101, Harvard University Center of Population Studies (Cambridge, Mass., 1977), pp. 11–14.

30. The real annual rate of growth of GNP in these countries approximated 6.5 percent in 1961–1974. World Bank, *Annual Report* (Washington, D.C.: 1976), p. 96. Nathan Keyfitz puts the rate at around 5 percent. "World Resources and the World Middle Class," *Scientific American,* CCXXXV, July, 1976, pp. 28–35, esp. 29–30.

31. David Pimental et al., "Land Degradation: Effects on Food and Energy Resources," *Science,* CXCIV, Oct. 8, 1976, pp. 149–55.

32. E.g., see Raymond Vernon, *The Economic and Political Consequences of Multinational Enterprise: An Anthology* (Boston: Harvard Graduate School of Business Administration, 1972), pp. 43–84. On the product life cycle of products of which the U.S. is the original producer and exporter see L. T. Wells, Jr., "International Trade: The Product Life Cycle Approach," in Wells, ed., *The Product Life Cycle and International Trade* (Boston: Harvard Graduate School of Business Administration, 1972), pp. 3–33, esp. 5–19. See also William V. Rapp, "The Many Possible Extensions of Product Cycle Analysis," *Hitotsubashi Journal of Economics,* XVI, June, 1975, pp. 22–29.

33. Vernon, *Economic and Political Consequences,* pp. 55–56; also W. H. Gruber, Dileep Mehta, and Raymond Vernon, "The R & D Factor in International Trade and International Investment of United States Industries," in L. T. Wells, Jr., ed., *The Product Life Cycle and International Trade,* pp. 111–39.

34. Vernon, *Economic and Political Consequences,* pp. 57–62. See J. B. Wiesner, "Has the U.S. Lost its Initiative in Technological Innovation?" *Technology Review,* LXXVIII, July–Aug., 1976, pp. 54–60.

35. Vernon, *Economic and Political Consequences,* pp. 86–123, 205–36; also Vernon, *Sovereignty at Bay: The Multinational Spread of U.S. Enterprises* (New York: Basic Books, 1971).

36. U.S. Bureau of the Census, *Current Population Reports,* Series P-25, No. 601, "Projections of the Population of the United States: 1975 to 2050," October, 1975, Tables 8–11, F-2; also ibid., Special Studies, Series P-23, No. 59, May, 1976, Table 6–10, p. 56.

37. E.g., see Munnell, *The Future,* chap. 4; U.S. Bureau of the Census, *Current Population Reports,* Series P-23, No. 57, "Social and Economic Characteristics of the Older Population 1974," pp. 31–35; Lenore E. Bixby et al., *Demographic and Economic Characteristics of the Aged,* DHEW Research Report No. 45, Publication No. (SSA) 75–11802, Washington, D.C., 1975, chap. 2.

38. Paul A. Samuelson, "The Optimum Growth Rate for Population," *International Economic Review,* XVI, Oct., 1975, pp. 531–38, and "The Optimum Growth Rate for Population: Agreement and Evaluation," ibid., XVII, June, 1976, pp. 516–25; also Alan V. Deardorff, "The Optimum Growth Rate for Population: Comment," ibid., pp. 510–15.

39. In proportion as economic power is concentrated, entry into entrepreneurial roles may be restricted even though numerous niches in the economy remain unexploited—perhaps because large-scale enterprise is uninterested in the limited profitability of small-niche exploitation. In a stationary economy "with room at the top limited" there may be relatively greater interest in exploring small-profit opportunities.

40. R. Hieser, "The Economic Consequences of Zero Population Growth," *Economic Record,* XLIX, June, 1973, pp. 259–60.

41. W. B. Reddaway, "The Economic Consequences of Zero Population," *Lloyd's Bank Review,* No. 124, April, 1977, pp. 14–30, esp. p. 29.

Epilogue

1. U.S. Bureau of the Census, *Current Population Reports,* Series P-25, No. 704, "Projections of the Population of the United States: 1977 to 2050," July, 1977, pp. 1–19.

2. U.S. Bureau of the Census, *Current Population Reports,* Series P-20, No. 308, "Fertility of American Women: June, 1976," Washington, 1977, pp. 1–3.

3. See their letter on "The U.S. Birthrate" in *Science,* CXCVII, July 8, 1977, pp. 108–10.

4. Michael L. Wachter, "A Time-Series Fertility Equation: The Potential for a Baby-Boom in the 1980's," *International Economic Review,* XV, Oct., 1975, pp. 609–23. See also Samuelson, "An Economist's Non-Linear Model of Self-Generated

Waves," *Population Studies* XXX, July, 1976; pp. 243–48; Marcel Fulop's critique, "A Survey of the Literature on the Economic Theory of Fertility Behavior," *The American Economist,* XXI, Spring, 1977, pp. 3–13.

5. J. C. Weldon, "On the Theory of Intergenerational Transfers," *Canadian Journal of Economics,* IX, Nov., 1976, pp. 559–79.

6. Harry G. Johnson, "Keynes's General Theory: Revolution or War of Independence," *Canadian Journal of Economics,* IX, Nov., 1976, pp. 580–94, esp. p. 593.

Bibliography

Aaron, Henry. "The Social Insurance Paradox." *Canadian Journal of Economics and Political Science* 32 (1966): 371–74.

Abrams, Elliott, and Adams, F. S. "Immigration Policy—Who Gets In and Why?" *The Public Interest* 38 (1975): 3–29.

Adams, Henry. *The Education of Henry Adams.* New York: Modern Library, 1931.

Adie, Douglas K. "Teen-Age Unemployment and Real Federal Minimum Wages." *Journal of Political Economy* 81 (1973): 435–41.

Adler, H. A. "Absolute or Relative Decline in Population Growth." *Quarterly Journal of Economics* 59 (1945): 626–34.

Advisory Council on Social Security. *Report to the Secretary of Health, Education and Welfare.* March 6, 1975, Washington, D.C., pp. 119–22.

Akerlof, G. A., and Stiglitz, J. E. "Capital, Wages and Structural Unemployment." *Economic Journal* 79 (1969): 269–81.

Almon, Clopper, et al. *1985: Interindustry Forecasts of the American Economy.* Lexington, Mass.: D. C. Heath, 1974.

American Economic Association. *Readings in Business Cycle Theory.* Philadelphia: Blakiston Company, 1944.

Anderson, C. A., and Bowman, Mary Jean, eds. *Education and Economic Development.* Chicago: Aldine, 1965.

Arrow, K. J. "Limited Knowledge and Economic Analysis." *American Economic Review* 64 (1974): 1–10.

Ascadi, Gy., and Nemeekeri, J., *History of Human Life Span and Mortality.* Budapest: Akademiai Kiado, 1970.

Atchley, R. C. *The Sociology of Retirement.* New York: Halsted, 1975.

Attah, Ernest B. "Racial Aspects of Zero Population Growth." *Science* 180 (1973): 1143–51.

Baer, W. C. "On the Death of Cities." *The Public Interest,* no. 45, (1976): 3–19.

Bain, J. *Barriers to New Competition.* Cambridge, Mass.: Harvard University Press, 1956.

Bancroft, Gertrude. *The American Labor Force.* New York: Wiley, 1958.

Barber, Clarence L. "Population Growth and the Demand for Capital." *American Economic Review* 43 (1953): 133–39.

Barnes, W. F., and Jones, Ethel B. "Woman's Increasing Unemployment: A Cyclical Interpretation." *Quarterly Review of Economics and Business* 15 (1975): 61–70.

Barnett, Harold, and Morse, Chandler. *Scarcity and Growth.* Baltimore: Johns Hopkins Press, 1963.

Barron, J. M. "Search in the Labor Market and the Duration of Unemployment: Some Empirical Evidence." *American Economic Review* 65 (1975): 934–42.

Barth, P. S. "Unemployment and Labor Force Participation." *Southern Economic Journal* 34 (1968): 375–82.

Bassie, V. L. "The Positive Relationship Between Unemployment and Price Changes." *Quarterly Review of Economics and Business* 15 (1975): 7–16.

Baumol, W. J. "Macroeconomics of Unbalanced Growth: The Anatomy of Urban Crisis." *American Economic Review* 77 (1967): 415–26.

Beale, C. L. "Natural Decrease of Population: The Current and Prospective Status of an Emergent American Phenomenon." *Demography* 6 (1969): 91–100.

Becker, Gary. "A Theory of the Allocation of Time." *The Economic Journal* 75 (1965): 493–517.

————, and Lewis, H. Gregg. "On the Interaction between the Quantity and the Quality of Children." *Journal of Political Economy* 81 (1973): S279–S288.

Beckerman, W. "The Determinants of Economic Growth." *Economic Growth in Britain.* Edited by P. D. Henderson. London: Weidenfeld and Nicholson, 1966.

Beckman, M. J. "The Limits to Growth in a Neoclassical World." *American Economic Review* 65 (1975): 695–99.

Bednarzik, R. D. "Involuntary Part-time Work: A Cyclical Analysis." *Monthly Labor Review* 98 (1975): 12–18.

Bell, Carolyn Shaw. "Age, Sex, Marriage, and Jobs." *The Public Interest* 31 (1973): 76–77.

————. "Lets Get Rid of Families," *Newsweek,* LXXXIX, May 9, 1977, p. 19.

Ben-Porath, Yoram. "First Generation Effects on Second Generation Fertility." *Demography* 12 (1975): 397–406.

Bennett, M. K. *The World's Food.* New York: Harper, 1954.

Berelson, Bernard. "Beyond Family Planning." *Science* 163 (1969): 533–43.

Bernard, Jessie. *The Future of Motherhood.* New York: Deal, 1974.

Beveridge, Sir William. "The Fall of Fertility Among European Races." *Economica* 5 (1925): 10–27.

————. "Mr. Keynes' Evidence for Over-Population." *Economica* 4 (1924): 1–20.

————. "Population and Unemployment." *Economic Journal* 23 (1923): 447–75.

Bixby, Lenore E. *Demographic and Economic Characteristics of the Aged.* DHEW Research Report No. 45, Publication No. (SSA) 75–11802, Washington, D.C., 1975.

Björk, L. E. "An Experiment in Work Satisfaction." *Scientific American* 232 (1975): 17–23.

Blackburn, J. O. "The Social Insurance Paradox: A Comment." *Canadian Journal of Economics and Political Science* 33 (1967): 445–46.

Blake, Judith. "Can We Believe Recent Data on Birth Expectations in the United States?" *Demography* 11 (1974): 25–44.

Blandy, R. "The Welfare Analysis of Fertility Reduction." *Economic Journal* 84 (1974): 109–29.

Bleakney, Thomas P. "Problems and Issues in Public Employee Retirement Systems." *Journal of Risk and Insurance* 40 (1973): 39–46.

Blinder, A. S. "Distribution Effects and the Aggregate Consumption Function." *Journal of Political Economy* 83 (1975): 447–76.

Bliss, C. J. "Prices, Markets and Planning." *Economic Journal* 82 (1972): 97–99.

Block, Maurice. *Statistique de la France comparée avec divers pays d l'Europe.* Paris: Guillaumin et cie, 1875.

Boak, A. E. R. *Manpower Shortage and the Fall of the Roman Empire in the West.* Ann Arbor: University of Michigan Press, 1955.

Bosanquet, N., and Boerringer, P. B. "Is There a Dual Labour Market in Great Britain?" *Economic Journal* 83 (1973): 421–34.

Boserup, Ester. *The Conditions of Agricultural Growth.* Chicago: Aldine, 1965.

Boskin, Michael J. "Social Security and Retirement Decisions." *Economic Inquiry* 15 (1977): 1–25.

Boudon, Raymond. *Education, Opportunity, and Social Inequality.* New York: Wiley, 1974.

Boulding, K. E. "Toward A General Theory of Growth." *Canadian Journal of Economics and Political Science* 13 (1953): 326–40.

Bowen, W. G., and Finegan, T. A. *The Economics of Labor Force Participation.* Princeton: Princeton University Press, 1969.

Brass, W., et al. *The Demography of Tropical Africa.* Princeton: Princeton University Press, 1968.

Bratt, E. C., et al. "Construction in an Expanding Economy: 1960–2000." Reprint from *Construction Review,* September 1961, pp. 151–67.

Brennan, M. J.; Taft, P.; and Schupack, M. B. *The Economics of Age.* New York: Norton, 1967.

Brentano, Lujo. *Die Schrecken des überwiegenden Industriestaats.* Berlin: 1901.

Bridbury, A. R. "The Black Death." *Economic History Review* 26 (1973): 557–92.

Briggs, V. M. "Illegal Aliens: The Need for a More Restrictive Border Policy." *Social Science Quarterly* 56 (1975): 477–84.

Brinkman, George L. "The Effects of Zero Population Growth on the Spatial Distribution of Economic Activity." *American Journal of Agricultural Economics* 54 (1972): 964–71.

Britto, Ronald. "Some Recent Developments in the Theory of Economic Growth: An Interpretation." *Journal of Economic Literature* 11 (1973): 1343–66.

———. "Steady-State Paths in an Economy with Endogenous Population Growth." *Western Economic Journal* 8 (1970): 390–96.

Brockie, Melvin D. "Population Growth and the Rate of Investment." *Southern Economic Journal* 17 (1950): 1–15.

Bronfenbrenner, Martin. *Income Distribution Theory.* Chicago: Aldine, 1971.

———. "Predatory Poverty on the Offensive, The UNCTAD Record." *Economic Development and Cultural Change* 24 (1976): 825–32.

Brown, A., and Deaton, A. "Models of Consumer Behavior: A Survey." *Economic Journal* 82 (1972): 1145–1236.

Brown, E. H. Phelps, and Brown, Margaret H. *A Century of Pay*. New York: St. Martin's Press, 1968.

————, and Jones, S. J. Handfield. "The Climacteric of the 1890's; A Study in the Expanding Economy." *Oxford Economic Papers* 4 (1952): 266–307.

Brown, Harrison, and Hutchings, Edward, Jr. *Are Our Descendants Doomed?* New York: Viking, 1972.

Brown, Lester. *Increasing World Food Output*. Washington, D.C.: U.S.D.A., 1965.

Browning, Edgar K. "Social Insurance and Intergenerational Transfers." *Journal of Law and Economics* 16 (1973): 215–37.

Browning, Harvey. "Speculation and Labor Mobility in a Stationary Population." *Zero Population Growth: Implications*. Edited by Joseph J. Spengler. Chapel Hill, N.C.: Carolina Population Center, 1975.

Brubaker, Sterling. *To Live on Earth*. Baltimore: Johns Hopkins Press, 1972.

Burgdörfer, F. *Volk ohne Jugend*. Berlin: 1932, 1933, 1935.

Burgers, J. M. "Causality and Anticipation." *Science* 189 (1975): 194–98.

Bush, W. C. "Population and Mill's Peasant-Proprietor Economy." *History of Political Economy* 5 (1973): 110–20.

Byrne, James J. "Occupational Mobility of Workers." *Monthly Labor Review* 98 (1975): 53–59.

Cain, Glen G. "The Challenge of Segmented Labor Market Theories to Orthodox Theory." *Journal of Economic Literature* 14 (1976): 1215–55.

————, and Weininger, Adriana. "Economic Determinants of Fertility: Results from Cross-Sectional Aggregate Data." *Demography* 10 (1973): 205–24.

Cairncross, A. K. *Home and Foreign Investment, 1870–1913*. Cambridge: University Press, 1953.

Cairnes, John. "The Cancer Problem." *The Scientific American* 333 (1975): 64–78.

Calot, Gérard, ed. "La population de la France," constituting the entire June, 1974, number of *Population* 29 (1974).

Cannan, Edwin. *Economic Scares*. London: P. S. King and Son, 1933.

————. *A Review of Economic Theory*. London: P. S. King, 1929.

The Cambridge Economic History of Europe. Vols. I–IV. Cambridge: University Press, 1941.

Carr-Saunders, A. M. *The Population Problem*. Oxford: Clarendon Press, 1922.

Castelot, Elvi. "Stationary Population in France." *Economic Journal* 14 (1904): 249–53.

Cépède, Michel. "Exportation de 'terre' et exportation de travail." *Economie Appliqueé* 22 (1969): 277–94.

Chambers, J. D. *Population, Economy, and Society in Pre-Industrial England*. London: Oxford University Press, 1972.

————, and Mingay, G. E. *The Agricultural Revolution 1750–1880*. London: Botsford, 1966.

Champernowne, D. G. "Expectations and the Links Between the Economic Future and the Present." In Robert Lekachman, *Keynes' General Theory, Reports of Three Decades.* New York: St. Martin's Press, 1964.

Chance, W. A. "Long-Term Labor Requirements and Output of the Educational System." *Southern Economic Journal* 32 (1966): 417–28.

Chang, H. C. "Natural Population Decrease in Iowa Counties." *Demography* 11 (1974): 657–72.

Chapin, Gene. "Unemployment Insurance, Job Search, and the Demand for Leisure." *Western Economic Journal* 9 (1973): 102–7.

Chapman, Guy. *Culture and Survival.* London: Jonathan Cape, 1940.

Charles, Enid. "The Effect of Present Trends in Fertility and Mortality Upon the Future Population of Great Britain and Upon Its Age Composition." *Political Arithmetic.* Edited by L. T. Hogben. London: Allen & Unwin, 1938.

————. *The Twilight of Parenthood.* New York: W. W. Norton and Co., 1934.

Chase, Richard X. "Keynes and U.S. Keynesianism: A Lack of Historical Perspective and the Decline of the New Economics." *Journal of Economic Issues* 9 (1975): 441–70.

Chen, Yung-Ping, and Chu, Kwang-Win. "Tax-Benefit Ratios and Rates of Return Under OASI: 1974, Retirees and Entrants." *Journal of Risk and Insurance* 41 (1974): 189–206.

Chenery, H. B. "Patterns of Industrial Growth." *American Economic Review* 50 (1960): 624–54.

————, and Taylor, L. "Development Patterns: Among Countries and Over Time." *Review of Economics and Statistics* 50 (1968): 391–416.

Christensen, L. R., and Jorgenson, D. W. "U.S. Income, Saving, and Wealth, 1929–1969." *Review of Income and Wealth* 19, no. 4 (1973): 329–62.

Cicchetti, Charles J. "Outdoor Recreation and Congestion." *Population, Resources, and the Environment.* Edited by R. G. Ridker. Commission on Population Growth and the American Future, Research Report III. Washington, D.C.: U.S. Government Printing Office, 1972.

Clague, Ewan, et al. *The Aging Worker and the Union.* New York: Praeger, 1971.

Clark, Colin. *The Conditions of Economic Progress.* London: Macmillan, 1951, 1957.

————. *Population Growth and Land Use.* New York: St. Martin's Press, 1967.

————, and Haswell, M. *The Economics of Subsistence Agriculture.* London: Macmillan, 1964, 1967.

Clark, J. B. *The Distribution of Wealth.* New York: Macmillan, 1899.

Clark, J. M. *Economics of Planning Public Works.* Washington, D.C.: National Planning Board, 1935.

————. *Strategic Factors in Business Cycles.* New York: National Bureau of Economic Research, 1934.

Clemente, Frank, and Hendricks, Jon. "A Further Look at the Relationship Between Age and Productivity." *The Gerontologist* 13 (1973): 106–10.

Coale, A. J. "Age Composition in the Absence of Mortality and Other Odd Circumstances." *Demography* 10 (1973): 537–42.

———, ed. *Demographic and Economic Change in Developed Countries.* Princeton: Princeton University Press, 1960.

———, ed. *Economic Factors in Population Growth.* New York: John Wiley & Sons, 1976.

———. *The Growth and Structure of Human Populations.* Princeton: Princeton University Press, 1972.

———. "The History of the Human Population." *Scientific American* 231 (1974): 40–51.

———. "Increases in Expectation of Life and Population Growth." International Union for the Scientific Study of Population, International Population Conference. Vienna: 1959.

———, and Demeny, Paul. *Regional Model Life Tables and Stable Populations.* Princeton: Princeton University Press, 1966.

———, and Hoover, E. M. *Population Growth and Economic Development in Low-Income Countries.* Princeton: Princeton University Press, 1958.

Cole, H. S. D., ed. *Thinking About the Future: A Critique of the Limits to Growth.* London: Chattux and Windus, 1974.

Cole, Robert E. "Optimal Population and Increasing Returns to Scale." *Demography* 9 (1972): 241–48.

Coleman, James S. *Youth: Transition to Adulthood.* Chicago: University of Chicago Press, 1974.

Conecion, E., ed. *The Mineral Position of the United States, 1975–2000.* Madison: University of Wisconsin Press, 1972.

Conley, R. W. *The Economics of Vocational Rehabilitation.* Baltimore: Johns Hopkins Press, 1965.

Corden, W. M. "The Economic Limits to Population Increase." *Economic Record* 31 (1955): 242–60.

Cornwall, J. "Diffusion, Convergence, and Kaldor's Laws." *Economic Journal* 86 (1976): 307–14.

———. *Growth and Stability in a Mature Economy.* New York: John Wiley & Sons, 1972.

Cotteritt, P. G., and Wadycki, W. J. "Teenagers and the Minimum Wage in Retail Trade." *Journal of Human Resources* 11 (1976): 69–85.

Council of Economic Advisers. *Annual Report.* Washington, D.C.: 1973, 1974.

Cox, Harold. *The Problem of Population.* New York: G. P. Putnam's Sons, 1923.

Culbertson, J. M. *Macroeconomic Theory and Stabilization Policy.* New York: McGraw-Hill, 1968.

Dalton, Hugh. "The Theory of Population." *Economica* 8 (1928): 28–50.

Daly, Herman E., ed. *Toward a Steady State Economy.* San Francisco: W. H. Freeman and Co., 1973.

Daugherty, C. and Selowski, Marcelo. "Measuring the Effects of Misallocation of Labor." *Review of Economics and Statistics* 55 (1972): 38–46.

Davidson, Donald, and Eaton, B. C. "Firm-Specific Human Capital: A Shared

Investment or Optimal Entrapment." *Canadian Journal of Economics* 9 (1976): 462–72.

Davis, Joseph M. "Impact of Health on Earnings and Labor Market Activity." *Monthly Labor Review* 95 (1972): 46–49.

Davis, Joseph S. *The Population Upsurge in the United States.* War-Peace Pamphlet No. 12. Stanford: Food Research Institute, 1949.

———. "The Specter of Dearth of Food: History's Answer to Sir William Crookes." *Facts and Factors in Economic History; Articles by Former Students of Edwin Francis Gay.* Cambridge, Mass.: Harvard University Press, 1932.

Davis, Kingsley, and Blake, Judith. "Social Structure and Fertility: An Analytic Framework." *Economic Development and Cultural Change* 4 (1956): 211–45.

Deane, Phyllis. *The First Industrial Revolution.* Cambridge: University Press, 1965.

———, and Cole, W. A. *British Economic Growth, 1688–1959.* Cambridge: University Press, 1962.

de Beauvior, Simone. *The Coming of Age.* Translated by Patrick O'Brien. New York: Putnam, 1972.

Deevey, E. S., Jr. "The Human Population." *Scientific American* 203 (1960): 195–205.

Demery, Lionel, and Demery, David. "Demographic Change and Aggregate Consumption UK: 1950–1973." *Population, Factor Movements and Economic Development.* Edited by Hamish Edwards. Cardiff: University of Wales Press, 1976.

Deneffe, P. J. *Die Berechnungen über die künftige deutsche Bevolkerungsentwicklung.* Leipzig: Hans Buske, 1938.

Denison, E. F. *Accounting for United States Economic Growth.* Washington, D.C.: Brookings Institution, 1974.

———. "Classification of Sources of Growth." *Review of Income and Wealth* 18 (1972): 1–25.

———. "The Shift to Services and the Rate of Productivity Change." *Survey of Current Business,* October 1972, pp. 20–35.

———. "Some Major Issues in Productivity Analysis: An Examination of Estimates by Jorgenson and Griliches." *Survey of Current Business* 69 (Part II, 1969): 1–27.

———. *The Sources of Economic Growth in The United States and the Alternatives Before Us.* New York: Committee for Economic Development, Supplementary Paper No. 13, 1962, pp. 204–206.

———. *Why Growth Rates Differ.* Washington, D.C.: Brookings Institution, 1967.

———, and Chung, W. K. *How Japan's Economy Grew So Fast.* Washington, D.C.: Brookings Institution, 1976.

Denton, F. T., and Spencer, B. G. "Health-Care Costs When the Population Changes." *Canadian Journal of Economics* 8 (1975): 34–48.

———. "Household and Population Effects on Aggregate Consumption." *Review of Economics and Statistics* 58 (1976): 86–95

Denton, F. T., and Spencer, B. G. "A Simulation Analysis of the Effects of Population Change on a Neoclassical Economy." *Journal of Political Economy* 81 (1973): 356–76.

———. "Some Demographic Consequences of Changing Cohort Fertility Patterns: An Investigation Using the Gompertz Function." *Population Studies* 28 (1974): 209–18.

Dernburg, T. F.; Rosett, R. N.; and Watts, H. W. *Studies in Household Economic Behavior*. New Haven: Yale University Press, 1958.

de Tray, D. N. "Child Quality and the Demand for Children." *Journal of Political Economy* 81 (Part 2, 1973): 70–95.

Deutsch, A. "Inflation and Guaranteed Pension Plans." *Canadian Journal of Economics* 8 (1975): 447–48.

Dewhurst, J. F. *America's Needs and Resources*. New York: Twentieth Century Fund, 1955.

Dillard, Dudley. *The Economics of John Maynard Keynes*. New York: Prentice-Hall, 1948.

Dirken, J. M. *Functional Age of Industrial Workers*. Groningen: Wolters-Noordhoff, 1972.

Domar, Evsey. "Expansion and Employment." *American Economic Review* 37 (1947): 34–55.

———. "Investment, Losses, and Monopolies." In B. Higgins and others, *Income, Employment and Public Policy, Essays in Honor of Alvin H. Hansen*. New York: W. W. Norton, 1948.

Dorfman, R.; Samuelson, P. A.; and Solow, R. M. *Linear Programming and Economic Analysis*. New York: McGraw-Hill, 1958.

Dougherty, C. R. S. "Substitution and the Structure of the Labor Force." *Economic Journal* 82 (1972): 170–82.

Douglas, Paul. "Elasticity of Supply as a Determinant of Distribution." *Economic Essays Contributed in Honor of John Bates Clark*. Edited by J. H. Hollander. New York: Macmillan, 1927.

———. *The Theory of Wages*. New York: Macmillan, 1934.

Dresch, Stephen P. "Demography, Technology, and Higher Education: Toward a Formal Model of Educational Adaptation." *Journal of Political Economy* 83 (1975): 535–70.

Dublin, L. I., ed. *Population Problems in The United States and Canada*. Boston: Houghton Mifflin, 1926.

———, and Lotka, A. J. "On the True Rate of Natural Increase." *Journal of the American Statistical Association* 20 (1925): 205–39.

———; Lotka, A. J.; and Spiegelman, M. *The Length of Life*. New York: Ronald Press, 1949.

Duesenberry, James. *Business Cycles and Economic Growth*. New York: McGraw-Hill, 1958.

Durand, John D. *The Labor Force in Economic Development*. Princeton: Princeton University Press, 1976.

———. *The Labor Force in The United States 1890–1960*. New York: Social Science Research Council, 1948.

―――. "The Modern Expansion of World Population." *Proceedings of the American Philosophical Society* 111 (1967): 136–59.

―――. "Population Statistics of China, A.D. 2–1953." *Population Studies* 13 (1960): 209–56.

Earle, E. M., ed. *Makers of Modern Strategy*. Princeton: Princeton University Press, 1943.

East, E. M. *Mankind at the Crossroads*. New York: C. Scribner's Sons, 1926.

Easterlin, Richard. *Population, Labor Force and Long Swings in Economic Growth*. New York: Columbia University Press, 1968.

Eck, Alan. "Occupational Mobility in the American Labor Force." *Monthly Labor Review* 100 (1977): 3–19.

Edgeworth, F. Y. *Papers Relating to Political Economy*. London: Macmillan, 1925.

―――. "Some German Writings About the War." *Papers Relating to Political Economy* 3. London: Macmillan, 1925.

―――. "The Stationary State in Japan." *Economic Journal* 5 (1895): 480–81.

―――. "The Theory of Distribution." *Papers Relating to Political Economy*. London: Macmillan, 1925.

Eichner, A. D., and Kregel, J. A. "An Essay on Post-Keynesian Theory: A New Paradigm in Economics." *Journal of Economic Literature* 13 (1975): 1293–1314.

Eilenstine, D., and Cunningham, J. P. "Projected Consumption Patterns for a Stationary Population." *Population Studies* 26 (1972): 223–31.

Eisele, F. R., ed. *Political Consequences of Aging*. Annals of the American Academy of Political and Social Science, Vol. 415, September, 1974.

Eldridge, Hope T. *Population Policies: A Survey of Recent Developments*. Washington, D.C.: American University, 1954.

Eshag, Eprime. *From Marshall to Keynes*. Oxford: Blackwell, 1963.

Espenshade, T. J. "The Price of Children and Socio-Economic Theories of Fertility: A Survey of Alternative Methods of Estimating the Parental Cost of Raising Children." *Population Studies* 26 (1972): 207–22.

―――, and Chan, C. Y. "Compensating Changes in Fertility and Mortality.' *Demography* 13 (1976): 357–68.

Evans, Archibald. "Flexibility in Working Time." Prepared for O.E.C.D. Labour / Management Programme, International Conference on New Patterns for Working Time. Paris: September 26–29, 1973.

Fabrycy, Mark Z. "Determinants of Total Factor Productivity." *Western Economic Journal* 9 (1971): 408–18.

Fair, Charles. *From the Jaws of Victory*. New York: Simon and Schuster, 1971.

Farmer, R. N.; Long, J. D.; and Stolnitz, J. J., eds. *World Population—The View Ahead*. Bloomington: Indiana University Bureau of Business Research, 1968.

Farrell, M. J. "The New Theories of the Consumption Function." *Economic Journal* 69 (1959): 678–95.

Fechter, Alan. *Public Employment Programs*. Washington, D.C.: American Enterprise Program, Evaluative Study No. 20, 1975.

Feldstein, Martin. "The Economics of the New Unemployment." *The Public Interest* 33 (1973): 3–42.

———. "Social Security, Induced Retirement, and Aggregate Capital Accumulation." *Journal of Political Economy* 82 (1974): 905–26.

———. "Temporary Layoffs in the Theory of Unemployment." *Journal of Political Economy* 84 (1976): 937–58.

Fellner, William. "Theoretical Foundations of the Failure of Demand-Management Policies: An Essay." *Journal of Economic Literature* 14 (1976): 34–53.

Ferber, Robert. "Consumer Economics, A Survey." *Journal of Economic Literature* 11 (1973): 1303–42.

———. "Research on Household Behavior." *American Economic Review* 52 (1962): 19–63.

Ferguson, C. E. *The Neoclassical Theory of Production and Distribution.* Cambridge: University Press, 1969.

Finkel, S. R., and Tarascio, V. J. *Wage and Employment Theory.* New York: Ronald Press, 1971.

Fisher, A. C., and Krutilla, J. V. "Conservation, Environment, and the Rate of Discount." *Quarterly Journal of Economics* 89 (1975): 358–70.

Fisher, F. M., and Temin, Peter. "Returns to Scale in Research and Development: What Does the Schumpeterian Hypothesis Imply?" *Journal of Political Economy* 81 (1973): 56–70.

Fisher, P. S., and Quinn, W. C. "A Cross-Section Analysis of Fertility." *The American Economist* 19 (1975): 64–68.

Fleming, Thomas F., Jr. "Manpower Impact of Purchases by State and Local Governments." *Monthly Labor Review* 96 (1973): 33–39.

Fogel, W. A. "Immigrant Mexicans and the U.S. Labor Force." *Monthly Labor Review* 98 (1975): 44–46.

Forrester, Jay. *World Dynamics.* Cambridge: Wright-Allen Press, 1971.

Forrester, R. B. "The Limits of Agricultural Expansion." *Economica* 3 (1923): 209–14.

Fortes, Michael. "Job Evaluation and Income Policy." *Lloyd's Bank Review* 114 (1975): 38–48.

Fourastié, J. "De la vie traditionelle à la vie tertiaire." *Population* 14 (1959): 417–32.

Fox, Alan. "Work Status and Income Change, 1968–72: Retirement History Study Preview." *Social Security Bulletin* 39 (1976): 15–28.

Frejka, Tomas. "Demographic Paths to a Stationary Population: The U.S. in International Comparison." *Research Reports,* Vol. I, Commission on Population Growth. Washington, D.C.: 1972.

———. *The Future of Population Growth: Alternative Paths to Equilibrium.* New York: Wiley & Sons, 1973.

———. "The Prospects for a Stationary World Population." *Scientific American* 229 (1973): 15–23.

———. *Reference Tables to the Future of Population-Growth, Alternative Paths to Equilibrium.* New York: Population Council, 1972.

————. "Reflections on the Demographic Conditions Needed to Establish a U.S. Stationary Population." *Population Studies* 22 (1968): 379–97.

Friedland, Edward. "Oil and the Decline of Western Power." *Political Science Quarterly* 90 (1975): 432–50.

Friedman, Milton. *Capitalism and Freedom.* Chicago: University of Chicago Press, 1962.

————. "Nobel Lecture: Inflation and Unemployment." *Journal of Political Economy* 85 (1977): 451–72.

————. "Population Change and Aggregate Output." *Demographic and Economic Change in Developed Countries.* Edited by Ansley J. Coale. Princeton: Princeton University Press, 1960.

————. *Price Theory, A Provisional Text.* Chicago: Aldine, 1962.

Frisbie, Parker. "Illegal Migration from Mexico to the United States. A Longitudinal Analysis." *International Migration Review* 9 (1975): 3–14.

Fullerton, H. N., Jr. "A New Type of Working Life Table for Man." *Monthly Labor Review* 95 (1972): 20–27.

————. "Sensitivity of Generation Tables of Working Life for Men to Different Projections of Labor Force Participation Rates and Mortality Rates." *Proceedings of the American Statistical Association,* Social Statistics Section, 1972.

————. "A Table of Expected Working Life for Men, 1968." *Monthly Labor Review* 94 (1971): 49–55.

————, and Byrne, James J. "Length of Working Life for Men and Women, 1970." *Monthly Labor Review* 99 (1976): 31–35.

————, and Flaim, Paul O. "New Labor Force Projections to 1990." *Monthly Labor Review* 99 (1976): 3–13.

Fulop, Marcel. "A Survey of the Literature on the Economic Theory of Fertility Behavior." *The American Economist* 21 (1977): 3–13.

Gallaway, Lowell E. "Age and Labor Mobility Patterns." *Southern Economic Journal* 36 (1969): 171–80.

————. "Labor Mobility, Resource Allocation, and Structural Unemployment." *American Economic Review* 53 (1963): 694–716.

————. *Manpower Economics.* Homewood, Ill.: Irwin, 1971.

Gellner, C. G. "Enlarging the Concept of a Labor Reserve." *Monthly Labor Review* 98 (1975): 20–28.

George, C. S. *The History of Management Theory.* Englewood Cliffs, N.J.: Prentice-Hall, 1968.

Georgescu-Roegen, Nicholas. "Dynamic Equilibrium and Economic Growth." *Economie Appliquée* 27 (1974): 529–63.

————. *Energy and Economic Myths.* New York: Pergamon, 1976.

————. "Energy and Economic Myths." *Southern Economic Journal* 41 (1975): 347–81.

————. *The Entropy Law and the Economic Process.* Cambridge, Mass.: Harvard University Press, 1971.

Gilroy, C. L. "Investment in Human Capital and Black-White Unemployment." *Monthly Labor Review* 98 (1975): 13–21.

Ginzberg, Eli, ed. *Jobs for Americans*. Englewood Cliffs, N.J.: Prentice-Hall, 1976.

Gitlow, A. L. *Labor and Manpower Economics*. Homewood, Ill.: Irwin, 1971.

Glass, D. V. *Population Policies and Movements in Europe*. Oxford: Clarendon Press, 1940.

————. *The Struggle for Population*. Oxford: Clarendon Press, 1936.

————, and Eversley, D. E. C., eds. *Population in History*. Chicago: Aldine, 1965.

————, and Revelle, Roger, eds. *Population and Social Change*. London: Arnold, 1972.

Glick, Paul C. *Some Recent Changes in American Families. Current Population Reports*, P-23, No. 52 (1975).

Goldenberg, Leon. "Savings in a State with a Stationary Population." *Quarterly Journal of Economics* 61 (1946): 40–65.

Goldsmith, Raymond. "A Synthetic Estimate of the National Wealth of Japan, 1885–1973." *Review of Income and Wealth*, Series 21 (June 1975): 125–51.

————, and Saunders, Christopher, eds. *The Measurement of National Wealth*. Vol. 8 in Income and Wealth Series. Chicago: Quadrangle Books, 1959.

Goldstein, Sidney. *Study of Consumer Expenditures, Incomes, and Savings*. Philadelphia: University of Pennsylvania, 1960.

Goodwin, Craufurd, D. W. *Economic Enquiry in Australia*. Durham, N.C.: Duke University Press, 1966.

Goodwin, R. M. *Elementary Economics from the Higher Standpoint*. Cambridge: University Press, 1970.

————. "Secular and Cyclical Aspects of the Multiplier and the Accelerator." In Higgins et al., *Income, Employment and Public Policy*. New York: W. W. Norton, 1948.

Gordon, Lincoln. "Limits to the Growth Debate." *Resources*, Resources for the Future (Summer 1976): 1–6.

Gordon, Robert A. "Population Growth, Housing, and the Capital Coefficient." *American Economic Review* 46 (1956): 307–22.

————. "Some Macroeconomic Aspects of Manpower Policy." *Manpower Problems in the Policy Mix*. Edited by Lloyd Ulman. Baltimore: Johns Hopkins Press, 1973.

Gordon, R. L. "Conservation and the Theory of Exhaustible Resources." *Canadian Journal of Economics* 32 (1966): 319–26.

Gordon, W. "The Case for a Less Restrictive Border Policy." *Social Science Quarterly* 56 (1975): 485–91.

Greville, T. N. E., ed. *Population Dynamics*. New York: Academic Press, 1972.

Griliches, Z., and Ringstad, V. *Economies of Scale and the Form of the Production Function*. Amsterdam: North-Holland Publishing Co., 1971.

Groat, M. G.; Workman, R. L.; and Neal, A. G. "Labor Force Participation and Family Formation: A Study of Working Mothers." *Demography* 13 (1976): 115–26.

Gronau, Reuben. "The Evaluation of Housewive's Time." *The Measurement of Economic and Social Performance.* Edited by Milton Moss. New York: Columbia University Press, 1973, pp. 163–92.

Grubel, H.; Maki, Dennis; and Sax, Shelly. "Real and Induced Unemployment in Canada." *Canadian Journal of Economics* 8 (1975): 151–73.

————. "Real and Insurance-Related Unemployment in Canada." *Canadian Journal of Economics* 8 (1975): 174–91.

Gruber, W. H.; Mehta, Dileep; and Vernon, Raymond. "The R & D Factor in International Trade and International Investment of United States Industries." *The Product Life Cycle and International Trade.* Edited by L. T. Wells, Jr. Boston: Harvard Graduate School of Business Administration, 1972, pp. 111–39.

Guillaumont, Patrick. "The Optimum Rate of Population Growth." *Economic Factors in Population Growth.* Edited by Ansley Coale. New York: John Wiley & Sons, 1976.

Gutman, David. "The New Mythologies and Premature Aging in the Youth Culture." *Social Research* 40 (1973): 248–68.

Haber, L. D. "Age and Capacity Devaluation." *Health and Social Behavior,* September 1970, p. 8.

Haberler, Gottfried. *Prosperity and Depression.* Lake Success: United Nations, 1946.

————. *The Theory of International Trade with Its Application to Commercial Policy.* Translated by A. Stonier and F. Benham. New York: Macmillan, 1936.

————, ed. *Readings in Business Cycle Theory.* Philadelphia: Blakeston, 1944.

Hägerstrand, Torsten. "Quantitative Techniques for Analysis of the Spread of Information and Technology." *Education and Economic Development.* Edited by C. A. Aderson and Mary Jean Bowman. Chicago: Aldine, 1965, chap. 12.

Hahn, F. H., and Matthews, R. C. O. "The Theory of Economic Growth: A Survey." Survey V, in *Surveys of Economic Theory.* Prepared for the American Economic Association and the Royal Economic Society. London: Macmillan, 1965.

Hajnal, J. "European Marriage Patterns in Perspective." *Population in History.* Edited by D. V. Glass and D. E. C. Eversley. Chicago: Aldine, 1965.

Hamilton, G. S., and Roessner, J. D. "How Employers Screen Disadvantaged Job Applicants." *Monthly Labor Review* 95 (1972): 14–21.

Hammermesh, D. S. *Jobless Pay and the Economy.* Baltimore: Johns Hopkins University Press, 1977.

————. "A Note on Income and Substitution Effects in Search Unemployment." *Economic Journal* 87 (1977): 312–14.

Hammond, A. L. "Lithium: Will Short Supply Constrain Energy Technologies?" *Science* 116 (1976): 1037–38.

Handler, Philip, ed. *Biology and the Future of Man.* New York: Oxford University Press, 1970.

Hansen, A. H. *Business Cycle Theory.* Boston: Ginn and Co., 1977.

————. *Economic Stabilization in an Unbalanced World.* New York: Harcourt, Brace and Co., 1932.

————. *Full Recovery or Stagnation?* New York: Norton, 1938.

————. "Economic Progress and Declining Population Growth." *American Economic Review* 29 (1939): 1–15.

————. *Fiscal Policy and Business Cycles.* New York: Norton, 1941.

————. *Economic Policy and Full Employment.* New York: McGraw-Hill, 1947.

————. *A Guide to Keynes.* New York: McGraw-Hill, 1953.

Hansen, Bent. *A Survey of General Equilibrium Systems.* New York: McGraw-Hill, 1970.

Hardy, C. O. "Schumpeter on Capitalism, Socialism and Democracy." *Journal of Political Economy* 53 (1945): 348–56.

Hareven, Tamara K. "The Last Stage: Historical Adulthood and Old Age." *Daedalus* 105 (1976): 13–28.

Harris, Seymour E. *The New Economics.* New York: Knopf, 1947.

Harrod, Roy. "Les relations entre l'investissement et la population." *Revue économique* 6 (1955): 356–67.

————. "Modern Population Trends." *Manchester School of Economics and Social Studies* 10 (1939): 1–20.

————. "The Population Problem." *Economic Essays.* London: Macmillan, 1952, 1972.

————. "Report of the Royal Commission on Population—A Comment." *Journal of Development Studies* 10 (1973–74): 252–53.

————. *The Trade Cycle.* Oxford: Clarendon Press, 1936.

Hart, B. H. Liddell. *History of the Second World War.* New York: G. P. Putnam's Sons, 1971.

Hassan, Zuhair, and Johnson, S. R. "Consumer Demand Parameters for the U.S.: A Comparison of Linear Expenditures, Rotterdam and Double-Log Estimates." *Quarterly Review of Economics and Business* 16, no. 1 (1976): 77–92.

Haufe, Helmut. *Die Bevölkerung Europas.* Berlin: Junker and Dünnheinpt, 1936.

Hayami, Y., and Ruttan, Vernon. *Agricultural Development: An International Perspective.* Baltimore: Johns Hopkins Press, 1971.

Haywood, R. M. *The Myth of Rome's Fall.* New York: Thomas Y. Crowell, Co., 1958.

Hedden, W. P. *How Great Cities Are Fed.* Boston: D C. Heath, 1929.

Hedges, Janice N. "How Many Days Make a Workweek?" *Monthly Labor Review* 98 (1975): 29–36.

————. "A Look at the 4-Day Workweek." *Monthly Labor Review* 96 (1973): 3–8.

Hedrick, C. L. "Expectations and the Labor Supply." *American Economic Review* 63 (1973): 968–74.

Heeren, H. J. "Declining Population Growth and Population Policy." *International Social Science Journal* 26, no. 2 (1974): 244–54.

Heien, D. M. "Demographic Effects and the Multiperiod Consumption Function." *Journal of Political Economy* 80 (1972): 125–239.

Helleiner, K. *Cambridge Economic History of Europe.* Chap. I. Cambridge: University Press, 1941.

Hendershot, Gerry E. "Population Size, Military Power, and Antinatal Policy." *Demography* 10 (1973): 517–24.

Henderson, P. D., ed. *Economic Growth in Britain.* London: Weidenfeld and Nicholson, 1966.

Henry, Louis. "Pyramides, statuts et carrières." *Population* 26 (1971): 463–86; 27 (1972): 599–636.

Heuckel, Glenn. "A Historical Approach to Future Economic Growth." *Science* 187 (1975): 925–31.

Hicks, J. R. *A Contribution to the Theory of the Trade Cycle.* Oxford: Oxford University Press, 1950.

————. "Growth and Anti-Growth." *Oxford Economic Papers* 18 (1966): 257–69.

————. "Mr. Keynes' Theory of Employment." *Economic Journal* 46 (1936): 252–53.

————. *Value and Capital.* 2nd edition. Oxford: Clarendon Press, 1946.

Hieser, R. O. "The Economic Consequences of Zero Population Growth." *The Economic Record* 49 (1973): 241–62.

Higgins, Ben H. "The Concept of Secular Stagnation." *American Economic Review* 40 (1950): 160–66.

————. "Concepts and Criteria of Secular Stagnation." *Income, Employment and Public Policy, Essays in Honor of Alvin H. Hansen.* New York: W. W. Norton, 1948.

————. "The Doctrine of Economic Maturity." *American Economic Review* 36 (1946): 133–41.

————. "The Theory of Increasing Underemployment." *Economic Journal* 60 (1950): 255–74.

Hill, C. R. "Education, Health and Family Size as Determinants of Labor Market Activity for the Poor and Nonpoor." *Demography* 8 (1971): 379–88.

Hirschman, A. O. *National Power and the Structure of Foreign Trade.* Berkeley: University of California Press, 1945.

Ho, Ping-ti. *Studies on the Population of China, 1368–1953.* Cambridge, Mass.: Harvard University Press, 1959.

Hoch, Irving. "City Size Effects, Trends, and Policies." *Science* 193 (1976): 856–63.

Hodges, Henry. *Technology in the Ancient World.* New York: Knopf, 1970.

Hofstee, Erland. "Birth Variation in Populations which Practice Family Planning." *Population Studies* 25 (1971): 315–26.

Hogan, T. D. "The Implications of Population Stationarity for the Social Security System." *Social Science Quarterly* 55 (1974): 151–58.

Hogben, Lancelot, ed. *Political Arithmetic.* New York: Macmillan, 1938.

Hohm, Charles F. "Social Security and Fertility: An International Perspective." *Demography* 12 (1975): 620–44.

Holdren, John P., and Ehrlich, Paul R. *Global Ecology*. New York: Macmillan, 1973.

Hollander, J. H., ed. *Economic Essays Contributed in Honor of John Bates Clark*. New York: Macmillan, 1927.

Hollander, Sam. *The Economics of Adam Smith*. Toronto: University of Toronto Press, 1973.

Hollingsworth, T. C. *Historical Demography*. Ithaca, N.Y.: Cornell University Press, 1969.

Hoover, E. M. "Basic Approaches to the Study of Demographic Aspects of Economic Development: Economic Demographic Models." *Population Index* 37 (1971): 66–75.

Hopkin, W. A. B. "The Economics of an Aging Population." *Lloyd's Bank Review* 27 (1953): 25–36.

Horst, Francis L. "Patterns of Output Growth." *Survey of Current Business* 46 (1966): 18–25.

Houthakker, H. S., and Taylor, L. D. *Consumer Demand in the United States: Analysis and Projections*. Cambridge, Mass.: Harvard University Press, 1970.

Howard, J. A., and Lehman, D. R. "The Effect of Different Populations on Selected Industries in the Year 2000." *Economic Aspects of Population Change*. Commission on Population Growth and the American Future, Research Report II. Washington, D.C.: U.S. Government Printing Office, 1972.

Hulten, C. R. "Technical Change and the Reproducibility of Capital." *American Economic Review* 65 (1975): 956–65.

Humphrey, D. B., and Moroney, J. R. "Substitution Among Capital, Labor, and Natural Resource Products in American Manufacturing." *Journal of Political Economy* 83 (1975): 57–82.

Hutchinson, E. P. *The Population Debate*. Boston: Houghton Mifflin Co., 1967.

Ironmonger, D. S. *New Commodities and Consumer Behaviour*. Cambridge: University Press, 1972.

Ishii, Ryoichi. *Population Pressure and Economic Life in Japan*. London: P. S. King, 1937.

Jaffe, A. J., et al. *Disabled Workers in the Labor Market*. Totowa, N.J.: Bedminster Press, 1964.

―――. "Labor Force." *International Encyclopedia of Social Sciences* 8 (1968): 469–91.

Jevons, W. S. *The Coal Question*. Edited by A. W. Flux. London: Macmillan and Company, 1906.

Johnson, A. H.; Jones, G. E.; and Lucas, D. B. *The American Market of the Future*. New York: New York University Press, 1966.

Johnson, E. A. J. *American Economic Thought in the 17th Century*. London: P. S. King, 1932.

―――. *Predecessors of Adam Smith*. New York: Prentice-Hall, 1937.

Johnson, George E., and Stafford, Frank P. "Lifetime Earnings in a Professional Labor Market: Academic Economists." *Journal of Political Economy* 82 (1974): 549–69.

Johnson, H. G. "Keynes's General Theory: Revolution or War of Independence?" *Canadian Journal of Economics* 9 (1976): 580–94.

——. "Minimum Wage Laws: A General Equilibrium Analysis." *Canadian Journal of Economics* 2 (1969): 599–604.

——, and Mieszkowski, Peter. "The Effects of Unionization on the Distribution of Income: A General Equilibrium Approach." *Quarterly Journal of Economics* 84 (1970): 539–61.

Johnston, D. F. "Illustrative Projections in the Labor Force of the United States to 2040." *Economic Aspects of Population Change*. Research Report II, Commission on Population Growth and the American Future. Washington, D.C.: U.S. Government Printing Office, 1972.

——. "The U.S. Labor Force: Projection to 1990." *Monthly Labor Review* 94 (1973): 3–13.

Jones, A. H. M. *Athenian Democracy*. Oxford: Blackwell, 1957.

Jones, David. "Projections of Housing Demand to the Year 2000, Using Two Population Projections." *Economic Aspects of Population Change*. Research Report II, Commission on Population Growth and the American Future. Washington, D.C.: U.S. Government Printing Office, 1972.

Jones, Martin V. "Secular Trends and Idle Resources." *Journal of Business of the University of Chicago* 17 (1944): Part 2.

Jorgenson, D. W., and Christensen, L. R. "U.S. Real Product and Real Factor Input, 1929–1967." *Review of Income and Wealth* 16 (1970): 19–50.

——, and Griliches, Z. "The Explanation of Productivity Change." *The Review of Economic Studies* 34, no. 3 (1967): 249–82, reprinted with corrections in *The Survey of Current Business* 69 Part II (1969): 29–64.

Kahn, E. *Der internationale Geburtenstreik*. Frankfort-am-Main: 1930.

Kahne, Hilda, and Kohen, A. I. "Economic Perspectives on the Roles of Women in the American Economy." *Journal of Economic Literature* 13 (1975): 1249–92.

Kaldor, N. *Causes of the Slow Rate of Growth of the United Kingdom; An Inaugural Lecture*. Cambridge: University Press, 1966.

——. "Economic Growth and the Verdoorn Law: A Comment on Mr. Rowthorn's Article." *Economic Journal* 85 (1975): 891–96.

Kamien, M. I., and Schwartz, N. L. "Some Economic Consequences of Anticipating Technical Advance." *Western Economic Journal* 10 (1972): 123–38.

Kaplan, Robert S. *Financial Crisis in the Social Security System*. Washington, D.C.: American Enterprise Institute, 1976.

Katona, George. *Psychological Economics*. New York: Elsevier, 1975.

——, and Strumpel, Burkhard. "Consumer Investment Versus Business Investment." *Challenge*, 18, January–February 1976, pp. 12–16.

Keesing, D. B. "The Impact of Research and Development on United States Trade." *Journal of Political Economy* 75 (1967): 38–48.

Keesing, D. B. "National Diversity and World Progress." *World Development* 3 (1975): 191–99.

———. "Outward-Looking Policies and Economic Development." *Economic Journal* 77 (1967): 304–26.

———. "Population and Industrial Development: Some Evidence from Trade Patterns." *American Economic Review* 58 (1968): 448–55.

———. "Small Population as a Political Handicap to National Development." *Political Science Quarterly* 84 (1969): 50–60.

Kelley, Allen C. "Demographic Change and the Size of the Governmental Sector." *Southern Economic Journal* 43 (1976): 1058–65.

———. "Demographic Changes and American Economic Development, Past, Present, and Future." *Economic Aspects of Population Change.* Research Reports II, Commission on Population Growth and the American Future. Washington, D.C.: U.S. Government Printing Office, 1972.

———. "The Role of Population in Models of Economic Growth." *American Economic Review* 64 (1974): 39–44.

Kelly, W. J. "Comment on Hendershot's 'Population Size, Military Power and Antinatal Policy'," *Demography* 11 (1974): 533–35.

Kendrick, John W. "Measuring America's Wealth." *Morgan Guaranty Survey,* May 1976, pp. 507–13.

———. *Productivity Trends in the United States.* Princeton: Princeton University Press, 1961.

Kennedy, C., and Thirlwall, A. P. "Technical Progress: A Survey." *Economic Journal* 82 (1972): 11–72.

Keyfitz, Nathan. "Age Distribution and the Stable Equivalent." *Demography* 5 (1969): 261–70.

———. "Individual Mobility in a Stationary Population." *Population Studies* 27 (1973): 335–52.

———. "On the Momentum of Population Growth." *Demography* 8 (1971): 71–80.

———. "Population Waves." *Population Dynamics.* Edited by T. N. E. Greville. New York: Academic Press, 1972.

———. "World Resources and the World Middle Class." *Scientific American* 235 (1976): 28–35.

———, and Flieger, Wilhelm. *World Population.* Chicago: University of Chicago Press, 1968.

Keynes, J. M. *The Economic Consequences of the Peace.* New York: Harcourt, Brace & Howe, 1920.

———. *The Economic Consequences of the Peace* (1919), vol. 2. of *The Collected Writings of J. M. Keynes.* London: Macmillan, 1971.

———. "The General Theory of Employment." *Quarterly Journal of Economics* 51 (1937): 209–23.

———. *The General Theory of Employment, Interest and Money.* New York: Harcourt, Brace and Co., 1936.

———. "A Reply to Sir William Beveridge." *Economic Journal* 33 (1923): 475–86.

————. "A Self-Adjusting Economic System?" *The New Republic,* Feb. 20, 1935, pp. 35–37.

————. "Some Economic Consequences of a Declining Population." *Eugenics Review* 29 (1937): 13–17.

————. *A Treatise on Money.* New York: Harcourt, Brace and Co., 1930.

Khang, Chilsoon. "Equilibrium Growth in the International Economy: The Case of Unequal Natural Rates of Growth." *International Economic Review* 12 (1971): 239–49.

King, A. Thomas. "The Demand for Housing: Integrating the Roles of Journey to Work, Neighborhood Quality, and Prices." *Household Production and Consumption.* Edited by E. Terlickyi. New York: Columbia University Press, 1975.

Kirzner, Israel M. *Competition and Entrepreneurship.* Chicago: University of Chicago Press, 1973.

Klein, L. R. *The Keynesian Revolution.* New York: Macmillan, 1947.

Knibbs, G. H. *The Shadow of the World's Future.* London: E. Benn, 1928.

Knight, Frank. "Issues in the Economics of Stationary States." *American Economic Review* 26 (1936): 393–411.

————. "Professor Fisher's Interest Theory: A Case in Point." *Journal of Political Economy* 39 (1931): 176–212.

————. *Risk, Uncertainty, and Profit.* Boston: Houghton Mifflin Co., 1921.

Knox, A. D. "The Acceleration Principle and the Theory of Investment: A Survey." *Economica* 19 (1952): 269–97.

Kolata, G. B. "!Kung Hunter-Gatherers: Feminism, Diet, and Birth Control." *Science* 185 (1974): 932–34.

Kolb, F. R. "The Stationary State of Ricardo and Malthus: Neither Pessimistic nor Prophetic." *Intermountain Economic Review* 3 (1972): 17–30.

Koyl, L. F. *Employing the Older Worker: Matching the Employee to the Job.* Washington, D.C.: National Council on the Aging, Inc., 1974.

Kramer, S. D. "State Power and the Structure of International Trade." *World Politics* 28 (1976): 317–47.

Kranz, Peter. "What Do People Do All Day?" *Behavioral Science* 15 (1970): 286–91.

Kravis, I. B. "A Survey of International Comparisons of Productivity." *Economic Journal* 76 (1976): 1–44.

Kregel, J. A. "The Modelling Methodology in the Face of Uncertainty: The Modelling Methods of Keynes and the Post-Keynesians." *Economic Journal* 86 (1976): 209–55.

Kreps, Juanita M. *Lifetime Allocation of Work and Income.* Durham, N.C.: Duke University Press, 1971.

————, and Spengler, J. J. "Equity and Social Credit for the Retired." *Employment, Income, and Retirement Problems of the Aged.* Edited by Juanita M. Kreps. Durham, N.C.: Duke University Press, 1963.

Kuczynski, R. R. *The Balance of Births and Deaths.* I. New York: McGraw-Hill, 1928.

————. *The Balance of Births and Deaths.* Washington, D.C.: Brookings Institution, 1931.

Kuczynski, R. R. "British Demographer's Opinions of Fertility." *Political Arithmetic*. Edited by L. Hogben. New York: Macmillan, 1938.

——. *Fertility and Reproduction*. New York: Falcon Press, 1932.

——. *The Measurement of Population Growth*. New York: Oxford University Press, 1936.

Kuipers, S. K., and Nentjes, A. "Pollution in a Neo-Classical World: The Classics Rehabilitated?" *De Economist* 21 (1973): 52–67.

Kuznets, Simon. *Capital in the American Economy*. Princeton: Princeton University Press, 1961.

——. *Economic Growth of Nations*. Cambridge, Mass.: Harvard University Press, 1971.

——. "Fertility Differentials Between Less Developed and Developed Regions: Components and Implications." *American Philosophical Society* 119 (1975): 363–96.

——. *Income & Wealth of the United States*. London: Bowes & Bowes, 1952.

——. *Modern Economic Growth. Rate, Structure, Spread*. New Haven: Yale University Press, 1967.

——. *Population, Capital, and Growth*. New York: W. W. Norton, 1973.

——. *Postwar Economic Growth*. Cambridge, Mass.: Harvard University Press, 1964.

——. *Secular Movements in Production and Prices*. Boston: Houghton Mifflin, 1930.

Lachmann, L. M. "From Mises to Shackle: An Essay on Austrian Economics and the Kaleidic Society." *Journal of Economic Literature* 14 (1976): 54–62.

Lafitte, F. "The Economic Effects of a Declining Population." *Eugenics Review* 32 (1940): 121–34.

Lambert, Paul. "The Evolution of Keynes's Thought from the Treatise on Money to the 'General Theory.'" *Annals of Public and Cooperative Economy,* 1969.

Lancaster, Kelvin J. *Consumer Demand: A New Approach*. New York: Columbia University Press, 1971.

Land, K. D., and Spilerman, Seymour. *Social Indicator Models*. New York: Russell Sage Foundation, 1975.

Landry, Adolph. "La révolution démographique." *Economic Essays in Honour of Gustav Cassel*. London: Allen & Unwin, 1933.

Lapp, Ralph E. *The Logarithmic Century*. Englewood Cliffs, N.J.: Prentice Hall, 1973.

Latouche, R. *The Birth of Western Economy*. London: Methuen, 1961.

La Tourette, J. E. "Economies of Scale and Capital Utilization 1926–72." *Canadian Journal of Economics* 8 (1975): 448–55.

Lebergott, S. *Manpower in Economic Growth. The United States Record Since 1800*. New York: McGraw-Hill, 1964.

Lee, Maurice W. *Macroeconomics: Fluctuations, Growth, Stability*. Homewood, Ill.: Irwin, 1967.

Lehman, Harvey C. *Age and Achievement*. Princeton: Princeton University Press, 1953.

Leibenstein, Harvey. "The Impact of Population Growth on Economic Welfare—Nontraditional Elements." *Rapid Population Growth*. Edited by Roger Revelle et al. Baltimore: Johns Hopkins Press, 1971, pp. 175–98.

————. "An Interpretation of the Economic Theory of Fertility: Promising Paths or Blind Alley." *Journal of Economic Literature* 12 (1974): 457–79.

————. Introduction to "Population: A Symposium." *Quarterly Journal of Economics* 89 (1975): 230–34.

————. *A Theory of Economic-Demographic Development*. Princeton: Princeton University Press, 1954.

Lekachman, Robert. *Keynes' General Theory. Reports of Three Decades*. New York: St. Martin's Press, 1964.

Leontief, Wassily. "Structure of the World Economy." *American Economic Review* 64 (1974): 823–24.

Levine, A. L. "Economic Science and Population Theory." *Population Studies* 19 (1965): 139–54.

Levitan, S. A., and Johnston, W. B. *Work is Here to Stay, Alas*. Salt Lake City: Olympus Publishing Co., 1973.

Linder, Staffan Burenstam. *The Harried Leisure Class*. New York: Columbia University Press, 1970.

Littman, Gary, and Keyfitz, Nathan. *The Next Hundred Years* (Working Paper No. 101) Harvard University Center of Population Studies, 1977.

Livingstone, R. S. "Unemployment—A Story the Figures Don't Tell." *U. S. News & World Report*, Nov. 18, 1974, pp. 43–45.

Lloyd, Cynthia B., ed. *Sex Discrimination and the Division of Labor*. New York: Columbia University Press, 1975.

Long, C. D. *The Labor Force Under Changing Income and Employment*. Princeton: Princeton University Press, 1958.

Long, Larry H. "New Estimates of Migration Expectancy in The United States." *Journal of American Statistical Association* 68 (1973): 37–43.

————, and Boertlein, Celia G. "The Geographical Mobility of Americans: An International Comparison." *Current Population Reports: Special Studies Series*, Series P-23, no. 4. Washington, D.C.: Bureau of the Census, 1976.

Lopez, A. *Some Problems in a Stable Population Theory*. Princeton: Princeton University Press, 1961.

Lösch, August. *Bevolkerungswellen und Wechsellagan*. Jena: Gustav Fischer, 1936.

————. "Population Cycles as a Cause of Business Cycles." *Quarterly Journal of Economics* 51 (1937): 649–62.

————. *Was ist vom Geburtenrückgang zu halten?* Heidenheim (Wurttiemberg): 1932.

Lotka, A. J. *Elements of Physical Biology*. Baltimore: Williams & Wilkins, 1925.

Lough, W. H. *High-Level Consumption*. New York: McGraw-Hill, 1935.

Loveday, A., et al. *The World's Future. The Halley Stewart Lectures, 1937*. London: Allen & Unwin, 1938.

Lovell, Michael C. "The Minimum Wage, Teenage Unemployment, and the Business Cycle." *Western Economic Journal* 10 (1972): 414–27.

Lucas, R. E. B. "The Distribution of Job Characteristics." *The Review of Economics and Statistics* 56 (1974): 538–39.

Luft, Harold L. "The Impact of Poor Health on Earnings." *The Review of Economics and Statistics* 57 (1975): 43–57.

Lutz, Mark A. "The Evolution of the Industrial Earnings Structure: the 'Geological Theory,'" *Canadian Journal of Economics* 9 (1976): pp. 473–91.

Macura, Milos. "The Long Range Outlook." *World Population—The View Ahead.* Edited by R. N. Farmer, et al. Bloomington: Indiana University Bureau of Business Research, 1968.

Mansfield, Edwin. "Contribution of R & D to Growth in The United States." *Science* 175 (1972): 477–86.

———. *The Economics of Technical Change.* New York: Norton, 1968.

Marbach, G. *Job Redesign for Older Workers.* Paris: OECD, 1968.

Marcin, T. C. "The Effect of Declining Population Growth on Housing Demand." *Challenge,* 19, November–December, 1976, pp. 30–33.

Marsden, Ralph W., ed. *Politics, Minerals, and Survival.* Madison: University of Wisconsin Press, 1974.

Marshall, Alfred. *Principles of Economics.* London: Macmillan, 1920, 1961.

Martin, Laurence. *Arms and Strategy.* New York: David McKay Co., 1973.

Mass, N. J. "Modeling Cycles in the National Economy." *Technology Review* 79 (1976): 43–52.

Matthews, R. C. O. *The Business Cycle.* Chicago: University of Chicago Press, 1959.

———. "Why Growth Rates Differ." *Economic Journal* 89 (1969): 261–68.

McCarthy, Michael D. *The Wharton Quarterly Econometric Forecasting Model Mark III.* Philadelphia: Wharton School, University of Pennsylvania, 1972.

McCulloch, J. H. "The Effect of a Minimum Wage Law in the Labour-Intensive Sector." *Canadian Journal of Economics* 7 (1974): 316–19.

McFarland, David D. "On the Theory of Stable Populations." *Demography* 5 (1969): 301–22.

McKeown, Thomas. *The Modern Rise of Population.* London: Edwin Arnold, 1976.

Meade, J. E. *The Growing Economy.* Chicago: Aldine, 1968.

———. *The Stationary Economy.* Chicago: Aldine, 1965.

———. *Trade and Welfare.* London: Oxford University Press, 1955.

Meadows, Dennis L., and Meadows, Donella H. *The Limits to Growth.* New York: Universe Books, 1972.

Mesarovic, Mihajlo, and Pestel, Eduard. *Mankind at the Turning Point.* New York: E. P. Dutton, 1974.

Metropolitan Life Insurance Company. *Statistical Bulletin* 56 (September 1975): 8–9.

Michell, H. *The Economics of Ancient Greece.* Cambridge: University Press, 1940, 1957.

Miles, R. E. *Awakening from the American Dream*. New York: Universe Books, 1976.

Mill, John Stuart. *Principles of Political Economy*. Edited by W. J. Ashley. New York: Longmans Green, 1921.

Mincer, Jacob. "Labor Force Participation of Married Women: A Study of Labor Supply." *Aspects of Labor Economics* (National Bureau of Research). Princeton: Princeton University Press, 1962.

——. "Unemployment Effects of Minimum Wages." *Journal of Political Economy* 84 (1976): S87–S104.

Modigliani, F., and Brumberg, R. *Utility Analysis and Aggregate Consumption Functions: An Attempt at Integration*. New York: Photocopy, 1953.

——, and Gruneberg, E. "The Predictability of Social Events." *Journal of Political Economy* 62 (1954): 465–78.

Mombert, Paul. *Bevölkerungslehre*. Jena: Fischer, 1929.

——. *Bevolkerungspolitik nach dem Kreige*. Tübingen: Mohr, 1916.

——. *Die Volkswirtschaft der Gegenwart u. Zukunft*. Leipzig A. Deichert, 1912.

Montgomery, Arthur. "Befolkningkommissionen Och Befolkningsfrågan." *Ekonomisk Tidskrift* 41 (1939): 200–21.

Moore, G. H. *Recession Related Unemployment* (Reprint No. 29). Washington, D.C.: American Enterprise Institute, 1975.

——, and Hedges, Janice N. "Trends in Labor and Leisure." *Monthly Labor Review* 94 (1971): 3–11.

Morishima, Michio. *Equilibrium, Stability and Growth*. Oxford: Clarendon Press, 1964.

Morth, J. "Human Capital: Deterioration and Net Investment." *Review of Income and Wealth* 19 (1973): 279–302.

Moss, Milton, ed. *The Measurement of Economic and Social Performance*. New York: Columbia University Press, 1973.

Mossen, Jan, and Bronfenbrenner, Martin. "The Shorter Work Week and the Labor Supply." *Southern Economic Journal* 33 (1967): 322–31.

Moulton, H. G., and McGuire, C. E. *Germany's Capacity to Pay*. New York: McGraw-Hill, 1923.

——, and Pasvolsky, Leo. *War Debts and World Prosperity*. New York: McGraw-Hill, 1932.

Munnell, Alicia H. *The Effect of Social Security on Personal Savings*. Cambridge, Mass.: Ballinger, 1974.

——. *The Future of Social Security*. Washington, D.C.: Brookings Institution, 1976.

——. "Private Pensions and Saving: New Evidence." *Journal of Political Economy* 84 (1976): 1013–32.

Myrdal, Alva. *Nation and Family*. New York: Harper & Brothers, 1941.

——. "A Programme for Family Security in Sweden." *International Labour Review* 39 (1939): 723–63.

Myrdal, Gunnar. *Population, A Problem for Democracy*. Cambridge, Mass.: Harvard University Press, 1940.

Namboodri, N. K. "Some Observations on the Economic Framework for Fertility Analysis." *Population Studies* 36 (1972): 185–206.

National Academy of Sciences and National Research Council. *Resources and Man*. San Francisco: Freeman, 1969.

National Bureau of Economic Research. *54th Annual Report,* September 1974, pp. 81–85.

National Resources Committee. *The Problems of a Changing Population.* Washington, D.C.: U.S. Government Printing Office, 1938, pp. 22–26.

National Resources Planning Board. *Estimates of the Population of the United States 1940–2000*. Washington, D.C.: 1943, pp. 3ff.

————. *The Structure of the American Economy,* Part II, *Toward Full Use of Resources.* Washington, D.C.: 1940.

Neher, P. A. "Peasants, Procreation, and Pensions." *American Economic Review* 61 (1971): 380–89.

Neisser, Hans. "The Economics of a Stationary Population." *Social Research* 11 (1944): 470–90.

Nerlove, Marc. "Household and Economy: Towards a New Theory of Population and Economic Growth." *Journal of Political Economy* 82 (1974): 200–22.

New York City's Financial Crisis. Study prepared for the Joint Committee, Congress of the United States, Washington, D.C., 1975.

Niehans, Jürg. "Economic Growth with Two Endogenous Factors." *Quarterly Journal of Economics* 77 (1963): 349–71.

Nordhaus, W. D. "World Dynamics: Measurement without Data." *Economic Journal* 83 (1973): 1133–55.

————, and Tobin, James. *Economic Growth*. New York: Columbia University Press, 1972.

North, Douglass C., and Thomas, Robert Paul. "The First Economic Revolution." *Economic History Review* 30 (1977): 229–41.

Notestein, F. W. "Population and Power in Postwar Europe." *Foreign Affairs* 22 (1944): 389–403.

————, et al. *The Future Population of Europe and the Soviet Union.* Geneva: League of Nations, 1944.

Nulty, Leslie. *The Green Revolution in West Pakistan. Implications of Technological Change.* New York: Praeger, 1972.

Odum, H. T. *Environment, Power, and Society.* New York: Wiley, 1971.

O'Hara, D. J. "Microeconomic Aspects of Demographic Transition." *Journal of Political Economy* 83 (1975): 1203–16.

Olson, E. C. "Factors Affecting International Differences in Production." *American Economic Review Supplement* 38 (1948): 502–22.

Olson, Mancur, ed. *The No-Growth Society.* Vol. 102, no. 4, *Proceedings* of the American Academy of Arts and Sciences, Fall 1973.

Oppenheimer, Valerie K. *The Female Labor Force in The United States.* Berkeley: Institute of International Studies, 1970.

Ornstein, M. D. *Entry into the American Labor Force.* New York: Academic Press, 1976.

Owen, John D. "The Demand for Leisure." *Journal of Political Economy* 79 (1971): 56–76.

———. *The Price of Leisure*. Rotterdam: Rotterdam University Press, 1969.

Owens, A. J. "Will Zero-Population Growth Hamper Scientific Creativity?" *Physics Today* 26 (1973): 9–13.

Ozga, S. A. *Expectations in Economic Theory*. London: Weidenfeld and Nicolson, 1965.

Panel on Social Security Financing. *Report* to the Committee on Finance, U.S. Senate, Pursuant to S. Res. 350, 93rd Congress, February 1975.

Pareto, Vilfredo. *Trattato di sociologia generale* (1916, 1923). Edited and translated by Arthur Livingston as *The Mind and Society*. New York: Harcourt, Brace and Co., 1935.

Parker, J. E., and Shaw, L. B. "Labor Force within Metropolitan Areas." *Southern Economic Journal* 34 (1968): 538–47.

Parnes, H. S. *Research on Labor Mobility*. New York: Social Science Research Council, 1954.

Patinkin, Don. *Keynes' Monetary Thought*. Durham, N.C.: Duke University Press, 1976.

———. "Keynes' Monetary Thought." *History of Political Economy* 8 (1976): 98–142.

Pearl, Raymond. "America Today and Maybe Tomorrow." *Quarterly Review of Biology* 8 (1933): 96–101.

———. *The Biology of Population Growth*. New York: Knopf, 1925.

———. *Introduction to Medical Biometry and Statistics*. Philadelphia: Saunder, 1923, 1930, 1940.

———. *The Natural History of Population*. New York: Oxford University Press, 1939.

Pechman, J. A.; Aaron, H. J.; and Taussig, H. K. *Social Security Perspectives for Reform*. Washington, D.C.: Brookings Institution, 1968.

Perlman, Mark. "Some Economic Growth Problems and the Part Population Policy Plays." *Quarterly Journal of Economics* 89 (1975): 247–56.

Perry, G. L. "Changing Labour Markets and Inflation." *Brookings Papers on Economic Activity* 1 (1970): 411–41.

Pesando, James E. "Inflation and Guaranteed Formula Pension Plans." *Canadian Journal of Economics* 9 (1976): 529–31.

Petersen, William. "A Demographer's View of Prehistoric Demography." *Current Anthropology* 16 (1975): 227–46.

Phelps, E. S. "Population Increase." *Canadian Journal of Economics* 1 (1968): 497–518.

———. "Some Macroeconomics of Population Levelling." In *Economic Aspects of Population Change*. Edited by E. R. Morss and Ritchie H. Reed. U.S. Commission on Population Growth and the American Future. Washington, D.C.: U.S. Government Printing Office, 1972.

Pick, James B. "Display of Population Age Structure." *Demography* 11 (1974): 673–82.

Pigou, A. C. "The Classical Stationary State." *Economic Journal* 53 (1943): 343–51.

Pigou, A. C. *The Economics of Stationary States*. London: Macmillan, 1935.
————. *The Economics of Welfare*. London: Macmillan, 1931.
————. *Industrial Fluctuations*. London: Macmillan, 1927.
————. *Keynes's 'General Theory'; A Retrospective View*. London: Macmillan, 1950.
————. *The Theory of Unemployment*. London: Macmillan, 1933.
Pimental, D., et al. "Food Production and the Energy Crisis." *Science* 182 (1973): 443–49.
————. "Land Degradation: Effects on Food and Energy Resources." *Science* 124 (1976): 149–55.
Pissarides, C. A. "Risk, Job Search, and Income Distribution." *Journal of Political Economy* 82 (1974): 1255–67.
Pitchford, J. D. *The Economics of Population*. Canberra: Australian National University, 1974.
————. *Population in Economic Growth*. Amsterdam: North Holland, 1974.
Plischke, Elmer. *Microstates in World Affairs*. Washington, D.C.: American Enterprise Institute, 1977.
Pohlman, Edward. *Incentives and Compensations in Birth Planning*. Monograph 11. Chapel Hill, N.C.: Carolina Population Center, 1971.
Political and Economic Planning. *Population Policy in Great Britain*. London: S.W.1, PEP, April 1948.
Pollak, Otto. *Social Adjustment in Old Age*. New York: Social Science Research Council, 1948.
Pollard, J. H. *Mathematical Models for the Growth of Human Populations*. Cambridge: University Press, 1973.
Post, John D. "Famine, Mortality, and Epidemic Disease in the Process of Modernization." *Economic History Review* 29 (1976): 14–37.
Postan, M. M., and Habakkuk, H. J., eds. *Cambridge Economic History of Europe* VI. Cambridge: University Press, 1966.
Prange, Otto. *Deutschland's Volkswirtschaft nach dem Kriege*. Berlin: Putkammer und Muhlbrecht, 1915.
Preston, S. H. "Effect of Mortality Change on Stable Population Parameters." *Demography* 11 (1974): 119–36.
Pryor, F. L. "Size of Establishment in Manufacturing." *Economic Journal* 32 (1972): 547–66.
Radner, Roy. "Satisficing." *Journal of Mathematical Economics* 2 (1975): 253–62.
Rajonc, R. B., and Markus, G. B. "Birth Order and Intellectual Development." *Psychological Review* 82 (1975): 26–44.
Rapp, William V. "The Many Possible Extensions of Product Cycle Analysis." *Hilotsubashi Journal of Economics* 16 (1975): 22–29.
Ratchford, B. U. "Institutionalized Inflation." *South Atlantic Quarterly* 73 (1974): 516–28.
Rawls, John. *A Theory of Justice*. Cambridge, Mass.: Harvard University Press, 1971.
Razin, Assaf, and Ben-Zion, Uri. "An Intergenerational Model of Population Growth." *American Economic Review* 65 (1975): 923–33.

Rea, Samuel A., Jr. "Unemployment Insurance and Labour Supply; A Simulation of the 1971 Unemployment Insurance Act." *Canadian Journal of Economics* 10 (1977): 263–78.

Reddaway, W. B. "The Economic Consequences of Zero Population Growth." *Lloyd's Bank Review* 124 (1977): 14–30.

————. *The Economics of a Declining Population.* New York: Macmillan, 1939.

————. "Special Obstacles to Full Employment in a Wealthy Economy." *Economic Journal* 97 (1937): 297–307.

Reed, H. L. "Economists on Industrial Stagnation." *Journal of Political Economy* 48 (1940): 244–50.

Reimers, Cordelia. "Is the Average Age at Retirement Changing?" *Journal of American Statistical Association* 71 (1976): 552–58.

Rejda, George E., and Sheply, Richard J. "The Impact of Zero Population Growth on OASDHI Program." *Journal of Risk and Insurance* 40 (1973): 313–25.

Resek, Robert W., and Siegel, Frederick. "Consumption Demand and Population Growth Rates." *Eastern Economic Journal* 1 (1974): 282–90.

Revelle, Roger, ed., *Rapid Population Growth.* Baltimore: Johns Hopkins Press, 1971.

Ricardo, David. *On the Principles of Political Economy and Taxation.* Edited by E. C. K. Gonner. London: George Bell, 1903.

Rich, E. E., and Wilson, C. H., eds. *The Cambridge Economic History of Europe.* Cambridge: University Press, 1967.

Ridker, R. G., ed. "The Economy, Resource Requirements, and Pollution Levels." *Population, Resources and the Environment.* Commission on Population Growth and the American Future, Research Report III. Washington, D.C.: U.S. Government Printing Office, 1972.

Riley, Matilda W., ed. *Aging and Society.* New York: Russell Sage Foundation, 1972.

Rivers, W. H. R., ed. *Essays on the Depopulation of Melanesia.* Cambridge: University Press, 1927.

Robbins, Lionel. "Notes on Some Probable Consequences of the Advent of a Stationary Population in Great Britain." *Economica* 9 (1929): 71–82.

————. "On a Certain Ambiguity in the Conception of Stationary Equilibrium." *Economic Journal* 40 (1930): 194–79.

————. "On the Elasticity of the Demand for Income in Terms of Effort." *Economica* 10 (1930): 123–29.

————. "The Optimum Theory of Population." *London Essays in Economics in Honour of Edwin Cannan.* London: Routledge, 1920.

Robertson, A. Haworth. "OASDI: Fiscal Basis and Long-Range Cost Projections." *Social Security Bulletin* 40 (1977): 20–48.

Robertson, D. H. "Word for the Devil." *Economica* 3 (1923): 203–14.

Robinson, E. A. G., ed. *Economic Consequences of the Size of Nations.* London: Macmillan, 1960.

————. "John Maynard Keynes: Economist, Author, Statesman." *Economic Journal* 82 (1972): 531–46.

Robinson, Joan. *The Accumulation of Capital.* London: Macmillan, 1958.
————. *Essays in the Theory of Economic Growth.* London: Macmillan, 1963.
————. *Essays in the Theory of Employment.* New York: Macmillan, 1937.
————. *Freedom and Necessity.* London: Allen & Unwin, 1970.
Robinson, Warren C., and McGinnis, Robert. "Limits to Growth." *Demography* 10 (1973): 289–99.
Rose, Sanford. "Third World 'Commodity Power' is a Costly Illusion." *Fortune* 94 (1976): 147–54.
Rosenberg, Harry. "U.S. Fertility Rates: What Birth Rates Specific for Age and Parity of Women Tell Us." *Proceedings of the American Statistical Association,* Social Statistics Section, 1976.
Rosenberg, Nathan. "On Technological Expectations." *Economic Journal* 76 (1976): 523–35.
Rosenblum, Marc. "On the Accuracy of Labor Force Projections." *Monthly Labor Review* 95 (1972): 22–29.
Rostow, W. W. "The Historical Analysis of the Terms of Trade." *Economic History Review* 4 (1951): 53–76.
————. "The Terms of Trade in Theory and Practice." *Economic History Review* 2 (1950): 1–20.
Rowthorn, R. E. "A Reply to Lord Kaldor's Comment." *Economic Journal* 85 (1975): 897–901.
————. "What Remains of Kaldor's Law?" *Economic Journal* 75 (1975): 10–19.
Royal Commission on Population. *Report.* London: His Majesty's Stationery Office, 1949.
————. *Reports and Selected Papers of the Statistics Committee.* II, London: 1950.
Rubin, P. H. "The Expansion of Firms." *Journal of Political Economy* 81 (1973): 936–49.
Russell, J. C. *British Medieval Population.* Albuquerque: University of New Mexico Press, 1948.
————. *Medieval Regions and Their Cities.* Bloomington: University of Indiana Press, 1972.
Ryder, Harl E.; Stafford, Frank P.; and Stephan, Paula E. "Labor, Leisure and Training Over the Life Cycle." *International Economic Review* 17 (1976): 651–74.
Ryder, N. B. "A Demographic Optimum Projection for the United States." In *Demographic and Social Aspects of Population Growth.* Edited by C. F. Westoff and Robert Parke. Commission on Population Growth and The American Future, Research Report No. 1, pp. 605–22.
————. "Notes on Stationary Populations." *Population Index* 41 (1975): 3–27.
Rymes, T. K. *On Concepts of Capital and Technical Change.* Cambridge: University Press, 1971.
Samuelson, Paul. *The Collected Scientific Papers of Paul A. Samuelson.* Edited by J. E. Stiglitz. Cambridge, Mass.: MIT Press, 1966.

————. "An Economist's Non-Linear Model of Self-Generated Fertility Waves." *Population Studies* 30 (1976): 243–48.

————. *The Foundations of Economic Analysis*. Cambridge, Mass.: Harvard University Press, 1947.

————. "The Optimum Growth Rate for Population." *International Economic Review* 16 (1975): 531–38.

————. "Optimum Social Security in a Life-Cycle Growth Model." *International Economic Review* (1975): 539–44.

————. "Scale Economies and Non-Labor Returns at the Optimum Population." *Eastern Economic Journal* 1 (1974): 125–27.

Sauvy, Alfred. *General Theory of Population*. Translated by Christophe Campos. New York: Basic Books, 1969.

————. "Les charges économiques et les avantages de la croissance de la population." *Population* 27 (1972): 9–26.

————. *Théorie generale de la population*. Paris: Presses Universitaire de France, 1966.

————. *Zero Growth*. New York: Praeger, 1976.

Schiffer, Lewis. *Consumer Discretionary Behavior*. Amsterdam: North Holland Publishing Company, 1964.

Schiller, B. S. "Job Search Media: Utilization and Effectiveness." *Quarterly Review of Economics and Business* 15 (1975): 55–64.

Schmöelders, G., and Biervert, B. "Level of Aspiration and Consumption Standard: Some General Findings." *Human Behavior in Economic Affairs*. Edited by B. Strumpel, J. N. Morgan, and E. Zahn. Washington, D.C.: Jossey-Bass, Inc., 1972.

Schultz, T. W., ed. *Economics of the Family: Marriage, Children and Human Capital*. Chicago: University of Chicago Press, 1975.

————. "The High Value of Human Time: Population Equilibrium." *Journal of Political Economy* 82 (1974): 2–10.

————. *Human Resources*. New York: Columbia University Press, 1972.

————, ed. *Marriage, Children and Human Capital*. Chicago: University of Chicago Press, 1975.

————. "The Value of the Ability to Deal with Disequilibria." *Economic Literature* 13 (1975): 827–46.

Schulz, James H. "The Economic Impact of an Aging Population." *Gerontologist* 13 (1973): 111–18.

————. *The Economics of Aging*. Belmont, Calif.: Wadsworth, 1976.

————, et al. *Providing Adequate Retirement Income: Pension Reform in The United States and Abroad*. Hanover, N.H.: University Press of New England, 1974.

Schumpeter, Joseph A. *Business Cycles*. New York: McGraw-Hill, 1939.

————. *Capitalism, Socialism, and Democracy*. New York: McGraw-Hill, 1945.

————. *History of Economic Analysis*. New York: Oxford University Press, 1954.

————. *The Theory of Economic Development*. Cambridge, Mass.: Harvard University Press, 1934.

Schwab, Stewart, and Seater, John J. "The Unemployment Rate: Time to Give it a Rest." *Business Review* of the Federal Reserve Bank of Philadelphia, May–June 1977, pp. 11–18.

Schwartz, Pedro. *The New Political Economy of J. S. Mill.* Durham, N.C.: Duke University Press, 1972.

Scoville, J. G. "Education and Training Requirements for Occupations." *Review of Economics and Statistics* 48 (1966): 387–94.

Security and Exchange Commission. *Annual Report* for the Year Ending June 30, 1975.

Selowsky, Marcelo. "On the Measurement of Education's Contribution to Growth." *Quarterly Journal of Economics* 83 (1969): 449–63.

Sen, S. F. *The Economics of Sir James Steuart.* Cambridge, Mass.: Harvard University Press, 1957.

Serow, William. "The Economics of Stationary and Declining Populations: Some Views from the First Half of the Twentieth Century." *Zero Population Growth: Implications.* Edited by Joseph J. Spengler. Chapel Hill, N.C.: Carolina Population Center, 1975.

———. "The Effects of Zero Population Growth on the Spatial Distribution of Economic Activity." *Journal of Agricultural Economics* 54 (1972): 964–71.

———. "The Implications of Zero Growth for Agricultural Commodity Demand." *American Journal of Agricultural Economics* 54 (1972): 955–71.

———. "Slow Population Growth and the Relative Size and Productivity of the Male Labor Force." *Atlantic Economic Journal* 4 (1976): 61–68.

Shackle, G. L. S. *Epistemics & Economics.* Cambridge: University Press, 1972.

Sheldon, E. B., ed. *Family Economic Behavior.* Philadelphia: Lippincott, 1973.

Sheppard, H. L., ed. *Towards an Industrial Gerontology.* Cambridge: Schenkman Publishing Company, 1970.

Shishko, Robert, and Rostker, Bernard. "The Economics of Multiple Job Holding." *American Economic Review* 66 (1976): 298–308.

Shiskin, Julius, and Stein, R. L. "Problems in Measuring Unemployment." *Monthly Labor Review* 98 (1975): 3–10.

Shorrocks, A. F. "The Age-Wealth Relationships: A Cross-Section and Cohort Analysis." *The Review of Economics and Statistics* 57 (1975): 155–63.

Shroeder, Larry. "An Information-Theoretic Analysis of Occupational Mobility Paths." *Quarterly Review of Economics and Business* 15 (1975): 15–23.

Siegel, Jacob S. "Development and Accuracy of Projections of Population Households in the United States." *Demography* 9 (1972): 51–68.

Simon, H. A. *The New Science of Management Decision.* New York: Harper & Row, 1960.

———. *The Shape of Automation for Men and Management.* New York: Harper & Row, 1965.

Sklar, J., and Berkov, B. "The American Birth Rate: Evidences of a Coming Rise." *Science* 189 (1975): 693–700.

Smith, Adam. *An Inquiry Into the Nature and Causes of the Wealth of Nations.* New York: Random House, 1937.

Smith, Warren L. *Macroeconomics*. Homewood, Ill.: Irwin, 1970.

Sobol, Marion Gross. "A Dynamic Analysis of Labor Force Participation of Married Women of Childbearing Age." *Journal of Human Resources* 8 (1973): 497–505.

Solomon, L. C. "Definition of College Quality and Its Impact on Earnings." *Explorations in Economic Research*. Occasional Paper, National Bureau of Economic Research, Vol. 2, 1975, pp. 537–87.

Solow, R. "The Economics of Resources or the Resources of Economics." *American Economic Review* 64 (1974): 1–14.

———. *Growth Theory: An Exposition*. Oxford: Clarendon Press, 1970.

———. "Technical Change and the Aggregate Production Function." *Review of Economics and Statistics* 39 (1957): 312–20.

Sommers, Dixie, and Eck, Alan. "Occupational Mobility in the American Labor Force." *Monthly Labor Review* 100 (1977): 3–19.

Sorokin, P. A. *Contemporary Sociological Theories*. New York: Harper, 1928.

———. *Social and Cultural Dynamics*. New York: American Book Company, 1937.

Spencer, B. G. "Determinants of the Labour Force Participation of Married Women: A Micro-Study of Toronto Households." *Canadian Journal of Economics* 6 (1973): 722–38.

Spencer, Vivian. *Raw Materials in The United States Economy: 1900–1969* (U.S. Bureau of Mines, Working Paper 35). Washington, D.C.: U.S. Government Printing Office, 1972.

Spengler, Joseph J. "Adam Smith on Population." *Population Studies* 24 (1970): 377–88.

———. "Cassel on Population." *History of Political Economy* 1 (1969): 150–72.

———. *Declining Population Growth Revisited*. Chapel Hill, N.C.: Carolina Population Center [Monograph 14], 1971.

———. "Economic Opinion and the Future of the Interest Rate." *Southern Economic Journal* 3 (1936): 7–28.

———. "Effects Produced in Receiving Countries by Pre-1939 Immigration." *The Economics of International Migration*. Edited by Brinley Thomas. London: Macmillan, 1958.

———. *France Faces Depopulation*. Durham, N.C.: Duke University Press, 1938, 1978.

———. *French Predecessors of Malthus*. Durham, N.C.: Duke University Press, 1942.

———. "Malthus the Malthusian vs. Malthus the Economist." *Southern Economic Journal* 24 (1957): 1–11.

———. *Population Economics*. Durham, N.C.: Duke University Press, 1972.

———. "Population Movements, Employment, and Income." *Southern Economic Journal* 5 (1938): 129–57.

———. "Population and Potential Power." *Studies in Economics and Economic History*. Edited by Marcelle Kooy. Durham, N.C.: Duke University Press, 1972.

Spengler, Joseph J. "Population Prediction in Nineteenth Century America." *American Sociological Review* 1 (1936): 905–21.

———. "Power Blocs and the Formation and Content of Economic Decisions." *American Economic Review / Supplement* 40 (1950): 413–30.

———. "Prospective Population Changes and Price Level Tendencies." *Southern Economic Journal* 38 (1972): 459–67.

Spengler, Oswald. *The Decline of the West*. New York: Alfred A. Knopf, 1926.

Stassart, Joseph. *Les avantages et les inconvienients économiques d'une population stationnaire*. The Hague: Nijhoff, 1965.

Staudinger, Hans. "Germany's Population Miracle." *Social Research* 5 (1938): 125–48.

———. "Stationary Population—Stagnant Economy." *Social Research* 6 (1939): 141–52.

St. Clair, Oswald. *A Key to Ricardo*. London: Routledge & Kegan Paul, 1957.

Steindl, J. *Maturity and Stagnation in American Capitalism*. Oxford: Blackwell, 1952.

Stephan, Paula E. "Human Capital Production: Life Cycle Production with Different Learning Technologies." *Economic Inquiry* 14 (1976): 539–57.

Stephenson, S. P., Jr. "The Economics of Youth Job Search Behavior." *Review of Economics and Statistics* 58 (1976): 104–11.

Stern, Irving. "Industry Effects of Government Expenditures: An Input-Output Analysis." *Survey of Current Business* 55 (1975): 9–23.

Stevens, Neil A. "Housing: A Cyclical Industry on the Upswing." *Review of Federal Reserve Bank of St. Louis* 58 (1976): 15–20.

Stevenson, Tom. "In Hock to Pensions." *New Republic* 175 (1976): 23–25.

Stigler, George J. *The Organizations of Industry*. Homewood, Ill.: Irwin, 1968.

Stodden, J. R. "Inflation-Temporary or Ongoing Is The Question for the 1970's," *Business Review,* Federal Reserve Bank of Dallas, June 1975, pp. 1–6.

Strausz-Hupé, Robert. *The Balance of Tomorrow*. New York: G. P. Putnam's Sons, 1945.

Strumpel, B.; Morgan, J. N.; and Zahn, E., eds. *Human Behavior in Economic Affairs*. Washington, D.C.: Jossey-Bass, Inc., 1972.

Swan, N.; McRae, P.; and Steinberg, C. *Income Maintenance Programs: Their Effect on Labour Supply and Aggregate Demand in the Maritimes*. Ottawa: Economic Council of Canada, 1976.

Sweet, James A. *Women in the Labor Force*. New York: Seminar Press, 1973.

Sweezy, Alan. "Declining Investment Opportunity." *The New Economics*. Edited by Seymour E. Harris. New York: Knopf, 1947.

———. "The Economic Explanation of Fertility Changes in The United States." *Population Studies* 25 (1971): 255–68.

———. "The Natural History of the Stagnation Thesis." *Zero Population Growth: Implications*. Edited by Joseph J. Spengler. Chapel Hill, N.C.: Carolina Population Center, 1975.

———, and Owens, Aaron. "The Impact of Employment Growth on Employment." *American Economic Review, Papers and Proceedings* 64 (1974): 44–50.

Sweezy, Paul M. "John Maynard Keynes." *Keynes' General Theory. Reports of Three Decades.* Edited by Robert Lekachman. New York: St. Martin's Press, 1964.

———. *The Theory of Capitalist Development.* New York: Oxford University Press, 1942.

Tabbush, Victor. "Underemployment." *Arizona Review* 24 (1975): 9–12.

Taeuber, Irene. *The Population of Japan.* Princeton: Princeton University Press, 1958.

Tarascio, Vincent. "Keynes on the Sources of Economic Growth." *Journal of Economic History* 31 (1971): 429–44.

Taubman, Paul T., and Wales, Terrence. "The Inadequacy of Cross-Section Age Earning Profiles when Ability is not Held Constant." *Annals of Economic and Social Measurement* 1 (1972): 363–68.

———. "Mental Ability and Higher Educational Attainment in the Twentieth Century." National Bureau of Economic Research Occasional Paper, No. 118, New York, 1972.

Taussig, F. W. *Selected Readings in International Trade and Tariff Problems.* Boston: Ginn and Company, 1921.

Taussig, Michael K. *Alternative Measures of the Distribution of Economic Welfare.* Princeton: Industrial Relations Section, Princeton University, 1973.

Taylor, Charles I., and Hudson, M. C. *World Handbook of Political and Social Indicators.* New Haven: Yale University Press, 1972.

Taylor, K. W. "Some Aspects of Population History." *Canadian Journal of Economics and Political Science* 16 (1950): 301–13.

Taylor, L. R., ed. *The Optimum Population for Britain.* New York: Academic Press, 1970.

Temporary National Economic Committee. *Report* Part IX, *Savings and Investment.* Washington, D.C.: U.S. Government Printing Office, 1940.

Terborgh, George. *The Bogey of Economic Maturity.* Chicago: Machinery and Allied Products Institute, 1945.

Terleckyj, N. E., ed. *Household Production and Consumption.* New York: Columbia University Press, 1975.

Terry, G. B. "Rival Explanations in the Work-Fertility Relationship." *Population Studies* 24 (1975): 191–206.

Thomas, Brinley. *The Economics of International Migration.* London: Macmillan, 1958.

———. *Migration and Economic Growth.* Cambridge: Cambridge University Press, 1954.

Thompson, D'Arcy W. *On Growth and Form.* Cambridge: University Press, 1917, 1942, 1961.

Thompson, Warren S. *Population: A Study in Malthusianism.* New York: Columbia University Press, 1915.

Thompson, W. S., and Whelpton, P. K. *Population Trends in The United States.* New York: McGraw-Hill, 1933.

Thurow, L. "The Optimum Life Time Distribution of Consumption and Expenditures." *American Economic Review* 59 (1969): 324–30.

Tinbergen, J. "Statistical Evidence on the Accelerator Principle." *Economica* 5 (1938): 164–76.

————. "Zur Theorie der langfristigen Wirtschaftsentwicklung." *Weltwirtschaftliches Archiv* 55 (1942): 511–49.

————, and Polak, J. J. *The Dynamics of Business Cycles*. Chicago: University of Chicago Press, 1949.

Tsiang, S. C. "The Effect of Population Growth on the General Level of Employment and Activity." *Economica* 9 (1942): 325–32.

Turchi, Boone. *The Demand for Children: The Economics of Fertility*. Cambridge, Mass.: Ballinger, 1975.

————. "Stationary Populations: Pensions and the Social Security System." *Zero Population Growth: Implications*. Edited by Joseph J. Spengler. Chapel Hill, N.C.: Carolina Population Center, 1975.

Ture, N. B. *The Future of Private Pensions*. Washington, D.C.: American Enterprise Institute, 1976.

Turnowski, S. J. "Empirical Evidence on the Formation of Price Expectations." *Journal of the American Statistical Association* 65 (1976): 1441–54.

Ulman, Lloyd, ed. *Manpower Problems in the Policy Mix*. Baltimore: Johns Hopkins Press, 1973.

United Nations. *The Aging of Populations and Its Economic and Social Implications*. New York: United Nations, 1956.

————. *The Concept of a Stable Population*. Population Studies No. 39. New York: United Nations, 1968.

————. *Demographic Aspects of Manpower*. Population Studies No. 33. New York: United Nations, 1962.

————. *Demographic Yearbook, 1975*. New York: United Nations, 1976.

————. *The Determinants and Consequences of Population Trends*, I. New York: United Nations, 1973.

————. *Growth of the World's Urban and Rural Population, 1920–2000*. New York: United Nations, 1969.

————. *Incomes in Postwar Europe: A Study of Policies, Growth, and Distribution*. Geneva: United Nations, 1967.

————. *Population Bulletin*. No. 7, 1963.

————. *Recent Trends in Fertility in Industrialized Countries*. New York: United Nations, 1958.

————. *The World Population Situation in 1970*. New York: United Nations, 1971.

U.S. Bureau of the Census. "Fertility of American Women: June, 1976." *Current Population Reports*. Series P-20, No. 308, June 1977, pp. 1–7.

————. "Demographic Aspects of Aging and the Older Population in The United States." *Current Population Reports*, P-53, no. 59, May 1976, pp. 3–10.

————. *Historical Statistics of the United States*. Washington, D.C.: 1960.

————. *Historical Statistics of the United States, Bicentennial Edition*. Washington, D.C.: 1975.

————. "Households and Families by Type." *Current Population Reports,* Series P-20, no. 296, September 1976.

————. "Social and Economic Characteristics of the Older Population, 1974." *Current Population Reports,* Series P-23, no. 57, November 1975.

————. *Statistical Abstract of the United States, 1972.* Washington, D.C.: 1972.

————. *Statistical Abstract of the United States, 1974.* Washington, D.C.: 1974.

————. "A Statistical Portrait of Women in the U.S." *Current Population Reports,* Series P-23, no. 58, April 1976.

————. *The Two-Child Family and Population Growth: An International View.* Washington, D.C.: 1971.

U.S. Department of Health, Education, and Welfare. *Acute Conditions.* (DHEW Publication No. HRA 75–1525), Series 10, no. 98, January 1975.

————. *Current Estimates from the Health Interview Survey, U.S., 1973.* Rockville, Md.: October, 1974.

————. *Health, United States, 1975.* DHEW Publication No. HRA 76–1232, Rockville, Md.: 1976.

U.S. Department of Labor. "The Length of Working Life for Males, 1900–60." *Manpower Report,* no. 8, Washington, D.C.: July 1963.

————. "Work Life Expectancy and Training Needs of Women." *Manpower Report,* no. 7, Washington, D.C.: May 1967.

U.S. Department of Manpower Administration. *Manpower Report of the President.* Washington, D.C.: 1975.

Unsigned. "The Great Rush for New Products." *Time,* October 24, 1969, pp. 92–93.

————. "Time for Recreation Desired More than Money." *Ohio State University Monthly,* April 1975, p. 9.

————. "A Wave of New Products for Work, Play, Travel." *U.S. News & World Report,* November 29, 1976, pp. 73–75.

————. "World Population." *Life,* September 3, 1945, pp. 45–51.

Urlanis, B. *Wars and Population.* Translated by Leo Lempert. Moscow: Progress Publishers, 1971.

Utterstrom, Gustaf. "Climatic Fluctuations and Population Problems in Early Modern History." *Scandinavian Economic History Review* 3 (1955): 3–47.

Verdoorn, P. J. "Fattori che regolano lo sviluppo della produttivita del lavoro." *L'industria* (1949).

Vernon, Raymond. *The Economic and Political Consequences of Multinational Enterprise: An Anthology.* Boston: Harvard Graduate School of Business Administration, 1972.

————. *Sovereignty at Bay: The Multinational Spread of U.S. Enterprises.* New York: Basic Books, 1971.

Von Foerster, H.; Mora, P. M.; and Amiot, L. W. "Doomsday: 13 November, A.D. 2026." *Science* 132 (1960): 1291–95.

Von Weiszsäcker, C. C. *The Political Economy of Stability in Western Countries.* Stockholm: Almqvist & Wiksell, 1972.

Wachlit, Paul. "The Effect of School Quality on Achievement, Attainment Levels, and Lifetime Earnings." *Explorations in Economic Research.* Occasional Paper, National Bureau of Economic Research, Vol. 2, Fall 1975.

Wachter, Michael L. "A Time-Series Fertility Equation: The Potential for a Baby-Boom in the 1980's." *International Economic Review* 15 (1975): 609–23.

Wallich, Henry C. "Is There a Capital Shortage?" *Challenge* 18 (1975): 30–43.

Watson, Cicely. Series of articles on France and Belgium. *Population Studies* 5 (1952): 261–86; 6 (1953): 3–38; 7 (1953–54): 14–45, 263–86; 8 (1954): 46–73, 152–87.

Watts, Harold W. "Long-Run Income Expectations and Consumer Saving." *Studies in Household Economic Behavior.* Edited by T. F. Dernburg, R. N. Rosett, and H. W. Watts. New Haven: Yale University Press, 1958.

Weinstein, M. C., and Zeckhauser, R. L. "Optimal Consumption of Depletable Resources." *Quarterly Journal of Economics* 89 (1975): 371–92.

Weintraub, E. Roy. " 'Uncertainty' and the Keynesian Revolution." *History of Political Economy* 7 (1975): 530–48.

Weiss, Y. "On the Optimal Lifetime Patterns of Labour Supply." *Economic Journal* 82 (1972): 1293–1315.

Weisskopf, V. F. "The Frontiers and Limits of Science." *Bulletin of the American Academy of Arts and Sciences* 28 (1975): 15–26.

Welch, Finis. "Human Capital Theory: Education, Discrimination, and Life Cycles." *American Economic Review* 65 (1975): 63–73.

Weldon, J. C. "On the Theory of Intergenerational Transfers." *Canadian Journal of Economics* 9 (1976): 559–79.

Welford, A. T., and Birren, J. E. *Behavior, Aging the Nervous System.* Springfield, Ill.: C. C. Thomas, 1965.

Weller, R. H. "Number and Timing Failures Among Legitimate Births in the United States: 1968, 1969, 1972." *Family Planning Perspectives* 8 (1976): 111–16.

Wells, L. T., Jr., ed. "International Trade: The Product Life Cycle Approach." *The Product Life Cycle and International Trade.* Boston: Harvard University Graduate School of Business Administration, 1972.

Westfield, F. M. "Technical Progress and Returns to Scale." *Review of Economics and Statistics* 48 (1966): 432–41.

Westoff, Charles F. "The Decline of Unplanned Births in the United States." *Science* 191 (1976): 38–41.

Wharton, Clifton, R., Jr. "The Green Revolution: Cornucopia or Pandora's Box?" *Foreign Affairs* 47 (1969): 464–76.

White, Lynn. *Medieval Technology and Social Change.* Oxford: Clarendon Press, 1962.

———. "Technology and Economics in the Middle Ages." *Speculum* 15 (1940): 141–55.

White, W. H. "Interest Inelasticity of Investment Demand." *American Economic Review* 46 (1956): 565–87.

Wiesner, J. B. "Has the U.S. Lost its Initiative in Technological Innovation?" *Technology Review* 78 (1976): 54–60.

Williamson, J. G. "Migration to the New World: Long Term Influences and Impact." *Explorations in Economic History* 11 (1974): 357–89.

Williams, R. H., et al., eds. *Process of Aging.* New York: Atherton Press, 1963.

Wilson, Ian H. "Socio-Political Forecasting: A New Dimension to Strategic Planning." *Michigan Business Review,* July 1974, pp. 15–25.

Winsborough, H. H. "Age, Period, Cohort, and Education Effects on Earnings by Race." *Social Indicator Models.* Edited by K. C. Land and Seymour Spilerman. New York: Russell Sage Foundation, 1975.

Wolf, Julius. *Die Volkswirtschaft der Gegenwart und Zukunft.* Leipzig: A. Deichert, 1912.

Wolfe, A. B. "Economic Conditions and the Birth Rate After the War." *Journal of Political Economy* 25 (1917): 521–41.

———. "Is There a Biological Law of Human Population Growth?" *Quarterly Journal of Economics* 41 (1927): 570–71.

———. "The Population Problem Since the World War: A Survey of Literature and Research." *Journal of Political Economy.* Pt. I–III, 36 (1928): 529–59, 662–85; 37 (1929): 87–120.

———. (criticism of Carr-Saunders argument) in "Superest Ager." *Quarterly Journal of Economics* 40 (1925): 172–75.

Worcester, Dean A. *Beyond Welfare and Full Employment: The Economics of Optimal Employment without Inflation.* Lexington, Mass.: D. C. Heath, 1972.

Woytinsky, W. S., and Woytinsky, E. S. *World Commerce and Governments.* New York: Twentieth Century Fund, 1955.

———. *World Population and Production.* New York: Twentieth Century Fund, 1953.

Wright, Quincy, ed. *Population* [Harris Foundation Lectures]. Chicago: University of Chicago Press, 1930.

———. *A Study of War.* Chicago: University of Chicago Press, 1947.

Wrigley, E. A. *Population and History.* New York: McGraw-Hill, 1969.

Young, A. A. "Increasing Returns and Economic Progress." *Economic Journal* 38 (1928): 527–42.

Zinam, Oleg. "Optimum Population Growth Concept and the Zero Population Growth Thesis." *Economia Internazionale* 27 (1974): 320–38.

Subject Index

Name Index